Held in Memory, Shared in Story

Teachings of the Middle Kuskokwim

Copublished by the Alaska Native Language Center and University Press of Colorado

Alaska Native Language Center
PO Box 757680
Fairbanks, AK 99775-7680

University Press of Colorado
1580 North Logan Street, Suite 660
PMB 39883
Denver, Colorado 80203-1942

ISBN: 978-1-55500-141-4 (paperback)

Library of Congress Control Number: 2026930974

Cover concept: Jonathan Samuelson, The Kuskokwim Corporation
Cover design: Allison Mcintyre, The Kuskokwim Corporation
Interior layout: Lillian Maassen, Alaska Native Language Center

The University Press of Colorado is a proud member of the Association of University Presses.

The University Press of Colorado is a cooperative publishing enterprise supported, in part, by Adams State University, Colorado School of Mines, Colorado State University, Fort Lewis College, Metropolitan State University of Denver, Regis University, University of Colorado, University of Northern Colorado, University of Wyoming, Utah State University, and Western Colorado University.

∞ This paper meets the requirements of the ANSI/NISO Z39.48-1992 (Permanence of Paper).

Let us honor the sacred languages of the Indigenous peoples of Alaska, whose words, stories, prayers, and guidance are respectfully recorded in these few pages. The origins of these languages are unknown, but they have been treasured, spoken, and lived by the first peoples of Alaska. As we read and learn, let us respect both the speakers who brought these languages to us and the ones who learned the written form to share with our peoples and our friends throughout the world.

Held in Memory, Shared in Story

Teachings of the Middle Kuskokwim

◇◇◇◇◇◇◇◇◇◇◇◇◇◇◇◇◇◇◇◇◇◇◇◇◇◇◇◇◇◇◇◇◇◇◇◇

Authored by Kuskokwim Elders, with help from

Mark John, Marie Meade, Alice Rearden, and Ann Fienup-Riordan

Including a foreword and essays by

Andrea Gusty, Cheryl Jerabek, and Chris Wooley

◇◇

THE KUSKOKWIM CORPORATION AND CALISTA EDUCATION AND CULTURE

Contents

Foreword

The stories in this book are more than reflections of the past; they are blueprints for the future. They carry the strength, knowledge, and resilience of the Middle Kuskokwim people. From Whitefish Lake and Butt Hill to Stone Woman, the Holitna, Barometer Mountain, and the Swift River, these stories ground us in who we are and remind us that no matter where we live, our roots remain strong.

Growing up in the Middle Kuskokwim, I had the opportunity to hear some of our traditional knowledge firsthand from Elders who spoke with quiet authority, from family members who passed down teachings through daily life, and from stories shared around tables, campfires, and fish racks. Those moments shaped who I am.

But I know that not every TKC Shareholder had the same experience. Many grew up outside the region, or were separated from these teachings by distance, time, or circumstance.

This collection of stories is an opportunity to change that. It's a way for those raised far from our villages to still learn from the voices that shaped them. It's a bridge reaching across geography and generations to make sure that the traditional knowledge of the Middle Kuskokwim is never out of reach.

And for those who did grow up in the region, these stories serve as a powerful reminder of who we are, where we come from, and what we carry forward. They reconnect us to teachings we may have heard as children and strengthen us as we steward the land and the gifts it gives us.

Each one of our communities is so unique, but common values and the stories of the Middle Kuskokwim weave us together. As I reflect on this project, I am incredibly proud to come from this beautiful place, rich with knowledge, strength, and tradition. These stories and teachings have been passed orally from generation to generation, strengthening our chain of connection to those who came before us.

For the first time, we are able to share them within these pages, preserved and available to everyone.

For those new to our story, The Kuskokwim Corporation (TKC) is an Alaska Native Village Corporation established under the Alaska Native Claims Settlement Act of 1971 (ANCSA). Along the Kuskokwim River, where the vast tundra gives way to mountainous, timbered terrain, you will find 10 communities that make up the Middle Kuskokwim, the original villages and the homeland of TKC.

Our leaders at the time knew that we could do much greater work for our people by coming together. On April 25, 1977, the villages of Lower Kalskag,

Kalskag, Aniak, Chuathbaluk, Napaimute, Crooked Creek, Georgetown, Red Devil, Sleetmute, and Stony River merged to form what we now know as The Kuskokwim Corporation.

Today, TKC has over 4,400 Shareholders living across the world, each one deeply rooted in the values and teachings of our Yupiaq, Deg Hit'an, and Dene ancestry. A confluence of culture, landscape, language, and community, TKC works to honor that ancestry by cultivating a sustainable future in which our people will thrive for generations to come.

Our mission is to create sustainable benefits for our Shareholders and descendants while protecting our land, preserving our culture, and investing in our people. Our values are rooted in stewardship, resilience, and responsibility. Whether we're investing in education, expanding workforce development, stewarding land and natural resources, or celebrating our cultural heritage, TKC's priorities remain clear: to support our Shareholders and protect the place that made us.

Preserving the values, knowledge, languages, and traditions of the people of the Middle Kuskokwim has been identified as a top priority by our Shareholders. Again and again, our people have told us how important it is to provide opportunities to connect, stay connected, or reconnect with the rich culture and heritage of our region.

In response, The Kuskokwim Corporation and our Board of Directors developed and launched the TKC ROOTS initiative: Raising Our Own Traditional Stewards. Through TKC ROOTS, we work to preserve and promote Middle Kuskokwim culture and traditions through cultural learning activities; tools and resources to share traditional knowledge and wisdom; and by providing access to opportunities beyond TKC. It is our way of ensuring that the knowledge held by our Elders is carried forward by the next generation.

As President and CEO of TKC, I am proud to help introduce this book as part of our commitment to stewardship, not just of land and resources, but of identity, language, and story. Our way of life is not a thing of the past. It lives on in the stories we share, the values we practice, and the connections we continue to strengthen.

May this collection remind you that we are a people of endurance and purpose. That our stories are our strength. And that preserving them is not just about honoring the past; it's about building a future rooted in who we are.

Quyana, dogidinh, thank you for taking the time to listen.

Andrea Gusty
President and CEO
The Kuskokwim Corporation

Acknowledgments

So many people have helped us in our work along the middle Kuskokwim that it is hard to know where thanks should begin. First and foremost, we are grateful to the elders who have shared so much, especially Agnes Andreanoff, John Andrew, Golga Effemka, Angie Kameroff, Wassily Kameroff, Clara Morgan, Olga Peterson, Sophie Sakar, Michael Savage, Elena Sergie, and Jennie Zaukar. My CEC partners and I knew less than nothing about the middle river ten years ago. You have taught us with patience and grace, and we are in your debt.

We also wish to thank tribal administrators and staff for their help and support during our village visits, including Muriel Morgan, Laura Simeon, and tribal chief Wayne Morgan in Aniak, Sleetmute Traditional Council member Ellen Yako, Tracy Simeon in Chuathbaluk, Bonnie Persson in Upper Kalskag, Nick Levi in Lower Kalskag, and Julie Zaukar in Crooked Creek.

Much of what we have included here was shared during gatherings of small groups of elders meeting for several days at a time to discuss a range of topics. These gatherings were organized by Calista Education and Culture (CEC), the primary heritage organization in southwest Alaska guided by an Elders' Committee including Moses White of Kasigluk, Annie Cleveland of Quinhagak, Ruth Jimmie of Toksook Bay, George Morgan of Kalskag, and Francis Thompson of St. Mary's. Beginning in 1997, CEC was under the able direction of Mark John, whose vision for CEC as an organization dedicated to documenting and sharing Yup'ik oral traditions set decades of work in motion. Until he passed away in August 2025, Mark served as cultural advisor for CEC, with the able assistance of CEC's new director Denise Brown-Chythlook, Robyn Kugtsun, and Dawn Samuelson. We could not do what we do without them.

CEC's topic-specific gatherings have been supported by many organizations over the years. We are particularly indebted to the National Science Foundation's Office of Polar Programs, Arctic Social Sciences, whose support of a traditional knowledge documentation project between 2000 and 2005 gave CEC the opportunity to develop and refine the gathering method that we have used in our work ever since. In 2020, NSF awarded CEC funds to host gatherings documenting place names and food knowledge along the middle Kuskokwim. Special thanks to our NSF program officers, past and present, including Anna Kerttula de Echave, Erica Hill, and Liam Frink.

This project could never have moved forward without the support and

Jacob Wise Spirit Camp staff and friends, August 2024. Cody Pequeno, Jonathan Samuelson, Megan Leary, Audrey Leary, and Piiyuuk Qungurkaq Shields. *AFR*

assistance of The Kuskokwim Corporation (TKC) – the for-profit corporation representing the ten middle Kuskokwim communities, including Upper and Lower Kalskag, Aniak, Chuathbaluk, Napaimute, Crooked Creek, Georgetown, Red Devil, Sleetmute, and Stony River. Spread out along a 200-mile stretch of the Kuskokwim River, running through mountains unlike anything one encounters on the lowland delta downriver, these communities are joined by deep family bonds, diverse cultural traditions, and a common love and respect for the land and waters they call home. We are particularly grateful to TKC President and CEO Andrea Gusty, Vice President of Shareholder Services Jonathan Samuelson, Vice President of Operations for the TKC Aniak Office Megan Leary, and Community Resource Specialist Rachelle Persson. Beginning work in an unfamiliar region was daunting, and Jonathan Samuelson was especially helpful in introducing us to elders from the region, now living in Anchorage. Denny Thomas also showed us much appreciated hospitality in Crooked Creek.

Also, in 2022, just as CEC's work was beginning in earnest, TKC's related non-profit, TKC Fish Wheel, acquired the old Aniak Elementary School from the Kuspuk School District (serving the TKC villages and based in Aniak), which TKC and TKC Fish Wheel have been renovating and transforming into the Arviiq Regional Training Center, a place for lifetime learning, vocational training, and cultural activities. Thanks to TKC's generosity, CEC staff and elders had a comfortable place to stay while in Aniak. We also ate many meals at the Arviiq and hosted several of our gatherings in the Arviiq's large dining area. Aniak is large, and villages are spread far apart on the Kuskokwim. Megan Leary smoothed our way not only by picking us up at the Aniak airport but taking us by boat to villages, near and far. Use of the Arviiq and help bringing elders together was an enormous contribution, for which we are truly grateful.

Audrey Leary, Executive Director of the Native Village of Napaimute, also generously invited other elders and me to attend their 2024 Jacob Wise Memorial Spirit Camp, just upriver from Napaimute, as well as the 2025 Cultural Wellness Week she organized at the Aniak School. Both experiences deepened and enriched my understanding of the middle river. Audrey and Megan's father, Mark Leary, visited the Culture Camp to share stories with the young people. Mark generously allowed me to record his stories and to include them here, for others to learn from and to enjoy. When asked to define what it means to be an elder, Mark John pointed out that those who share are given another day, meaning long life, and are true elders, while those who don't share just get old. Mark Leary has paid attention to what elders have said over the years, and he shares what he has learned – something that makes him a true elder.

Another invaluable contribution was made by Carrie Longpre, who lived in Sleetmute in the 1970s and has a homestead on the Holitna River. While in Sleetmute, Jack Egnaty told her the story of how the Holitna River came to be, which she wrote down in 1986 with the intention of sitting down again with Jack someday to "get it right." Jack was known as a great story teller, but today, even Jack's daughter, Mary Margie, does not remember this story. Thanks to both Carrie for writing the story down forty years ago, and to Mary Margie for her permission to share it in this book.

Many individuals have also helped us in our work. Archeologist Chris Wooley of Chumis Cultural Resource Services worked with colleagues on the 2007 Cultural Resources Survey for the Donlin Creek Project, and subsequently led excavation work at a prehistoric village site just downriver from Canoe Village. All through our project Chris's guidance has been instrumental – leading us to archives and museum collections as well as individual elders. Chris took Crooked Creek elders to the UA Museum of the North, and in April 2024 we followed. Chris took elders to Washington, DC where they visited the National Anthropological Archives, and in December 2024 I followed. Recently I told him that he should warn his wife: "I follow you everywhere!"

We would also like to thank Senior Collections Manager Angela Linn at the UA Museum of the North for making our work in collections both possible and a complete pleasure. Though our visit was short, we also enjoyed the hospitality of my friends Uma Bhatt and her husband David, as well as Uma's graduate student in Atmospheric Sciences (now Ph.D), Amy Hendricks. Also thanks to Micki LeClair Sievers, who did follow-up work in collections, taking photographs of all the objects we looked at for inclusion in this book.

We are also indebted to both the Association of Village Council Presidents and DOWL Engineering, especially Adison Spafford and Mike McKinnon, for sending both Marie Meade and me to Aniak and Lower and Upper Kalskag in

June 2018 to do elder interviews and document place names as part of their Portage Mountain Transportation Corridor Project. This was Marie's and my first visit to these communities, and it left us wanting to learn more. Also thanks to Chris McDevitt, Jeff Parks, and Katie Hayden for including me in their fieldtrip to the upper Kuskokwim in May 2021, traveling from Bethel to Nikolai in *The Famous Karl*. Their love and respect for the river were infectious, and I am in their debt.

Along with hosting elder gatherings at the Arviiq in Aniak, at the UA Museum of the North, and at my home in Anchorage, we had a great three-day gathering in Bethel at the US Fish and Wildlife Yukon Delta National Wildlife Refuge. Particular thanks go to Refuge manager Spencer Rearden for allowing us to use the Refuge conference room and bunkhouse, giving us both a comfortable place to stay as well as space to cook and enjoy meals together.

Thanks also to the many friends and colleagues who shared stories, made suggestions, and read pieces of this book to ensure that, to the best of our abilities, we got things right. These include Cheryl Jerabek, Carrie Longpre, June McAtee, Jonathan Samuelson, Mike McKinnon, Brenda Pacarro, Chris Wooley, Matt O'Leary, Steve Street, and Janine Stewman.

Finding pictures for this book was a complete pleasure. Illustrations are thanks to many individuals working in many archives and institutions, including Dawn Biddison at the Smithsonian's Arctic Studies Center in Anchorage; Amy Valentine and Monica Shah of the Anchorage Museum; Sandra Johnston at the Alaska State Archives and Alaska State Library in Juneau; Alex Brown at the National Anthropological Archives, National Museum of Natural History, in Suitland, Maryland; Alessandro Pezzati at the Penn Museum Archives in Philadelphia; Becky Butler Gallegos at the Archives and Special Collections, UAA Consortium Library in Anchorage; Fawn Carter and Monica Oatman at the UAF Alaska Polar Regions Collections and Archives in Fairbanks; Angela Linn and Micki LeClair Sievers at the UA Museum of the North; and the Moravian Archives in Bethlehem, Pennsylvania. Additional photos were contributed by Megan Leary, Audrey Leary, the family of John and Edith Kilbuck, June McAtee, Joe Spein, Terry Bissonnette, Andrea Gusty, Will Hartman, Cally Phillips, Rachelle Persson, Jonathan Samuelson, Maxine Laszlo, Chris Arend, Mariah Polty, Annie Mary K. Michaelson, and Chris Wooley. As in many of our past books, cartographer Ian Moore, assisted by his wife Jen Jolliff, has prepared our book's maps.

Last but not least, thanks to Lillian Maassen and the Alaska Native Language Center for their consideration. Quyana!

Agusta Gusty of Stony River; elders Seraphine and John Borowski of Napaimute; Kirerslyn Vaska of Chuathbaluk/Anchorage; and Zoey Morgan of Chuathbaluk at the Jacob Wise Memorial Spirit Camp, summer 2023. *Megan Leary*

Elder Tradition Bearers

Name	*Birth place*	*Residence*	*Birth year*
Golga Effemka / *Ungagpak*	Sleetmute	Sleetmute	1933
Jack Egnaty	Tatlawiksuk River	Sleetmute	1914
Pete Mellick	Sleetmute	Sleetmute	1942
Angie Kameroff / *Agyaq*	Sleetmute	Sleetmute	1948
Seraphine Kameroff Borowski / *Uulliarneq*	Kalskag	Napaimute	1946
John Borowski	Pennsylvania	Napaimute	1944
Sophie Sakar / *Cugluaq*	Old Aniak	Chuathbaluk	1942
Lucy Simeon / *Uullaq*	Crow Village	Chuathbaluk	1949
Olga Phillips	Napaimute	Chuathbaluk	1949
Nastasia Avakumoff	Crooked Creek	Chuathbaluk	1951
Eric Morgan	Anchorage	Chuathbaluk	1956
Olinka Sakar	Waskey's Landing	Aniak	1927
Marie Kameroff / *Guulak*	Aniak	Aniak	1938
Clara Morgan / *Kutuspak*	Igyaraq River	Aniak	1940
Agnes Andreanoff / *Atsaruaq*	Crooked Creek	Aniak	1949
Olga Peterson	Crooked Creek	Aniak	1966
Annie Morgan	Crooked Creek	Aniak	1958
Bob Aloysius / *Elliksuuyar*	Iinruq	Upper Kalskag	1935
Elena Sergie	Ayimqeryaraq	Lower Kalskag	1945

Name	*Birth place*	*Residence*	*Birth year*
Steven Gregory / *Araalek*	Kessigliq	Upper Kalskag	1946
George Morgan Jr. / *Aqsaq*	Kessigliq	Upper Kalskag	1946
Kerilia Wise	Upper Kalskag	Lower Kalskag	1950
Michael Savage Sr. / *Aqum'aq*	Upper Kalskag	Lower Kalskag	1954
Stanley Michelson / *Puuliyagaq*	Upper Kalskag	Upper Kalskag	1960
John Andrew / *Alegyuk*	Eek Mountains	Kwethluk	1945
Peter Gilila / *Anguarun*	Kassigluq	Akiak	1955
Mark Leary	Kalskag	Bethel	1964
Jacob Black / *Nasgauq*	Qaurragyagaq	Napakiak	1940
James Charles / *Ayagiaq*	Kuiguyulleq	Tuntutuliak	1940
Mary Sakar	Crooked Creek	Anchorage	1936
Jennie Zaukar	Waskey's Landing	Anchorage	1947
Wassily Kameroff / *Matarcuilnguq*	Chuathbaluk	Anchorage	1949

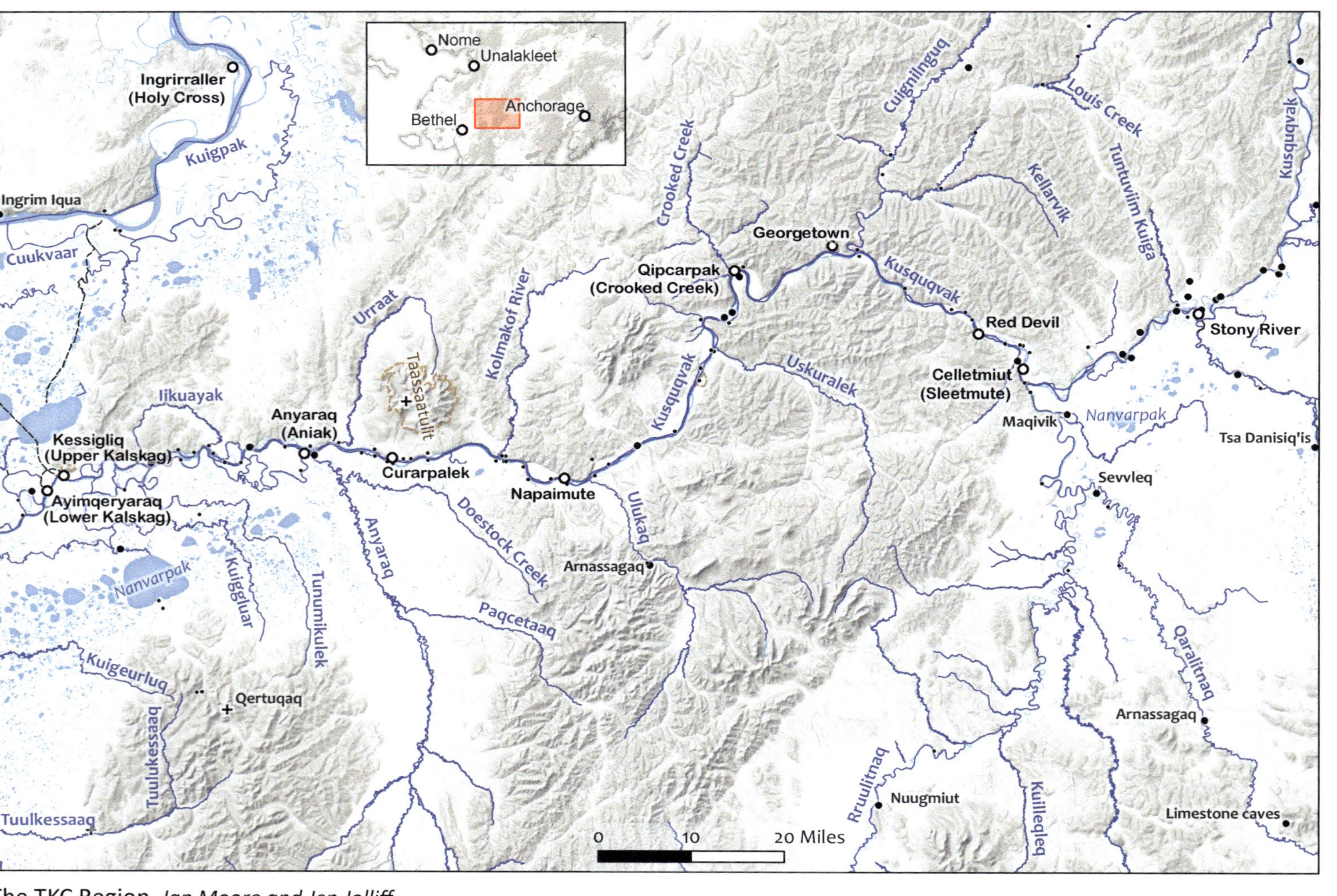

The TKC Region. *Ian Moore and Jen Jolliff*

Introduction

Over the last decade, Mark John, Marie Meade, Alice Rearden, and I have had opportunities to meet with middle Kuskokwim elders and to begin to learn about the area they call home. We did this through village visits and through elder gatherings like those the Calista Elders Council (CEC), and more recently Calista Education and Culture, have hosted over the last 25 years in efforts to document traditions in the Yukon-Kuskokwim region. Until this project, we had always focused on Yup'ik traditions, shared primarily in the Yup'ik language. The middle Kuskokwim, however, is populated by men and women of Yup'ik, Deg Hit'an, Dene, German, even Yugoslavian ancestry, and most of our conversations were in English. Speaking of his many relatives, Bob Aloysius once called himself "United Natives of Alaska."

The book is divided into two parts. The first includes essays describing five different gatherings with middle Kuskokwim elders – the first in June 2018 and the most recent in April 2024 – as well as one essay on middle Kuskokwim oral traditions generally. The remainder of the book includes stories by individual elders, in their own words. The stories by Golga Effemka, Joshua Phillip, and Frank Andrew were originally shared in Yup'ik. CEC published bilingual versions of Joshua Phillip's story in *Anguyiim Nalliini: Time of Warring* (Fienup-Riordan and Rearden 2016:240-52) and Frank Andrew's stories in *Ircenrraat / Other-than-human Persons* (Rearden et al. 2021:262-65) and *Angalkut / Shamans in Yup'ik Oral Tradition* (Fienup-Riordan, Rearden, and Meade 2025). We wanted to share them again here in English especially for middle Kuskokwim readers, as they represent important events in their history. Golga's stories have not been published in either Yup'ik or English, and we share them here for the first time as originally spoken and in translation, providing a fine example of the linguistic abilities of middle Kuskokwim elders.

How and why we work together: Topic-specific gatherings[1]

To better understand the elder gatherings that are the basis for the first part of the book, I will share a bit of history. I have worked as an anthropologist for the Calista Elders Council (CEC) since 2000, which was reorganized and renamed Calista Education and Culture in 2014 – the "new CEC." The "new CEC" remains the primary heritage organization in the Yukon-Kuskokwim delta region, an area the size of Kansas. Until he passed away in August 2025, Mark John was CEC's cultural advisor. Our principal translators have been Alice Rearden and Marie Meade – with help on this project from Corey Joseph – and I am their anthropologist. I tell people anthropology in Alaska today is a team sport, and I'm fortunate to be part of a great team.

Mark, Alice, Marie, and I have worked together on a variety of CEC projects over decades. In the beginning all projects were initiated by CEC's board of elders, including nine men and women, representing villages throughout the region. Under the new CEC, this board has been replaced by a six-member elders' committee which continues to guide the work we do. Both the original CEC board as well as the new CEC elders' committee actively support the documentation and sharing of their oral traditions, which they view as possessing continued value in today's world.

Almost from the beginning, CEC's primary information-gathering tool has been the topic-specific gathering. The CEC pioneered this format while working with elders between 2000 and 2005 during a major traditional knowledge project funded by the National Science Foundation's (NSF) Arctic Social Science program. We found that meeting with small groups of elder experts, accompanied by younger community members, for two- and three-day gatherings devoted to a specific set of questions was an effective and rewarding way of addressing topics. We use the term *gatherings* to describe these open-ended exchanges between generations as opposed to the term *meetings*, which are more often viewed as goal-oriented, decision-making events. Gatherings are also unlike interviews, during which elders answer questions posed by those who often do not already hold the knowledge they seek. Gatherings (like academic symposia) encourage elders to speak among their peers at the highest level. CEC board member John Phillip (October 2006:284) of Kongiganak observed during one gathering: "Hearing the story you just told, I learned what I didn't know. It is like we are still learning."

It is important to emphasize that these gatherings build on each other, and long and careful listening provides unique perspectives on local history and oral traditions. Over the past twenty years, CEC has hosted dozens of gatherings on numerous topics including: family values; traditional discipline; survival strategies; traditional technology; harvesting patterns; ocean hunting; snow and ice; and weather conditions. Our work together has resulted in more than 1500 hours of recordings and 25,000 pages of transcripts. I'm reminded of the proverb: "If you want to go fast, go alone. If you want to go far, go together." These deep collaborations go beyond consultation and cooperation to the true co-conceptualizations of knowledge.

In gatherings, elders teach not just facts, they teach listeners how to learn. They share not only what they know but how they know it and why they believe it is important to remember. CEC staff and community members value topic-specific gatherings not merely as tools for documentation but also as contexts of cultural transmission, and youth often accompany the elders who attend. The gatherings themselves are meaningful events that enrich lives locally at the same time their documentation has the potential to increase cross-cultural understanding globally.

Some of our gatherings are held in villages, others in Bethel, and many at my home in Anchorage. During the Anchorage gathering for this project, for example, two elders arrived by air while one (Wassily Kameroff) lives here in town. While elders usually stay as my guests – sleeping in the rooms vacated by our grown children – due to COVID restrictions our out-of-town visitors stayed at an Anchorage hotel. Mark brought all three up to my house in the morning, where Marie joined us for the day. Sitting comfortably in the living room, and after an opening prayer giving thanks for our health and gratitude for being together, I turned on the tape recorder and we began. Marie led the discussion, with me chiming in with questions. I made salmon soup, Mark brought beluga to cook for lunch, and we all enjoyed our shared meal. Time went fast. By mid-afternoon, we stopped for the day, and Mark took the men home for a steam bath. The second day followed the same pattern, and by day's end we all agreed it had been time well spent.

CEC topic-specific gatherings and our work with elders are ultimately shaped by the concerns and choices of individual participants. When elders have been asked whether questions are appropriate in storytelling contexts, many said that stories should be "just told." Yet in our topic-specific gatherings we have found elders ready and willing to answer our questions, especially when these questions show we have listened to what has gone before.

It is difficult to adequately convey the compassion and loving spirit that fill their accounts. Mark John's father, Paul John once told us that children should never be talked to harshly, as it blocks their minds and prevents them from learning: "If those who are giving them advice speak with compassion, it would be like giving them strong, healing medicine and would help bring them happiness." We remain deeply grateful for the gifts these elders have given us and their trust that we will treat these gifts responsibly and respectfully and share them in our turn.

The instrumental value of what we do is in the forefront of our work together. The image of the igloo-dwelling Eskimo still smiles out from many a gift shop window in Alaska. Though few elders directly confront this simple-minded and insidious stereotype, they sense that sharing their detailed narratives strikes its foundations, destabilizes it, and sends it crumbling down. Their contemporary narrative references to the past are active efforts to shape the future – a future in which they believe their history should be recognized and valued.

As noted, in gatherings elders are not just trying to *say*, but to *do* something. They know they possess a narrative tradition and knowledge system second to none, and they want others to give it the respect it deserves. In 2009, Nelson Island leader Paul John declared, "If white people see these books, they will think, 'These Yup'ik people evidently are knowledgeable and know how to take care of their own affairs through their traditional ways.'"

Boating on the Kuskowkim. *Will Hartman*

A Brief History of the Middle Kuskokwim

The Yukon-Kuskokwim delta

Yup'ik people have made their homes in the delta lowlands of southwest Alaska for thousands of years. They have done so in large part because, from the time people first settled on the headlands of the Bering Sea coast, they found that both the land and sea were rich in animals. Although the subarctic tundra environment may appear cold and unforgiving to the first-time visitor, in fact it is among the richest habitats in the Far North supporting a correspondingly large and diverse human population.

Today the Yukon-Kuskokwim delta is home to 48 modern villages, complete with infrastructure, located along the banks of both the Yukon and Kuskokwim Rivers as well as the Bering Sea coast stretching from Kotlik in the north to Quinhagak and Goodnews Bay in the south. The presence of particular plants and animals varies throughout the delta, depending on factors such as terrain, soil composition, annual snowfall and weather conditions generally, and distance from the Bering Sea coast. These variations, in turn, serve to define different regions, each dependent on a unique resource base. Coastal hunters, for example, have ready access to sea mammals, shorebirds, and saltwater fish – especially herring – while upriver hunters can more easily trap the larger furbearers and hunt for moose and bear.

The lowland delta of southwest Alaska is comprised of a network of lakes, rivers, and streams that cover close to half the region's surface with water supporting freshwater fish of every size – from tiny needlefish to gigantic northern pike, and everything in between, including blackfish, burbot, sucker fish, lampreys, five species of whitefish, and five species of salmon. The delta is bordered by the Kilbuck and Kuskokwim Mountains to the south and the Nulato Hills to the north. Caribou migrate through this high country, some herds moving north to south and others east to west. The mountains provide ideal habitat for ground squirrels and marmots. Larger fur bearers are found in the wooded country away from the coast, including wolverine, marten, lynx, wolves, and black and brown bears.

The same small fish that people harvest in abundance are also hunted by smaller furbearers, including mink and river otter. In the past, muskrats made homes in every lake and pond, feeding on water plants like poison water hemlock and pond lilies. Farther inland red foxes can also be found hunting for tundra hares along riverbanks and meadows, while Arctic foxes roam the coast where they grow fat on eggs, baby birds, and voles. Moose and beaver have always been present upriver – though not always plentiful – feeding on young willow shoots, pond greens, and spruce tips. During the last twenty years, as the climate has warmed and shrub growth has expanded toward the coast, the populations of both beaver and moose have also exploded, moving west following the new growth.

While each of the 48 villages in southwest Alaska is unique, common subsistence patterns and histories join them into distinct regional groups including the Qaluyaarmiut (people of Nelson Island), the people of the lower and middle Yukon River, the Caninarmiut of the lower Kuskokwim coast, the Akulmiut west of Bethel, the people of the middle Kuskokwim River, as well as the Cup'ik and Cup'ig speakers of Chevak and Nunivak Island respectively. The total population for this vast region – covering an area the size of Kansas – is close to 28,000.

The middle Kuskokwim

The ten villages located along the middle Kuskokwim – from Lower Kalskag upriver as far as Stony River – form a unique part of the Yukon-Kuskokwim delta. While sharing language, cultural ties, and many subsistence resources with their Yup'ik neighbors downriver, both their history and environment have presented challenges and determined solutions unlike those faced by any other regional group. While much of southwest Alaska lacked the commercial resources – sea otters, bowhead whales, gold, and timber – that drew non-Natives North, the commercial advantages of the middle Kuskokwim attracted trappers, traders, miners, and reindeer herders – many of whom made their homes along the middle river and contributed to the rich cultural blending of traditions that characterizes the region to this day. As it embraces the borderlands at the eastern extent of the Calista region, the middle river also includes men and women of Deg Hit'an and Dena'ina as well as Central Yup'ik heritage.

The climate of the middle Kuskokwim is continental, with cold winters and warm summers. As travelers move upriver, away from the coast, they encounter a wooded shoreline, including spruce, cottonwood, and birch, as well as willow and alder. Rocky ridges and alpine tundra are found atop the hills bordering the middle river. More than fifty varieties of edible greens and berries also flourish here, which people actively harvest, filling freezers with regional delicacies including *elagat* (alpine sweet vetch, "Eskimo potatoes"), red berries, and blueberries, to name but a few.

All ten middle Kuskokwim communities are built on the banks of a 200-

mile stretch of river. When people first moved inland from the Bering Sea coast approximately 2,000 years ago, they followed this river highway. As they left the flat, open tundra behind, they entered woodlands inhabited by Athabascan people along both the upper Yukon and upper Kuskokwim Rivers, as well as Dena'ina people along the headwaters of the Stony River.

Languages of the middle Kuskokwim

The ethnic and linguistic relationships of the middle river are complex, as the area is the meeting ground for four distinct Alaska Native language groups – Central Yup'ik, Deg Hit'an (formerly known as Ingalik), Upper Kuskokwim, and Dena'ina. Unlike other regional groups in southwest Alaska, Yup'ik and Deg Hit'an shared the middle river, sometimes living side by side (Oswalt 1980a:51-53). The Russian explorer Lieutenant Lavrentiy Zagoskin visited Kwigiumpainukamiut in 1843, noting 89 "Eskimos" (Yupiit) living adjacent to 71 Ingalik (Deg Hit'an) (Redding-Gubitosa 1992). Archaeological surveys of Little Mountain Village (Ingricuar), a site just upriver from Napaimute occupied for at least 1,000 years, also found Yup'ik and Athabascan people living together (Oswalt 1980a:53; Street 1998:6). Linguist Priscilla Kari (1985:180-81) recorded both Yup'ik and Deg Hit'an place names for important middle river settlements, including Crow Village, Kolmakov, Chuathbaluk, Napaimute, Crooked Creek, George River, Georgetown, and "Eight Mile" Village (Wooley et al. 2008:22). While our focus has been on Yup'ik place names and oral traditions, Deg Hit'an people also knew and used the middle river.

Anthropologist Wendell Oswalt (1962) noted that the people of the middle Kuskokwim had more contact with diverse Athabascan groups than any other segment of the Yup'ik population. He also noted that since subsistence resources were relatively plentiful and there were no major geographic barriers, Yup'ik people moved steadily upriver during historic times: "When they met already established Indian populations, they found a compatibility with them that did not deter their penetration of the area. No other historic Alaska Eskimos found conditions for venturing inland quite as favorable" (Oswalt 1990:14). As Yup'ik people moved into Athabascan territory, their contact was largely compatible, resulting in a blending of riverine Yup'ik and interior Athabascan lifestyles (VanStone 1974:42, Jerabek 2014:23).

Cheryl Jerabek (2014:9) noted that when she did her research on cultural identity and heritage on the middle Kuskokwim, local people referred to languages spoken by their parents and grandparents as Lime Village way (Dena'ina), Nikolai way (Upper Kuskokwim), Yukon way (Deg Hit'an), and downriver way (Yup'ik). In the past, many middle Kuskokwim residents spoke multiple languages – one or more Athabascan languages, as well as Yup'ik, Russian, and some English. Multi-lingualism was not a luxury but a necessity for living in such a culturally diverse environment. Jerabek (2014:10) quotes the late Ray Collins, a scholar in Athabascan culture living in the Nikolai-McGrath area, as saying that along the middle river, Yup'ik replaced Athabascan through intermarriage. Athabascan languages were very difficult to learn, and while Athabascan speakers were able to pick up Yup'ik and were often bilingual or trilingual, if Yup'ik people were not raised speaking Athabascan, they did not easily learn it. As a result, people of Athabascan descent ended up speaking Yup'ik as it was used over a broader area and gradually became the dominant language along the middle river. As noted below, in 1907, Yup'ik was the dominant language spoken in Sleetmute by both Athabascan and Yup'ik residents (Gordon 1917:110).

Most of the elders we worked with spoke Yup'ik but using a distinctive middle Kuskokwim vocabulary, including words such as *cikultaal* or *cikultall* (stone fly) which is likely Athabascan in origin. The "na" ending for names of rivers, as in Holitna and Hoholitna, is Athabascan for "river." Even using the same Yup'ik language, elders noted distinctive speech patterns as one moved downriver. During one of our gatherings, Wassily Kameroff commented that the upriver Athabascans speak fast, like the current, while people downriver speak slower. Finally, from just above Bethel where the tides go in and out, people start slurring words, just like the tides (see Chapter 3).

The Russian period

Although Russian influence was felt in other parts of southwest Alaska, including Iqugmiut (Russian Mission) on the Yukon River and St. Michael at the mouth of the Yukon, especially in terms of population disruption accompanying the introduction of communicable diseases, the middle Kuskokwim experienced more sustained Russian contact and influence than any other region.

Before contact with Euro-Americans in the early 1800s, there was already extensive trade between groups living along the river. Archaeologist Chris Wooley (2008:24) notes that trade networks have great time depth in the middle Kuskokwim as evidenced by the presence of obsidian in one 2000-year-old site. Well-known trade items included wooden bowls and birch-bark canoes which upriver and Yukon River Athabascan people traded for seal oil in downriver communities (Oswalt 1958:63). Russian fur traders built on these existing networks, including the Kuskokwim-Nushagak connection. When Russians built

Objects from the UA Museum of the North archaeology lab, including an ivory story knife found at Kolmakovsky and an obsidian biface found at the Angyaruaq site, downriver from Crooked Creek, dating from between 2200 and 1500 years ago. The obsidian source is Batza Tena, approximately 450 km north in the Koyukuk River region – evidence of ancient long-distance trade networks (Wooley et al 2008). *UA77-043-4382, UA2006-141-0059. Micki LeClair Sievers*

Aleksandrovskiy Redoubt at the mouth of the Nushagak River, people of the upper Nushagak traveled to the central and upper Kuskokwim to trade for more beaver and foxes.

Wooley (2008:24-25, 97-98) notes that along with the portage trail connecting Kalskag with the Yukon (still in use today), there was another winter overland trail between Crow Village and Paimiut Slough running along the east flank of the Portage Mountains and the Oskawalik (Uskuralek) to the Nushagak winter portage trail. There were also winter and summer portages from Sleetmute and Napaimute connecting with trails up the Holitna and Hoholitna past the Taylor Mountains and into the Nushagak Hills. Far from a backwater, the middle Kuskokwim was the center for travelers and traders moving north, south, east, and west.

Even before the arrival of Russian traders, Russian goods were already present. Chukchi and Iñupiaq traders in Siberia transported reindeer skins, iron and copper manufactures, beads, and tobacco to Seward Peninsula. From there, Iñupiat carried goods both north and south. Central Kuskokwim people also acquired Russian goods indirectly through Aleksandrovskiy Redoubt in Bristol Bay and from Cook Inlet stations (Oswalt 1980b:7). The success of Russian trading activities in the region built on a long history of indigenous trade and established relationships between Yup'ik and Athabascan peoples in the region (Burch and Correll 1972:30-31; Jerabek 2014:31).

Russian explorers and traders followed these well-established aboriginal trade routes through the region. Russian explorer Vasiliy Ivanoff visited the region in 1790 (Oswalt 1980a:9). A fur-trading station was built near present-day Sleetmute at the junction of the Holitna and Kuskokwim Rivers in 1832, another small trading station at Lukin's Odinochka at the village of Kwigiumpainukamiut in 1833, and at Kolmakovsky Redoubt in 1841 (Oswalt 1980a:10, 54-55; 1990:49-50). Kolmakovsky was built across the river from Kwigiumpainukamiut, already a central trading center for the region that brought together indigenous and Russian traders and was a stopping point for traveling Russian Orthodox priests. Although Kolmakovsky was abandoned by the Russians in 1866 in anticipation of the US purchase of Alaska, Hutchinson, Kohl, and Company (soon reorganized as the Alaska Commercial Company) continued to operate it as a trading center for several more decades.

Along with Russian traders came Russian Orthodox priests bringing the rudiments of Christianity to the people of the Yukon-Kuskokwim delta. Like the traders, they were few in number. Father Iakov Netsvetov served at Iqugmiut from 1845 to 1863 (Pierce 1984). As the single priest for the entire region, Netsvetov traveled by dog team over the Kalskag portage and up and down the Kuskokwim in winter, and by boat down the Yukon to Mikhailovskiy Redoubt (St. Michael)

Kolmakovsky Redoubt photographed by Adolphus Hartmann during his Kuskokwim reconnaissance in 1884. *Moravian Archives, Bethlehem, PA*

each summer. Aided by a handful of converts in the communities he visited, as well as by the few traders along the middle river, Netsvetov and the Russian Orthodox clergy who came after him were remarkably successful in introducing people to the fundamentals of Christianity and in planting the seeds for future Orthodox congregations. Today the Russian Orthodox church remains the major Christian denomination along the middle Kuskokwim.

The Russians who came to trade and to preach were few in number. They were, in fact, not ethnically Russian but rather Russian-speaking Creoles – the children of Russian men and Siberian or Alaska Native women – many of whom married local women and raised families of their own along the middle river. Petr Kolmakov and Ivan Lukin were two Creole sons who took over their fathers' trading duties. They had grown up along the Kuskokwim, and they spoke Russian as well as more than one Alaska Native language. After 1867, when others returned to Russia, these Creole men and their families stayed and became part of the local population (Jerabek 2014:58).

Relations between different Yup'ik groups, as well as between Yup'ik and Athabascan peoples, were not always peaceful before the arrival of the Russians. The bloody battle of Maqallartuli, fought between attackers from the Yukon and defending Kuskokwim warriors living north and south of the Kalskag portage, is but one example of long-standing animosities between regional groups (see Joshua Phillip's account, this volume). Whatever hostilities existed in the early 1800s were largely put aside by the end of the Russian period, due to Russian pressure to reduce conflict in favor of trade coupled with the drastic region-wide population decline that accompanied Russian expansion (Fienup-Riordan and Rearden 2016:81-82).

As in other parts of southwest Alaska, the most significant impact of the arrival of the Russians was the introduction of communicable diseases, including the 1838-39 smallpox epidemic. The smallpox epidemic was the first of many deadly new diseases, including diphtheria, measles, scarlet fever, mumps, typhoid, pneumonia, and influenza (Fortuine 1992:209-215, 230, in Jerabek 2014:50). This onslaught continued into the 1900s, with the arrival of influenza and measles in 1900, followed by the worldwide influenza pandemic of 1918-1919.

Deaths brought about the abandonment of entire villages. As much as 60 percent of the Yup'ik population with whom Russians were familiar in Bristol Bay and along the Kuskokwim were dead by 1838 (Fienup-Riordan 1994:30, 2000:10). It is estimated that the population of the entire Kuskokwim River drainage was about 4,000 in early historic times. By 1889 the population was estimated to be 2,743. It continued to decline to 1,114 ten years later, and by the turn of the century was only 600, with the lowest recorded population at 514 from 1910-1919 (Fortuine 1992:215-226, 235; Oswalt 1980a:17-18). Losses of this magnitude are difficult to comprehend. Yet people persevered. Although the introduction of communicable disease damaged social groups and patterns of intergroup relations, it left largely intact many of the routines of daily life throughout the remainder of the nineteenth century. Small bands of extended family groups continued to move over the land, seeking the animals they needed to survive.

A snapshot in time: George Byron Gordon's 1907 visit to Sleetmute

The foregoing brief history can help us understand the various influences reshaping life along the middle Kuskokwim during the nineteenth century. It may also be useful to consider first person observations of life along the river at the turn of the century to get a fuller picture of changing times. Euro-Americans began fur trapping in the central Kuskokwim area in the early 1900s when fur prices rose. Between 1907 and 1909, the number of non-Native fur trappers and prospectors along the Kuskokwim rose from twelve to 200 (Charnley 1984:25). Although fur prices would decline with World War I, in a boom-and-bust cycle that would continue throughout the twentieth century, a closer look at the early 1900s can shed light on changes already wrought as well as changes to come.

In the summer of 1907, then 37-year-old anthropologist George Byron Gordon traveled down the Kuskokwim with his brother MacLaren, on behalf of the University Museum in Philadelphia. He described his trip as a "mere reconnaissance," as the time was too short for further work. Gordon was, however, able to make a small collection of objects from the lower river, as well as to take some wonderful photographs along the middle river, especially during his two-and-a-half day stay at Sleetmute.

To access the upper Kuskokwim, the two young men traveled down the Yukon River after breakup to the mouth of the Tanana River, then up the Tanana to its junction with the Kantishna. They then followed the Kantishna upstream to Lake Minchumina, crossed the lake by canoe, and hiked the ten-mile portage to the North Fork of the Kuskokwim ("Tichininik") – country that white men had rarely visited at the time.

Traveling downstream, the pair passed no villages and met few people until they arrived at "Sikmiut" (Sleetmute) at the mouth of the Holitna. They landed below the village and a "tall Indian" took them to the chief's house. In his book describing his journey, *In the Alaskan Wilderness*, Gordon (1917:109) wrote: "At no other point on our journey, either before or after, were we treated with so much attention or with any show of ceremony." Communication with the Sleetmute leader was helped by the fact that the man had visited the Moravian Mission in Bethel where he had acquired a small English vocabulary.

In all, Gordon (1917:10) counted 60 men, women, and children at Sleetmute, although he was told that more than half of the people were away hunting. He judged the people "comely" and noted "Tinneh" (Dene) features and stature for the majority, a second group with mixed features, and a third group with "Eskimo" features. He wrote: "The first class and the last were sharply distinguished." Gordon also noted that although Athabascan in appearance, the people spoke the Yup'ik language: "The second fact by which we were struck was that our new friends spoke a language that was not Tinneh but Innuit and that corresponded closely to the language of the coast Eskimo" (which Gordon recognized from his previous visit to the Bering Sea coast in 1905).

Gordon (2017:113) went on to comment on the Sleetmute leader's reaction to the increasing number of white men traveling on the river:

> Although he had visited the Mission, the Sikmiut chief had not been converted or baptized and he had not been greatly impressed by what he had seen and heard. The teaching, he said, was good, but it was not better than the things that his people had taught and practiced always. He had encountered traders on his journeys down river and lately white people had made their appearance in his neighborhood on their way to the Tacotna. Reports had come to him, moreover, from the Yukon and from other parts of the country touching the doings of the white men. From his observations and from reports, he was convinced that the presence of the white men in Alaska was an evil and that they deliberately practiced evil. That being the case, what did their good teaching matter.

Gordon (1917:114) continued: "Sikmiut had just arrived at that unfortunate period in its history, for it lay on the route of the miners on their way up to the Tacotna, and the little stampede of the early summer was having its effects." The chief, he observed, was understandably anxious, as already "some of their young men had gone astray, strong drink made its appearance, and sickness had increased during the summer."

Gordon observed (and photographed) houses of logs like "Tinneh" houses of the far interior, noting that two houses had glass panes for windows: "The floors were on the level of the ground and never sunken, as are the Eskimo houses. On the other hand, the arrangement of the village was in the Eskimo style, with a kozgee [*qasgiq*] or public hall occupying the central position. This kozgee was of relatively small size; it was not built underground and was not used for sweat baths. It was used as a meeting place and a council chamber." The unmarried men sometimes slept in the *qasgiq*, but it was not the rule. In addition to the "kozgee," the village also had a bath house, a "mukeiawik" (*maqivik*) where the men took their sweat baths.

Sleetmute sub-chief, 1907. *George B. Gordon, courtesy of the Penn Museum, image no. 11799*

Gordon also noted mixed Athabascan and Yup'ik material culture, including birch-bark dishes and wooden bowls. He made a dozen photographs of men, women, and children in handsome parkas displaying both familiar Yup'ik designs as well as designs unique to the middle Kuskokwim. One woman, wearing a ceremonial headdress and holding a birch-bark container in one hand and a feather wand in another, appears to be performing a blessing or purification ritual.

Toward the end of his account, Gordon (1917:197) affirms the devastating impact of the diseases that followed the arrival of Russians on the middle river: "Diseases introduced with terrible effect among the Eskimo were no doubt carried to the far interior where they swept away the Indians in their distant fastnessess. In 1848 a terrible epidemic of smallpox swept over Alaska, and since that time successive visitations of disease, becoming more frequent, have nearly left the country of the Upper Kuskokwim without a population."

Son of Sleetmute sub-chief, 1907. *George B. Gordon, courtesy of the Penn Museum, image no. 11797*

Sleetmute girl, 1907. *George B. Gordon, courtesy of the Penn Museum, image no. 11802*

Sleetmute man, 1907. *George B. Gordon, courtesy of the Penn Museum, image no. 11804*

Sleetmute girl, 1907, whom Gordon referred to as "a belle of Sikmiut." *George B. Gordon, courtesy of the Penn Museum, image no. 11451*

Woman wearing a headdress and carrying a birch-bark basket and feather wand, 1907.
George B. Gordon, courtesy of the Penn Museum, image no. 11453

Sleetmute woman, 1907. *George B. Gordon, courtesy of the Penn Museum, image no. 11790*

Sleetmute woman, 1907. *George B. Gordon, courtesy of the Penn Museum, image no. 11791*

Daughter of the Sleetmute sub-chief, 1907. *George B. Gordon, courtesy of the Penn Museum, image no. 11795*

Mining

Crooked Creek, showing Dennis Parents' store in 1930.
Aleš Hrdlička papers, National Anthropological Archives, Smithsonian Institution

Writing about southwest Alaska as a whole, it is fair to say that the abundance of edible animals and plants – what have come to be known as "subsistence resources" – was matched by the region's lack of commercially valuable resources. A notable exception to this broad generalization was the middle Kuskokwim, which drew prospectors in numbers which would have a lasting impact. The sedimentary rock layers of the Kuskokwim Mountains contained deposits of cinnabar, which could be mined for quicksilver mercury, as well as gold, and placer gold mining has been conducted in the Iditarod region since the early 1890s (Wooley et al. 2008:6).

Numerous prospectors who had traveled to Nome in the Gold Rush of 1898 headed south to the Kuskokwim in 1900 to continue their search along Kuskokwim tributaries, including the "Yellow River" (Aniak River). By 1908 Crooked Creek (then known as Portage Village) became the stopping-off point for miners, who would travel up the Kuskokwim by boat, then overland to the mining camps at Iditarod and Flat. Gold was also discovered at Donlin Creek in 1909 and worked by various prospectors. Dennis Parent set up a trading post at Crooked Creek in 1914, followed by a post office, Russian Orthodox chapel, and territorial school (Oswalt 1980a:36-38; Wooley et al. 2008:32).

By 1910, nearby Georgetown had exploded into a gold rush community with more than 300 prospectors, whose cabins and out-buildings were mostly destroyed during a fire in 1911 (Oswalt 1980a:41). George Hoffman built a trading post downriver at Napaimute in 1906, and established a territorial school for his growing family in the 1920s. Napaimute continued to be occupied year-round into the 1950s, after which most residents moved to Aniak (Oswalt 1980a:62).

Red Devil was among the largest mining developments along the entire Kuskokwim when rich deposits of quicksilver mercury were found there. The Red Devil cinnabar mine continued in operation from 1939 through 1946 – supplying much needed mercury for the war effort – as well as 1952 through 1972 (Oswalt 1980a:13-15). Wooley (2008:34) notes that Red Devil was Alaska's largest mercury mine in the 1950s. Descendants of those who worked the Red Devil mine continue to live in the region today.

Hundreds of prospectors and miners traveled the Kuskokwim during the first half of the twentieth century. Although many left, many also stayed, marrying locally and establishing settlements in places where few had lived before. They came following severe epidemic disruption to the Yup'ik and Deg Hit'an populations, and they found space to build homes, gardens, and satisfying lives. Living side-by-side with Yup'ik families – often including in-laws – they introduced new techniques and traditions. In the beginning, Yup'ik families sold

Georgetown was still well populated when this photo was taken in 1912. *Robert Acheson Collection, Anchorage Museum B2009.061.26*

Napaimute Territorial School. In 1942, 13 students were enrolled. *ASL-MS146-05-33*

The sprawling mining operation at Red Devil, 1961. *Wein Collection, Anchorage Museum B1985.027.1676*

Men entering the Red Devil mine, 1961, from left to right, George Fredericks, Douglas Burd, Fred Drucky, and Jack Pruett. *Wein Collection, Anchorage Museum B1985.027.1680*

them fish for their dog teams, and cut wood to feed the sternwheelers that carried their equipment and supplies upriver. Beginning in the early 1900s, salmon were harvested with fish wheels introduced by miners from the Yukon. The middle Kuskokwim had become a center for cultural exchange unlike any other part of southwest Alaska.

Reindeer herding

Another immigrant population that had a lasting impact on the middle Kuskokwim were the Sami herders who came to the Kuskokwim with their families in the early 1900s to tend the reindeer that Dr. Sheldon Jackson had brought to Alaska from Finnmark in northern Norway. Jackson's motivation for this experiment in animal husbandry was in part to alleviate periodic food shortages in Alaska but, more important from the point of view of "Manifest Destiny," to help "civilize" Alaska Natives – transforming them from hunters to herders. The first deer and their Sami herders arrived on the Seward Peninsula in 1894, with a more permanent colony recruited from Finnmark during winter 1898. By 1901, ten missions in Alaska owned deer. The Moravians brought the first herds to Bethel in 1901 with Sami herders in charge and Yup'ik men taken on as apprentices. By 1903, the Kuskokwim herd had grown to close to 800 reindeer, with Sami herders Nils Persen Sara and Per Spein in charge (Henkelman and Vitt 1985:308; McAtee 2010).

Akiak became the regional center of herding activities along the Kuskokwim, and John Kilbuck, then superintendent of schools, helped to organize reindeer fairs in Akiak beginning in 1915. Local herds prospered, as both the Kilbuck and Kuskokwim Mountains, as well as the tundra lowlands between them, provided excellent grazing grounds. Although limited transportation made it difficult for the Moravians to sell meat beyond the region, they were able to market reindeer meat to miners in Iditarod. Jens Kvamme Anderson, a Norwegian immigrant who married Nil Sara's daughter, Ellen Marie, bought reindeer from Native herders in Unalakleet and from Sami families in Akiak and drove the deer to Flat, where he sold the meat to the miners (McAtee 2010:27; Wooley et al. 2008:30).

In 1914, the Kvamme family established a new herd in the headwaters of the Buckstock and Aniak Rivers, constructing trails, brush corrals, and cabins.

Sami herders arriving at Akiak, March 1915. Note the boat-shaped freighting pulks (sleds). According to John Kilbuck, each sled held about 200 pounds, and one man usually handled seven sled deer. *Kilbuck family photograph*

Their herds grazed among the high ridges dividing the Swift and Holitna River headwaters south of the Aniak, Holokuk (Ulukaq) and Oskawalik (Uskuralek) Rivers. The family spent winters in the Napaimute area, moving to Aniak in 1930 (McAtee 2010:28).

Local herds continued to grow and prosper until the 1937 Alaska Reindeer Act restricted ownership of deer to Alaska Natives, forcing the Sami herders and other local non-Natives who had acquired herds, such as A. H. Twitchell, to sell out at the low price of $3 per deer. After the Reindeer Act, the herds rapidly declined, then disappeared. For Yup'ik men, subsistence harvesting activities continued to take precedence over close attention to the herds, and finding herders was a problem. Overstocked ranges, predation by wolves, and losses to migrating caribou were also given as reasons for the decline of the herds (Lantis 1950). Some Yup'ik narratives lay blame for the decline of mission herds on owners who failed to share meat, with the arrival of the wolves the consequence of their "stingy" behavior (Benedict Tucker in Fienup-Riordan et al. 2025:131).

Jens Kvamme and his family provide a significant addendum to the history of

Ellen Sara with her daughter, Mary Spein, several years after the Speins arrived on the Kuskokwim in 1903, probably at Akiak where the Speins and Saras settled. Ellen is still wearing the northern-style of clothing from St. Lawrence Island where the Sara and Spein families taught reindeer herding for the Bureau of Education before coming to the Kuskokwim. *June McAtee family collection*

mining along the Kuskokwim. While obtaining reindeer from Sami herders on the Kwethluk River, Jens discovered a small but rich placer deposit and filed claims on the Kwethluk River tributary, Canyon Creek, in 1913. He and his brothers worked the mine for nearly thirty years, thus providing income for their family after they were forced to sell their deer (McAtee 2010:28). Geologist and family historian June McAtee points out that Canyon Creek continued to be a source of income for the next generation as well, as it was passed on to Jens' son and later his grandson.

Although herding as a commercial activity failed to take permanent root on the Kuskokwim, the Sami and Norwegian herders did. After they were forced to sell their herds, many – like the Kvammes – lived out their lives on the Kuskokwim, as have their descendants. The Spein, Sara, and Kvamme families in Akiak, Aniak, Kwethluk, and Bethel are all descendants of Sami herders, adding their "Laapat" (Lappland) traditions to local community life (McAtee 2010:29-30; Wooley et al. 2010). Spein Mountain stands tall on the shores of the Kiseralik River, and when invited to the Aniak school Francine Kvamme continues to show students how to make "brain bread," replacing reindeer brains with moose brains.

Missionary activity

With the American purchase of Alaska in 1867, the era of Russian dominance ended. Although the Russian Orthodox chapel at Kolmakovsky closed, vestiges of Russian influence remained, especially a familiarity with the Russian Orthodox faith and its teachings. Creole traders and Yup'ik converts continued to hold services and observe holy days without the direction of a resident priest.

Beginning in the 1890s, new mission groups began to work to capture souls along the middle Kuskokwim. The Moravians, who built their first mission house in Bethel in 1885, sent missionaries upriver and established their farthest upriver mission outpost at Ogavik (Uuravigmiut), just below Kalskag, in 1892 (Henkelman and Vitt 1985:168).

Catholic missionaries also arrived on the Yukon-Kuskokwim delta in the 1880s. In the face of competition from the Moravians, they focused on the Bering Sea coast south as far as Nelson Island, and Yukon River communities, including a major mission station and orphanage at Holy Cross (established in 1888), where children from the middle Kuskokwim continued to be sent into the 1960s. The Jesuits did little direct work along the Kuskokwim. In 1892, they built a mission house at Ohagamiut (Urraarmiut), just a few miles upriver from Kalskag. Smallpox had shrunk this once-thriving community, and the French Jesuit Father Robaut served there in 1894. In the face of continued epidemic disruption, many residents of Ohagamiut moved to Upper Kalskag, where a Catholic church was built in 1926, along with another Catholic church in Aniak in 1930. Both churches served the many Catholic families who had moved from the Yukon as well as those who had attended school in Holy Cross.

While the middle Kuskokwim represented a "frontier" for both the Moravians and Catholics, it remained then – and continues today – as the heartland for Russian Orthodoxy in southwest Alaska. Introduced by itinerant priests such as Father Netsvetov, Orthodoxy was slowly but surely adopted by communities as a form of "Yup'ik Christianity" more compatible with village life than the more recent (and notably stricter) Catholic and Moravian denominations.

A new Russian Orthodox chapel was built at Little Russian Mission (Chuathbaluk) with a priest and reader in 1894, and consecrated eleven years later (Smith 1980:31-34). The church endured with the help of Creole and Yup'ik community leaders who remained in the region and continued to support village chapels and hold Orthodox services. As success of the Moravian church owed a great deal to the early conversion of Yup'ik "Helpers," who spread the word within their own communities, the rootedness of Russian Orthodoxy in middle Kuskokwim communities derived from local church and community leaders who related church teachings to older Yup'ik beliefs in such areas as burials and mid-winter celebrations (Fienup-Riordan 1991:195-211).

One noteworthy Yup'ik transformation of a Russian Orthodox tradition is the celebration of Slaaviq, a Christmas celebration that remains an important part of community life to this day. Winter feasting, intercommunity visiting, and gift-giving had always been important in Yup'ik community life, and the house-to-house feasting and gift-giving of Slaaviq provided a new vehicle for these familiar traditions (Fienup-Riordan 1990:94-122). The late Father Michael Oleksa (1992:188) noted that the only Ukrainian missionary to serve in southwest Alaska, Father Iakov Korchinskii, likely introduced the singing of Carpatho-Russian folk carols (Koliady) in 1905, providing the foundation for the unique Slaaviq tradition: "Winter was the ancient traditional season for feasting and distributing gifts, associated with the Bladder Festival [and Messenger Feast], and the Yup'ik quickly adapted the caroling customs to their own needs...The Yup'ik celebration of Selaviq [Slaaviq], derived from the Slavonic 'Slava,' represents an obvious synthesis of Orthodox liturgical, Ukrainian folk, and ancient Eskimo traditions."

Pride in their Orthodox heritage is seen today in the ways contemporary elders talk about their own parents and grandparents. Chuathbaluk elder Sophie Sakar, for example, noted that her father used his trapping money to build a Russian Orthodox chapel in Aniak in the 1950s, "no donations, no volunteers, no

Sleetmute Russian Orthodox Church, 1948. *George A. Morlander Photographs, UAF-1997-108-555*

fundraisers." Likewise Lucy Simeon recalled how her grandfather, Sam Phillips (Crow Village Sam) moved his family from Crow Village to Chuathbaluk to care for the Russian Orthodox church that had been abandoned there when the community was depopulated due to disease. When discussing village leadership, Jennie Zaukar and Wassily Kameroff both noted that the *tuyuq* (lay pastor) and village chief were one and the same.

It should be noted that while Orthodoxy remains the dominant Christian denomination along the middle Kuskokwim, co-operation rather than animosity characterizes the relations between the different churches today. For example, although Lower and Upper Kalskag remain divided – with a Catholic Church in Upper Kalskag and a Russian Orthodox Church in Lower Kalskag – many families today are mixed and all come together for Slaaviq as well as community feeds to honor a first hunt or a forty-day memorial feast (Jerabek 2014:176). This ecumenism is in sharp contrast to the inter-denominational feuding – often between the missionaries themselves – reported in journals and official reports from the late nineteenth and early twentieth centuries (Fienup-Riordan 1991:184-212).

Village formation and regional challenges, past and present

Fish camp near Stony River, 1930. Note the canoe alongside a narrow upriver-style skiff with motor. *Aleš Hrdlička papers, National Anthropological Archives, Smithsonian Institution*

The first half of the twentieth century was marked by continued cultural mixing and the slow but steady ascendancy of a cash economy along the middle Kuskokwim. Mining and trapping continued as viable income sources. Men like Dennis Parent and his son Sam, Paul Kameroff, and George Hoffman managed independent trading stations where local hunters would exchange their furs for supplies for the coming year, including flour, coffee, tea, rice, bullets and – increasingly – gasoline for the motors used to power boats up and down the river. Many of the elders we spoke with described traveling with their parents to spring camps to harvest the muskrat, squirrels, beaver, and bear their families needed for both skins and food. They also traveled to winter trapping camps in the hills to harvest furbearers including wolf, wolverine, marten, lynx, and fox. As Wassily Kameroff reminded us, each family had their own territory with invisible boundaries others knew and respected.

Among the most significant changes in the mid-twentieth century was the abandonment of many of these small camps and settlements (ranging in size from five to 30 persons) and the gathering of people into more permanent villages near trading posts, churches, and schools. This population concentration occurred throughout rural Alaska, in part as a consequence of federal mandates requiring that children receive formal education or the government would take them from their families. George Hoffman built a school in Napaimute to meet this requirement. Raised in Crooked Creek, Jennie Zaukar and Agnes Andreanoff remember their families moving to nearby Georgetown so that they could attend school. Angie Kameroff's family had spent winters at Cotton Village (Avungalek) on the Hoholitna when she was young. When she was older, they moved to Sleetmute in part to be closer to a school.

While these villages were small by urban standards, they represent unprecedented population concentrations in the delta environment, with direct consequences for community viability – especially people's ability to harvest animals. Among the most striking features of life in southwest Alaska today are the uses people continue to make of the products of their land and waters. Their lives remain inexorably bound to the seasonal cycling of fish, land and sea animals, plants, and birds. Yet as people gather closer together, animals and fish are more distant. As many middle Kuskokwim hunters point out, hunting and fishing along the middle river has always been challenging. Michael Savage recalled his father's comment that coastal hunters were rich – on the Bering Sea coast, food was always close at hand. On the middle Kuskokwim, however, men had to continually travel to meet their families' needs. Michael remarked, "[My grandfather] said that he went wherever the animals are going to be." Today, many people still harvest from the fishing sites and hunting camps their parents used when they were young, but the cost is much higher, as men have to travel with gasoline-hungry snowmobiles or skiffs, to set their nets and traps. At a time

Crooked Creek Territorial School, replaced in 1934. *ASL.MS146.03.12a1*

when the market economy of southwest Alaska continues to founder, hunting and fishing activities become increasingly difficult to afford (Alaska Department of Labor 2010).

While mining, trapping, and commercial fishing were reliable sources of income during the first half of the twentieth century, unfortunately this is no longer the case. Fur prices are low, salmon are scarce, and mining – with the notable exception of the controversial Donlin prospect – may have run its course. Today, the middle Kuskokwim – like other parts of southwest Alaska – is among the poorest regions in Alaska. Poverty and its attendant social problems continue to plague the region. Southwest Alaska has among the highest rates of suicide and domestic violence in the nation (Alaska Injury Prevention Center 2007, Berman 2014). Residents have repeatedly assessed recent suicides as a consequence of the conditions existing at the time. They maintain that although individuals are responsible for their own actions, they cannot be expected to act appropriately if they are not in control of their land, language, and life. This assessment implies that many have lost such a sense of control. Economic recessions past and present only make the situation worse.[2]

While gathering a seasonally mobile population into year-round communities was among the most significant changes in the mid-twentieth century, the passage of the Alaska Native Claims Settlement Act (ANCSA) in 1971 and the formation of both regional and village corporations laid the groundwork for life along the middle Kuskokwim today. With the passage of ANCSA, middle Kuskokwim communities joined other Yup'ik villages to become part of the Calista regional corporation. As noted, they are on the eastern edges of the region, where their contact with both Athabascan as well as non-Native immigrant populations – including traders, miners, and herders – have produced a cosmopolitan blending of cultures unlike anything their downriver relatives experienced. Although the majority of the elders we worked with speak the Yup'ik language fluently, their children and grandchildren do not. Instead, English provides a common denominator for this diverse population.

Along with their cultural diversity, middle Kuskokwim communities present a uniquely unified face to the world around them. Following the passage of ANCSA, leaders of their ten individual village corporations made the very wise decision to merge and form The Kuskokwim Corporation in April 1977, promoting both economic growth and cultural revitalization in the region – something that no other regional group in southwest Alaska has accomplished. George Morgan of Kalskag noted that if the ten village corporations had stayed separate, many would have been broke years ago. Instead, The Kuskokwim

Corporation (TKC) has over 4,300 shareholders living all over the world, many in Anchorage. Sophie Sakar closed a January 2023 gathering with middle Kuskokwim elders by thanking the first TKC board members, many of whom have since passed on, for getting the villages together:

> If we didn't have Nixie [Mellick] and Tiny [Glenn Fredricks], and so many others, we would have nothing. I always thank them for forming The Kuskokwim Corporation for our future....
>
> Nixie and Tiny, they start traveling to see if they wanted to form a corporation of this area. Because we always feel left alone, nobody bothered to help us....
>
> And now, we have CEO, managers. And those kids we see when they were small, they grow up. I can't believe our younger generation that we watch grow up.

Today, the population of the middle Kuskokwim continues small and spread out. In 2023 Sleetmute had 78 people, Crooked Creek 90 (down from 105 ten years before), and Chuathbaluk was 103 (down from 118) for a total population of 271. The upriver village of Stony River had a population of 57, pushing the total to 328. The populations of Aniak (507), Lower Kalskag (278 in 2020), and Upper Kalskag (212 in 2020) are somewhat higher, with the regional total reaching close to 1350. These low numbers reflect both limited subsistence resources and a struggling economy.

Traveling downriver by boat, people continued to tell us the names of the people whose homes we passed. Some cabins and fish camps were full of life, but many are now deserted. Gradually a picture of the middle Kuskokwim emerges as one windy, 200-mile-long community, where most people have extended family throughout the region, rather than in a single village. Anchorage rather than Bethel is their nearest "regional hub," where many middle Kuskokwim elders have moved to be closer to health care while younger families come for jobs and to attend school.

When sharing personal histories, elders continually referred to the places where their own parents and grandparents were born and raised, who they married, and where they settled to raise their families. They take great pride in their middle river homeland, and rightly so. Many place names refer to the humans who have lived there – English surnames, more akin to coastal names like Nelson Island and Cape Vancouver than Qaluyaat or Nuiget. Yup'ik place names are also plentiful, referring to old stories. Rather than no stories, people are creating new stories reflecting their special place in the wider world.

Fish hanging in Esther Donhauser's smokehouse, Aniak. *Andrea Gusty*

Part I
Gatherings

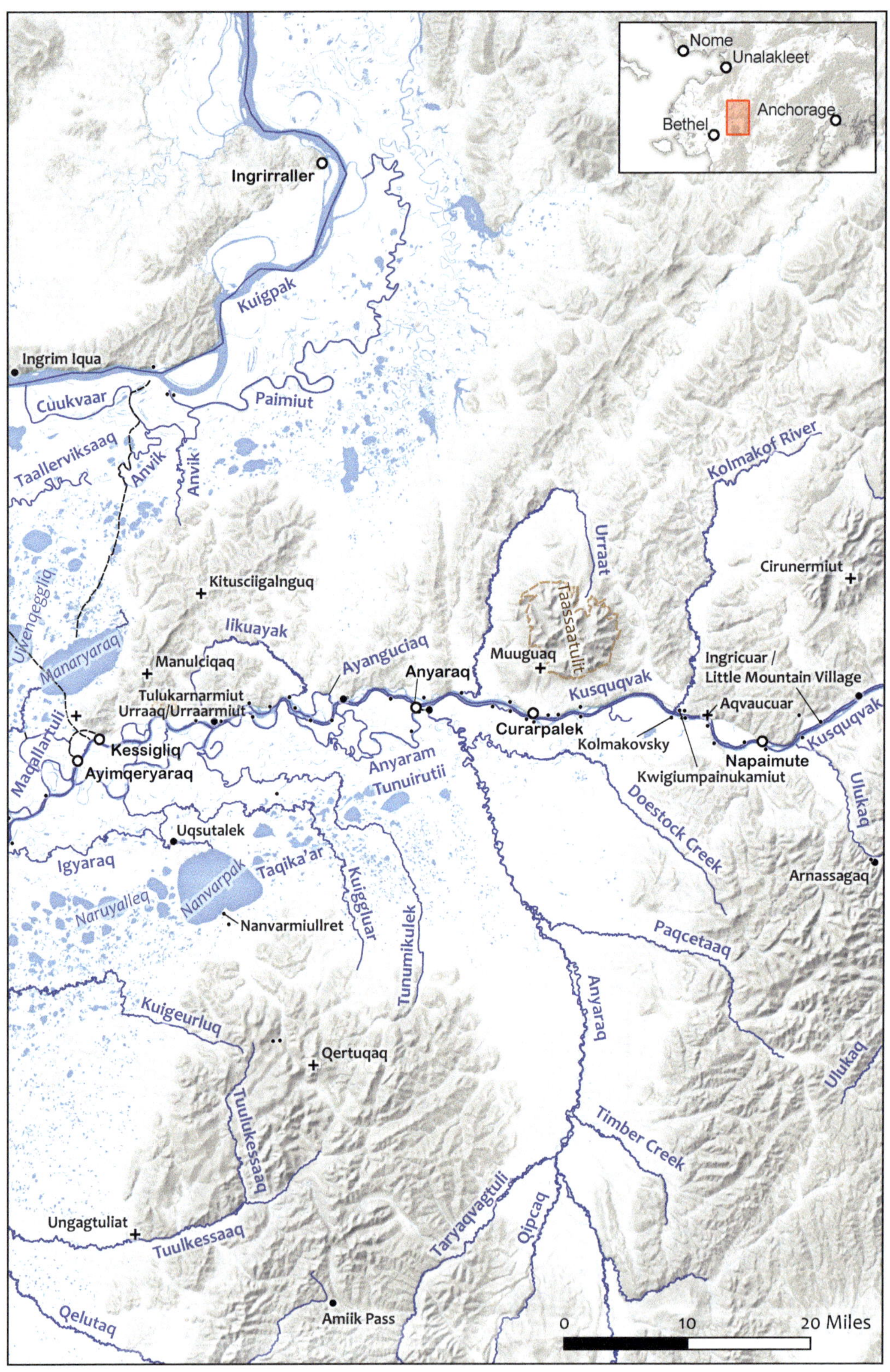

The TCK Region, West. *Ian Moore and Jen Jolliff*

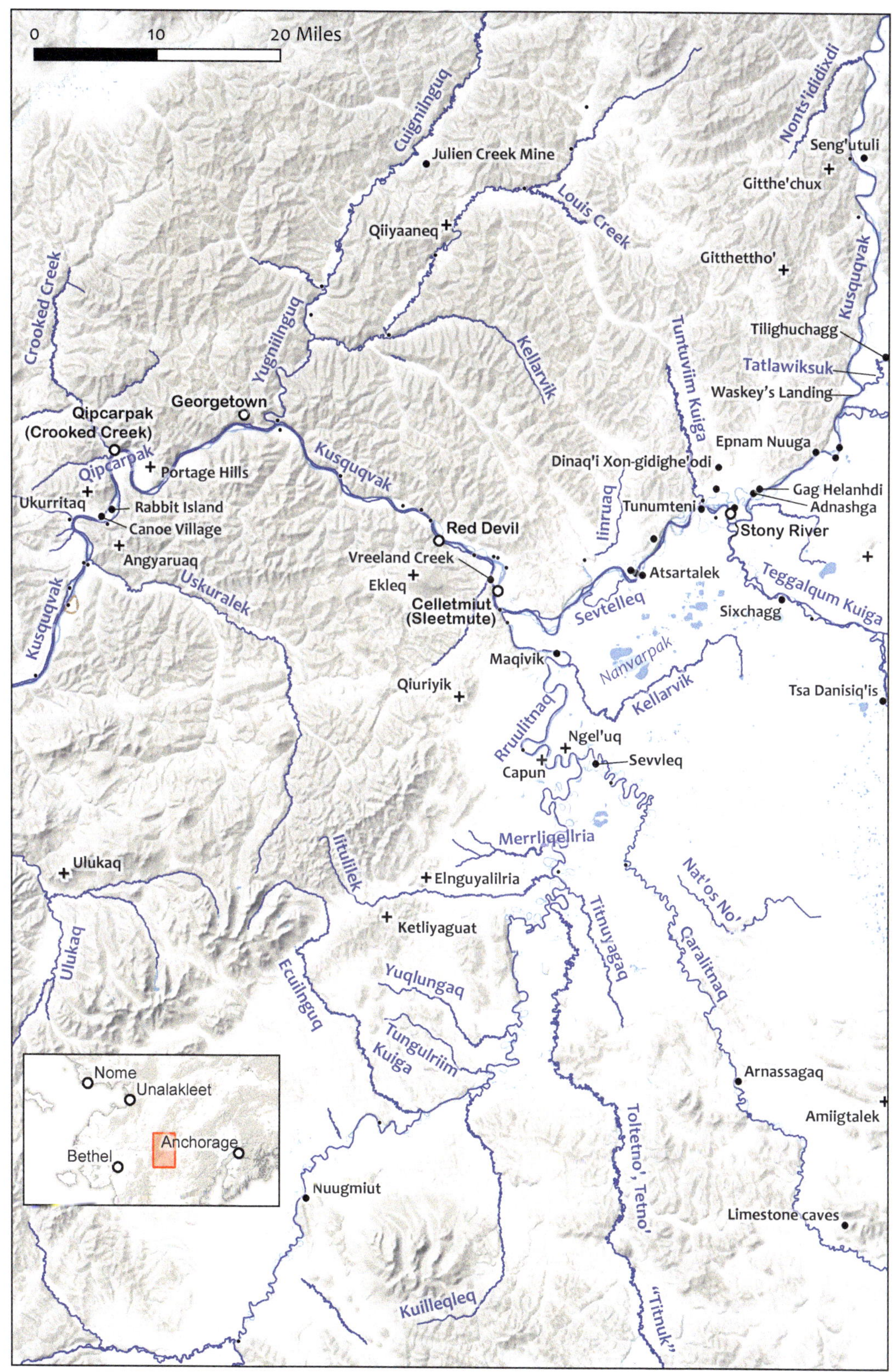

The TCK Region, East. *Ian Moore and Jen Jolliff*

Winter in Aniak.
Maxine Laszlo

Chapter 1

Aniak and Kalskag: Community Histories and Elder Recollections

◇◇

Aniak elders' gathering

During the first week of June 2018, Marie Meade and I traveled to Aniak to meet with elders in the Aniak Tribal Office conference room. Our primary purpose was to document place names in the area as part of the Portage Mountains Transportation Corridor Project. We also asked elders to speak about their personal histories and the changes they have witnessed in the region during their lives. This was our first visit to Aniak, and we were both excited, as we knew we had a great deal to learn.

Aniak (Anyaraq, lit., "Way to go out") is the largest middle Kuskokwim village, with a population in 2018 of approximately 550 (70 percent Native and 30 percent non-Native) with daily flights to Anchorage as well as more than a dozen surrounding villages. A large precontact village existed along the bank below the mouth of Aniak River, but it was abandoned before the Russians arrived in the early 1800s. Present-day Aniak was established downstream from the mouth of Aniak Slough following the Nome Gold Rush when gold seekers were prospecting the Aniak River area in the early 1900s. By 1910 the settlement consisted of three or four cabins, and the non-Native homesteader, Tom Johnson, established a store there in 1913. Sam Simeon from Ohagmiut (Urraarmiut) and Willie Pete were among the first Yup'ik men to settle with their families at Aniak. A territorial school was established there in 1936, construction of a large paved airfield was begun in 1938, and the White Alice radar-relay station was built in 1956. The local population – both Native and non-Native – increased abruptly in the mid-1950s as people moved to Aniak from Upper Kalskag and other places to take advantage of job opportunities at the airport and White Alice facilities (Oswalt 1980a:24-26).

Our Aniak gathering included three women suggested by the tribal administrators – Clara Morgan and Marie Kameroff from Aniak, and Sophie Sakar from Chuathbaluk. All knew each other well, as they had worked together

Aniak elders' gathering with Marie Meade, Clara Morgan, Sophie Sakar, and Marie Kameroff, June 2018. *AFR*

for years as health aides in Aniak and Chuathbaluk. All three were knowledgeable and friendly, and the longer we met the more they enjoyed what we were doing. They are all fluent Yup'ik speakers, and much of our discussion was carried out in the Yup'ik language. When we finished our three-day meeting, they all said they hoped we would do this again soon.

Our gathering started with Marie Meade explaining that we were in Aniak to document place names. Over the last ten years, Calista Education and Culture (CEC) has documented more than 6,000 Yup'ik place names in southwest Alaska and made them available on the online Yup'ik Atlas, which can be found at yupikatlas.org. Following this gathering, we hoped to add more place names from the middle Kuskokwim – an area that CEC had not previously had an opportunity to work in. After her explanation, Marie then introduced herself in Yup'ik, and I did the same, both to share our backgrounds and to show our group what we hoped to learn about them in turn.

Marie Kameroff (Guulak) was born in Aniak in 1938. Her adopted mother was from Aniak and married Paul Kawagley from Akiak. When young, Marie traveled with her adopted parents, who followed the reindeer throughout the Kuskokwim and Kilbuck Mountains, traveling up to McGrath and down to the Bering Sea coast. She described herself as mischievous around the deer when she was young; to keep her out of the way, her father once hung her in a tree.

When she was five, Marie and her mother moved back to Aniak. While still young, she was sent to Holy Cross for five years, where they spoke English and she was punished for speaking in Yup'ik. She moved to Chuathbaluk when she married, then back to Aniak in 1986 where she lives today.

Clara Baldwin Morgan (Kutuspak) was born in 1940 at a winter camp along the banks of Igyaraq, where both her and her younger brother's umbilical cords are buried. The family moved several years later: "When my younger sibling was born in 1942, my grandfather and all of the family moved to Ayanguciaq, Birch Crossing. My grandfather built a house there, and my father and my uncles made three sod houses."

Clara's great-grandmother was from Shageluk, and Clara's mother was born and raised in Paimiut on the Yukon, where Clara's two older brothers were born. After the birth of her youngest brother at Ayanguciaq, Clara's father – a *kass'aq* (non-Native) – planned to build a village there: "But during that time, a school was established in Kessigliq [Upper Kalskag]. Then before winter, my family moved here [to Aniak] from Ayanguciaq."

Clara noted that the first airport was under construction in Aniak in 1943, and that her father worked on it. He died two years later, in 1945, and Clara's mother, Olinka, remarried Joe Gregory (Cuussacuar) from Tuluksak. Clara described her early years traveling with her family between their winter camp at Uqsutalek (near Whitefish Lake) and their spring camp at Taqika'ar:

> When I was little we stayed [at Taqika'ar] in the spring several times. I remember I was with my mom when we landed there in a boat and I stood up and said, "Ugly Taqika'ar."
>
> And when I was about 13, we came to Taqika'ar by dog team from Uqsutalek. And when ice was gone, we went from there and came out to the Kuskokwim River above Tuluksak. Then we went up the Kuskokwim River to Igyaraq River, and we would travel on and go to Uqsutalek. And after we stayed there for a while we'd go on Lewis Creek and go out to Kusquqvalleq (the Old Kuskokwim Channel) and continue on to Kessigliq.
>
> One spring there were no muskrats; we traveled and looked for muskrat and stayed in 17 camps. I was 13 years old, and my two little siblings were with us. I got tired of camping at times, but I liked the wilderness.
>
> When we stopped we'd take the dogs out of the boat and tie then to trees. We'd gather spruce tree branches and use them as a mattress in the tent.

Muskrat skins drying in the sun, 1948. *George A. Morlander Photographs, UAF-1997-108-367*

Clara also described her years attending school at Holy Cross on the Yukon:

> When my mom remarried, my younger sibling and I were sent to the mission at Holy Cross. My two older siblings, my father told my mother to send them to the mission in Holy Cross when he was gone. And when my younger sibling and I went to the mission, the two older siblings, they left the school and moved here [to Aniak]. And when my younger sibling and I came home, the two older siblings were already attending high school at Mt. Edgecumbe. They were gone from 1949 to 1982, and we never saw each other. When school was done, they stayed there and worked.

Clara was in school at Holy Cross from 1949 through 1952. Describing her years there, she recalled:

> When I was little I already spoke English [and Yup'ik]. At the mission we weren't allowed to speak Yup'ik. The other children there only spoke in English and no other language.
>
> Then one day a girl came from the Bethel area, and she spoke only in Yup'ik. I was so happy and spoke to her in Yup'ik, and we'd criticize the nuns. [*laughter*]

> While at the mission, our relatives from the village would come and get my younger brother and I; my mother's aunt and her daughters. We'd visit then on Sundays; we'd all speak in Yup'ik....
>
> Other children there didn't speak in Yugtun. Some were from upper Yukon River area villages, some were from Koyukuk, Nulato; children came from those villages to attend school in Holy Cross. I never heard them speak their language.
>
> In the dining room while eating we weren't allowed to speak [in either Yup'ik or English]. If we talked they let us kneel facing the other children eating. Several times they let me kneel for talking. [*laughter*]

When Marie asked Clara if her experiences were good at Holy Cross, she answered: "Yes. Probably because I didn't want to be home."

In 1953, Clara's stepfather built a house four miles downriver from Aniak. She recalled the 1956 flood, when a helicopter took their family to high ground where they stayed in a tent until the water went down. Clara remembers walking to school in Aniak with her brothers: "We never took four-wheeler or snowmachine, we would just walk from our house to attend school here. We didn't mind at all."

After the flood, Clara's mother was sent to the hospital for treatment for tuberculosis, and her father followed soon after: "My mother stayed with him. It was during that time I went out on a date with my husband-to-be, Billy Morgan. He'd hike from [Aniak] to our house to see me. I left my mom and moved here to Anyaraq. Raphael Kupanak, we call him Ap'a [Grandfather]. His wife had me stay here [in Aniak] and I went to school." Clara graduated from 8th grade in 1958 and was married to Billy Morgan in November of the same year.

Clara said that she has always cut and dried salmon in Aniak and never moved anywhere else after she married. She has, however, traveled up and down the Kuskokwim, from Bethel to Lime Village, during her 35 years working for the Yukon-Kuskokwim Health Corporation (YKHC). In the beginning Clara had no training and worked out of her house as a volunteer health aide. In 1967 she went to Bethel for her first training, taking her baby with her. In all, she had nine children, and in 2018 she already had two-dozen grandchildren and three dozen great-grandchildren, with a great-great-grandchild on the way. She describes herself as a "genealogist" interested in everyone's family tree or, she laughs, just nosy.

Sophie Sakar (Cugluaq) was born in old Aniak in 1942. She became aware – had her first memories – in old Aniak, and she attended school in the new village on the south side of Aniak Slough. Her father was Old Man Kelila in English and Ikamrarrluk in Yup'ik, and her mother Marie (Caqilaq in Yup'ik) was from

Chefornak. Along with her younger sister Annie, Sophie had two stepbrothers and two stepsisters after her mother died and their father remarried.

Sophie was seven years old in 1949 when her father used his trapping money to build a Russian Orthodox church on the north side of Aniak Slough: "He told us the church was an heirloom and a family treasure to everybody.... He used to get flour, sugar, tea, coffee, Crisco out of his trapping money. And his leftover money, he used it for the church." Sophie remembered packing lumber for the church with her younger sister, Annie, who was spoiled and just sat down in the middle of the job and refused to continue. Sophie chuckled as she told the story.

Sophie told another lively story about rolling down hills with her friend Balasa Tom, then putting moss in the bottom of their berry buckets to make them look full. Later she forgot what she had done and gave the bucket to her mom. She laughed and said, "We were goofy, we used to have fun."

Aniak during breakup, 1956. *Bill Ray White Alice Collection, Anchorage Museum B1994.009.405*

Sophie estimated that around 80 people lived on the north side of Aniak Slough in 1950, and today ten Native families still live there, as well as a number of non-Natives. Like Clara, Sophie remembers the flood in Aniak during breakup in 1956. Her father had a two-story building, and everyone on the north side of the slough stayed with them during the flood. Aniak often flooded in the spring before the dike was built in 1982 and extended in 1998.

Sophie moved to Chuathbaluk in 1967 when she married. In 2018 she had seven children (some of whom send her food from the Yukon), 30 grandchildren, and 52 great-grandchildren (beating Clara), "coming down like a Christmas tree." She is the last of her siblings still living and considers herself rich, with a large family in Chuathbaluk, where today she is the eldest woman.

Chuathbaluk (Curarpalek, lit., "Place with large *curat* [blueberries]") was a seasonal camp into the 1800s, when St. Sergius Russian Orthodox Church was built there in 1894 by local residents. The settlement (on the north side of the Kuskokwim) was unoccupied after 1929, although church members continued to hold services in the church and bury their dead in the cemetery. The site was reoccupied by Sam Phillips and his family from Crow Village (Tulukarnarmiut, from "*tulukaruk* [raven]") in 1954 and soon joined by other families from Aniak and Crooked Creek. The old church was torn down in the late 1950s and replaced by a new church, and a school was established there in 1967 (Oswalt 1980a:34-35). Originally called Little Russian Mission, the name was changed to Chuathbaluk to avoid confusion with the Yukon River village of Russian Mission. Sophie recalled that there used to be many houses at the original Curarpalek before people relocated to the present site. The 1956 flood, which happened after Curarpalek was abandoned, wiped out the remaining homes.

Although brief, these personal histories make clear the complex character of family relations, marked by death, adoption, and remarriage. Not only did families move between seasonal camps, but many relocated from the Yukon to the Kuskokwim and vice versa. Having close relatives living along both rivers was not uncommon. These histories also give some indication of the areas through which people moved before formal education was made mandatory and schools were established in select villages along the middle Kuskokwim. A major change throughout southwest Alaska in the 1950s and 1960s was the concentration of people into 48 permanent, year-round villages, including Aniak and Chuathbaluk. Until then people were scattered in hundreds of winter settlements – such as Tulukarnarmiut and Ayanguciaq – many of which have since been abandoned.

Place names

Our discussion of family history led directly into a discussion of place names, as each woman described her family's movement between winter, spring, and summer camps when she was young. With the map spread before us, the women located Bogus Creek, Lewis Creek, and Discovery Creek, none of which have Yup'ik names that they knew of. When asked about the Yup'ik name for Whitefish Lake, they suggested naming it Qaurtussurvik or Qaurturvik (from *qaurtuq*, "humpbacked whitefish"). Later we learned from an interview with Sinka Williams (1988) that the lake's original name is Nanvarpak (lit., "Big *nanvaq* [lake]"). They also did not recognize several long abandoned precontact sites, including Siimartulirmiut and Nanvarmiullret.

What the group did know, however, in great detail, were the locations of dozens of camps and homesteads used by families into the present day, including Sophie and Sinka Sakar's fish camp near Curarpalek; Jim and Olga Smith's homestead, where they lived year-round; Sam and Helen Tom's homestead, where they also lived year-round before they died; Evan Wassillie's allotment and house, abandoned after he died; Raymond Peterson's trapping and fishing camp; and Morris Hofseth's place, where his family stayed year-round before moving to Aniak and where their children still have a house.

The group also shared Yup'ik place names for geographic features, including Urraat River, along the mouth of which Sophie's father, Ikamrarrluk, had a building long before she was born; Ulukaq River (lit., "Slate"), above Napaimute; Taassaatulit (Russian Mountains, from *taassiq*, "dishpan," from Russian *taz*); and Qassuq (Betty and Jerry Simeon's camp). Looking over my shoulder and trying to identify places she knew, Marie Kameroff declared, "Too bad they don't have names." That was what we had come to remedy. To get a good look at the map, Clara announced, "I better go climbing" and slid onto the table.

Eyagyarat / *Abstinence practices*

During our Aniak gathering, we discussed a special class of rules known collectively as *eyagyarat* – the traditional abstinence practices following birth, death, illness, and first menstruation. Diverse *eyagyarat* practiced in a variety of situations were tied by a common purpose – restraining and guiding behavior during life's transitions to avoid annoying or frightening human and nonhuman companions in a sentient universe. Because these rules cover different phases of a person's life, *eyagyarat* are often dealt with separately in discussions of the relationship between men and women, illness and wellness, and death and dying.

Many elders, however, understand these abstinence practices as interrelated, allowing men and women in a vulnerable condition to safely coexist with their fellow humans and animals in a knowing and responsive world.

Eyagyarat codified the restraint and special care people must exercise during critical phases in their lives. Marie Meade noted that women in downriver communities – especially Napaskiak – still follow these rules: “The rules are especially followed by young girls who have their first menstrual period. People also follow the rules when they lose their family members.... Our ancestors adhered to the rules of *eyagyarat* mainly for their health and well-being and to show respect to all of life on earth.”

Marie also noted that these rules differed in different places. Clara was not familiar with *eyagyarat*, and she asked Marie to clarify which rules she should follow under what circumstances. Marie Kameroff recalled what her mother-in-law had told her about *eyagyarat*:

> When she was alive she gathered all of us and she told us, when one of our relations passes away, like my husband, son, or daughter, people are going to tell you that you cannot fish, you cannot pick berries; she said, “Don’t listen to them.” Because they’re not going to come and say, “Here’s five gallons of berries” or “Here’s a bundle of fish.” She said, “You have to keep going.” She said, “It’s not followed anymore.”

Marie Meade noted: “Back in those days it was okay for those who didn’t have providers to ignore the rules and go out and gather and hunt.” Clara added that in the past people used to share food, but that they no longer do that.

Sophie (who is Russian Orthodox) then spoke at length about *eyagyarat* she practiced when she had her first menstruation:

> When I was young I heard about *eyagyarat* all the time. My mother and my late father used to tell us about the rules. She said, “When I die you will follow rules. You will not pick berries, and you will try to follow rules I’ve taught you.” And when a family member died, they told me to put some beaver castor in a piece of cloth and sew the bundle on a belt and wear it for one year.
>
> They also instructed me to take one strand of my hair and use it as a string to tie a salmonberry, blueberry, or red berry plant to the ground if I went out to pick after abstaining [not picking berries] for a year.
>
> They also said if our sibling died to restrict our hunting. They said it was okay for our children to go out and hunt if our main provider was unable to go or was gone.

> They also talked about raw frozen foods and raw uncooked foods; we were not to eat such foods for one year. But today people don't follow the rules anymore.

Sophie then shared her own experience, following her first menstruation:

> When I bled for the first time, I sat on a black-bear skin for five days. And when I finally got ready to go outside, they told me not to look at the sun directly. They said if I did I would lose good eyesight.
>
> They also said that while I was on restriction and someone brought an animal, I was not to handle it, but to have my children or my grandchildren take care of it.
>
> However, today people don't follow these rules anymore.

Sophie also described food restrictions:

> My grandchildren get curious and ask me, "Why can't you eat that food?" Like the *kuucenak* [hind quarters, pelvic bone] of beaver; my mom told me not to let girls eat those. I ask her why...and she said, "If you start having babies, you will not be able to open up."
>
> But if you stop having babies, it's okay for you to eat that part of a beaver....
>
> Only women are restricted from eating that part. Some women have labor pains for a long time. My mom said that they suffer like that because they hadn't adhered to the rule.
>
> And bird wings, too; don't eat those while you are pregnant. I asked my mom, "Why can't you eat them?" She said that when a baby is born, the baby would flap its arms like a bird does with wings.

Later Sophie added that when pregnant a woman should not eat a beaver's hind feet or their child's hands will look like beaver hands. Sophie had been taught other rules surrounding pregnancy as well: "And if you are pregnant and go out the door, don't go out backwards; when going out, face forward immediately. My mom said that when my baby is born, he'd come out feet first. She'd say the baby would come out backwards."

Later when we were discussing animals generally, Sophie spoke of her experience with porcupines:

> My dad came back and he catch female *issaluuq* [porcupine]. So they burn it and gut it, and it had two or three babies inside. Then those baby *issaluuqs*; My mom said, "Come." I was looking, and my dad was

watching. She take one baby *issaluuq*. I said, "What are you going to do with it?" "I'm going to drop it down inside your dress." I said, "Why?" She told me if I did that and start having babies I wouldn't have problems. I was just feeling queasy.

My sister Annie, [my mom] tried telling her to come to her, but she said, "No way." She take off.

She pulled the neck opening of my dress and dropped it down head first. When I asked why she did that she told me that if I start having babies I wouldn't have problems delivering.

They were little babies. I closed my eyes thinking of the quills.

Care of animals

Speaking about *eyagyarat* reminded Sophie of rules surrounding the treatment of animals generally. These rules ensured that the animals were well-received as guests and so would want to return in future.

> They also instructed me about animals. Animals like moose and bear, I was to take care of them right away and not leave their bones scattered around. They said if I hadn't properly cared for an animal, they would avoid the hunter. And if I saw an animal bone out in the open I was to move it aside so it would not be trampled, or [I should] bury it in the ground. If my family...had not adhered to that teaching our Provider will not allow them to receive that sustenance....
>
> Those were the rules my mom and dad talked about; they said we must teach our grandchildren to bring all of the catch home to us. The only thing left out is the intestines of the animal.
>
> And when a hunter caught a black bear, he was told not to bring the head home. He was instructed to bury the black bear's head facing the east where the sun rises.

Clara was also familiar with these rules: "I've heard that if people begin throwing bones of moose, caribou, and bears in the water, those animals will begin migrating downriver. It's the truth; already they are catching moose and caribou all the way down in Eek."

Finally, Sophie noted the importance of sharing one's catch:

> You know, some people go through hardship, those who have no income or get food stamps. If you see someone suffering, bring them food or things they need. Hunters were told to share their catch with elders.

> Today they say if you share your food to someone in need, it will return to you more than what you gave. So true.
>
> Nowadays, I recognize what my mom and dad talked about. They said provide for those who are in need. Even we don't have much, we used to share with this family that didn't have much.

Sophie described an experience she had when young that brought home the importance of respecting animals:

> Me and my baby sister, we were so goofy. My dad, over there he made beaver snares. We were crazy. My dad let us bring [the beaver home]; I bring the medium size beaver, he tied string around my waist, and me and my baby sister Annie bring the *aqsatuyaaq* [small beaver]. He tied it to each foot, he let us drag 'em home to the tent.
>
> Our mom, she was cooking in the tent. We look around; of course it was me; look around and see if my dad's coming. Go on top of the bank, I tell my sister, "Annie come." I sat on top of the beaver and take the ears, and I slide down. We got carried away.
>
> We were sliding down the bank. Suddenly my dad appeared. It was too late for us to hide. We stayed there and wait for him. He came over. He was quiet, humble man. My heart was beating. I told my sister that he was going to scold us. My sister said, "Your fault."
>
> He get close, and he try not to laugh. We wait for him. He didn't scold us, but talk to us. He said, "These animals we have caught, you don't play with them. If you played with them I will not be able to catch animals anymore." Boy, after that we never mess around with beavers.
>
> After he tell my mom he laughed, and she said, "These two crazy ones! You don't play with animals!"

We also spoke briefly about the animals hunted and eaten along the middle Kuskokwim, including moose, bear, lynx (which Clara said tasted like chicken), porcupine, beaver, rabbit, muskrat, ptarmigan, even snowy owls. Clara recalled: "In those days we never ate turkey. When my stepdad went out he heard a snowy owl. He came in and took his .22 rifle, went out again, and we heard the gun shot. He came in with a snowy owl. My mom cleaned it and made soup with it. It was good. They eat mice and rabbits." Clara added that her children like beaver half-dried and boiled:

> It's fixed like *egamaarrluk* [half-dried fish boiled before serving]. One time while I was eating, one of my grandkids came in. As soon as he

> walked in he came to me and said, "Great-grandmother, what you eating?" I said, "I'm having *pukuk* [bones with meat] and seal oil." He said, "Could I try some?" I said, "Go ahead." So, I got him leg, and he eat it with seal oil. He said, "Mmm, I like this, Amau [Great-grandmother]."
>
> My grandkids, even my daughter, youngest one; when I have anything they eat with me; eating beaver feet, moose nose, and the innards.

Speaking of bears, Clara noted that people eat the whole animal except the head:

> In the spring is when they get out [of their dens], and they are good and fat. And summer they eat fish, and in the fall; they wait till they start eating roots and whatever they eat, vegetation; they wait until they start eating those and they get 'em. I couldn't eat it for a while.
>
> Billy didn't eat bear meat; he said when you skin a bear, their bodies looked like human's body. He never ate bear meat. I now eat bear meat again....
>
> You can't eat bear fat raw. But you can boil it and cut it up and eat it with dried fish....
>
> Black bear meat tastes like pork, but you got to cook it. I always get these two mixed up. Trichinosis and trichomonas. Trichinosis is from the pork. Trichomonas is [*whispering*] vaginitis. [*laughter*]

Moose meat is another staple. Clara continued: "We do dry moose meat; jerky. In the winter, we used to freeze moose meat and cut and shave it with a knife; that's how my husband ate frozen moose meat. Our four-year-old son used to eat roe of whitefish raw. He cried when a whitefish had no roe inside." Clara concluded: "I used to feed my children everything I fixed and cooked; when kids are little they like everything I feed them, and they get older they begin to dislike the food. And when they turn into adults they'd start eating the food again."

Youth today

At the end of our discussion of *eyagyarat*, Sophie noted that today she tries to pass these instructions on to young people: "Today I pass it on to the girls not to eat that [beaver pelvis].... They invite me to the school to tell stories. Boy, those kids could ask so much questions." Sophie maintains that one should share what one was taught as a child. She says it is not the children's fault that they don't know these things but rather the parents who did not teach them: "So I started calling their parents or Ap'as [grandfathers] to teach your kids.... Today, our traditional knowledge is no longer taught. Even they blame the younger generation what they are doing today. I have said it's not their fault. We parents, we are the first teachers to our children."

Sophie's parents spoke to her only in Yup'ik. She remembers the first English word she learned in school was "yes," and the second was "no." Clara was also a fluent Yup'ik speaker when young. She remembered listening to stories, in both English and Yup'ik: "When I was little, I'd see old men gather and tell stories. I used to go with my grandfather and listen. And one of them would read Western pocketbooks; he'd translate them into Yugtun and share stories to other old folks. I learned the word *luussitaq*, Yugtun word for horse from him."

Sophie also described her experience raising her own children:

> Fr. Michael, he always came to our house when he arrived in our village. My Marie was maybe four or five. My late husband, daily, when we were alone, he used to cuss all the time. My kids grow up with it. That one day, Fr. Michael and him were eating. My baby Marie was sitting on a gasoline box playing with her dolls. While playing one of her dolls fell on the floor, from the start to the end she cussed at her doll.
>
> My husband turned and looked at me. Then Fr. Michael said that children, they grow up conscious of everything we do. Children's first learning come from their fathers and mothers. We as parents are teachers. So true.

Sophie reiterated the well-known Yup'ik admonition that talking to one's children is a way of showing love: "My mother talked to me and said, 'If I leave [die] don't think you are alone; *ellam ilua ilakan* [you are related to everything on earth]. You have a family with many children, and grandchildren and will get great-grandchildren eventually. *Kenkekuvci qallautaqluki; kenkekuvki inerquraqluki* [If you love them, talk to them; if you love them, instruct them about right and wrong].'"

Traditional healers

On our last morning together, we also discussed healers in the past – a good topic for women who had spent their lives working as health aides in their communities. Marie asked if they had heard about *angalkut* (shamans) when they were young. Clara replied that a man named Migtuli was said to have been a shaman, and Migtuli's brother was also a healer: "One time my mom had pain on her back; he placed his hand on her back; my mom said that his hand almost got stuck on her back. So, being a shaman, I think he worked to help people. However, his brother

Migtuli was dark.... They say he moved to Kessigliq from the Yukon River. Many people moved to Kessigliq from the Yukon."

Marie then asked about women healers, and Sophie described her experience:

> That Mary Sakar's mom; one time in 1964, I must have had a tumor in my head.... I used to have headache from right here all the way back behind my ear. I was very, very sick and couldn't walk around no more. And when she came, that old lady asked Mary how I was doing. She told her I was sick. We were in a little house. I prayed and made sign of the cross and watched my kids, "I have to say good-bye to you kids."
>
> That old lady, Mary's mom, she said, "My cousin, I have come to see you. I am going to help you." She told me not to be scared. I told her that I wasn't scared and told her that I wasn't afraid to die.
>
> They had me sit down in bed and have somebody hold me. She worked with my body all over. She keep going to the pain area, like she was feeling something. She said, "Don't be afraid for I'm going to help you."
>
> Then she said, "I have found it. I am going to remove it." Then she pull out something. She open her palm and said, "This is what made you sick. You are going to get well." It look like to me it was spider; puss oozing. [She said,] "I am removing the thing that made you sick. You are going to get well. Apparently, I have come at the right moment so I can help you."
>
> So in the morning I wake up, my eye feel like it was better; every morning I feel just a little bit better.... Maybe about a month, I feel better and better.

Clara also mentioned that Big Sinka Gregory from Stony River was a healer, as well as Billy Morgan's aunt Agafia who made medicine for her people.

We then spoke briefly about medicinal plants, including *chaga*, a fungus which grows on birch trees. When dried and made into tea it helps those with cancer and other illnesses. *Ayuq* (Labrador tea) was another well-known medicinal plant. *Caiggluk* (wormwood) could be made into tea or used as a poultice on cuts or boils. Clara noted: "I use wormwood on boils and other infections. I dry wormwood plants like my mom had done, and rub them in my hands till it gets like cotton. I add a little shortening to it and place it on a boil and cover it."

Closing comments

We ended our Aniak gathering just after noon on Wednesday, but it took us time to say good-bye. We took a group photo, and everyone thanked us for coming and invited us to come again. Sophie declared: "So good to be telling stories with others." Clara noted:

> It's good to gather and talk with joy like this; sharing stories and memories of our ancestors. Sharing allows us to heal....
>
> I just like this [gathering]. I wish we'd do it again. Can I go Kalskag with you?

Before we left, Clara asked, "So, are you going to print our words into a book?" I told her that was our hope, and this is the result.

Kalskag elders' gathering

From Aniak, Marie and I traveled by boat to Kessigliq (Upper Kalskag), landing by the old schoolhouse. Tribal administrator Bonnie Persson met us at the riverbank and drove us to the Kalskag tribal office building where we would be staying and where our meeting would start the next morning. On the way, we passed the older section of Upper Kalskag, with houses close together along the river and small yards and bushes growing up between them. Kessigliq has a Catholic Church – the first one built by George Morgan (the father of George Morgan Sr. and the grandfather of George Morgan Jr.) – and cemetery, along with a Church of Calvary that has been there for several decades. We continued on past the new housing development on the side of the hill – resembling AVCP housing in other villages – toward the airport and tribal office building, both in the middle of the two Kalskags. At the airport, one road headed down to Lower Kalskag. The other headed to the right uphill, and taking this road we reached Kalskag's gravel pit, at about 800 feet elevation. From this point we could see the Yukon River mountains to the north and Whitefish Lake to the south. Below us both Upper and Lower Kalskag were visible, as well as the gravel road connecting them.

Lower Kalskag has a community hall, a three-year water and sewer project to provide indoor plumbing, and a Russian Orthodox cemetery and church (destroyed by a fire in 2021). Religion divided these relatively new villages in the beginning, with priests discouraging intermarriage between the two churches. Today the two Kalskags share a common post office, gas station, and elementary, middle, and high schools. Both communities are increasingly working together, though differences remain.

View of the Yukon from the gravel pit on the side of Kessigliq Hill, Kalskag, June 2018. *AFR*

Looking across the Kuskokwim toward Whitefish Lake, June 2018. *AFR*

Our Kalskag gathering began the next morning in the upstairs apartment of the tribal office building. Three of the five elders who the two tribes had suggested attended, including Bob Aloysius and George Morgan Jr. from Upper Kalskag, and Elena Sergie from Lower Kalskag. Bob had also invited his friends Stanley Michelson and Kerilia Wise, along with Kerilia's wife Catherine.

As in Aniak, Marie and I started by introducing ourselves and explaining the purpose of our visit – to document local place names as well as community and family history. The elders then introduced themselves in turn. First was Elena Sergie, a lively woman well able to hold her own. What is today Lower Kalskag was the site of her family's fish camp. She gave Qalqaq as the name of the old village, located several miles to the south. Elena said that her parents were from Russian Mission and had moved to Qalqaq. Elena has a large family, with relatives on the Yukon, in Kwethluk, and up and down the Kuskokwim River. She noted: "I don't forget our family tree," and, indeed, she told us about her family in great detail.

Elena was born in September 1945. When she was young her family moved back to Russian Mission, but then returned to the Kuskokwim because of tuberculosis in that village. By then a number of houses had been built at the site of their old fish camp. They called the place Ayimqeryaraq (probably from *ayemqar-*, "to take a shortcut, to cut across") as it was a place to portage from Kuicaraq (the Johnson River) over to the Kuskokwim. Elena remembers the early

Kalskag elders' gathering with Bob Aloysius, Stanley Michelson, Kerilia and Catherine Wise, George Morgan, Elena Sergie, and Marie Meade, June 2018. *AFR*

days in Ayimqeryaraq, when people helped each other and everything was shared. To this day, Elena says she can't go back to Kuicaraq, remembering the good times they used to have there, camping and picking salmonberries. At camp her father used to gather them and talk to her and her brothers when they ate.

Elena also spoke about her late husband's family. The Sergie's have relatives in Bethel and Togiak, where she stayed one summer with her children while her husband fished.

Kerilia Wise was born in 1950 in the older section of Upper Kalskag. This was a fish camp where Kerilia's grandmother stayed. His father was from Tuluksak. George later praised Kerilia (known by all as "Connector," because Elena's younger sister couldn't pronounce his name) who was the night driver on barges moving up the Kuskokwim and knew all the river channels. Unfortunately, Kerilia recently had a stroke and has difficulty speaking.

Stanley Michelson (Puuliyagaq, lit., "Little Bullet") was born in Upper Kalskag in January 1960. His father, Joseph, was from Holy Cross and his mother, Olga, from Paimiut. His grandfather, Sergie Matthew, was also from Paimiut.

George Morgan Jr. (Aqsaq) was born in 1946 and raised in Upper Kalskag. His mother was Mary Tugumcunaq and his father George Morgan Sr. His grandfather, George Morgan, was a head reindeer herder. George Jr. remembers the BIA having a big meeting at Pike Lake, planning to charge herders for the reindeer that grazed there. His grandfather was against it. After that disagreement, he said, the reindeer left.

While in Aniak, Clara had told us that the first George Morgan had married a Peterson from the Yukon. Clara named the original Morgan siblings as Matt, Barbara, Mary, George Sr., Theresa, Carlie, her husband Billy, Johnny, Irene, and Maggie; the tenth child died as well as the twins. Of these, the first five spoke Yup'ik fluently while the others could understand a little. Clara also noted that four of the children of George Morgan Sr. live in Upper Kalskag – George Jr., Earl, Francine, and Kenny – while Herman lives in Aniak. She jokingly told us, "When you see Georgie, tell him 'I know all your history.' Little birdie thinks she knows everything."

George spoke highly of the people of Kalskag, who had to protect their land from people coming from the Nushagak, the Yukon, and the lower Kuskokwim. He then told a brief version of the story of the battle of Maqallartuli, which took place during the period of bow-and-arrow warfare which predated the arrival of the Russians in the early 1800s. Two men hunting muskrats saw warriors coming up the Kuicaraq River. They subsequently warned their Kuskokwim relatives, who ambushed the would-be attackers at Maqallartuli (Mud Creek), which remains red with their blood to this day.

George also shared a story about how the Kuskokwim River got its name – a mystery to many Yup'ik language experts:

> Long time ago there were two Yup'ik guys come over [from the Yukon]. And they saw this beautiful river. They were trying to be quiet because of warriors from here. And so they were trying to be quiet, admiring this river, and his partner *quspak* [coughed loudly]. "Shshsh, be quiet, they might hear." So they went back to their village and they said they found a good river. Lots of animals, trees, and everything. "What you call it then?" He said his buddy had *quspak* [coughed loudly]. So, its first name was Quspak, the Kuskokwim River.

Bob Aloysius (Elliksuuyar) was the next to speak. He was born in 1935 in a fish camp called Iinruq on the Yukon River, just below Arulaqurviaq at the mouth of Paimiut Slough. When six months old his grandmother took him to Aniak to raise him. He grew up with two old women, speaking only Yup'ik. His father's mother was Sophie Belcoff from Anvik, and her husband was William T. Vanderpool. Bob emphasized his big family and many relatives – Yup'ik, *kass'aq* (non-Native), Athabascan, Russian, German, even Cherokee. He jokingly called himself "United Natives of Alaska."

During Bob's young years he was an only child living with his grandmother, occasionally camping with other families. During a Calista Elders Council gathering in 2010, Bob described how he longed to travel out on the land. He pestered his grandmother until she allowed him to accompany a nearby family to their well-established spring camp where Bob helped to gather wood, haul water, and hunt and fish in the surrounding area all spring. He remembers sitting behind his host, Qaleqcuuk, in a kayak, falling asleep watching for muskrats. Finally, in April, the family began getting their wooden boat ready for summer use, complete with a two-horsepower motor. They remained at camp until May, when they knew by the sound that the ice was breaking on the Kuskokwim and it was time to move to the main river for summer salmon fishing. When they arrived at fish camp, his grandmother had them eat a small bit of land and drink from the river as protection for the year ahead (Rearden and Fienup-Riordan 2016:118-33).

The first fish harvested in the spring were sheefish, which people eagerly boiled for their oil. Then they harvested salmon non-stop all summer long. Bob remembered all the delicious foods people enjoyed – *akutaq* made with pike and grayling flesh, berries, and a bit of lard but no other shortening or sugar; fry bread cooked in sheefish oil, made with flour and salt but no leavening; and another *akutaq* made in the fall from a combination of berries, sheefish oil, and "mouse food" (the tiny tubers gathered by tundra voles and stored for winter use).

Bob also mentioned gathering *elagat* (lit., "things dug from underground," alpine sweet vetch or "Eskimo potatoes") from gravel beaches in spring and making them into *akutaq*. He described gathering mouse food on islands in the fall, and he concluded: "The subsistence way of life, the entire land can provide every kind of food to us. That's why our ancestors were always eager to gather things from the land and the water."

In the past, Bob said, people didn't know about money but everyone was rich, owning their own homes and dogs. Resources abound in a 50-mile radius, including six varieties of salmon (kings, reds, chums, fall chums, silvers, and pinks): "We don't go to them; the fish come to us." People moved to their fish camps after breakup each year and stayed there through the fall taking care of fish. Today people just travel back and forth. Bob also noted five species of whitefish, as well as different varieties of pike and ptarmigan. Bob lived in Bethel for 27 years but returned to Kalskag because, as he said, this is a place of plenty.

During our CEC gathering, Bob also spoke briefly about harvesting practices, including egg gathering, drying meat of beaver, bear, and moose, and hooking for smaller fish such as rainbow trout and Dolly Varden. He then spoke passionately about the concrete, "natural education" he received from the time he was born, and the stories he was told to prepare him for the future. After these experiences, Bob spent years at the Catholic mission school at Holy Cross, and he still resents the non-Native educational process he experienced there. Yup'ik people, he said, need to take back their role as parents and educate their young people:

> If there's anything that we can do, it would be to break away from depending on other people to do our education. We have to take it upon ourselves to be the leaders and bring back the way we're supposed to live as human beings and teach our children.
>
> But the federal government and its attitude of divide and conquer has done a magnificent job. They literally cleaned out our society. They took away our land, they took away our spirituality, they took away our culture...and values and dumped theirs on top of it. And we have to push theirs away and take back our rightful place and teach and show.

Bob's grandmother died when he was fourteen, and he came to live with his grandfather in Upper Kalskag. Bob described how the government wouldn't allow him to stay, as he was considered a burden on the old man. He was also barred from living alone in his grandmother's house. From that point on, Bob says, he has had trouble with authority and no patience.

All regretted the death of Sinka Williams (Elena's brother and Bob's mentor, whose Yup'ik name was Aanarakaq) in 2014. Sinka really knew the land. Bob had just returned to Kalskag and bought a boat to follow him and learn from him. Then Sinka died and went where Bob could not follow.

Place names

Following introductions, our first order of business was to look at the maps and identify and share the histories of important places in the vicinity of Upper and Lower Kalskag. Qalqaq (Old Kalskag) was located just above the mouth of Maqallartuli Creek. It was first mentioned in the mid-nineteenth century in Lieutenant L. Zagoskin's description of the portage route between Russian Mission and the Kuskokwim. Zagoskin visited the village in June 1844 and counted 120 people in five houses (Michael 1967:306 in Oswalt 1980a:72). Following an epidemic (possibly the influenza pandemic of 1918-19), people began to move to the fish camp site at Ayimqeryaraq, four miles up the Kuskokwim, and Qalqaq was abandoned.

Bob reiterated that Upper Kalskag is a relatively new village. People moved there from Qalqaq, as well as from Urraarmiut (Ohagmiut) and Tulukarnarmiut (Crow Village) on the Kuskokwim. Over the years, a significant number of families from the Yukon – both Russian Mission and Paimiut – also moved to Upper Kalskag. The first George Morgan, who was born in Germany in 1870, made his way to Alaska and became a trader at Paimiut before settling along the Kuskokwim and opening a store at Urraarmiut, which was thriving in 1910 when he took the census. After the store burned in the late 1920s he moved to Upper Kalskag and became the first postmaster in 1932. A Bureau of Eduction School was established there in 1931. A 1932 census lists five whites and 55 Natives living there, and a local teacher noted that 90% of these Natives could not speak English (Oswalt 1980a:85-86).

Bob described Paimiut on the Yukon River as a hub community the location of which has changed over time, in part because of flooding. The first Paimiut was on the upper part of Paimiut Slough. People then moved to Arularqurviaq, which was a large village. Bob described how Jake Aloysius pitted people against each other in the community, and after a fire destroyed many homes, the village broke up. People from Paimiut scattered to Urraarmiut, Upper and Lower Kalskag, Holy Cross, and Russian Mission.

In the 1920s and probably for many years before, Ayimqeryaraq (Lower Kalskag) was seasonally occupied as a fish camp. In the 1930s, however, people

Crow Village, with a new cabin built by Sam Phillip's grandson, David Phillips, June 2018. *AFR*

"Chief's home" in Lower Kalskag, 1950. *George A. Morlander Photographs, UA-1997-108-559*

Kalskag family, February 1940. *George Dale, ASL.P306.405*

began living there year-round. Community members moved there from Upper Kalskag at least partly because of religious differences. Upper Kalskag residents were predominantly Roman Catholic, and those who settled at Lower Kalskag were primarily Russian Orthodox. A BIA school was established there in 1959, and the village incorporated as a Second Class City in 1969 (Oswalt 1980a:54). While in Aniak, Clara had noted that people in Kessigliq and Ayimqeryaraq weren't united in the past:

> The Kameroffs and Morgans lived in Kessigliq, and there was a school there. They would bring children by dog sled [from Ayimqeryaraq] to Kessigliq to go to school. I lived in Kessigliq when I was seven in 1947. Henry Jung and his wife were there, and Gladys was my first teacher.
>
> Soon, people from both sides started to intermingle and get along. And today, members from both sides live in a housing complex together below

Upper Kalskag, February 1940. *George Dale, ASL.P143.844*

the mountain. Some people from Ayimqeryaraq moved up to Kessigliq to live in the housing complex.

Clara said that today more people live in Ayimqeryaraq (about 300) than in Kessigliq (about 230). The high school for both places, as well as the ANICA store across from the school, are in the middle along a three-mile road that connects the two villages. People also go back and forth by boat.

Portage routes

Bob noted that in the past first Qalqaq and then Lower Kalskag were transportation hubs, with trails leading to Paimiut and Russian Mission. The group described the main portage route from Lower Kalskag to Paimiut on the Yukon. One enters the north end of Maqallartuli (Mud Creek), then takes a short portage (Tevyaraq) to Pike Lake (Manaryaraq), follows the little lakes along the hills, portaging into Paimiut Slough. George noted that this was a winter trail. Once, however, when he was young, he was staying at Pike Lake in spring when a family came down that route from Paimiut after the village burned.

In a 1988 interview with Sinka Williams and Stanley Nook of Lower Kalskag,

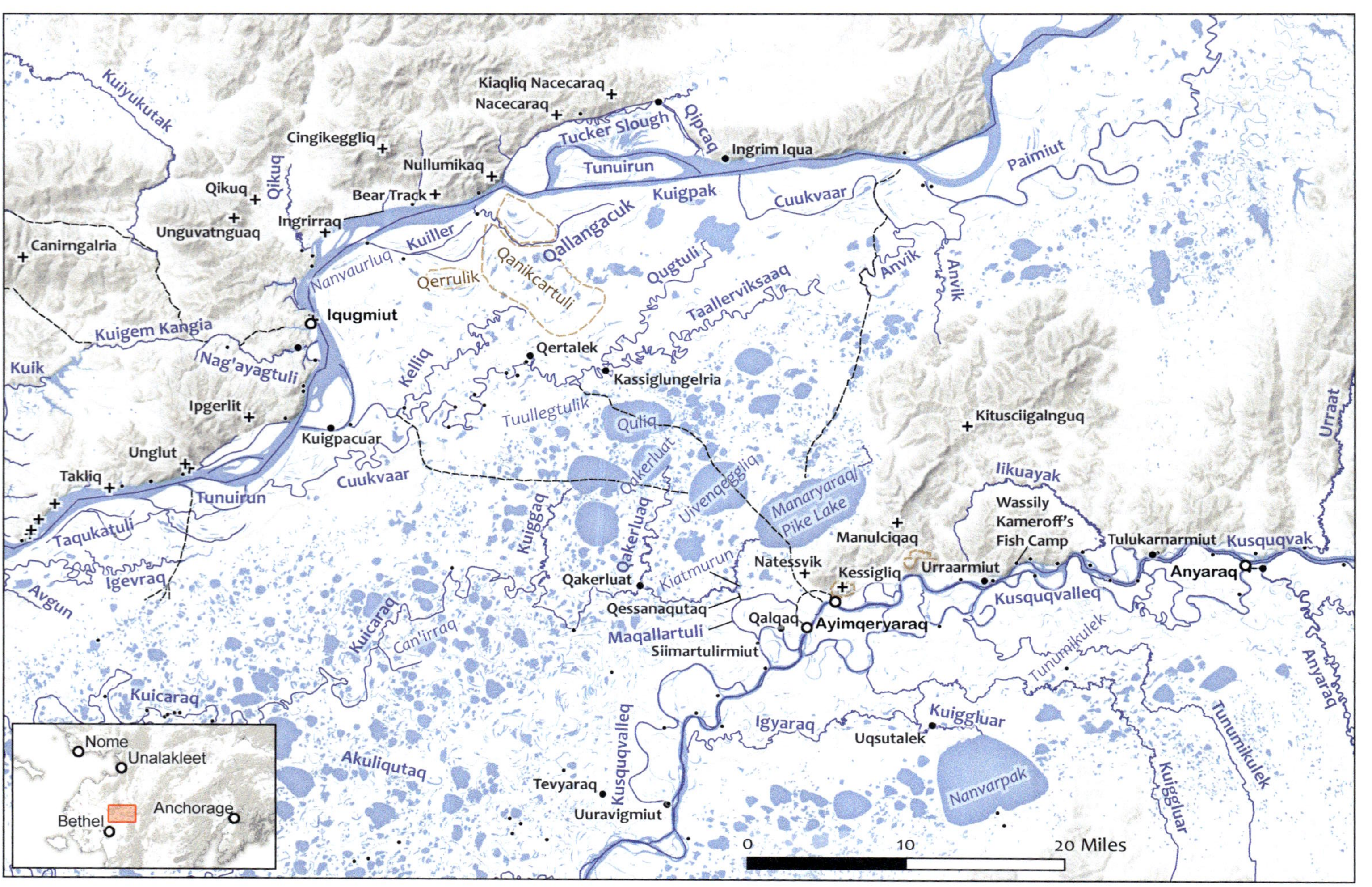

Portage routes between the Yukon and Kuskokwim Rivers. *Ian Moore and Jen Jolliff*

the two men described the summer portage route between the Kuskokwim and the Yukon River below Russian Mission. From Lower Kalskag, they followed Maqallartuli Creek until they reached the portage at Qessanaqutaq. From there they crossed a small lake, Kiatmurun, and took another portage into the upper Kuicaraq (Johnson River). To reach the Yukon, they followed Kuicaraq downstream to Qakerluat (Crooked Creek). They then followed Qakerluaq Creek to its headwater lake, Qakerluat, then into Quliq Lake. At the northwest corner of Quliq Lake they took another portage through a man-made creek into upper Taallerviksaaq River. Finally, they followed Taallerviksaaq downstream until it entered the Yukon River below Russian Mission.

In December 2014, James Nicholai of Atmautluak described using the summer portage to the Yukon River from the upper Kuicaraq when moose hunting in the area:

> From the lower side of the Kuicaraq River you'd portage over through a channel to a lake...and go across to a little *akuluraq* [stream between two bodies of water] on the other side and find a tramway. Years back when we used to go moose hunting over there, we took that tramway and portaged over and checked out the river on the other side. There evidently were two tramways there not far apart.
>
> They said that was the place where Kalikiurta [Oscar Samuelson, lit., "Mailman"] used to portage over when traveling to the Yukon River. The place where we portaged is old. You'd go over the bluff and on the other side you'd get to [Taallerviksaaq] river.

Clara also recalled the portage that went between Kessigliq and Russian Mission: "My mom used to talk about Taallerviksaaq River. In May they went to a spring camp in Taallerviksaaq from Paimiut." Later, she added: "This portage years ago; I remember when I was little, we had a spring camp [on Taallerviksaaq] and we were coming back, they put the dogs and the sled on the tramway. They put the boat on it, and they had the dogs pull." She noted that although the summer portage is rarely used today, people still go by four-wheelers and snowmachines to Russian Mission in winter.

When discussing the portage route in Kalskag, Bob Aloysius described the line of low hills running south of Taallerviksaaq and referred to by many as High Portage. Bob explained: "What they call High Portage starts down by Devil's Elbow [on the Yukon River]. That highest hill back there goes north, then west all the way down to Devil's Elbow. You can't miss it because it's higher than the Yukon side and higher than the Kuskokwim side."

Marie later spoke with her cousin Henry Parks of Nunapitchuk about the route he took when he and three other men ran out of gas along the upper Kuicaraq. Henry said that they walked to Pike Lake, continued along the bank to the end of the lake, then followed the edge of the mountains to Lower Kalskag. It took them ten hours round trip. Akulmiut hunters like Henry all know Sinka Williams' cabin and camp at Angilarterpak, which are landmarks in the upper Kuicaraq River area.

Akulmiut hunters living west of Bethel also used the portage that led from the upper Kuicaraq to the Kuskokwim, but in 2014 this route was known to be in bad condition. In December 2014, Johnny Berlin of Nunapitchuk recalled: "The portage to the Kuskokwim River is quite long. The portage way leads to a river, but the tramway wasn't stable. Though they weren't good, people would portage over to the Kuskokwim River from Kuicaraq."

One famous account of the use of this portage is in Tuluksak elder Joshua Phillip's story of the Battle of Maqallartuli – sometimes referred to as the Bloody

Fishing at Manaryaraq (Pike Lake), February 1940. *George Dale, ASL. P306.0416*

Men and gear on the last leg of the portage trail into the Kuskokwim, summer 1930. *Aleš Hrdlička papers, National Anthropological Archives, Smithsonian Institution*

Canoes crossing the portage, summer 1930. *Aleš Hrdlička papers, National Anthropological Archives, Smithsonian Institution*

Maneuvering boats through the ice over the Yukon-Kuskokwim portage, summer 1930.
Aleš Hrdlička papers, National Anthropological Archives, Smithsonian Institution

Creek Massacre – fought during the period of bow-and-arrow warfare on the banks of Maqallartuli Creek, where it enters the Kuskokwim just below Qalqaq (Fienup-Riordan and Rearden 2016:240-253). This battle is well documented in both Yup'ik oral tradition and non-Native accounts (Fienup-Riordan, ed. 1988:32; Oswalt 1990:40-42 based on Anderson 1940:119-120). According to Joshua Phillip, Yukon warriors and their allies planned to cross over to the Kuskokwim by the portage route beginning below Russian Mission, then travel downriver killing everyone in their path. Their guide was a captive from Qalqaq who led them past Akulmiut settlements following a shortcut into the upper Kuicaraq. There – as George had described – two hunters from Qalqaq spotted them and hid along the riverbank as the warriors paddled by. An older man traveling with the warriors detected these two men when he smelled their newly made parkas. His warnings, however, were dismissed, and the Yukon warriors continued overland to within sight of the Kuskokwim.

Meanwhile, the Qalqaq hunters returned home and warned their village, which sent messengers both upriver as far as Uskuralek and downriver as far as Siimartulirmiut. The Kuskokwim warriors gathered along both sides of Maqallartuli Creek. When the Yukon warriors entered the creek traveling single file in a long line, they were taken by surprise. The Kuskokwim warriors decimated their foes, leaving only one man alive to tell the story. So many died, they say, that the water turned red with blood and remains discolored to this day, and the river – originally called Currlugliq (from *currluk*, "murky water") – became known as Bloody Creek. To commemorate the battle, men of Qalqaq and middle Kuskokwim villages began painting a red line on their paddles to mark the depth of the blood (see also Fienup-Riordan and Rearden, 2016:258-264). To this day, elders recall this battle and many know the story.

Eyagyarat / *Abstinence practices*

Among the high points of our Kalskag visit were conversations with Elena Sergie, whose sharp memory and vivid descriptions brought the past to life. Like Sophie Sakar, Elena is Russian Orthodox. Many Orthodox families still know and follow traditional *eyagyarat* (abstinence practices) frowned on by Roman Catholic priests who arrived along the middle Kuskokwim more recently. Elena spoke at length about these practices. She described how when she menstruated for the first time, she took a piece of a beaver castor, chewed it, put it in a little piece of cloth and tied it with a string, then tied the string around her waist. She then put her saliva on her fingertips, rubbed them over her eyes, nose, mouth, and ears, and "pretended to put on a beaver", that is, travel on land and water like a beaver, avoiding obstacles: "After that my mom say, '*Cangerliit avitarturciqaten* [You will dodge and avoid sickness and misfortune for one year].' That's how we abstain for one year." After the year she took the castor and burned it. Beaver is a valued animal along the middle Kuskokwim. Recall the admonition shared by Sophie Sakar not to eat a beaver's pelvic bone while pregnant.

During the year after she first menstruated, Elena was also told not to chop live trees or her life would be shortened. She could not eat frozen fish. Boys, she said, had different *eyagyarat*. As Sophie and Clara had explained, Elena was instructed to tie down a berry with a strand of her hair so that the berry harvest would be abundant.

Elena also described how, when Sakar Levi was going to die, her cousin offered water to the sky's four corners to change the weather. First she placed a bit of dried fish and water in each of four corners. Then she wet her pinky fingers with her saliva and lifted them up toward the sky, opening up each corner in turn. She did this three times, then took the pieces of fish and burned them in the stove for good weather. Elena had seen Mary Ann Kameroff do this once during very windy weather, making it got calm "just like magic." Elena recalled:

Elena Sergie at home in Lower Kalskag, May 2024. *AFR*

Sakar Levi told me, "Watch what your cousin is doing so you can learn how to do it later." Because lots of people don't know how to abstain anymore. So when I went home I took a cup and put four fish inside and offered water to the sky for them. Then the sky finally cleared.

The weather is against those people who don't abstain.... But I was taught long ago how to offer water to the sky because they say, "*Ca tamalkuan nunam qaingani unguvaut* [Everything on earth is alive]."

Youth today

Elena later noted that in her opinion today's problems are in part due to the fact that people no longer abstain. Three situations, she maintained, require abstaining: becoming a woman (first menstruation), the death of a spouse, and graves washing into the water. Elena learned these things from her brother, Sinka. She said she was careful for one year after her mother and father died, but after her brother died the only thing she didn't eat was raw frozen fish.

Elena noted that old women say that today the weather is never good because people don't abstain. She said that she teaches these things to students in the cultural heritage classes at school:

> I go in there [to the school] and tell those kids about *eyagyarat* [abstinence practices] and about everything we have to do, fish every year for four seasons; winter, spring, summer and fall. We have to get ready for that month – hunt, prepare food, or get what we need.
>
> I tell my kids, "I'm not gonna be here to teach you all the time; so I'm just telling you messages that you will remember. And if you have kids, talk to them."

Bob agreed that they should share what they know with their grandkids. It frustrates him that people say "they don't know it": "Ap'a and Grandma are responsible to teach. Right now, grandparents are nothing."

Elena recounted the teachings she received from her own father, who spoke to both her and her brothers when they were young:

> But the memories of them; they were good; they leave us something. 'Cause my dad gather us to where he'll talk to us. When we're eating...he used to talk to us: "As you go forward in life you'll run into problems and distress. You will also experience good things. Even though other's actions and words hurt you, you got ear right here and the other ear. You have ears... If they tell you something, hurting your feelings, you'll hear the words with this ear and let them go out through the other ear. Never think of it no more."
>
> Those hurting us; those who are jealous; we all have bad deeds and thoughts inside us. They take our bad deeds and thoughts. And he say, "Go hunting. If somebody take 'em leave 'em alone."
>
> He said that person who stole the food, he won't ever get satisfied with food as long as he lives. The one who stole, he will never get full even though he ate. My dad used to gather us to pick berries and then when we eat he give us; he advised us before he left us: "I will not be here forever to take care of you." He said that we talk to others because we love them.

Bob commented that today's youth take his advice as criticism: "Right now these young people think we're scolding them." Elena agreed:

> Yaa. Their feelings get hurt when we talk to them because they have parents who never talk to them while growing up. Back when we were

growing up our fathers and mothers were strong. They give us one little word that stretch out lots.

To this day, I'm by myself.... I have no mom and dad, no more brothers. But their memories are in here. Sinka used to say, "Even I leave you, I'm always being with you." Their spirit will always be with us and their good memories.

Animals

We also talked briefly about animals – lynx snared in the upper Salmon River country, with delicious meat tasting like chicken. Stan noted that wolves run in packs of five to six animals and make a kill every two or three days in their 30-square-mile territory.

Elena also noted the rule to place land animal bones in the water and to bury fish scales in the land.

Elena's most unusual stories were about her pets. They were sparked when George mentioned that porcupines are jealous and want to be the first to be caught. Elena noted that she didn't eat porcupine meat because she once had a baby porcupine as a pet. When small it made a quacking noise, and she let it go after several months when it was able to eat on its own.

Elena said that she also had a black bear as a pet. Her father had killed its mother and brought her the cub, which she kept for four years. She called it Tan'gerliyagaq (Small black bear). She slept with it and fed it with a bottle when it was small. Later when it was bigger, they had it haul small loads of fish up from the boat at fish camp. It never bothered or bit her and was completely tame.

Elena's bear loved fish, turnips, and sugar. She fed it sugar cubes, but it also sometimes got into her mother's table sugar. To get turnips it dug up her mother's garden – the sandy soil made rich with mud and smelt juice – until her brothers built a fence around the garden patch. Her father would fix a place in their smokehouse for it to hibernate in winter. It didn't like Peter Volga or Mary Nook because they threw rocks at it. After four years, her father took the bear down to Tuluksak after Elena went to school in Wrangell in the fall, where it escaped and was shot. Elena never eats black bear meat, remembering her pet.

Ghosts and ircenrraat

On our last day, Stan commented that everywhere they hunt and trap, they see graves. George talked about men seeing *alangrut* (ghosts) and *ircenrraat* (other-than-human persons) at Whitefish Lake. People also hear voices at the old village site, Nanvarmiullret, at the end of Whitefish Lake, as the spirits of the dead are still there. They said that was why people moved to a new, clean spot following a death.

Bob told the story of Joe Simeon and Evan Wassilie who couldn't cross the slough in front of Urraaq because *ircenrraat* pushed them back. So Joe hit Evan in the nose and it started bleeding, and he took the blood and scattered it all over, and the *ircenrraat* disappeared so they could cross. Bob explained that *ircenrraat* are super clean and any kind of dirt stops them. Bob added that *ircenrraat* move to camps, just like people: "Sometimes they wake up and there's all kinds of noise; and those *ircenrraat* are moving out of the hills, going to fish camp or going to fall camp or going to spring camp. They are just like people here, they move to different locations for subsistence."

Elena talked about how her brother Sinka was cured by the spirit of their mother when he was staying at his spring camp by himself. There his dead mother cooked for him and let him eat. Sinka told Elena that if someone died she should burn his things: "Burn them, because even if you exchange for it [replacing it with something else], the same fate will follow you." She didn't do that but gave Sinka's motor to her son after Sinka died, and her son drowned, too.

Elena told the story of her father finding tea at the base of a tree. But he forgot to tie his shirt around the tree, and the tea disappeared:

> They always tell us that when we find something, to take off our shirt and tie it around it; put something or my scarf and tie it around it, and it won't disappear....
>
> Then my dad say, "Long ago, out of compassion, *ircenrraat* reveal food for us." They say we can smell them from far away.

Closing comments

At the end of our gathering, Bob regretted that we had not done this work sooner, before Sinka's generation had passed away. He voiced a concern shared by all – that youth in their communities today are experiencing hardships directly related to the fact that they are not well instructed in Yup'ik values and traditions.

George, however, was more optimistic. Today Kalskag is at the center of one million acres of rich country. George concluded, "They say we're living in the poorest country, but it's the richest country. Others tried to take it, but we still have it." Though George regrets the lose of good people who knew the *qaneryaraat* (teachings), he sees a better future for the people of his community because of the abundant resources in the area – moose, fish, berries, and more.

Throughout our discussions, George was the voice of hope. He thanked both Elena and Bob for talking to young people. We closed our gathering on a positive note.

In listening to elders from Upper and Lower Kalskag, as well as Aniak and Chuathbaluk, tell their stories, two things stood out. First and foremost, their personal histories reflect widespread family connections with brothers, sisters, and children living in communities up and down the Kuskokwim as well as the Yukon River. Most – like Bob – can describe themselves as "United Natives of Alaska." Many families have non-Natives in their ancestry, including the first George Morgan and Clara's father, Mr. Baldwin. Also, in the not-too-distant past, families moved regularly between the Kuskokwim River and communities such as Russian Mission, Holy Cross, and Paimiut on the Yukon. In many cases, these family connections are still strong and provide a base communities can build on.

View looking upriver from Aniak, 1952. *Reich Collection, Anchorage Museum B1998.022.007*

Chapter 2

Food and Family on the Middle Kuskokwim: Women's Stories

> I was born in Sleetmute at my Ap'a's house. And I grew up there, up the Holitna, but mostly up the Hoho. Winter camp. Spring camp. Summer camp. And Fall camp. We used to go wherever food was, we follow the food. I remember that.
>
> – *Angie Kameroff, Sleetmute*

> We who are now elders, things we learned from our parents, the knowledge we have is legacy from our parents; knowledge on how to care for food. Food may be fresh – moose, black bear, porcupine – everything from the land was our food because store-bought food wasn't available. You all, the knowledge you have about food, [give] to our descendants. Those of you who are grandmothers, mothers and fathers, if you love your children, your grandchildren, show them and tell them about the parts of fish and animal that are edible. They won't forget what they learned.
>
> – *Sophie Sakar, Chuathbaluk*

Our food knowledge is our legacy

During the last week of September 2023, ten women from the middle Kuskokwim came together in Aniak to share their experiences harvesting and preserving food when they were young. The three-day gathering was hosted by The Kuskokwim Corporation (TKC) and Calista Education and Culture (CEC) with funding from the National Science Foundation. Some of the women lived in Aniak, but the rest of us came to town for the gathering and stayed at the Arviiq – Aniak's old elementary school that was given to TKC in 2022 when the Kuspuk School District built a new school, and which TKC has since turned into offices and a comfortable training center. TKC put up cots for the elders in the old classrooms, and we met in the large, well-lit school cafeteria. A newly renovated kitchen gave us everything we needed to prepare big meals of baked whitefish, salmon

Angie Kameroff and Agnes Andreanoff attending our gathering on food and family, September 2023. *AFR*

soup, and moose stew, along with plenty of dry fish and blackberry and red-berry *akutaq*.

This gathering was a long time in the making. In 2021, CEC had been funded to continue documenting place names and food knowledge along the middle Kuskokwim. With COVID widespread, however, traveling and meeting with elders was put on hold. We were finally able to hold another small meeting in Aniak in January 2023, followed by day-long meetings with a handful of elders in Anchorage and short village visits in April and August 2023. Thanks to the help of TKC and many village administrators, these brief meetings were enough to set the stage for what turned out to be a richly rewarding week in Aniak.

Just before noon on Tuesday, Mark John, Marie Meade, and I arrived in Aniak on Ravn's flight from Anchorage. That same day Lake and Peninsula Airlines picked up Angie Kameroff in Sleetmute and Jennie Zaukar in Crooked Creek, and brought them downriver to Aniak, while Megan Leary (in charge of TKC's Aniak office) took a boat to nearby Chuathbaluk to pick up Sophie Sakar and Nastasia Avakumoff, as well as Lucy Simeon and Olga Phillips. Marie spotted Seraphine Borowski returning to Aniak on the Ravn flight and asked her to come as well. Three more women living in Aniak – Agnes Andreanoff, Olga Peterson, and Annie Morgan – were also able to join us.

After a quick lunch of soup and sandwiches, we moved the tables into a large square and sat down together. The eldest, Sophie Sakar, led us in the Lord's Prayer. After Sophie, I began by saying how grateful we were that everyone was able to join us. Then I explained the purpose of our visit and our hope to work together to begin to document traditional food knowledge on the middle Kuskokwim. I told how CEC had held small gatherings like this in other parts of southwest Alaska – including Nelson Island, the lower Yukon, and Kuskokwim communities below Bethel. Just as we were doing here, in the past CEC staff has met with groups of elders over several days to discuss a particular topic. Over the years, we have found that this way of working together gives everyone an opportunity to share: We all learn from one another and have fun at the same time. I also briefly introduced my partners, CEC cultural advisor Mark John and Yup'ik language expert Marie Meade. Both Mark and Marie would be leading the discussion, organized around harvesting during the different seasons. I would be recording our discussion on my trusty Sony 5000 tape recorder, and during the months ahead Marie and I would transcribe what was shared so that others could hear what the elders had to say. Although most of our discussion was in English, Marie would also translate comments made in Yup'ik. Sharing knowledge is as valued as sharing food in southwest Alaska, and everyone agreed that this was important work.

Our next step was to circle the room introducing ourselves, as not everyone knew each other. I spoke briefly about my own background. I was born on the East Coast and moved to Alaska with my husband more than fifty years ago, in 1973. A year after coming to Alaska I was sent to Nelson Island to help with a pottery project. After that I continued to work in the region, which I love. I told the group: "I've learned a little Yup'ik, but I'm not fluent. I'm learning, and I'm going to die still learning. But I've been so fortunate to know and work with such knowledgeable elders, and with Mark and Marie now for more than thirty years. And that's who I am."

Marie followed, speaking in Yup'ik and sharing her Yup'ik names – Arnaq and Cupluar. She said that she was born in 1947 and raised in Nunapitchuk, in the Akulmiut area west of Bethel, and that her ancestors come from Kayalivik just north of Nelson Island, as well as Qissunaq and the lower Kuskokwim.

Angie Kameroff from Sleetmute was the next to speak. Angie said that her father's family came from the lower Yukon and moved across to the Kuskokwim, then upriver to Canoe Village. Her mother's father was Goosma Effemka, and her mother, Annie, was born around Crooked Creek. Her father, Steve Derendy, was born in Canoe Village, later moving with his family to Sleetmute, where Angie was born in October 1948. Angie was their only child:

> There was a boy after me, but he died when he was two months old. Long time ago they'd say when you catch something [don't bring it in the

> house]..... My dad had caught a wolf, and he brought it into the house. And not too long after that my brother died.
>
> So I was the only kid for a long time. But I had four boys that were bigger than me [her mother's two brothers and two uncles]. And they help me learn how to set traps, all the things that boys do. Because we didn't have no girls. That's how come I was a tomboy.
>
> I was born in Sleetmute at my Ap'a's house. And I grew up there on the Holitna, but mostly up the Hoho. Winter camp. Spring camp. Summer camp. And fall camp. We used to go wherever food was, we follow the food. I remember that.

Sophie Sakar was the next to speak. She noted in her introduction that everyone there already knew her:

> You all know me. I'm Sophie Kelila Sakar. I live up in Chuathbaluk, but I'm from Aniak, here across the slough. We moved up to Chuathbaluk in 1967 because my late husband wanted to move up there.
>
> My dad was John Kelila, but everybody called him by his Yup'ik name Ikamrarrluk. The reason why they started calling him Ikamrarrluk, [which means] "bum sled," was because he was always making basket sleds for everybody that needed them and for his family.
>
> I was born January 1942. My dad was from here in Aniak. And my mom is Marie Kelila. She was from Chefornak. So I've got some relatives downriver, and I'm still meeting some of my relatives that my mom grew up with.
>
> My mom was married three times. First, she married somebody from Napaskiak. Then after he passed away, she got married with my dad. When my dad went downriver they met somehow.
>
> Anyway, I thank our elders that passed on, to give us messages to go after them and raising our families, our kids.

Sophie spoke briefly about her childhood: "I grew up here in Aniak, across the slough. And those years we used to walk across the slough to go to school in the morning, cold or not, deep snow or not. And we have very strict teachers. If we're late three or four minutes, we have to write, 'I won't be late no more' hundred times without stopping. It was painful to write those words without stopping, when your fingers start hurting. If we don't listen to him, if we don't write, he'll pull your ear and tell you, 'When are you going to get done?'"

After sharing her ancestry, Sophie spoke of her own marriage and family: "You know, long time ago, our elders used to force their sons and daughters to marry somebody that some of them don't even know.... I was forced to get married with my husband, 1958. I was only sixteen years old when I got married. And together we had eight kids – three boys, five girls." She then returned to her extended family that were her riches when she was young:

> I was raised up by my family. I was rich with family. I have mom and dad. I have brothers and sisters. I have uncles and aunties. I don't know my Ap'a and grandma by my mom and dad, they left before I was born. So I don't know who they are....
>
> Anyway, all of my families that I grew up with, all of my riches that I grew up with, my immediate family, all of them are gone. My uncles, my aunties, my Ap'as, my grandmas. My mom and dad. My brothers and sisters. But before my mom got senile, before she start poor hearing,... when we were alone she talk to me about life, about family. You could be rich with family, but they start going, they go one after another. She told me that she and I are left, and she'd say, "I don't want you to go before me. Because if you go before me, I don't know who's going to help me, because I can't move around much anymore."

Sophie then shared a long, moving account of traveling to Anchorage in 1990 when her mother was dying and her youngest daughter was in a coma in the Native Hospital. Sophie is a strong woman, but she broke down describing holding her daughter's hand but not being able to tell her that her grandmother had died, fearing the shock would be too much for her: "It broke my heart like a knife... I prayed to God, 'At least save me one of them.'" Sophie concluded:

> I thank God for sharing me who I have left in my family, which is my kids, my sons and daughters... I have eight kids, two of them died. One year-and-half old, she died in my arms. My youngest son got killed last year. His one year [feast] was on September 17. I thank God for letting him be found, so we wouldn't wonder where he is, what happened to him. I thank God for bringing my son home.

Agnes Andreanoff was the next to speak. Agnes said that she was born in May 1949 at her grandfather's place (Waskey's Landing) above Stony River on the Kuskokwim. She didn't know her grandparents, as both passed away when she was young. Agnes was raised in Crooked Creek, where she married and had three children. Although her husband passed away several years ago, her mother, Olinka Sakar (who was born and grew up just above Devil's Elbow) was still alive at the time, passing away at age 98 in Aniak in 2025. Marie asked Agnes what her Yup'ik name was, and Agnes said that she didn't have one until she traveled to St. Mary's to attend a language workshop. There two elders from Nunam Iqua gave her the Yup'ik name Atsaruaq, which she uses to this day.

Sitting beside Agnes was Jennie Waskey Zaukar, who was born in 1947. Jennie was also born at Waskey's Landing and lived there with her parents, Evan and Annie Waskey. When Jennie was two or three, the family moved to Crooked Creek, where Annie was from, and Jennie grew up there. After she married Peter Zaukar, she moved to Sleetmute, where she raised six children and worked as a health aide for close to twenty years.

Next to Jennie was her younger sister, Olga Waskey Peterson. Olga explained that their father, Evan Waskey, was the brother of Agnes's mother Olinka: "I never knew my dad's side of the family because I was too young, or my mom's side of the family.... I remember my two uncles a little bit. Only one I really knew was my auntie Olinka. She's the only one living now, out of all my dad's side. She's really strong for her age, still walking around the house using a cane." Born in 1966, Olga was also raised in Crooked Creek and moved to Aniak in the 1970s when she was married. Together the couple had four children before Olga's husband passed away in 2005.

Nastasia Avakumoff was also from Crooked Creek, where she was born in 1951. Nastasia remembered: "I used to be John, but when I got married it changed to Avakumoff. And my dad was Johnny John, but he married three times, so I have stepbrothers. My mom was Martha Waskey, but I never got to see her. I was maybe two years old. I was raised with stepmom. I didn't mind because I thought she was my mom. Nowadays I start thinking, 'Gee, I wish I could've seen my mom.'"

Nastasia said that she didn't know much about her father's or mother's side of the family. Agnes noted, "We're all related upriver." Jennie agreed and added, "When we were growing up we never used to ask about our ancestors. To me, they never used to tell us, we just grew up with them."

Olga Phillips from Chuathbaluk was the next to share:

> I was born in 1949 [in Napaimute]. I remember my Ap'a, my mom's dad. His name is Abruska. He was blind. His Eskimo name is Arnacuaq. My mom said I had 19 sisters and brothers. There's just three of us now. I have only one sister left.
>
> And I got married when I was 16 years old. But we were married for 21 years.... I moved down to Aniak when my mom and dad went to Mt. Edgecumbe, when they had TB. I went to school there, to third grade.

Mark John was the only man attending our gathering, and he introduced himself at length in a mixture of Yup'ik and English. He shared his many Yup'ik names, noting that he was the first grandchild of two large families, so he was picked on a lot as a child. Mark's parents are Paul John from Chefornak and Martina John from Nightmute. Paul moved to Nightmute when he married Martina, and Mark was born there in 1954. In 1964 the family was one of many that moved to the new village of Nunakauyaq, Toksook Bay, to be closer to spring sealing and summer fishing. After elementary school, Mark attended high school at St. Mary's Catholic Mission, then college at the University of Alaska, both in Fairbanks and in Anchorage. In 1997, he was offered the job of running the Calista Elders Council, to work on documenting traditional knowledge and passing this knowledge on to youth. Soon after he started, Mark brought both Marie and me on board to help CEC accomplish these goals. Mark noted that when he initially took the job directing CEC, he planned to return to social work (his profession) in a year or two. In fact, he has continued to work with CEC ever since. Mark has also fished commercially in Bristol Bay for more than 50 years – an activity that means as much to him as his work with CEC.

Lucy Simeon was next. Lucy's father's father was Sam Phillips from Crow Village downriver from Aniak, and her mother Lucy Pitka was from the Holitna. Lucy was born in Crow Village: "My grandma, Ap'a Sam's wife, she passed away in January, and I was born that same year. So I'm named after her, Lucy, and my Yup'ik name is Uullaq." Lucy shared that in 1957, her Ap'a Sam and his family moved up to Chuathbaluk: "You see that Russian Orthodox church up there? It was by itself, nobody around. So he moved his family up there, his wife and his daughter and one son who wasn't married." The next year, Lucy's family as well as her other uncle and his wife moved up to Chuathbaluk: "My grandpa's relatives are downriver, at Akiak and Akiachak. And my mom's relatives are from upriver on the Holitna....They were way up in Holitna River when my Ap'a's wife died, my mom's mom. And my mom said that they had to leave those kids in the camp while my Ap'a Andrew bring my grandma down by dog sled."

Lucy remembered how the church was relocated farther up the bank and rebuilt after people moved to Chuathbaluk: "I used to see mostly Ap'as and uncles helping out with that, moving the whole church back to the [present] location."

Talking about her growing up, Lucy recalled how much she enjoyed moving with the seasons: "I used to love going spring camp and fall camp with dog team way back. I remember going to pick berries when the snow melted, where the berries grow and they're left behind. Every time the snow melt around the berries and they're still there, my mom used to tell us, 'Go pick the berries.' So we listen

Seraphine Borowski at her homestead near Napaimute, May 2024. *AFR*

and go pick." Angie added with a smile: "They say those are the sweetest berries, because they lasted through the winter. Low bush cranberries. We used to go pick them, too."

Speaking of berries, and recalling Agnes's Yup'ik name Atsaruaq (lit., "Pretend berry"), which is the Yup'ik name for chamomile, Lucy continued: "My mom used to always tell us, 'Watch those, and when they get bigger, the berries are ready to pick.' And they call those [chamomile flowers] clay berries."

Seraphine Borowski introduced herself with a laugh: "My name is Seraphine Kameroff, used to be. And it changed, 'cause I got married. My daddy's name is Paul Kameroff. And my momma's name is Rita Kameroff. We never call her by her Native name... She went to Holy Cross." Seraphine said that she was born in 1946 after an old woman had passed away: "They gave me that name. Her name was Uulliarneq. My daddy say, 'What's her *kass'aq* name?' Nobody knows. So, my dad's first wife was Seraphine. So they named me Seraphine."

Sharing food

Our introductions had taken time, but everyone had heard something new – both about their friends and family and about the reasons we had come together. Mark followed with more detail on the purpose of our gathering and what we hoped to accomplish, stating our themes in both Yup'ik and English:

> They say food is a way to make family. When you share food, it's a way to gain friends, to have family, to keep family together. That's why

> they used to eat in large gatherings, sharing the same large bowl.
>
> And it's a way to keep family and also to have good friends. People never forget what food they were given. And they want to repay, reciprocate. Like when you feed a stranger from another village. They'll want to have you over to their house because you had them.

Mark mentioned the story he'd heard from a woman from Egegik in Bristol Bay. She wrote about her fish cutting table, where her mother and sisters worked together: "It was a special place for them. And while they work on fish, they tell stories and their mom and grandmother tell them stories, they pass on knowledge of how to take care of the food." Finally Mark spoke about the custom of *kalukaq* (feasting) well known in southwest Alaska: "They used to subsist all summer, gather food, wherever they are, wherever the camp is. And then they go back to their winter place. Then they'd have *kalukaq*, where a family gives a big feast."

Marie noted that people still share food today, especially during Slaaviq: "I know it's a big thing up here, too. The feasting, sharing the food you harvested. And my parents used to put food away just for the Slaaviq feed." The forty-day and one-year feasts following the death of a family member are other opportunities to share food. Mark added that in the past, after everyone had eaten well, whatever was left was shared with those who were lacking: "Those that have food, they don't want to have them take food from there, but only the elders, widows, and people without providers."

Following Mark and Marie, I asked the group if they could talk about their experiences sharing food. Angie had been listening and had a story to tell:

> Getting back to this food sharing. When I was growing up I remember my mom and dad and me. We lived in this lumber frame house across the river. And when I think about it now, we only had breakfast and lunch at our house, me and my mom and dad, only breakfast and lunch.
>
> And for dinner we always went over to my dad's sister. She would have the whole family, all of our family in her house. And she would cook with a big old pot. And there were so many of us. But everybody had enough to eat....
>
> It was like that for a long time. I remember, my mom used to get mad at my dad, "How come we don't eat over here?" And my dad would tell her, "Because my sister will get mad if we don't show up." Even the three of us, she said, it made a big hole in the family dinner [when they weren't there]. So, we always tried to go over there. And now you don't see that anymore.
>
> But that's one thing I remember about the families eating together.

Angie also remembered families working together harvesting eels in the fall, and the tasty results:

> I remember, one time they were catching eels in the falltime. This was so funny. They make a long, skinny opening in the ice, kind of even with the bank. And then they said that the eels are running. So we went down to watch them. And they put a pole in the water that had nails sticking out all over. When they put it up, they pulled up these eels. I remember seeing them the first time, I was so excited. I went up and I grab one and it poked me. Oh, that hurt!
>
> And then when it was time to eat, my auntie had cooked those eels. But she had cut them in tiny pieces. And she put them in a baking pan, one layer of eels. And when we take them out from the stove, the fish would be floating on top of the grease, the eels. And I remember tasting it. It was so good! And you could even eat the bones. I was so impressed with that. Boy, I tried to eat all the bones I could get.

Later the women observed that people rarely harvest eels these days, as there is no more shore ice in the fall to stand on, and no dog teams that require the rich, fatty food.

Once she got started, Angie was full of food memories. She remembered the fish heads her grandmother fermented in a sack at her fish camp, then shared with her extended family:

> My grandma, one time, we stop at their fish camp. We always stop in their fish camp. One day I noticed that she had a gunny sack that was tied up to the *segvik* ["fish pond," the dock for fish processing, including holding tanks and cutting tables]. And it was floating. That gunny sack looked like it was full. So, I asked her what it was. She said, "Our food." And I was more and more curious. 'Cause it took a long time to get it ready.

Later Angie added: "My grandma aged them in the water. She had the gunny sack float back of her *segvik* for a long time. After two weeks, I kept asking, 'When we gonna eat 'em gram?'" Marie asked how long she kept them in the water, and Angie responded: "Seem like forever. And forever is a long time." Finally, the fish heads were ready to eat:

> When it was ready, those guys brought the sack back to the *salayaq* [summer storehouse and smokehouse for fish], and they start cooking

> them. And since there were three families there, they put a head in a big *taassiq* [dishpan], three *taassiqs*, one family per *taassiq*. Boy, when we finished ours, I went looking for more, but there was no more. My grandma tell us to only eat the *tatangquq* [cartilage], the crunchy part. It was so good!

Continuing to talk about food sharing, Angie remembered the Slaaviq feast her extended family had one winter in Cotton Village on the Hoholitna River when she was young. The family usually traveled to Sleetmute for Slaaviq, but heavy snow made travel too difficult:

> That was the year we had all the singers living in Cotton Village about Slaaviq time. Before we started making road down to the village, to Sleetmute, there had been a big snowstorm. And we were trying to get down to Sleetmute for Slaaviq...But after two days of trying to get out, we decided that we can't do it. So we had Slaaviq in Cotton Village. Seven houses. And it took us three days. And we ate in every house in those three days, I remember.

As the only girl in the family, Angie grew up doing boy's things outside. She recalled successfully setting a mink trap and selling the pelt to buy herself winter clothes:

> They tell me to set trap one time. So I set one. But I set it where you shouldn't set traps. Nobody told me that I couldn't set one in there. So I just put it there. But first I had to find the ring, so you can put that ring and put your trap in, and [when] they catch, [the animal] can't pull it because they're stuck.
>
> Right along the creek side where animals go there's a little shelf.... So I put the trap in there, and that's where the animals bring their fish up to eat. And I got that mink in there. I remember long time ago, it sold for 65 dollars.
>
> And I got myself a winter coat, winter boots, and a pair of pants, I think. That's all I had money for. Boy, I tell you, when my boots and my coat came, I was happiest person.

Angie shared many experiences of harvesting food out on the land. As a youngster she liked to help a neighbor woman pick greens and berries: "I used to like to go picking stuff with a woman named Aanaurluq. She was a single lady at the time that I knew her. But she had raised boys before I got to know her. She would tell me the night before what she's gonna do tomorrow. She want to go pick salmonberries tomorrow. I say, 'Okay. I'll go with you.' And we pick 'em. Next day when I go see her, she'd give me *akutaq*. Boy, it was so good."

Angie also recalled encounters with bears:

> I wouldn't carry a gun if I'm gonna get berries. If I was not hunting I wouldn't take a gun. And I come across some bears that were so close, and I got away from them.... You could see his eyes. And I looked up and saw him.
>
> You know how you have a folder in your head. You know, everything what they tell you when you're growing up, all the stuff that they tell you. I saw that bear, and right away I could feel my brain, "Where's the bear ones?!" You know, thinking about, "Where did I put it?" And then finally I remembered it. My dad always told me, "A bear can't see very good. He isn't good at judging distance. So, if you come across a bear, you watch him. Don't look into his eyes. If you look into his eyes he'll feel you. Look at his ear. And soon as he put his head down, move."
>
> So when he put his head down, I moved back little bit. Just right behind me there was a little tree. I even leave my *piicikaq* [birch-bark basket] in there. Next day I had to go get it.
>
> But soon as I got behind that tree I went running home. My dad was standing in the door, and I say, "Hi, Dad!" And I went running in the house, and I run upstairs and I sat on my bed and, boy, I couldn't stop breathing loud for a long time.
>
> Then my mom, the next day, she goes, "I wonder how come that kid never go out today?" And my dad tell her, "She must've run into some kind of animal." She goes, "How you know?" "You see her when she come running home? She didn't stop and talk to us downstairs, she just went running upstairs and go to her bed. You didn't notice that?" Mom said, "Yaa, I noticed it, but I thought she was just in a hurry."

Angie said that after that experience she started being more careful. Still, it took her hours to walk down the beach or over the hills to her Ap'a's house, checking the trees and eating berries and plants as she went.

Fish camp on the Kuskokwim: "We never waste any kind of food"

After Angie's lively stories, Sophie took her turn, describing the way her family worked together at fish camp each summer to harvest and store the abundance of salmon that used to run up the Kuskokwim River:

> Long ago when we were growing up, when our parents were raising us up, we came to gather food for the winter. Summertime catching salmon, all kinds of fish. They used to have fish wheels. Now you hardly see fish wheels anymore.
>
> And the fish wheel, when it was set across there on the island, it used to catch about four [or] five hundred fish a day. And morning we cut fish, we all get together, the family get together and cut the fish.
>
> And they used to have poles on the beach [fish drying racks called *iniviit*]. After they cut fish they hang those fish for the slime to drip before they bring 'em up to smokehouse.
>
> And my parents took care of the fish, the food. We never waste not one piece of fish anywhere. They let us cut all the fish, all of us get together as family, help each other. Cut fish all day. Hang them up.
>
> There was two [smokehouses] – one for eating fish, one for the dog fish. Mostly the king salmon they cut was blanket fish, and they save their backbones for winter. Some of them, they save 'em for *egamaarrluk* [half-dried fish or meat]. Some of 'em they save for dogs.
>
> Anyway, they never let us waste any kind of food, the body, the head, the stomach... And not throw away the fish eggs, they put 'em in the gut. You know, when you see the black bear gut, they save them, they hang them and make something out of 'em, like bullet-bag purse. They put those king salmon eggs, or any kind of fish eggs like dog salmon, silvers, reds. They put them in those little stomach [bags], and they hang 'em. And they half-dry some of 'em. When they go hunting they bring some of those.

The next day, the women also discussed drying fish eggs in the fish's airbag or "bubble sack," which is tied at one end and put in the *salayaq* to smoke. Angie explained: "Inside the stomach, [all] fish have a bubble sack." Marie was surprised, as the bubble sack is thin and looks easy to tear. Angie remembered: "You tie up one side. We used to like to rob them and eat them [as snacks]. When we run into the *salayaq*, grandma knew exactly what we're doing. Stealing some eggs.... And when you eat them, they're really gummy, better than Bubblicious." Angie noted that you need two people to put the eggs in the sack – one to hold the sack open, and one to drop the eggs inside. Jennie added that fish eggs were also routinely saved in 55-gallon drums for dog food in winter: "They'd chop them and add it to dog food. They used to add fish heads into the eggs they saved for the dog."

Sophie continued, talking about fish heads: "They never waste nothing. Even their heads, they make stink heads out of 'em. They put them together [underground]. And when they're ready we'd dig them out, and we'd have some." Like Angie's grandmother, Sophie's family had also fermented fish heads in the river at the *segvik*: "[Other] fish heads, we leave them in the fish pond, we don't throw them away. Some of 'em we cook for the dogs. Make the fish heads like brine, when the head come up to the water, you just take the skin off and eat the *tatangquq* [cartilage]."

Sophie then told a story about curing salmon heads at her fish pond, and what happened one day when her children were playing nearby:

> You know, up here we always have those fish ponds for cutting fish. There's a lumber [frame in the water] and cutting table. One time I was cutting fish and my two girls, the oldest one, Lulu, she was enjoying eating those [heads], take those skins off, enjoying those crunchy parts. And her

Two men bend over a fish wheel at Sleetmute, while someone watches from shore, 1948. *George A. Morlander Photographs, UAF-1997-108-296*

> sister come around this way, she wanted to pass her sister, but older sister never listen. And there was other people cutting fish in their fish pond.
>
> Anyway, her sister try to get back there, then she take 'em by the neck, and the older sister push her back. They were using dresses. They fell in the water.
>
> When they stand up, my oldest daughter was still chewing on the *tatangquq*. Everybody start laughing.

Our group laughed as well.

Sophie continued describing the teamwork that went into processing fish at fish camp:

> After the slime drip from the fish, they bring 'em up to the smokehouse. Everything by hand. No Hondas, no nothing.
>
> And my dad had a little [wheelbarrow].... And he make a lumber basket and put wheels, from old parts of something that's not useable anymore. He load up those fish in the basket, and he walk up and push that little tractor to bring all [the fish] to the smokehouse. And they gather up smudge wood.
>
> My goodness, there used to be so much fish to cut. They never let us waste nothing, not even those little fish. Us kids would scale them and [make] dry fish out of them.

Sophie also spoke briefly about putting the fish away for winter: "We put away the fish, the dog fish. They used to bundle them up and bring 'em up to the cache for the dogs. And they bundle up the eating fish. They take the back bones off, bundle them up and put 'em away. They never spoil. They never get moldy." In those days before freezers, Sophie's father built a cold-storage cellar:

> And these fish that we take care of. We didn't have no freezers, no cooler. But my dad made a big cellar, a cooler, outdoors. He shoveled off the mud and built a lumber shed in the top for tools, nets, whatever hunting gear that they have, and gather 'em inside. And on the third part, they get grasses for the dogs for wintertime and hang their harness up in the top one. And the cooler, we used to put moose meat there, [and other things] like salt fish, salmonberries, blueberries, put 'em in the barrels. But the red [berries] and blackberries, they put 'em in the cache in a gasoline box. They never spoil.

Others recalled the cold cellars in use before freezers were available. Angie described storage caches made against the side of hills. "[They] dig it out. And then you put poles to make it sturdy. And inside they keep all their valuables." Lucy agreed: "My grandpa had one of those. Like igloo going into hillside. He dig way back. And the flooring is just the mud. He made door. That's where they used to store all their subsistence [foods]. Berries, *sulunaqs* [salted fish], all your *egamaarrluk*... The red berries in the gasoline box. And those almost like stink heads, I think they leave some in the ground for their dogs. And they make *passiaq*, smash up the fish eggs and put berries. My uncle make them with red berries. I liked it. It was like yogurt."

In addition to fish, Sophie's family also had a summer garden: "Besides those, my dad make a garden, grow potatoes, carrots, lettuce, turnips, and save 'em for winter. Keep them cool where they wouldn't get spoiled right away. Sometimes we're short of those, 'cause we never had much." At summer's end, her family added wild fruits and berries:

> It was fun to take care of those foods for winter all by hand.... It was fun how they raised us up.
>
> And the fruits that we used to have was rhubarb. My mom would cook rhubarbs and sugar, and we eat them for fruit. Even the blueberries or salmonberries. We never waste nothing.

Our parents talked to us

Sophie spoke at length about how her parents spoke to her when she was young, as well as the consequences of not listening.

> And then my parents, they talk to us while we're growing up. They let us sit on the floor and listen. [They spoke] in Yup'ik. We didn't know how to talk English.... I was seven years old. My first words in English were "yes" and "no."
>
> My parents used to teach us everything....
>
> And they never used to holler at us when they talk to us. But some people, they never watch the person talking or listen to them. They just fiddle around.
>
> And then one day there was a man and a woman talking to us about food, and how we take care of them the best we can so that they wouldn't spoil, every part of the food.
>
> Anyway, one lady, she must've been about middle age. She was fiddling around, not listening, not facing the person that was talking. And they tell her to stop fiddling around. She got mad, she stand up. "Oh, those

> old people, they just talk superstitions." They never said nothing. She walk out. And then after she walk out, those elders said, "*Akleng augna* [That poor one], she's making her life shorter."
>
> Sure enough, how many years later, during Slaaviq time she got sick. They medivac her, but she didn't make it. The elders tell us, "Listen. Listen, what they tell you." It's true.

One of the first lessons her parents imparted was the importance of sharing:

> And they used to tell us, "Especially, share with those orphans that have no parents, or widows, or those that have no boat or motor to go fishing or hunting. Share with those people when you catch anything."... Those that have no help, "Help them bring food. Share with them."
>
> And it's so true. I have one girl in my house, her parents both died.... And now their kids, their daughters and sons, they never look away from me. And they tell me, "You helped us when we needed help. You helped us when we were hungry. You share with us, even you didn't have much to share."
>
> This one that's staying with me now...since my youngest son passed away. She always tell me, "Auntie, I never forget you guys helping us when we needed help." Because their dad had no motor, no boat.

In the past, Sophie recalled, they were not rich, but people took care of each other: "That's how my parents taught us when we were growing up. Never waste nothing. And to watch out for somebody. You know, lot of us grew up, we were not rich. Everybody didn't have boat and motor. And the time they go with dogs, when they go out camping or get wood." Sharing food had practical value in helping families survive, creating friends in the process: "And always share the food to the ones that have nothing to go hunting with.... I always tell my kids, for the ones that are poor like us, bring them something to cook. Bring them a piece of dry fish. They'll be happy. They'll be glad. That's how our families brought us up."

Sophie remembered the days before store-bought food was readily available:

> We have no juice, no birthday parties, no cakes, no Jell-O, no nothing.
>
> And my stepsister's daughters used to live in Holitna. When they first hear plane above our old house across there, they used to run under the bed, get scared. They used to be scared of planes.
>
> And I don't know who make Jell-O, when they start buying Jell-O. My niece, nephews they never see Jell-O before in Holitna. You know they

have no store up there. They were going to eat. Their mom put Jell-O in their bowl, start moving, "*Iliii*! It's moving!"

We all laughed at the recollection. Sophie returned to how carefully people treated their limited food when she was growing up:

> And the only time they let us eat is breakfast, lunch. You're lucky if they let you have piece of bread in the afternoon for snack. And these small kids sit down and eat, no running around. And they tell us, "When you don't finish your food, you could eat it later and finish it. If you waste that food, when you go hungry, when there's nothing to eat, you'll think about the food you waste."

Many today, Sophie fears, have forgotten this essential instruction:

> Long ago those elders never waste nothing....
>
> And then some forget about how they grow up, to take care of the food. Oh, my goodness. After they start these freezers, my mom was so upset. She came home...the person that was poor when they had nothing. They take the meat out, leftover part of soup, maybe it spoiled. Oh, my God, she was shocked. She said, "Boy, if they go hungry, they're going to think about the food they smell around." And she tell us, "Don't ever smell around food that you take care of unless you know it's spoiled."

Sophie ended our first afternoon with thanks and a funny story:

> Thank you, all of you, for listening. This is what our parents teach us when we were growing up.
>
> You know, we didn't know about birthday parties...no cake, no Jell-O, no juice, no fancy foods, no salad. Anyway, one time, for the first time I had a birthday present. I didn't know what it was. It was something silver. And I ask my mom, "What is it?" My *aataq* [father] gave me something silver. I didn't know what it was. Before I ask my mom [what it was] we went to store. Me and my baby sister we wanted candy bar. Then my mom ask me, "*Nauwami akiuten* [Where is your money]?" I look at her and I said, "*Akiutaitua* [I have no money]." "*Nauwami imna aatavet cikiutii* [Where is the gift your dad gave you]?" I look at her. I was kind of scared to tell her. And in the beach summertime, you know, we used to race and skip rocks. I run back and I go get that silver thing, I throw it and I win.

Everyone laughed, and Sophie concluded her story:

> And she tell me, "*Angill'elpeni usviipaa* [You are so crazy]!"
> I look at her and said, "*Ciin* [Why]?"
> "That was money."
> Quyana. But don't throw money.

Fish is our food

Our second day also began with the Lord's prayer. Marie observed that twelve women along with one man – Mark John – were gathered together. Annie Morgan of Aniak had joined us, and she briefly introduced herself. Annie is Agnus Andreanoff's younger sister. Both have the same mother – Olinka Sakar – but different fathers. Annie noted that her mom, Olinka, was born and raised just above Devil's Elbow, in Athabascan territory. Olinka's mother was from Nikolai, and Olinka's first husband (Agnes' dad) was Pete Bobby from Lime Village. So Olinka spoke Upper Kuskokwim Athabascan and Dena'ina until she married her second husband, Oscar Sakar. Annie's father, Oscar, was born in Crooked Creek and drove the barge from Bethel to McGrath. He taught his wife, Olinka, to speak Yup'ik, Russian, and English. Like Agnes, Annie grew up in Crooked Creek speaking mostly English, and she considers herself Athabascan. The middle Kuskokwim is noteworthy for bringing different people together. Not surprisingly, Annie said that she respects every culture.

Following Annie's introduction, we continued our discussion of summer fish camp and processing salmon. In the past everyone went to fish camp. Though today many people work on their fish in the village, Nastasia Avakumoff still goes to fish camp every summer. Nastasia noted that she has been going to fish camp all her life, starting with her parents: "As a girl, I mostly used to babysit, but I was watching what they were doing. That's how I learned." Nastasia married when she was sixteen and moved from her home in Crooked Creek to Chuathbaluk: "My in-laws used to live in Napaimute. So we all go up there to fish camp. First we were living in one house, and then we made our own house not far from them. [My in-laws] had already set up their place at fish camp. But me and my husband, we had to start on our own."

Today, Nastasia moves up to fish camp in late May or early June, right after breakup, to get camp ready before they set their nets. Once she is at fish camp, she doesn't leave:

> 'Cause you know, there's lots of bears. Lotsa things, animals come by and break in our smokehouse. Somebody has to be there to watch. I'm always there with them.

> Even if my grandson is working, I would have phone and CB. And he used to say, "If I hear you shoot, I'll come and check on you."
>
> So I did one time. Brown bear came, and I was all by myself. I was in the smokehouse, and I saw it come out of the trees. I didn't get excited. I just walk slowly over to my house and [took] that gun. I didn't aim at it, I just scare it away. Well, if I shoot at it, it'll be wounded and get me. So, Jake said he hear me shoot. So he came right over and ask me, "What's going on?" "There's a brown bear back there."
>
> He said, "Are you scared?" I said, "No, I have this dog here." Dog protect me.
>
> Lot a times I did see animals come. Even bear come by the house, and I just go out and I tell him, "Gee, don't bother. You should go where you come from." And slowly it would turn around. I said, "I'm not bothering you, so you shouldn't come bother me." Then it turn around and go back.

Soon after breakup, people start catching fish. First come the sheefish, then the king salmon. Nastasia explained:

> First set net we always get sheefish, first of the summer. We scale them and hang them to dry or half-dry fish.
>
> King salmon [are next]. [We make into] strips or blankets.
>
> I smoke the heads for *egamaarrluk*, too.
>
> First king salmon back bones are good for *egamaarrluk*, half-dry them and put them away.

Today *egamaarrluk* is put away in freezers for winter, to be taken out and boiled when people want to eat them. In the past before freezers *egamaarrluk* was eaten in the summer: "We only had *egamaarrluk* while we were at fish camp."

Mark asked if they got humpies (pink salmon) this far upriver, and Nastasia said yes, though not this past summer. Angie added: "They always say humpies are good luck. So more fish would be coming."

The end of summer is not the end of fishing, as different fish become available as the seasons change. People go for whitefish in the fall. Broad whitefish (*qaurtuq* here and *akakiik* in the Akulmiut area) and humpback whitefish make the best *akutaq*. The women agreed, however, that any kind of fish, even king salmon or pike, makes good *akutaq*. Angie recalled: "You could make *akutaq* with bread, with rice. Moose meat. Whitefish. One time we go berry picking and when we come back we had so many berries and wanted *akutaq* so bad. I look in our lunch box, we had lots of bread. So, I cut it up and mix with berries. It was good."

Seraphine recalled making *passiaq* (*akutaq* made from crushed, aged fish eggs with berries, oil, and sugar) as well as *qayussaak* (a mixture of broth, greens, oil, and fish eggs).

Angie remembered her family spearing whitefish just before freeze-up:

> We used to go spearing falltime. And when we go spearing, we spend the day outside, all day. My dad said, "We gonna go fishing." And I tell him, "Can I take my ice skates?" "Yah, you could."
>
> So we got to where we were gonna go fishing; nice smooth ice. So I skated around for a while. And then after that I start fishing. And then we ate while it was getting dark. And we were gonna start going down pretty soon. And they light [a] gas lamp. And they put it inside open five gallon can. You hold it in the middle of the boat; you shine it into the water. And you could see them fish coming, whitefish.
>
> My dad spear one. I tell 'em, "I'm so cold." Mom tell me, "Hold this gas lamp and you'll warm up." So I was holding the gas lamp; I'm just shaking.
>
> My dad catch that whitefish and put it in the boat. He hurry up and bend down, cut it open, and he give me one side of the *meluk*, eggs. "Here, eat this." I kind of look at it and look at him. He said, "Just eat it." So I ate it. And I swear, from the inside of my belly, warm came all over, nice and warm. That's when I realized we need lots of grease [in cold weather].

Marie asked how Angie could skate and fish in open water at the same time, and she explained that there was ice along the shore but open water toward the middle of the Kuskokwim River: "You hold the gas lamp by the edge of the boat.... You have one spear person by the motor and one spear person at the bow, and you have the gas-lamp-holding person in the middle. I used to get so excited. 'There's one coming, dad. There's one over there!'"

Angie said that after freeze-up, people also went ice-fishing for grayling, lush fish (burbot), and trout. She remembered the three large, wooden *taluyat* (conical fish traps) set in front of the village, and lush fish piled like cordwood on the bank for people to take. Nastasia noted that once in a great while they catch trout in the set net, though they are mostly caught when "hooking," jigging through holes in the ice. Annie added that people get trout up the Aniak River. And Jennie said that during the ice-fishing season, you'll see lots of people jigging for fish on the Kuskokwim River.

Segvik / *Fish pond*

In summer in Aniak and the upriver villages, fish are cleaned and cut along the shore rather than on the bank as is customary downriver. Every year families put together logs, with cutting areas on the side and a basket of netting in the middle where fish can be stored before they are cut. Lucy noted that the cutting table is covered with spruce bark so that the fish won't slide off. Today some use gunny sacks for the same purpose. Annie explained: "Up here we call it a *segvik*. And it consists of logs, maybe three on this side and three on this side, and in the middle is where the fish goes. That's the fish pond, the *segvik*. And on both sides is our table. And long ago we used spruce trees, the bark. That way the fish don't move around."

Marie asked if they put water in the *segvik*, and Annie replied: "It's already in the river. Once it's in there, we push it out, and when we get our fish we put our fish in there." Annie noted that when the river went down, they pushed the *segvik* farther out: "You follow the tide. The water just go down, we gotta push it out. And when our water come up we pull it back again."

Annie added that the basket is usually made from chicken wire or an old fish net so that the fish don't float away. When working on fish, women can throw fish guts in the river, where gulls gather to eat them. Everyone was interested in hearing about how women work on fish on the lower river. Marie explained: "We do have fish baskets on the ground with no water. We call it *qikutaq* [temporary storage bin]. And right along the side of the *qikutaq* is our cutting table. We'd put grass in the bottom and put the fish in there. And on the side we'd have a big container to wash the fish before splitting for drying."

Mark observed that on the coast where he's from, the tidal variation is so great that using a *segvik* wouldn't work: "We pack water, and after cutting the fish we'd wash them in that water, in the tub. Tide comes in and out and sometimes it goes a long ways down, like in Toksook [Bay]. Water is not steady. Nowadays there's running water. We wash [our fish] in tubs."

Mark went on to share more about how fish are processed on Nelson Island, including leaving herring in the net for several tides to give them a little sea salt taste. He also described preserving fatty herring in seal pokes full of seal oil – "good food for cold weather." All the women were interested. Mark shared that when herring is preserved in seal oil, and some of the oil is left over, it has a slightly different taste, and people consume it with other foods. Mark also mentioned aged seal oil, called *piuciqaumalria*, that elders like to use for a dipping sauce. He added that people from the coast use seal oil to process many foods, including dried seal meat, tom cod, cooked walrus skin, and cooked

Upriver-style fish-cutting raft, including a table as well as a floating "fish pond" or *segvik* made of chicken wire or old fish netting where the fish are stored before they are cut, 1950s. *Wein Collection, Anchorage Museum B1985.027.0798*

beluga. People also used seal oil as a medicine, rubbing it on their chests to ease congestion. Annie asked Mark what kind of oil, and he explained that different kinds of sea mammals have different-tasting oils, including bearded seals, spotted seals, hair seals, and beluga. He shared that although people didn't make much oil from walrus blubber, sometimes he mixed beluga oil and spotted seal oil together for dipping, joking that it was "specially brewed." All the women were impressed. Annie enthused, "Awesome. Cool. I like that." And Lucy admitted, "I always thought seal oil came from one kind of seal. I learned now. My eyes are open. Thank you."

John and Seraphine Borowski's two-story *salayaq* (smokehouse), built to hold fish for both people and dogs, May 2024. In the old days, when they were feeding dogs, John and Seraphine filled it with more than 2300 fish – 2000 for the dogs and the rest for themselves. John remembered once getting 450 fish in his fish wheel on the first day, then 300 on the days following until their smokehouse was filled. Lots of work. *AFR*

Annie shared that while seal oil was hard to get this far upriver, people boiled sheefish for their oil: "We'd boil it, and the grease comes to the top. And boy, it makes some good [fry] bread."

Our food is our legacy

Talk of seal oil reminded Sophie of how oil was used as medicine in the past:

> And oils, and also seal oil, they used them as medicine. Some of my children, I teach them what I had learned as a little girl.... Remember back in those days many of us had impetigo and sores. Since there were no clinics and we had not seen much Western medicine around, some children had impetigo on their faces that couldn't heal....
>
> One time a girl had rash on her face. My mom used fish oil. They also used seal oil when it was available. They used fish oil or seal oil on the sores and impetigo. They were better than Amoxicillin, *kass'aq* medicine from clinic. The sores and impetigo healed faster using home remedy.
>
> Today, I don't see anyone using animal oil as medicine anymore.

> Also some people suffer from asthma or breathing problems. Maybe one teaspoon in the morning before breakfast, they'd let us drink oil.
>
> Also when we suffer from earaches, they put oil in our ears to ease the pain.

Sophie reflected that many foods used in the past are no longer eaten:

> The foods we ate, today many of our people don't eat them anymore. Some forget about their past and don't eat traditional foods. They'd just throw away parts of fish that were used as food in the past. I guess their parents don't teach their children anymore.
>
> Also my daughter, because she was a girl and had seen how care was given to parts of the fish, she has tried to follow and use what she learned. And when her own children complain about foods she prepared, she'd say, "You poor one, when you are hungry, if hunger hits us, the fish parts you used to throw away, you will remember them."
>
> Every fish or animal – moose, black bear – the oil was saved. Today, I never see anyone saving oils from those kinds of fish and animals anymore.
>
> Also sometimes, when invited, I go to the school to talk to the children. Many are curious and ask a lot of questions about fish and animals and how we care for them, saving every part of the fish and animal.

Sophie went on to describe their food knowledge as their legacy, and how important this was to share with children today. Lucy noted that it was not only young children who asked questions but young adults as well, so that they can answer the questions of their own children: "I'm a grandma and a great grandma. I have twelve grandchildren, seven great [grandchildren].... Even though I taught Yup'ik in school, I mostly talked English at home because there was nobody else [speaking Yup'ik]. My husband was part Yup'ik, but he couldn't speak it." Lucy went on to say that even though children want to know how it was in the past, and ask questions, like about the oil we had just been talking about: "Even we tell them, they won't understand."

Annie Morgan noted that modern technology has replaced the old ways: "I believe this modern technology took most of that away. But it hasn't taken that away from me yet." She said that although we think children aren't listening, they hear and remember what we say: "What our parents told us as a very young child, I remember. And when I grew up, I still remembered all they taught me. And I still cherish the time I had with them." Our conversations were bringing many of these cherished memories to mind. Annie concluded with feeling, "This sure is opening my eyes to stuff I've never known."

Foods from the land

Closing our discussion of fishing, Marie asked the women if there were any plants they used to clean or purify their hunting equipment to attract animals. First she turned to Angie and asked: "How do you attract animals?" Without missing a beat, Angie responded: "You just got to be there." Everyone chuckled.

Later in the day, the women described one delicious plant that some people continue to gather each year along riverbanks after breakup – *elagat*, the roots of Alpine sweet vetch. Olga Peterson explained:

> They grow underground. I get mine in springtime. I [used to] go across [from Aniak]. I don't go there anymore because it's all full of willows. I go to different places, like on the island. Try not to get in rocky areas because they're hard to pull. I get them from the sand.
>
> And they're a lot of work. You use a shovel. If you do it right they come out good. I go home and soak 'em in tote container. And I use scrubber to clean 'em. And rewash them again. After they get clean, I dice 'em.

Marie asked how long the roots are. Olga answered that they're long if you dig them correctly, but that they break if you don't do it right: "You try to get down to the root. Some of them have lots of roots. You have to try to get as much as you can."

Lucy commented that *elagat* are sweet in the spring. Olga noted that when she gets lots, she preserves some by chopping them and freezing them in quart-size bags filled with water: "I take 'em out when I'm going to use 'em and boil them. I give it 15 minutes after it boils and put in a tablespoon sugar. It's a lot of work but it's worth it." Olga noted that half-a-dozen women in Aniak still gather *elagat* each spring, adding it to *akutaq*. Marie remarked: "I've never had *elagaq akutaq* in my life." A visiting student piped up, "I have." Marie responded, "You're lucky."

Sometimes *elagat* are found on the surface. Olga recalled: "If you go early where the ice breaks, they're [on the ground].... I remember that one time that ice stayed for a week or nine days.... It never moved. Right after that dam broke, after the ice clear out, me, my aunt, and my late husband, we went across [and] we just pick 'em off the ground. Man, that was the most *elagat* I ever picked. We were

Elagat ("Eskimo potatoes") growing on the river bank at Napaimute, August 2024. *AFR*

so happy. It was the easiest, I didn't have to work hard. After that, to this day [I haven't seen that]."

Lucy also described gathering *elagat* and other roots such as "waterberries" (*qet'get*, root nodules of horsetail plants) in the fall from the underground caches of tundra voles, often referred to as mice:

> Way back, maybe early 1950s, I went with her dad and mom. They were hunting mouse holes. There was so many mice in one island. There were so many holes.... Where the mouse have holes, on the ground they find a soft spot, they break that, the mouse ran out, they open it, they gather all their *elagat*. And they cut off the ends where mouse chew on them. They're really clean.
>
> They gather all those, leaving those black berries, and bring 'em home. And took *elagat* that were small enough and dice it. There were so many mice that year, all those holes in the sand. I went with her mom and dad, and they pick all those clean *elagat*. They just cut off where they bite. They didn't have to wash them.

Finally, Angie mentioned another plant – not edible but with medicinal value: "They were round [puffball] mushrooms with a hole on top. And if you press that mushroom, clouds come out, puffs of something [spores]. If you put that on *pupicuks* [infected sores, impetigo] it cleared right up."

Harvesting animals in spring

Our conversation turned to spring camp and the beginning of summer harvesting after the long winter. Nastasia shared that in April her parents pulled her out of school in Crooked Creek and traveled to the George River. There the men hunted for beaver, muskrat, ducks, and geese. The women hung the meat to dry and then smoked them: "Smoke all of 'em 'cause we have no freezer to put them away." Women and children also gathered red berries on patches where the snow had melted. Nastasia explained: "Springtime just go up the hill and pick those red berries, they call them *uruneq* [from *urunret*, 'open ground surrounded by snow']. [We use them] for *akutaq*." At the same time, her father set a whitefish net: "My dad always bring set net to get whitefish...and grayling. We eat anything out in spring camp."

To this day, Nastasia dries and smokes beaver. First she spreads the meat into a flat round, then turns it over on the drying rack to make sure both sides are dried before smoking:

> I just like them. Every spring I always make them.... I still put away dried beaver meat. Even when they give me porcupine.... Then I take it up to my fish camp and smoke it; half-dried and smoked [is good]. Even half-dried muskrat is good.
>
> But my dad used to burn the skin.... Beaver or porcupine. He liked them burnt. But we used to take the burnt part off and eat the inside....
>
> I liked going to spring camp while growing up. Nowadays we don't go. No one to take me out.

Annie and Angie said that beaver tail is also good, either baked fresh or half-dried and smoked. Angie added that beaver feet are another tasty dish: "You can eat the feet, beaver feet. My son made a mistake of letting his youngest daughter taste it. She really liked beaver feet. So every time we go hunting, she's looking for beaver, for the feet." Chuckling to herself, Angie then shared a story:

> We used to always go camping on holidays. This happened to be Fourth of July. We like to go out camping, go enjoy ourselves outdoors. We don't do games or things like that, but just go out and go camping,

Beaver feet cooking in Anchorage, December 2024. *AFR*

> eat out and bring your goodies that you baked, maybe you bring *egamaarrluks*.
>
> Andrew and Natalia and their little girl [who they] adopted. She grew up with her grandparents, and she never be quiet. Always yakking, talking.... And she'd be whining and not listening to her Ap'a. And she happen to like beaver. And it was getting towards evening. Every time she start trying to cry around.... [Her] Ap'a had cooked bunch of beaver feet and took it along. Her beaver feet was keeping her calm.

Everyone laughed at the role beaver feet played in managing a talkative child. Angie added that beaver was a staple in the past, especially during summer: "Before the freezers came out, we used to always keep them in a dry cool place. In the summertime when we get tired of eating fish, you take it down, you soak it for days, and filled up gas box and boil it practically all day. When evening comes [it's ready to eat]." A break from eating fish in summer was welcome. Jennie later told the story of how her father, Evan, came and sat at his sister, Olinka Sakar's, table in Crooked Creek and teased, "You eat so much fish. Just like otters."

Sophie also remembered harvesting beaver in the spring and saving the castor to use as medicine:

> And my goodness, when my parents go spring camping, we gather food, beaver, muskrats, ducks. And we work on 'em, skin 'em, and clean

> every part inside the beaver, like the beaver castor. They tell us that was a good medicine for infection. They hang 'em up and dry it. And it is true....
>
> One time my husband had an infection on his ankle. So I take that beaver castor, cut it with knife, take the hard part in the top and soft part in the infection. Man, that puss drain out so much. That's how they taught us.

Talking about land animals, Marie and Mark noted that dried and boiled mink meat and otter meat were also good. All agreed that people did not eat the meat of weasel, fox, wolf, or brown bear, but that the meat of black bear is good. Jennie said that black bear fat is also good with dry fish, but it needs to be rendered. She explained:

> We don't eat [bear fat] fresh. We boil it and put them in jars.... We use the oil for *akutaq*, too.
>
> You cut up the fresh bear fat. You boil it with water.... The oil comes up to the top. Then you spoon it out.... The fat part with the oil.

Marie compared these pieces of bear fat to *tangviarrluk* (rendered seal blubber). Jennie added that you can eat the rendered fat with dry fish or pan fry the pieces of bear fat like bacon. Annie said that her father made bear bacon: "My dad used to make [bacon] out of that bear fat. And he put [the bacon] in those wooden barrels... And we never had to buy [bacon]. We only had bacon bear. Growing up, I always thought the bacon we have now was bear bacon."

Angie noted that bear fat and moose fat, both called *tunuq* (tallow, back fat), can be used to make *akutaq*. Annie said that when she was young she watched her father and Jack Egnaty of Sleetmute make *akutaq* in a big pan, stirring it with a wooden paddle. Angie observed that moose fat is stiffer than bear fat and gets hard and lumpy.

We spoke briefly about brown bears, and the women agreed that people don't eat them along the middle Kuskokwim. Annie said that for Athabascan people, both brown bears and eagles are sacred and must be treated with respect: "I was taught that as a very young child." Annie continued, talking about thanking other living things: "And when you take a bark from a tree, you tell that tree [thanks]. I'm a basket maker. So, my mom taught me to tell the birch, 'I'm gonna be taking your bark to make me a basket to pick berries or to sell.' And I gotta thank it after I'm done taking that bark. Because it's alive, a living thing. That's how my mom and dad taught."

Annie's mention of the respectful treatment of animals and plants reminded Angie of a story:

> Like lush [burbot]. Long time ago, I guess, they never used to eat it. And the lush cried. This was a story I heard. Lush cried to somebody [because they didn't want to eat it]. And they put a bone cross in his [throat, near the gills]. When you eat the lush you'll find a cross. That's how come now we eat lush....
>
> I used to be curious about everything. When I saw that [bone] I ask Ap'a, "How come it got this? It look like a real cross." And I carried it around for about two, three days until I lost it.

Mark mentioned snowy owls, which are hunted and eaten on the coast and considered delicious. Annie was surprised: "Wow, we're scared of them... They can talk. And they could say our names." Jennie agreed: "We up here have heard that *iggiayulit* [great horned owls] can talk like people. If somebody drowns, they let the family know." Angie explained that when owls speak, some hear their words, while others only hear, "Hoo, hoo":

> And it's so funny how they talk. If they wanted to talk to me and you were with me, you would hear him just singing, "Hoo, hoo, hoo." And he would talk to me.
>
> And I found that out when Marie Mckindy was alive. We were up there by Government Cabin. And in the evening after we get done picking berries, we went over to camp. And just when we stopped, there was an owl right above us. And to me it was hooting, and it told Marie that her grandbaby had died. That was when Darrel and Gina lost their boy. But she said she heard 'em just plain. The owl talk to her. And we were there, but to me all he said was, "Hoo. Hoo. Hoo."
>
> My brother used to be so scared of them. He used to be so rough, especially on the rocks going back down to Sleetmute. We get by Maqivik, we hear this [owl]. Boy, soon as my brother heard that owl, he stopped. Just stop in his tracks, and he listened. And it make noise again. He went right to the tent and go to bed. Nothing could take him out of bed, nothing. Not even candy bar.

Sharing stories

Jonathan Samuelson had stopped to visit before traveling to Kalskag for a TKC meeting and to thank us for coming together. He had been listening to us talk about fish earlier, and he said that Angie had a story about fish that she might share – about a family that was hungry in winter and how they survived. Jonathan left, and Angie began:

This was a long-time-ago story my grandma had told me. And I just remembered I told him about it.

During the winter, you know, first of the winter, this family had food. And then getting toward the end of winter, their food supply was going down. So before they completely ran out of food, the husband and dad, he decided he's gonna go hunting. So, he go hunting; all day he go around. And then evening time, he go home. Next day he did the same thing; never see nothing. On the third day he went out, and when he go out he saw a bear. And that bear tell him, "Don't be scared of me. Come with me if you want to live."

So that guy, he was getting weak from hunger, so he follow him. And they went to a mountain, at Amiik [the Door Mountains, lit., "Door"]. That bear go in, so that guy go in after him. But soon as he go in, that bear took off his hood; take it off. And he turn into a person. And this guy was so amazed, but he didn't say anything, didn't show his fear. He was desperate. He needed food for his family.

So, that bear had invited him. When he went in he saw a guy sitting by the door. And he told him, "You remember which door you come in. You go out the same way. If you don't go out same way, you gonna end up in different country." So that guy that was watching the door, he tell that man, "You can drink water. You can drink tea. But don't eat nothing." No matter how hungry he was, he didn't eat.

And then [the man] said, "Well, I gotta go home, it's getting dark. I gotta go home to my family." And they ask him if he had tarp for his sled. He said, "Yaa." So they take the tarp and they spread it out all over the sled. And all these people come. They got sticks, wood; they bring [the sticks] to that tarp, and they put it inside. Last one, really white coat; and his hood was white.... He had big wood. He put it on top of pile of wood. And they cover it and tie it up.

And they tell him, "Don't open this until you get home." And white guy, he was that [bear] person, "When you see me drifting in a river, in the summertime, don't bother me. I'm catching fish for my family. I'm catching fish for my family, so don't bother me." And [the man] said, "Okay."

And he got home; and his wife come to the door. "Did you find any game today?" He said, "No. But I found this guy with a black coat and he took me to his home. And all the people that were there gave me wood." And he tell his wife, "You will help me unload this sled." His wife said,

> "Yaa." They untie it. Take it apart. They opened it. Right on top was king salmon. That [bear] had given king salmon; and [the bear] tell 'em, "Leave me alone when you see me on the river, 'cause I'm fishing for my family."
>
> And all the rest of it was all different kinds of meat, bear meat, anything. That guy with a black coat saved this guy and his family. So the animals, you know. That story was so great. [My gramma] had put embellishments here and there, just to make it interesting, but that was the most important thing I took away from that story. If you treat others good, it'll come back to you. That's what I try to tell my kids and their kids. "Somebody be bum to you, let 'em go." What comes around, goes around.

Smiling, Angie added: "Somebody's gonna make me laugh like heck one of these days." And we all laughed. Then she continued:

> My dad [was] like that. He used to like to tease people. And I notice that me and my boys are the same way. If we like somebody, we pick on 'em. If we don't really like 'em, we just let 'em be. We don't talk to 'em, unless he talk to us. But if it's somebody we like... You know how you could smell people. When they're good people we always pick on them. Like we're playing with cousins. You know, cousins always like to pick on each other; like our *uicungaq* [woman's male cousin].
>
> But that's the story I had told Jonathan. I was running out of stories, and I come up with that one.

Angie remembered how elders used stories in the past to instruct her and to help her settle down:

> It was one of my relatives. I can't remember which one. But every time I was mischief, they would tell me, "Sit down. You're gonna hear a story." They never spanked. They never said cross words to us. Really patient with me. I don't know why I was so rough. I was like one of these people that don't like to listen. I didn't like to listen, unless they tell me story, then I listen.

Stories told as a way to discipline with love reminded Angie of another personal experience which she shared at length. It fit right into our conversation about sharing food and family:

> My grandson went to school one day. And while he was in school he decided to push his luck. And he got one of the teachers mad at him,

really, really mad at him. My other grandkids come, "Gram, you shoulda seen BJ today. Boy, he made that teacher so mad."

And we always ate dinner together, fourteen of us. We put our food together 'cause we were starting to run out, end of the month. And we were trying to stretch our food, so we ate together and made our food last longer that way, it seemed like. I don't know if it's true.

They tell me, "Boy, BJ got the teacher so mad today." I waited until everybody was done eating. I called BJ, "BJ."

"What, Gram?"

I said, "Come over here, sit down by me."

"Okay."

He come over, you know, just bouncing boy. Then I ask, "How was school today?" And all of a sudden you could see the fear coming into his eyes.

And he said, "It was good, I guess."

I ask, "Did you learn anything?"

"Aaa, I don't really know, Gram."

And I said, "You know, that's not what I heard."

And he looked up at me. I swear, you can see the fear in his eyes.

Because he knew that I knew what happened today. "What did you hear, Gram?"

You know, when you're talking to kids, if you put them down too much, it'll hurt their feelings. I didn't want to hurt his feelings because I knew he had a reason for trying to get this teacher mad at him. But he didn't want to share his reason with anybody.

And I tell him, "That's not what I heard BJ."

"What did you hear, Gram?"

I said, "I heard you piss somebody off today." And they looked at me and turned around, and he started laughing. Everybody in the house started laughing, too. But I go, "You know, that's not a very good thing for you to be doing, trying to get your teacher mad at you. That's not right. You shouldn't try to do that."

And then after that, his younger brother bit somebody that same day. And I tell him, "It's not nice to bite people."

So next day when they were getting ready for school, I hollered at BJ, "BJ."

"Yeah, Gram."

"Don't piss anybody off today."

> I tell Ethan, "Ethan."
> "Yeah, Gram."
> I say, "No tasting anybody either."

At this point our group was laughing, too. Angie continued:

> You should find different ways to put a spin on some things, and you know accidently make their feelings hit the floor.
>
> It was really funny. One of teacher's husbands was at my house when the kids were gonna get ready for school. I tell every one of them, "Have a good day. Be good." And when I got to BJ, "Don't piss anybody off again today BJ." And Ethan was gonna go out, and I said, "And no tasting anybody either, Ethan."
>
> The teacher's husband waited until they were all gone, and he just busted. And I ask him, "How are they doing now?" And he said, "They're doing a lot better." They're thinking before they do something.

Knowing the land

Our conversations had ranged widely. We returned to discussing animals. Annie mentioned using bear gut for windows, and Angie added that beaver intestines were also used:

> When I was a little girl, one of my relatives catch beaver. And since it was so late, we didn't set up a tent. We just put tarp on the ground and slept underneath the stars.
>
> And in the morning when I wake up, I looked and there was [inflated] beaver guts hanging all over around us. And when my mom got up, she go up and she touch it. She said it was nice and dry. So she took it down and rolled it up.
>
> And when we got to where we gonna build our cabin, she took that beaver gut and she cut it. Our window in the back was not very big. And mom measured it with beaver gut; she cut it there. Then she cut some more. She sewed them together and put it in the window. And you couldn't see out, but it let the light in.

Marie commented that the gut dried fast, in one night. Angie noted that they also got intestines from moose and bear: "Always save them for something. And I hear they used to make rain gear out of fish skin."

Speaking of fish reminded Angie of the giant pike in the Hoholitna:

> They used to want us not to go swimming in Hoho. Too big fish out there. And I didn't believe 'em until my brother caught one. You know the biggest pike. And its mouth was huge. It could swallow human child. And that was the biggest pike I ever saw.
>
> A lot of people tell us that. There's couple of lakes up there that you can't even put your finger in the water. There's too many *patqayulit*. I don't know what kind [of fish they are], maybe suckers? If they break into your skin, they'll suck your blood out.

The women described *patqayulit* as round, but not eels. Some call them "kissing fish." Angie said there were two lakes they were told to stay away from, one close by on the Kuskokwim and one farther upriver.

We followed by asking if there were other places that people were warned about. Angie mentioned Maqivik near the mouth of the Holitna:

> This is what they tell me. When you go to that Maqivik and pick berries, you're not supposed to holler around. You know, when you go pick berries some place, when you wanna find somebody, you [call out], "Hoh!" And pretty soon you hear somebody else, "Hoh!" Just letting you know where everybody is. In Maqivik, there's something [that answers], "Hooh."

Jennie called it Uurayuli (lit., "One who whistles"), and Angie agreed:

> It'll make you get lost. It'll just totally confuse you.... This is when there's [different dimensions] in the world. Because this will stay where it is, but the other side will move farther. And you can get lost like that.
>
> I've been lost like that lots a times. And once I decide I'm lost, I could see something that I know where it is. But since I made up my mind I'm lost, I'm lost. Crazy, eh?
>
> So, Maqivik is one of these places that has a portal between dimensions.

Remembering things she had been told in the past, Angie recalled: "[They] used to tell us stuff long ago. Some of the stuff that they tell, you could see it coming true.... They're coming true today. How did they know it long ago? They had no phones. They had no reading material. No nothing. And still they know what's going to happen. How? Well, we live in a weird world. You know, I always thought so. 'Cause I know I'm weird."

Everyone laughed, and Angie continued: "*Atam* [Look], if you're out in the *yuilquq* [wilderness] sometimes, especially where you have stories about these flying things, you could watch them. Some of them even follow you.... You know, there's flying lights, flying blobs. Whatever you're going to call 'em."

Marie asked if they were birds, but Angie said no: "Birds, you expect them to be there. But you don't expect a light to be flying around, with nothing to fly around with. Yet it's flying there." Annie said that sometimes people see rolling balls of light coming out from Kalskag: "I've seen them. And then they roll on the hill. We see them at night in wintertime." Angie added that they also see northern lights: "They can actually pick you up and take you away. That's how come they tell us not to whistle around outside, not to walk."

Special foods of the middle river

Early on our second day, Lucy had invited us all to the one-year memorial feast for her nephew, Jerry Simeon, starting at 4 that afternoon at her house. Adrian from TKC (who had spent all day helping her family prepare the food) picked us up in her truck and brought us over. When we got there just after five, people were already walking out, carrying full plates covered with tin foil. Going inside the tiny crowded house, a table full of two dozen different dishes greeted us, including smoked and boiled beaver, roast beaver tail, moose stew, moose stomach rolled and baked, goose soup, ptarmigan legs, salmon *egamaarrluk*. Rolls, *assaliaq* (fry bread), and many different kinds of fish *akutaq* were also served, as well as bags of gifts for the elders. A young woman gave me new socks and pieces of candy wrapped in a washcloth. So much food! I took more than I could eat and, like many others, brought my leftovers home.

Our final day gave us a chance to talk in detail about some of the special foods we'd been discussing and that we'd had a chance to sample the day before. Once again, Mark began with a short prayer, asking for good minds to say words that would help the younger generation. Marie then shared a comment about the memorial feast we had all attended. The extended family had filled tables with enough food for dozens of guests. Marie observed:

> Yesterday all day the discussion was on traditional foods our ancestors harvested and consumed. And when it was time to eat lunch, I told you all that I was suddenly craving for such foods that you talked about all morning.
>
> When our meeting was done, we all went to a memorial feast. There we were served the foods you had talked about during our meeting. We had half-dried and smoked beaver, tail and all. We also had cooked moose nose, and dried and smoked boiled king salmon heads and tails, cooked

> goose and ptarmigan, and fresh blueberry *akutaq* with whitefish. Yummy! I was so amazed and grateful for the gift of foods that nourished my spirit, mind, and body.

Before we began our meeting, Jennie had mentioned moose hoof Jell-O, and Marie asked her to explain how it was made. Jennie began:

> The moose leg below the hock on down has no meat, but it has a lot of *yualuq* [tendons, sinew]. They'd remove all the tendons and take the hoofs and wash them and cook them all day long, till the tendons get soft. You could add some rice, too. When done cooking, dish out the tendons and hoofs to a pan, including the broth and rice.
>
> The marrow from [the] leg bone has oil, and if there's lots you spoon some of the oil out. Then you gel it overnight. And the next morning you'd have Jell-O for breakfast.

Jennie Zaukar removing the cartilage from cooked moose hooves to make Jell-O, March 2025. *AFR*

Jennie added that people call the Jell-O *yuurleqtaaq*, and that some save and put away whole moose legs to make moose hoof Jell-O at a later time.

Jennie also described how the moose's nose and other parts of the head are cooked. Sometimes the nose was cooked with part of the moose's cheek. Jennie said that her mother skinned the nose before cooking it. Olga commented: "Today we do it new way, lazy way. Cut off the nose and boil it and afterwards skin it." Jennie added that some cook moose nose in chunks, while others make moose meat stew and add moose nose.

Olga noted that the moose's brain could be used

to make brain bread, a Sami specialty. Jennie continued: "My dad skin the whole moose head and split it. We used to use five-gallon cans to cook. He'd split the moose head right in the middle and cook it. We ate the eyes and the marrow when done, and eat whatever is left in the skull." Olga said she likes the cheeks, as well as the tongue and eyes. Once she cut a moose head in half and cooked it in a big pot and made soup with it.

Earlier Angie had shared another well-remembered upriver specialty: roasted moose horns.

> Lots of different things we used to eat. In springtime when we happened on a moose, the horns were not too big. My dad took an axe and chop them off. And then he put them by the fire, both of them. Then every once in a while he'd come over, he turn them over. So, after watching him do that, I ask him if I could [turn them]. "No, I'll do it." So when it was done and time to eat, we were really wishing there were some more moose

Jennie pouring the hoof broth and rice over the cooked moose cartilage and sinew. Once set, the *yuurleqtaaq* (moose hoof Jell-O) was ready to eat. March 2025. *AFR*

> horn to eat. It tasted like a cross between *pateq* [marrow] and moose nose. It was so good.

Angie said that her father cooked the horns of bull moose that were just starting to grow: “It looks like a loaf of bread,...but with fur on it.... You don’t cook it directly in the flame.... [When cooked] the skin on the horn can easily come off like bandage. It’s really rich, and tastes so good.”

Speaking of roasting moose horns reminded Angie of the moose dogs her father trained to help the family harvest big animals:

> And we used to have to train our dogs to go hunting. ’Cause sometime we can’t catch ’em on our own. We need help. The only problem was that every one of our dogs was a moose dog. And if you were helping get wood or something, and you are the only one in the sled with seven moose-crazy dogs, and you see two moose running across the bank, and your dogs are about to go nuts, you’re sitting there crying your head off. And then try to turn around and make the dogs come back to you, ’cause I cry too much. I used to be so rough, and I hardly used to cry. And when I cried, my lead [dog] always listen, really listen.
>
> Every time we came around the bend and we saw moose coming, my dad would land where we saw them and hurry up and run up and let

Jennie removing the skin before cooking the moose nose during Aniak’s Cultural Wellness week, March 2025. *AFR*

> one dog loose [to] go bark at [the moose]. And while the dog was gone, my daddy takes axe or knife on a bunch of willow, makes a willow bed on the ground. And then when he gets done, he makes cigarette, and my dog come with the moose.... And then he'd check, he take another puff, and he look at them. And then the third time he look, he'd go and kill [the moose]. But that dog would put that moose right in the middle of the willow bed. That's how we train them....
>
> My dad shoot it right there, and it just fall. The dog would bring it right there. And whatever dog went that day, he got first choice after we start cutting up the moose.

Angie noted that you need to wait at least an hour after killing a moose before butchering it: "You wait before you make hole in the body. If you cut the throat, the blood comes out, it wouldn't help it relax. You know, when something dies, before they die, some of them tense up. And then when you cut it, it's gonna be tough." Angie continued:

> I always tell my boys to shoot them in the head, so they take 'em out of their misery. Because I don't want them to cut nothing, I don't want them to cut the throat because of the blood loss. It won't let the muscles relax. Some of them, when you cut 'em, they're just like rubber, really chewy no matter how long you cook 'em. And some people get moose, and their meat is so tender. It just depends on who gets it and how they treat it.

Having discussed moose heads, Marie asked about bear heads, and the women agreed that bear heads are not eaten but buried facing east. Angie declared: "You have to point the nose toward the sunrise.... Anything that you kill; if you're going to bury it, you have to let them face the east. So they can see the sun rise. Because God calls us back, he's going to call us from over there. So, everyone want to be facing that way."

Olga and Jennie knew that Orthodox burial crosses faced east, but hadn't heard this about animals. Angie explained: "If you stop to think about it, animals are people, too. Because long time ago, in the story that they told us, every time they put their hood on, they turn to whatever animals. And when they take it off they turn to humans; and you can talk to them." Marie agreed: "Elders have said that all living things have sense, *elpengqertut cat tamarmeng.* Animals are able to smell, able to hear, able to talk, just like us humans. Animals are people like us."

Wassily Kameroff showing an Aniak student one technique for cutting moose during the school's Cultural Wellness Week, March 2025. *AFR*

Olga added:

> What I hear, too, is that if they're gonna go out hunting, they don't brag and say, "I'm gonna go get me a moose." Because we don't know, we can't predict....
>
> You're not to talk negative about them. They can sense you.

Continuing talking about the uses of moose, Lucy recalled her family skinning the moose and using its hide as a mattress. Some also made moose-hide line: "My grandpa saved the moose hide and soaked it in the water for how many days, until all the hair came off. And he used the skin [to] make string to make snowshoes and also use it for the sled."

Moose are ruminants with stomachs with four compartments, including the ruman (the largest chamber where feed is stored and regurgitated as cud), the reticulum (also called the honeycomb, where feed is further broken down), the omasum (that increases surface area and ensures nutrients are absorbed), and the abomasum (the regular stomach). Angie remembered eating the reticulum, known as *erurciigalnguq* (lit., "one that cannot be washed"). Lucy also recalled this part: "My mom used to always have the guys look for that, and cut it up into pieces and boil it." Angie explained:

> It's the stomach where the [moose] grind up what they eat. Then it goes back up and they rechew it, and it goes to the regular stomach. It is the first place the food goes to grind. And if you see it, it's about [nine inches].
>
> And when you cut it in half, there's so many layers. That's how come they call it *erurciigalnguq*. You can't wash 'em. That's the first thing that they [cook] in our house....
>
> They boil the whole thing. And when it's done, it's cut up.

Jennie noted that they eat this with a little bit of fat, as it is lean. Angie explained that they eat the regular stomach as well. People also fry the liver and kidney, and they boil the tongue. Moose fat is also cooked to render it. Angie noted: "Those little pieces of fat. After you render it, if you put salt and eat 'em, boy they taste good." Lucy also noted that after the fat is cooked, it can be put in a jar and kept in a cool place: "And when you eat dry fish, you use the oil." People also peel off the membrane that surrounds the stomach and intestines and hang it to dry. It comes off as a sheet with pieces of fat attached, and can be cooked and eaten as well. Angie noted that the stomach lining is like bacon, with fat and meat attached.

Jennie Zaukar holding up the moose's stomach membrane, laced with fat, March 2025. *AFR*

Marie asked if people ate bear innard, and Jennie replied: "We don't eat those parts like we do with the moose. We eat only the meat and fat, and the bear feet and their hands." Lucy added that people eat the meat and save the fat but not the bones or marrow:

> You don't use the bone. You don't cut it up like we cut moose.
>
> I never heard anybody *pateq*ing from a bear. And if you cook the bear, you leave the ribs whole, you don't cut 'em. The bear meat and fat, that's the only part you eat.

Today some people save the *cungak* (bile, gall) and sell it on the Asian market. Angie shared another use:

> We went upriver one time, and my dad somehow throw his back out. And he was walking really slow. They say *qukairtuq* [he sprained his back]. They went back up there, and they catch bear. And my dad take the *cungak*, put it in his hand and rub on his back. Then he carried half of the bear back down to the boat. And after that, like nothing ever happened to his back. He used it for medicine.

Speaking of bears, Marie recalled a custom downriver when a boy catches his first bear: "They let him put his hand and arm inside the mouth and throat of the bear." Lucy agreed: "That's how it is up here, too. When a boy catch his first bear, they put their hand in their mouth." Mark noted that John Andrew of Kwethluk had explained that it was done so that the boy would not fear bears in future. Jennie and Angie said they were hearing this for the first time.

Salmon indicators

After talking about these special foods, the discussion turned to the natural indicators people used in the past to let them know the salmon were on their way upriver. Olga was the first to share: "The only way I would understand fish are coming is when I start hearing that bird, *tevicuuk* [likely *tekciuk*, "Savannah sparrow"]. When they make that noise, that's when I always say, 'Oh, fish are coming!' I used to hear that growing up.... It's a fish bird. They let you know when fish are coming." Olga added: "It's a little bird, and they make that noise, *tevicuuk, tevicuuk*."

Olga mentioned an abundance of mosquitoes as another indicator that many fish are on their way: "And if there's hardly any mosquitoes, there's hardly any fish." Seraphine agreed: "Yaa, that's what they say."

Jennie noted that chamomile flowers were also used as "calculators," indicating that salmonberries were ripening. Olga added that when high bush cranberries start to get red, blueberries are half-ripe as well.

Angie added other indicators for king salmon:

> Another way my Ap'a used to tell me, when there's thunderstorms, they say, "The fish are coming." 'Cause before any fish come, there's always bum weather. Not really bum weather, but you could hear the thunder, you could see the lightening. That's when they say the king salmon are coming.
>
> And another one is monarch [swallowtail] butterfly. When you see monarchs [swallowtails] on the beach, that's when you know that there's king salmon in the river. My grandkids always keep an eye on that kinda butterfly, because they know the salmon are here and they can go swimming. Some people have ulterior motives.

Angie and Jennie also mentioned *cikultaal* or *cikultall*, the Athabascan name for stonefly (order Plecoptera) – a cold-hardy insect, between one and two inches long, that spends its larval stage in water along stream bottoms. They come up around the sides of holes in the ice, and people saw them when they packed water. They come on land in spring, and they grow wings and fly later in summer. Olga noted that they used to see them in Aniak as well. Like mosquitoes, lots of stoneflies are an indicator of lots of fish to come.

The women also mentioned frogs, called *peleqpalaat*. They say the more noise they make in spring, the more fish will be coming. Jennie also noted that they were told not to play with them or kill them: "They say that they can retaliate, pay back."

Food shortage

We now turned the conversation to another important topic – something we had already touched on but hoped to better understand. Mark asked the group what their elders told them to do during times when food was not abundant. Sophie replied:

> Some discard the food that was not eaten at this time. Back then, we never discarded food. My parents told us, those that do that, when they experience hunger, they will remember the foods they had discarded when there was plenty. The foods we have, they told us not to waste them. They said during food shortage we'll remember them.
>
> And many hunters today waste body parts or the bones; leg bones,

back bones, sometimes you see dogs out there scatter them, even meats that they didn't put away.... Today, I do see that kind of waste.

And these sportsmen, they hunt only to get their horns. And their meat, they threw them away as trash. When hunger hits us, those foods we had wasted, that will come back to us. For that reason, my Uliggaq, my grandson, when they catch a moose, those who live with me, I teach them; if they catch, to immediately welcome the hunter who had caught. And today, my grandchildren and great-grandchildren, as soon as they hear, they'd get the *uluaq* ready, or a knife.

Though they are little, my Apeng'aq, from the age of four years old, I have talked to him about these things. He would also get ready and would take his little knife and say that he's going to skin a moose.

And Jr. Girl, the legs of moose, hoofs. She loves to skin those parts, all the way to the hoof. And one time I asked her, "How come you like to skin those legs?" Then she replied, "'Cause I like their marrows." Kids that learned early do and say things that tickle your stomach.

Wassily Kameroff skinning a moose leg and removing the thin bone behind the shin used to make spear points in the past, March 2025. *AFR*

Lucy noted that the same thing is true all over – people catching and not taking care of all that they catch: "They take the meat and leave the bone and throw it away. I believe what she said. It'll come back to one who don't take care of it." Lucy recalled riding in a plane that landed in an upriver village to pick up hunters. The men brought moose heads with antlers into the plane, wrapped in plastic, leaving the meat behind: "It was really odorous smell.... I wish they would stop that. Just for the horns and the head, not the meat. That's waste."

Marie agreed that what they were sharing was true. While downriver communities have easier access to food, living in villages today is not easy, even for families that continue to hunt and fish. Many are in need and run out of food. In the past, in some areas, people suffered from *piitnaq* (famine, food shortage). People still run out of food today. Marie asked Angie to share the story she had told Marie that morning, about her experience living in Bethel, when all she could put on the table was one bowl of rice and beans for her and her four children, giving a spoonful to each child in turn. Angie explained:

> It was when I try to go college. And I couldn't swing it. I couldn't do what they wanted me to do and take care of my kids at the same time. So, I opted for my family because they were more important to me then these books....
>
> And when you're alone. My dad died in '79 I think. And that year we went home [to Sleetmute] for the funeral, and they tell me that I'm not supposed to leave the village for one year after my dad died. "You got to take care of his house," they tell me. So, I tried.
>
> There was days that we didn't have water, because by the time I got the wood home, it was too late for me to go down and get water. I used to have to carry birch home. I cut down four trees every day and carry them home. And when I get home, I use hand saw to cut 'em up, bring them into the house. Next day I do the same thing. My kids go to school. I get the woods. But when you have to do stuff like that, you do it. Because that's the only thing that you can do. You can't depend on anybody.

Marie asked Angie to continue her story of eating with her children from one bowl in Bethel when a neighbor woman visited. Angie recalled:

> She went and checked my cupboards. "How come you never come over?" [I told her,] "I can't. Your house is not my house." She went out from my house, and not too much later the phone ring, and her husband tell me, "You bring your kids over here right now."

> So, I tell my kids we got to go. We went in their house and already she had...

At this point Angie was in tears, but she continued: "She had already put all her leftover on top of the table. And she give us plate, every one of us, and told us to eat. After that they told me I should not try to be alone. I got *ilaqs* [relatives]. I'm sorry." Angie apologized for breaking down:

> I know it hurt when it was happening. [The pain] is still here [in my heart].
>
> And when you don't have food, you think about the little ones that are in your house. You've already gone through lots, and you don't have to eat as much. But still, you have to eat to keep up your strength.
>
> I used to make sure my kids eat before me. I still do it. I didn't realize how much hurt I'm still carrying. But, you know, all that hardship make me who I am today.

Lucy noted that she, too, had experienced food shortage when her father left his family in Chuathbaluk to go trapping in winter:

> I've encountered no food in the house. I don't know how old I was. We had nothing in our house. Nothing to cook. Nothing to make anything. And even though we had neighbor, we never go and ask for food. And what my mom used to do is, she had some of those bones. She take couple of those and boil it, and me and my sister sip on that broth. And whatever she could find in the porch, the fish skin, she burn it over the fire and let us eat, and we had water, just for me and her.
>
> And she would not have anything to eat. I don't know how many days we were like that. We had no food. I know how it feel, your stomach being empty. My mom used to have us eat first and leave herself out. But she would have the broth from the bones. That's the one I remember. My heart hurts for her. I'd tell my kids it's not fun to have empty stomach.

Olga agreed: "That's why I always remember what the old people used to tell us. Go get what God put on the land for you to go and get, put it away while you can. 'Cause you don't know what the winter is going to bring us."

Sophie had been sitting quietly while the others spoke. Now, with a deep sigh, she began:

> What we're talking about, being hungry when we have nothing to eat. I had two stepsisters, two stepbrothers.... Our mom and dad go spring

camping, and they left us to our stepsisters and brothers. I hardly talk about this. But now I'm starting to talk about it. When we keep talking about food.

I was eight years old. I don't know what I do to my stepsisters or stepbrothers. My dad used to call me "Aanaka. Aanaka. My mom." They stay over a month spring camping. What I went through; lots of food in the house, in the porch; dry fish, everything. What my two stepsisters and brothers did. When they eat something, I was lucky; they give me one piece of bread, enough to put in your mouth. That was my breakfast. Lunch time...my baby sister was small. They go in front of me, they let me watch them eat. And, in my mind, I pray for them to someway, somehow stop it.

And as time passed, I was getting weak. Once I went to the porch, knowing there's lots of cut up dry fish. So, in those brown bags there's fish. I take one piece of dry fish so I could hide and go outdoors and eat it. I was hungry. One of my stepsisters caught me, just when I go like this to the bag. I get thrown around in the porch for taking. She tell me I was stealing. I never tell them that I was hungry. One piece of bite of bread in the morning, one piece of dry fish lunchtime. One bite of whatever they cook for supper. That was my breakfast, lunch, and supper.

And when I got weak, I couldn't walk around no more. There was lump right here, like rock in my stomach. Thinking about those who had suffered from hunger; what they go through. My baby sister she used to run out, see if Mom and Dad come. Not yet. I'm glad they didn't let my baby sister starve. Pretty soon I couldn't walk around no more, 'cause my legs were too weak. My body was too heavy.

So, what my baby sister used to do. We have those iron pumps [for] water. She filled the cup, half a cup of water. So, I would hide it behind my pillow, not let my stepsisters and brothers see me. When I got hungry, I put my fingers in the water and I wet my mouth, 'cause it was too dry.

Then when I was getting sick, I couldn't move around no more. And I started to fall asleep. And baby sister, she used to shake me, "Sophie, wait for Mom and Dad." So, I open my eyes. I tell her, "Don't tell Mom and Dad. What they do to me, don't tell 'em." 'Cause I didn't want them to get scolded.

Sophie was crying now, but she continued:

My dad never used to get mad. Only one time I see him get mad. I didn't want them to scold them. I tell my sister, "Don't tell them."

I couldn't walk around no more. I start to sleep. Oh, so good sleep. Every time I do that, my sister would shake me, "Wait for Mom and Dad." For her sake, I start to be strong. Then I went to sleep. I couldn't help it no more.

You could have broken nose. You could have toothache. You could have headache, earache. That's nothing. It's nothing compared to being hungry. It's nothing. I have too many broken bones. They're nothing. Only when you have nothing to eat, when your stomach is empty, that's something that hurts.

But I tried to be strong. After so many times of going out, my baby sister ran to me. I was half sleeping of course. She shake me up, "Sophie, Mom and Dad are here. They are coming up to the house. Wait for them."

So, I tried to keep my eyes open. Pretty soon the door open little bit. I recognize my mom's face, and while she was walking to me, I blacked out. I don't know what happened.... I don't even remember my dad coming in the house.

Then I smell incense; first right here, second time right here. Third time it was all the way to my body and my face. Apparently, they had got incense from the church. There's lots of people. I heard them laughing, talking. Then I was [blacked] out. I don't know what happened.

Then I started to wake up. I woke up and hear people laughing, talking. Then somebody was holding me right here, maybe checking my pulse. I woke up and saw my dad. He was holding me. When I woke up, like he cried. He said, "My mother, you have returned. You have come back."

And I tried to shake my head. My stepsisters and one stepbrother, Wally, they don't know what to do. They kept quiet and never moved. They never look at me. Then, I was out again. When I woke up again, those people that was eating, they come over and made a sign of cross and kissed me. They tell me I come back.

After that my mom and dad asked me again and again, how I get sick. I always tell them, "I don't know." I didn't tell on my stepsisters and stepbrother, 'cause I knew they were scared. You could have any kind of body problem...

I'm glad my stepsisters and my stepbrother teach me how to be strong. When they start being sick, they used to tell me, "Eat anything you want from the fridge. Eat anything you want to eat." I know they were trying to

> tell me, "I'm sorry."
>
> Then I made sign and forgive both of my stepsisters and my stepbrother. When I started walking, I thanked them all for making me strong.
>
> To tell you the truth, no wonder them elders used to say, "Someday we will experience hunger." I went through that when I was eight years old. I thank them for letting me be strong, to teach me the tough way of life. Mom and Dad used to tell us not to pay back the wrong done to you. Someday the same pain will get to them, worse than what you experienced.
>
> Thank you very much for listening to me. I never talk about this. This is the second time I talk about it.

Tears still stood in Sophie's eyes, and the room was hushed. Both Olga and Agnes quietly said that they had never heard Sophie share this story. All were grateful. Olga said: "That's a heart-breaking story. But we learn, strengthen. Always forgive from the heart."

Mark recalled what his own grandmother had told him years ago:

> She used to tell us that when someone goes through hunger, it is the worst pain. She herself remembered running out of food twice. Even though they didn't completely run out, they started to eat a little of what they had.
>
> But she used to instruct us and say if we knew of those who were in need of food, that if we had enough, we should share our food with them.

Olga agreed: "It's always good to share. And when you share you give it from your heart. The more you share, even a little bit, it comes back, and more. I always used to do that growing up."

Food preservation before freezers

Our morning had been emotional, with tears and comforting hugs. We stopped for a good lunch of baked whitefish, enjoyed by all. When we began again, I suggested talking about how food was preserved before freezers. This was something we had already touched on, but we knew we had lots to learn. Sophie added detail to what she had shared earlier:

> Back in those days when we had no freezers, we had under-the-ground freezer, [and] food was put in those – salt fish, salmonberries, blueberries with a little bit of sugar added. They'd put them in wood barrels and put

them in those storages. They said they were coolers.

And when they catch moose, we'd carve off the meat from the bones and some of the meat was salted. And after the meat from the bones was removed, they'd hang them in the porch to dry. And the meat was hung and dried in the smokehouse; they make fire and smoke them.

My parents took care and process everything edible. And the bones, when they were half-dried, they'd cut them up and eat them. They were eaten first, bones with marrow in them. And they'd hang the ribs to dry; some were eaten half-dried, and some were dried all the way.

Though we had no freezers, food was never allowed to spoil.... And the dried fish in the *salayaq*, food for the dogs, they gathered them in tied-up bundles, they'd put them in caches. And the dried backbone of the fish, fold them over and tied them up in bundles and store them in the cache.

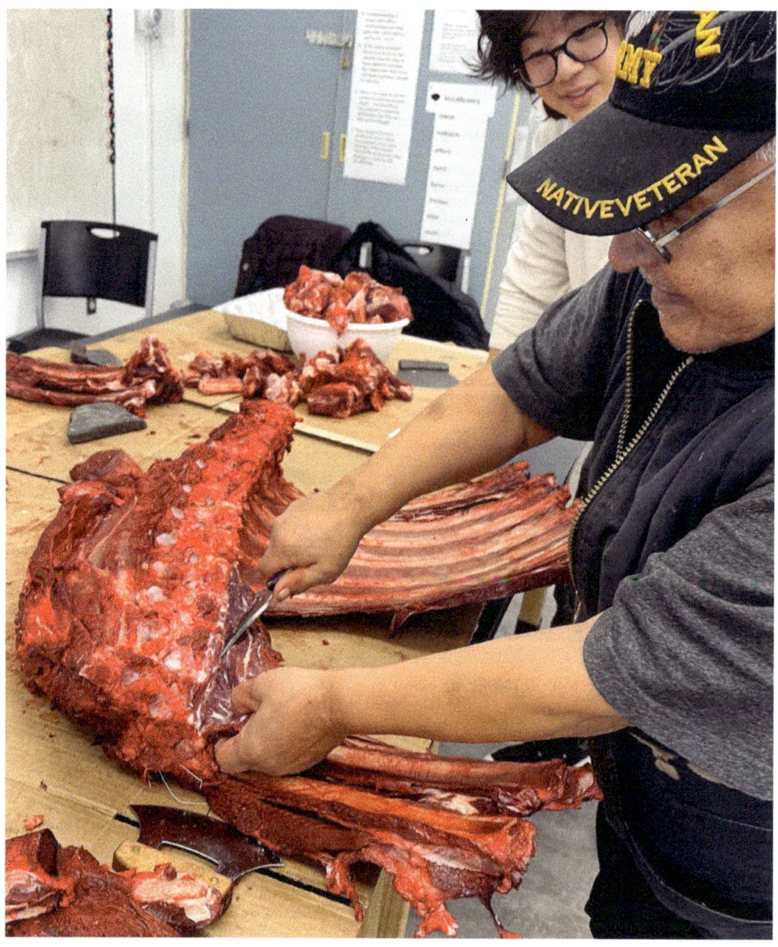

Wassily showing Chris Kim how to cut moose ribs "uptown, downtown." March 2025. *AFR*

> Everything, also the beavers, they'd split them like fish and hang them and make half-dried beaver, including the bones and other body parts. The whole thing was tied around the neck and hung and smoked. And after those were done and put away, they'd put them in things and store them, making sure they don't spoil. In the elevated cache, they never spoil.
>
> And since we used to use fish wheels.... The whitefish, trout, our parents used to let us young children clean and split them. They'd make skinning pole and hang them, saying they were *segg'aruat* [split and dried fish].
>
> Everything was processed with care when freezers were introduced. I never forgot what we used to do back in those days; while growing up our parents teach us how food was processed and used. And now at this time, to my children and to my grandchildren, I've passed that knowledge down to them. I instruct them and tell them to take good care of everything we use for food and not to waste them or leave them out and let dogs or others scatter them around.

Sophie then shared the story of a memorable experience while listening to elders in the past:

> And, to elders, when they share their knowledge, I listen to them talk about food and how food was cared for and preserved back when they were growing up. And Olga's dad Capun and Agnes Charles, whenever they were going to talk [and] tell stories about old time, I'd go with my children to listen to them. Then one time when we went to listen, Olga's dad, he sometimes try to speak in English to his grandchildren. They were telling stories.

Chuckling, she continued:

> While he was talking, viewing how people live today. He said, back then when they went out to attend dances, they'd put on better clothes. He said they'd play music on those old phonographs, and they would dance. Then he suddenly spoke in English and said, "Good dance, long time ago." Them kids were listening. He spoke in English and said, "You fellas, today, no good. No good. You dance just like frogs, jumping around."

We all laughed, and Sophie concluded: "I used to like to listen to them old people when they tell stories. They were funny when they tried to speak in English."

Angie picked up where Sophie had left off:

> I remember, too when I was a little kid, we used to go pick blueberries. And they put 'em in wooden barrels. And then they put rainwater and put it away. No sugar, nothing, just rainwater. In winter when they want some, they bring it in and thaw it out, take however much they need, and they bring the rest of it out. Used to be good, like fresh blueberries.

Lucy's grandfather had also built a cooler in the hillside at Crow Village:

> On a little hill on our right side, my Ap'a had a hole inside that little hill. Inside he had shelves, and outside he put door. That's where they store all their berries – blueberries, red berries, salmonberries, and their salt fish. They never spoil.
>
> But dry fish they keep 'em in the cache.
>
> And in the middle of the house they have cellar. I think that's where they kept mostly their eating stuff down there. And what they need, they bring it up. Those are the ones I remember.

Agnes was listening, and when Lucy was done, she added: "What they said is what we always do. Seem like everything is the same, taken care of like that long ago. It just reminds me of how I used to do, too, and my mom. Same thing, same story." Agnes then added detail on how her mother stored sheefish oil and harvested potatoes from the garden:

> And in springtime they used to catch lots of sheefish long ago when I was growing up. And she would put guts in a big pot, and heads. And after it cook off, we put 'em in those gallon containers. And she tell me to dig a hole. "You gotta put 'em in there. Make sure you cover it well." I'd say, "Okay."
>
> So, all of that grease from that fish, we always put in the hole. Just stay cold all summer long. I used to make a lot of fried bread with that grease, over the fire....
>
> And we had a cache in the falltime. In the springtime they made garden. And in the falltime, they start putting away those potatoes and whatever they planted, and they keep 'em. We used to use them all the time.
>
> The fishing is similar to what I hear of everybody's story. It's the same.

Jennie noted that men hunted moose late in the fall, so that the meat would freeze: "They tried to go hunting late so the meat will stay preserved. They hang them outside." Olga remembered her father catching a moose one spring: "They used to have big plastic barrels. I remember my mom hurry up and *sulunaq* [salt] that whole moose for the summertime. When you're tired of eating fish, she would take it in gunny sack and cook 'em by the fishing rack. That's how they preserved outlaw [moose] from springtime." Angie added:

> Even now we still outlaw. The hunting season that they have [in September], there's too many bugs out. If you leave your meat on the ground trying to dry them up, they have so many flies.
>
> Boy, so scary nowadays. When you catch something right now, you've got to take it home right away. But they used to wait until first frost to go moose hunting. But danger too, 'cause the bulls are rutting, run over anything.

Animal stories

Our time together was drawing to an end, but we found time to share a handful of animal stories. Talking about bear hunting, Angie mentioned brown bears in winter, with frozen fur: "Some of those brown bears don't go to bed in the winter. 'Cause one time my dad found brown bear that had been [awake]. He go in the brown bear track, and it led to hole in the water. And when [the bear] jumped in the water and came back out the other side, he rolled in the snow." One of the women asked, "Was it to get the water off?" Angie replied: "No, to make the fur freeze. And he would do it over and over again. Those bears are really hard to kill. 'Cause the only place that they're [soft] is right here [under the arm] when they walk. And if you can't see [they're hard to kill.] They're really dangerous, them ice-covered bears."

I asked about animals having different personalities, and I gave porcupine – who is said to be jealous – as an example. Olga recalled: "You know it's the other way around from what I heard. If you see a porcupine before you see a moose, get the porcupine so it'll bring you luck. That's my understanding." Angie, however, also viewed porcupines as jealous.

Olga and Angie agreed on raven bringing people luck, when it hears a person's request and flips and drops its load. Olga shared:

> One time I was going out hunting and we saw raven. I talk to it. I go, "Okay. Flip! Do your thing, you know. Flip! Give me good luck. I want to catch moose." Sure enough, when moose season open, my son caught his moose. I say, "Oh yaa, that raven didn't lie." I told him, "Talk to the raven and tell him to give you luck." When it flip over, sometime it works and sometime it doesn't. And I told him I talk to that raven.

Angie had also experienced raven bringing animals – perhaps too many:

> One time I tell one of them [ravens], "Gee, I really need moose soup!" And then he took off. I said, "See you!"
>
> And we went go pick berries. And the baby, she was sleeping right underneath blueberry bush, so when she wake up she would see them berries and maybe go after them. And that raven come and talk to me. And when I tell 'em, "I need moose," he send two of 'em to me.
>
> They were coming right at me, baby was right there, right where that moose is gonna run. And her mom was closer; and I reach her [baby] before. I just grab her and keep running. Next time I see that raven, "I don't want to talk to you." And my cousin Agnes say, "How come you tell 'em that?" [I say,] "He want to bring the animals too close."

Everyone laughed at Angie's story.

Our gathering was almost done. Before the afternoon ended, however, we had a visit from a group of Aniak third and fourth graders, all of whom had grandmas and aunties among the women. Their teacher had asked if they could come and listen, and the women greeted them warmly. The students introduced themselves and then one by one the elders spoke to them, always noting how they were related. Sophie began, telling them that although she lives in Chuathbaluk today, she grew up in Aniak and went to school here. She said she was glad to see them, as they were the next generation. She admonished them to think about what they wanted to do when they finished school: "You're not always gonna be small. We need you kids to take over, as teachers, pilots, city council members."

Angie was next, letting them know that she was from Sleetmute:

> I come from a little village. My people, like my parents, my grandpa... they tell me when I was growing up, "Please listen. Use your ears. Listen. Put it in your head. Some people will give you stuff. And all you have to do is put your hands out and take it."
>
> See, your teacher right there. He come and give you part of his brain, because he has given you what you need to know.
>
> Sometimes it's kinda hard to listen, especially rough kids. You know how I know? I was a rough kid. And it was very hard to listen. But if we need to, we listen good, and we treat people good, and everything will come out okay.

Agnes was next, telling the students that she first went to school in Crooked Creek, then at Georgetown: "And I finish school there. I had all kinds of teachers.

Some of them are good, and some of them are bad. But I make it through eighth grade." Jennie told the students that she had gone to school in Crooked Creek, too, graduating from eighth grade. Although she wanted to go to high school, her dad was in bad health and her mom needed her to stay home. Later in life she married and moved to Sleetmute, where she was a health aide for more than twenty years: "From graduating from eighth grade to going to health aide training, it was kinda hard, but if you put your mind to what you want to do you can succeed."

Olga followed. She welcomed the students again, saying how glad she was to see them here. Then she told them that this was the last day of our gathering, talking about how they used to put away food: "I'm originally from Crooked Creek. I moved from there in 1978. I lived in Aniak and got married. A lot of you know me 'cause I used to sub at the school. Always listen to your teachers, respect your teacher, respect your elders, and try to listen to what they're telling you. Hope you all have a good afternoon. And thank you for coming."

We could not have asked for a better ending for our gathering. We had been talking about the past, and here was the next generation – the very reason it is so important to remember.

The George River. *Ian Moore and Jen Jolliff*

Chapter 3

Mountain Hunting along the Middle Kuskokwim

Of all the regions in southwest Alaska, the middle Kuskokwim is unique in the extent to which people know and travel in mountain country. The delta lowland between the Yukon and Kuskokwim Rivers consists of vast stretches of tundra – as much water as land – flanked on the south by the Kuskokwim and Kilbuck Mountains and on the north by the Andreafski Hills. In the past, hardy hunters from villages like Kwethluk and Akiak traveled seasonally into the mountains to trap squirrels and hunt caribou and bear. But few wintered in the mountains, where snow was deep and animals could be scarce. Traveling up the Kuskokwim from Bethel, however, hills draw closer and closer to the riverbank until just past Chuathbaluk these hills dominate the landscape, shaping the lives of the people who call the middle river home.

On the last day of February and the first day of March 2024, CEC staff – Mark John, Marie Meade, and I – met with three men who shared their experiences hunting and fishing along the middle Kuskokwim. Since he was a child, John Andrew of Kwethluk had spent springs hunting with his father and uncles in the mountains along the headwaters of the Kwethluk River. Although not a mountain man himself, Michael Savage was born and raised in Kalskag and had intimate knowledge of the resources available both upriver and down from his hometown.

Both John and Michael had attended previous CEC gatherings and were familiar with the focused conversations that were the hallmark of our work with elders. Our third group member was Wassily Kameroff who we were meeting with for the first time. Wassily was born in Chuathbaluk and raised in Crooked Creek. After he married, he lived in Kalskag for twenty years where he hunted with Michael and got to know a different part of the river. While all three men recognized that harvesting patterns differed along the river, depending on geography and animals available, Wassily's personal experiences of these differences provided an invaluable perspective.

After an opening prayer, Wassily was the first to introduce himself:

> My name is Wassily Kameroff. And they call me Matarcuilnguq. I was born in Chuathbaluk in December 1949. My mom was married to Andrew Kameroff from Kalskag. But, you know, that TB epidemic got him.
>
> And the family is mostly from Crooked Creek, my roots. My mom is from Crooked Creek. I was pretty much raised up in Crooked Creek. And most of our relatives, the Johns and Sakars, were up there, and Alexies.
>
> It's amazing. People always say, "Kids are raised by a village." Even though they have parents, they have the village. We were raised by my mom and stepdad. When one kid gets into trouble, all the kids are in trouble. That's how they teach us, how to respect each other, not to put anybody down. You help somebody that needs help. So that's what we used to do.

Even before our introductions, Wassily had told a story to demonstrate this point: "When I was a kid going to school, there was this one kid that used to cause trouble. When that one kid made [that other kid] cry, everybody else, all the boys got scolded. There was no discipline for one person, it was for everybody. I'm still mad at that guy, even he passed away."

Wassily continued with his personal history:

> William Alexie was my stepfather. Andrew Kameroff was my real father. That's how [Michael Savage] and I are related; my dad's sister [was Michael's mother]. And there was Father Alexie from Kwethluk. And him and my stepfather were related; they're both Alexies. And families, they never really talked about how they grew up. They tried to teach us how to respect each other, not to try to hurt anybody, help somebody. When you have something little you share with them.

Later during our gathering, Wassily described how he foiled plans his parents were making to find him a bride.

> Me, too, I almost got forced marriage. Their parents were talking with my stepdad and mom.
>
> I plan lots. I'm not gonna get married. Too much trouble. I plan and get big stash. Got nine horse engine. Plan, gonna run away. One night I take the boat. Got the gas in there, and I pole way up around the bend past portage, start the nine horse, and go to George River. Run away.
>
> I was up there, maybe wait two weeks. Caught a moose, bear. I was drifting down, I was in no hurry. Then I hear boats, motors coming up. I stop. Make fire, put the kettle on.

> Around the bend I see boat. See my mom and stepdad, that girl's parents. They stop. They cook. That girl's mom and my mom, they cook. Another boat come; my uncles, come looking for me.
>
> They were sitting down. My mom go, "You're not marrying nobody. You'll marry somebody you care for. I don't care what anybody say, but you're not marrying nobody." The boss was talking.
>
> None of the men say anything. And that girl's mother said, "Yes, that's true. My daughter is not gonna marry anybody that she don't love." But we can be friends, you know. "You guys talk to each other, but don't do nothing."
>
> My dad get in the boat. After we get done eating with them, my mom tell that girl's mom, if she want to have the meat and stuff. So they take it and they go.
>
> Paddle down the George River. Once we hit the Kuskokwim we start the engine. Go down. My stepdad look at me, I was sitting in the front. So I go back, start the nine horse, go down. Them other boats behind us, go to our place. And that was the end of everything.

Wassily was drafted in 1971 and spent two years in the army at the tail end of the Vietnam war. After that he married a woman of his own choosing and moved to Kalskag in 1974 where he worked in the city office and served as mayor. Between 1996 and 2016 he worked at the Donlin Creek mine, first as Calista's shareholder hire coordinator and later as the camp boss, working directly for Donlin. Today Wassily lives in Anchorage along with his children and grandchildren, noting that he misses working for the people in the villages:

> I used to have fun, even it was hard work. I used to have to teach the people that are coming in to work on schedule. And the people that come in [from Outside], I teach them the culture of the villages. 'Cause they didn't know. These guys coming from down states, all they think about is money. If you can't get this thing done right away, you gonna be losing money. And I had to try to teach both.

Michael Savage followed with details of his personal history:

> I never really know [Wassily] until he moved down to Kalskag and my mom told me that we were relatives.
>
> I'm Michael Savage. My name is Aqum'aq after my grandpa on my mom's side. My dad is originally from Yukon, Paimiut. And his grandpa was up by McGrath, Nikolai, that was his homestead. I think their last

names were Nikolai, but I think he was a loner away from people so they call him Savage. So that's how we got our name. But they moved down to Holitna after Holy Cross, that area. But my dad was born in Paimiut.

But my grandpa was born around Mt. Mckinley, in that area. That's how they migrate down that way. They've been in Kalskag since the 1930s. And they lived there until 1969 [when] we moved down to Lower Kalskag. I heard that they had a sawmill in Lower. They were cutting logs, and a guy told my dad to work there. He said my dad wanted a house to move my mom down closer to the church. And that's how we lived there. After that we moved down to the fish camp [every summer], six miles below Kalskag. We been there since, fishing.

I was taught like Wassily said. I listen and pay attention when elders talk, especially during Slaaviq. When I'm watching [it's] like they were looking at only me, like they were scolding me. I was kind of bashful. So I listen and pay attention. Even when Wassily talks, I pay attention, 'cause

Wassily Kameroff, right, and Michael Savage in Lower Kalskag, May 2024. *AFR*

we were taught to respect our elders. So when he talk I always try to listen to him 'cause he knows a little more than I do. You're about five years older than me? I just turned 70. My birthday is January 15, 1954.

I was born in Upper Kalskag. Been in Kalskag area, hunt in that area mostly. Until Wassily move down, we start going upriver hunting. But my dad traveled, hunted all over; they make a big circle. When Native Land Claims came up, we started hunting where my dad claimed land; went hunting in that area only. My grandpa was Mesak; my mom's dad.

When we work together in the summer, we work all together with family. There was the three of us [siblings]. All three of us, we gotta help each other out.

Although he was our eldest group member, John Andrew was the last to introduce himself, speaking in Yup'ik. John is not shy, but he has great respect for others attending our gatherings and shares what he knows in an effort to encourage them to share in their turn:

They call me Alegyuk in Yugtun. They say my dad Cungauyaq, his father's name was Alegyuk. And the father of Alegyuk, my great-grandfather, his name was Anguksuar [lit., "Small man"]. He was named that even though he was a huge man. Maybe that's where I got my body frame. They say he was big and had long hair. They say when his wife died, he married a woman from Quinhagak and moved there. They say his two daughters there in Quinhagak, their many children there are my *nuliacungaq* and *iluraq* [female and male cross-cousins of a male].

My mother, they called her Nayagaq and Nanugaq, also. My mom's mother was from Dillingham. Her name was Sophie Nickolai. She was Cakayak's [John Samuelson's] wife's *ilungaq* [female cross-cousin of a female]). Father of Cakayak; Oscar Samuelson brought my mom's *ilungaq* over. They say her parents were living in Akiak....

But my relatives on my father's side, starting from Anguksuar; in Kwethluk and their relatives, his cousins, they referred to them as Ingrimiut [Mountain people]. Last of the nomads that moved down to the villages, maybe 1940s.

They say I was born along the mountains in the area of Iigmiut [Eek]. They say I was born in a sod house, March 7, 1945. That's why I called [Marie, born in 1947] a young one. They called me Alegyuk. They say, Alegyuk had a brother named Tupilluk. They called me both names. I had other names, but they mostly called me Alegyuk and Tupilluk.

Hunting land animals in the mountains

John immediately followed his biography with a brief description of hunting in the mountains when he was young:

> When I was little and became aware of my surroundings, we were always staying in the mountains, hunting squirrels. We'd move up in March by dogsled. And while staying up there, when bears began coming out, my father would hunt them to use their hides to make *angyaqatak* [shallow-draft skin boat meant for one-time use].
>
> When he caught four brown bears, he'd stop hunting them, when it's just our family in a camp. However, when another family was in our camp, they'd get up to eight bears and quit. One spring, I remember he caught eight brown bears for two families to use as *angyaqatak* to go down, along with their sled dogs and camp gear.
>
> But the moose they had caught, they'd dry the meat; same way with the brown and black bears. However, they didn't get much caribou.

Constructing the frame for an *angyaqatak* (shallow-draft skin boat) in the mountains before traveling downstream, spring 1980s. *Joe Spein*

Though there were a lot of caribou around, they didn't hunt them much, saying their hides were too thin and easy to tear. But some people did make *angyaqatak* out of reindeer or caribou hide, those who didn't catch bears.

And when they go down[river] with them and the skin got a tear, they'd quickly land and sew and repair them. I used to watch my mother sewing *angyaqatak*. She would mend and repair holes. They also used pitch from spruce trees and applied it to the seams to make it waterproof.

Sometimes, when they catch a lot of squirrels, one family would catch up to 500 or more in a season. The squirrel meat was eaten by campers, and the meat from the skinny ones was fed to the dogs.

But when they were almost done hunting squirrels, they'd let their dogs go on a diet and fed them less...to clean their guts so they wouldn't defecate in the skin boat as they headed downriver. One time, when one of my grandfathers, Sam Jackson, was with us, one of the dogs was about to defecate. My mom turned to Sam and said, "That dog, put your paddle under it to defecate." The guy was holding the paddle, and when the dog pooped, he started gagging loudly. I was laughing 'cause I was young and didn't know anything; I laughed at him. That old man got angry and said I was laughing at him. I didn't know anything or how to behave.

From the time I was little, the tiny squirrels, they had me set traps and snares for them. I hunted animals, starting from little animals. And as I got older and older, the animals I caught got bigger and bigger. I'd hunt otter, beaver, fox. As a teenager I hunted lynx, and occasionally I'd catch wolverine. I mostly caught animals using a snare. But I used to watch my old man.

John continued, talking about the seasonal round he and his family followed when he was young:

We went and stayed in camps season to season. During summer, we'd return to the Kuskokwim River. After we stayed in our village [Kwethluk] for a few days, we'd bypass our village and move to our summer camp, after we had a feast in the village. And we'd give some of our catch to the elders in the village. And again in the fall, we'd move to our fall camp [in the foothills]. Using gill nets we'd get silver salmon for us and the dogs. And a little later, right after freeze-up, near our base camp, we'd hunt for mink and beaver for a while.

Then when ice was thick enough, we'd go up to the mountains and hunt mostly lynx and fox. The pelts, they were the ones we used to buy goods and merchandise in those days. The whole year when we hunted, we were always getting for next quarter or the next season.

And we didn't hunt in the same valley. We'd make a base camp, we'd hunt in the other valley first, either toward Eek or toward the Kwethluk River where it splits into two rivers or toward Canyon Creek area. We didn't stay much in our base camp. But when it got closer to the time to move down, we'd hunt around our base camp and start getting ready to move down. We'd use skin boats and return home.

Year round, we were always out in wilderness. But after the 1950s we stopped going up much, we'd go on and off. Since we don't get much snow anymore, we'd go up by plane sometimes. There are a very few people that still do it. Even one of my nephews goes over as far as Denali to hunt squirrels. That's why when I started working, my relatives started calling me Trapper [John]. When I didn't get much cash in the winter, I'd go to Bristol Bay to commercial fish. And I did two summers in Kodiak. Most of the time I'm the pilot of the boat. I do have a lot to say.

A lively series of hunting stories followed these introductions. Wassily described running down a caribou and killing it with a knife. John followed with three stories of killing bears at close quarters, including an account of one of his uncles tracking and killing a bear in deep snow:

> These two uncles of mine, in springtime, it was really wet. They were tracking one bear. They had snowshoes on, and the bear was getting tired. And when it got bogged in the snow not able to lift itself up, one of them shot it. And he told his brother, "Go hold it down with a pole." He ran to it, he poked the pole by it. He held it by the neck and his brother jumped on it and slit its throat. And they said when they pulled it up and skinned it, there was no bullet hole. One brother would say this to his brother, "You must be crazy."

These stories reminded Wassily of something he'd witnessed when he was young in Crooked Creek:

> Maybe I was nine years old, we were up on the hill, a bunch of us boys. That one kid, he was older than us. He was talking. He said that he was going to fight the black bear with a knife.
>
> We see bear. We tell him to go. That bear grab him. [The bear] was like this [with its arms around the boy]. We run over and we shoot [the bear]. It

> fall down, still holding that guy. We tried to take its arm off. No. Go to the pack sack, take knife; we was gonna cut [the bear's arms] off.
>
> Took [the knife]. [The bear's arms] came off and it rolled. Maybe from there to the trees. He sit down with his back to the black bear. We laughed at him. Tell him, "We see another one, we say, 'Time to go.'"

That experience was something the young man never forgot:

> Every time he saw a bear, he sit down with his back on it. When we get home we told the story about it. They said, "He now has respect for it." Even when they go by boat and they see one, he'd turn his back on it.
>
> [He was] one of them kids from home.... You are not to talk about animals, what they gonna do to them.

John agreed: "We were taught about that, too. We're not supposed to say the animal by name, though we're out there hunting them." Michael had heard the same thing: "Me, too. I'm usually not scared of bear, but lately I've been. One time I run into a bear, from here to you. I had my gun. I wanted bear meat. I couldn't even grab my gun because I could see his eyes and mouth, just right here." Wassily noted the reason not to talk about hunting bears: "They hear you by the ground." John had been admonished in the same way: "They talked to us when we were small. Even older people never hunt them. They are afraid of them. They won't even come near them."

Winter hunting on the George River

After a short break, I asked Wassily about the seasonal cycle at Crooked Creek, noting that he had mountains, too, like John. Wassily demurred:

> We got only two mountains, Horn Mountains and Russian Mountains.... Horn Mountains in Yugtun is Cirunermiut. The other one, they call Russian Mountains.
>
> But for Crooked Creek, it's not the same as from Kalskag down [where] they pretty much have fish camps. [Around Crooked Creek] the hills provide everything that we need. We don't go spring camp. We only go fall camp, go hunting and trapping. We never do spring [camp], even though we have spring game and stuff.
>
> For the falltime, everybody goes out, all the men. And in George River, they have the main river and the East Fork [of the George]. The East Fork had about twelve camps, all the way to the end, and we were almost the last one.

> But everybody has a place. They have a little cabin in each, and nobody never cross that imaginary line when they're trapping. Because when they trapped, they trapped both sides of the river, the valleys.
>
> Before snow fall, when they're up there and the ice is thin, they make [fish]traps, but they take it out after they're done. And they hunt mink then. And mink is not as big as on the coast. Then they hunt mink and otter.
>
> And then when it gets more snow, they start trapping marten. And each person that traps in the area has imaginary line. Sometimes they meet and they have lunch. But most of the time, they turn around from [the end of their area] when they're trapping.

Wassily noted that his family was not alone wintering on the George River: "There's lots [of other families].... My uncles used to be in the mouth of North Fork. They call them Johns, Johnny John and Ignaty [John]. That's my mom's brothers."

Wassily told us that most of the time families left the George River after break-up, and I asked if they came down by large skin boats, as in John's area. Wassily laughed: "No. They had wood to make boats." Then he explained:

> In the fall, before freeze-up, we go up by boat and dogs. Dogs pull the boat, and we push to keep the boat out [from the shore]. And once we get to our camp, we'd pull up the boat and then take care of everything. And then they had canoes, and they'd go down. Usually one person stay up at the camp.
>
> And before freeze-up, guys go up with rest of the dogs, what we left behind. And that's what we do. And then springtime we just come down with the boats.
>
> There was certain families that make boats, houses, nets. And they all share. And that's what we used to do. But now it's different, you can just jump in your boat and go. Few hours to where it used to take a week [to get to our camp] up the George River.

Wassily, along with all fourteen members of his family, spent the winter at their camp. They brought dried fish from their summer harvest. They also fished below their camp and hunted nearby for fresh food: "Make a [fish]fence like that and a hole, and then we'd dip for lush or grayling or mud suckers and pike; anything that comes out. For about four or five days. And then we'd pull out the fencing.... And then two, three moose and bear; pick berries back in them hills."

When Wassily mentioned moose, he included a description of the "moose dogs" his stepdad trained to hunt them. John had mentioned training dogs to hunt moose by having them chew on moose tendons when they were young. Wassily explained:

> My stepdad used to let them chew rawhide. But they used to make moose dogs different up there. They set fire to an old rotten stump, let it smolder and smoke, and hold that pup [over the fire]. And all that foam and stuff come out [of its nose]. And when he starts having nose bleed, they're done.
>
> And they don't make more than two dogs for moose dog. And they say they can smell easy, when they clear out everything.
>
> And when my old man don't wanna go out too far, always tell one of them dogs to go and get moose to bring. They always get moose and bring 'em; they keep 'em right there in front of the house until the old man shoot it. And then go lay down. That's how they were trained.
>
> And that's something that nobody does anymore. 'Cause they got boats and snowmachines.
>
> Those dogs would drive the moose in, and he would shoot it. The dogs don't let it go.... They just go right [around it] like that. The moose is in the middle; every time it turn, they move.
>
> He had three [moose dogs]. They'd hold it until they shoot it; then they go lay down in the house.

Wassily concluded: "That's the cycle. It's kind of different than downriver. But we have pretty close to everything that we need there around the hills and river." Later, he added:

> We stayed there [on the George River] through the winter. Never used to drink coffee or smoke cigarettes in them days. We used to go trapping. And I still remember my mom say, "You have to learn how to make bread. You might not get married." We have to learn early to fend for ourselves when we're away from family.
>
> [We stayed in] just one [cabin]. We had cabin, double, inner and outer. Long ago there's no rooms in the houses. They had one, and if the family grow, they added.
>
> One of us, they usually leave me in the camp; I don't know how come, I was not the oldest of the family. Maybe because I was the craziest. [*chuckling*]

"Indians towing boat and canoe upstream with dogs five miles below Kolmakof, August 1914." *A. G. Maddren UA-hmc-0166-apu-b2-f5-25*

"Towing boat up Kuskokwim River, August 1914." *A. G. Maddren UA-hmc-0166-apu-b2-f5-28*

Food shortage and abundance

Wassily shared another story about wintering on the George River that brought home the hardships families endured in the past:

> I can tell you a true story. You know, long ago, we used to starve out there. Used to have hardly anything to eat. We save everything. You know bacon, they come in slabs. When you cook the bacon, you save the skin. You don't keep it whole, but you cut it up and put it away; you save it.
>
> Same way with fish skin. If you eat dry fish, you save the skin. Those things can save your life. And it happened to me and my stepdad. For some reason, the plane couldn't come and bring our food.
>
> We was up in George River hunting, trapping in winter. All our excess foods that we saved were gone. There was nothing. Not even a mouse or birds or anything around. Nothing. I was sitting outside, and I hear something. I run in and tell my stepdad, "Sounds like airplane." Come out with his coat. Sam Parent [who ran the trading post at Crooked Creek] wave [from his plane].
>
> We had lots of fur, lots of marten. Twenty marten in one bundle. We go back and sit down and drink fishskin broth. And I hear a plane turbine. Sam Parent never stop his airplane. He come in and they talk. He give him twenty or thirty bundles of twenty marten; [my dad] give it to 'em. "You bring us food." My old man tell 'em. Hold the keys to the cache.
>
> Sam Parent go. Them guys say [it would be] 40 below, 40 [or] 50 below; never used to be warm. [He] kept his airplane warm with them heaters. Come back with bundle of fish. Instead of holding it in bundles, [he] break it up so he can put more food in the plane. Soon as he come, he never stop his airplane, throw everything out, just take off and go.
>
> Our dogs were just skinny. Make 'em dog food. One pilot bread cracker with little butter, break it in fours. Dad tell me, "You just eat that one little part. Only when you get hungry, you eat the next one." That little piece of quarter of that cracker, I was full. I cook for them dogs. Two hours later, I eat that other part. All day, that one cracker. Something, you know, I don't think our kids would ever experience.

Wassily told another story that brought home the power of sharing food, not only to avoid starvation but to create abundance. He was in his early twenties and already living in Kalskag. From there, he traveled all the way to the George River with other young hunters in search of beaver. At first they had no luck.

Another thing is, when you're out hunting, especially wintertime. You can't catch nothing, you know. Whatever you have, when you go back to the village, you pass it around.

There was me, my brother, and couple other people. I do my hunting, beaver trapping up George River all the time every year. And we couldn't catch nothing. We only got one beaver and one moose. Two weeks, nothing, almost run out of food. I tell them boys to cut up whatever moose we have, but keep the ribs. Ribs are good, they dry out; wintertime they dry.

We go down to Crooked. We stop at this old man, I give 'em moose meat, liver, kidney. Tell them boys to go pass some to all them old people – my uncle, auntie Annie, and them. And if you have leftover, you give to them other younger ones. Go down to store; Evelyn and Dennis [Thomas] was there.

You remember them moon boots. One of the first winter boots. Guys was sitting down reading books. One of them, he was cussing. I ask, "What's the matter?" His moon boots had melted; too close to the stove. Even I wanna laugh, I didn't laugh.

We were heading down to Crooked [from the Thomas's store]. Oh gee, I cut canvas. I still believe in canvas. I make him wrap on his leather boots, put grass, tie 'em up round. We go.

We go first time, and we keep stopping. Getting close to Kuskokwim, my younger brother go, "Man, them guys from Crooked, if they come up, 'What kind of animal or person with round feet.'" [*laughter*]

Then we laugh; even him. We go and we stop above Crooked, and look at Tim. He was taking [the boots] off. I ask, "How come you're taking them off?" "I ain't gonna go to Crooked like this!"

But we pass all that meat out. I camp with that old couple, Golga Sakar and Bedusa, his wife, that's their name. That's my stepdad's brother-in-law and sister. I went down. Bedusa had cooked that liver and kidneys; that old guy, he finish the whole thing, all the liver. And he said, "Boy! Taste good. Not gamey, just good." Good kidneys.

He ask me, "When you gonna go?" I tell him, "Tomorrow." He said, "Gee, stay one more day." He said, "It's so good to see you again." "Yaa, I guess so."

Them boys come next day, 10 o'clock; ready to go. I tell 'em, "That old man told me stay one more day." They say, "What about our snares, traps?" He said, "They'll still be there."

At my camp, I had ten beaver houses; three holes [each]. That guy that melt his boots, he stay.

We go [next day], 10 o'clock. All the way up to our first beaver house. Psssss. Holy cow! And go to the next one. He said, "Maybe we catch in there, too." I pull out beaver; clean it out. Go there. Pssss. "Look like we catch in here, too."

We had ten beaver houses, with three holes in each. From that last beaver house to our cabin, we catch 30 beaver. So we sit down; gutting them. Those boys come in and sit down, and we're eating. I tell 'em, "You know, when I was growing up, dad, everybody used to tell us, 'When you can't catch nothing, you take whatever you got, bring to that village, next village, and pass it. Those guys are so thankful for that meat, it come back like this. Look at how much we have.'"

So, next day then five beaver [houses] going up, they come back with 15 beavers. I say, "Gee, you guys better go take them snares out. There's too much beaver." In that four days we were up there, we got 90 beaver. "Ah gee, that's too much."

So I went down to Crooked. I bring 20 beaver down there – whole beaver, skin and all. I tell 'em just pass it around. After I get gas, I go back. Next day I go down, bring 20 beaver to Chuathbaluk. Them guys they were busy gutting. They would go down and go down, last trip going home. Got two snowmachines with sleds, all full of beaver meat.

We stop in that old man's place. He give me bag. I tell him, "What's that?" "Beaver skin, them guys bring beaver skin." They're happy for beaver meat.

I stop by the store, [take out] the money to fill up. He go, "No." I say, "Look." He said, "You can fill up all your cans. They're already paid for." Everybody that had take beaver meat and stuff, they were so happy they put a little bit of money in. Even them, they give me cash for gas. Go Chuathbaluk, stop at that old man, he give me bag. I tell 'em, "I don't want no bag. Got too much beaver skin." "What you gonna do with 'em?" I tell him, "You stretch 'em, that's yours."

I go down, I go home. Aggie call everybody that need meat. I think your [Michael's] wife came over, too. Ninety beaver! I couldn't believe it. Holy cow! They were so thankful for the little bit meat we had give 'em. Those boys, they couldn't believe it. Those people were so thankful for fresh meat.

Throughout southwest Alaska, they say the gratitude of elders is strong, bringing prosperity to those who share. Wassily's experience was testament to the truth of this admonition.

Listening to Wassily's story, Michael remembered the days when beaver were scarce around Kalskag: "Long time ago there was hardly any beaver down in Kalskag area. They used to come up all the way to right around Mt. Mckinley and hunt for beavers. That's how my grandpa, great-grandpa moved down.... That's how we get food, different areas." Michael noted that his father envied coastal people for their rich resources:

> My dad always tell me, he really liked those coast people. And he said the hardest time they have is during winter. But summer, spring, they got everything, get all the food they can eat. That's what he always used to tell me.
>
> They got fish, big dogs, berries, just right there. 'Cause we have to travel far to get berries. My dad said he really envied people down coast; they have everything.

Michael's dad was not alone. The middle Kuskokwim had seasons of abundance but also a long winter when food could be scarce.

Food was not always abundant for John Andrew and his family in the past, and he was carefully instructed in how to make the food they had last:

> Sometimes we had nothing with us and traveled all day long. Even if we were really hungry, we got a tiny piece, keep it under the tongue so it makes saliva, keeps the mouths from getting thirsty.
>
> And they told us not to eat snow. If we try to eat snow, especially ice, you burn up too much energy. But sometimes we let it melt in the mouth and swallow it, a little bit of it.
>
> But I used to hear from a person from Yukon River, around St. Mary's area. He said when they had no food, even one little egg from salmon eggs, they keep it under their tongue so they can taste the food and keep the mouth moist. This kept you from getting dehydrated.
>
> We apparently were lucky. Our parents, they'd bring provisions, but we'd try to make them last. We ate only when they gave us food. Out on the land, we'd look for animals so we'd have more food while traveling out there. We'd be traveling all day long and eat in the evening, trying to get to our destination. Anything, we'd get beaver or birds for supper.

> And if we had gotten fresh fish, we eat certain parts of it raw – their liver and other innards and also their fat. And when you get to the camp, we'd either boil or fry the fish.
>
> We tried not to eat from the provisions we brought along while traveling. Especially the dried fish, we'd keep them as long as possible without eating them, unless you really need to eat it. And when you get hungry, you'd cut a little bit of dried fish and put it in your mouth and keep it in there for long time instead of swallowing it right away.
>
> And when we caught caribou, we used to eat their liver raw. They'd cut a little piece and put it in our mouth and keep it in our mouths for a while before swallowing. And then later another tiny little piece. Though we were tired, we'd be satisfied and not hungry. But if they had cooked it in the fire and they gave you too much, you'd get thirsty. But if you eat a little pretty far apart, it'll be good.

John also described saving animal hides when out hunting to use in case of emergency:

> If you get caught in a blizzard, and after you dig a hole to shelter, you'd use the hide as a blanket, fur side in. Or they'd make parkas out of the animal skins.
>
> I used to use one a few times when I'm too far out. And when I bring my grandchildren and great-grandchildren, when they got cold, I'd make them coats out of animal skins. One of them said, "Wow, am I going to use this as cover, even though it's not dry?" I said, "No, it's the Eskimo way of keeping you warm." I made him a coat and wrapped his feet with the skin. When he got warm, he was happy.
>
> When we got a caribou, the skin, I made an overcoat and put it on the boy when we were going home. And when we got home, that caribou skin was given to his great-grandmother as a gift. He went down to his great-grandmother's house wearing the caribou overcoat. When he went in he said, "Make me a caribou coat. They can keep you warm." She made him a parka out of the skin right away.

Times have changed. John concluded: "Long ago when people camped out, some people would run out of food when they weren't able to carry a lot of provisions with them. And during that time there would be a lot of snow in the winter. But today, when people go out camping, they come home fat because they bring a lot of extra food with them when they go."

Spring hunting

Once back in the village in late spring, Wassily described another distinctive practice along the middle river – hunting bear and moose in the hills close by and bringing the meat home in small, round skin boats.

> And springtime [in Crooked Creek], they used to send us up [into the hills], when it's warming up like this, to hunt moose for spring meat. And it's not only for one family. Maybe it's for about three or four families.
>
> And like [John] was saying, them skin boats. We make round ones with the skin outside, fur is inside, round like that. With willows. We don't use string or anything. And we hunt moose and bear.
>
> [We use] moose skin [for the boats]. One moose skin can hold a moose, me and my partner, and maybe a bear or two. And when we catch moose, before you cut it up or anything; from the neck, below the head, all the way to the *kuucenak* [rump] you cut. They call it backstrap. They tell us to save that, don't cut it. You save that meat.

John added: "All the way to the tail bone." Wassily continued:

> Yaa, to there. That's where the sinew is.
>
> And my mom take that, take all the meat off. Then she dry it up. After it dry, go like this [rubbing with both hands]. And it becomes thin strip for *kameksak* [ankle-high skin boots]. You take the meat off the sinew and dry the sinew.
>
> When you cut the back strap off, bring it home. My mom always tell us, "Don't try to take the meat off. I'll do it." She knew how to take the meat off and dry the sinew to make thread.
>
> "And make sure you save [the bone] from the moose [leg]." That's what we used to do. In springtime we never save. We use 'em for rope for the boat. Come out of Crooked Creek, and then go up [one person] pulling 'em [walking on the shore], somebody stay in the boat, little round canoe, [and we] go home to Crooked Creek.
>
> And there's a little creek up there they call Bell Creek. You climb up the hill and we watch for moose and bears. Go up the hill and hunt. When we got older, that was our job to do that. We just walk up the hill from the village. It's not only us but there's maybe six or seven boys that hunt for the whole village. Go up the hill, eat fresh red berries. Good in springtime, sweet.

Wassily continued, talking about how the moose was cut up and every part saved and used, including the colon:

> The first thing you cut is the back strap, after you skin 'em. Then you take the arms and legs off. And the brisket, cut around the stomach. Sometime they're fat, you know, in the stomach. Take all the fat, hang 'em up.
>
> And the *anauteq* [large intestine, colon] where the moose turds are, they're long. They call 'em *anauteq*, the colon part of it. You save that, you turn it inside out and wash it out, 'cause it's all fat. And when we go

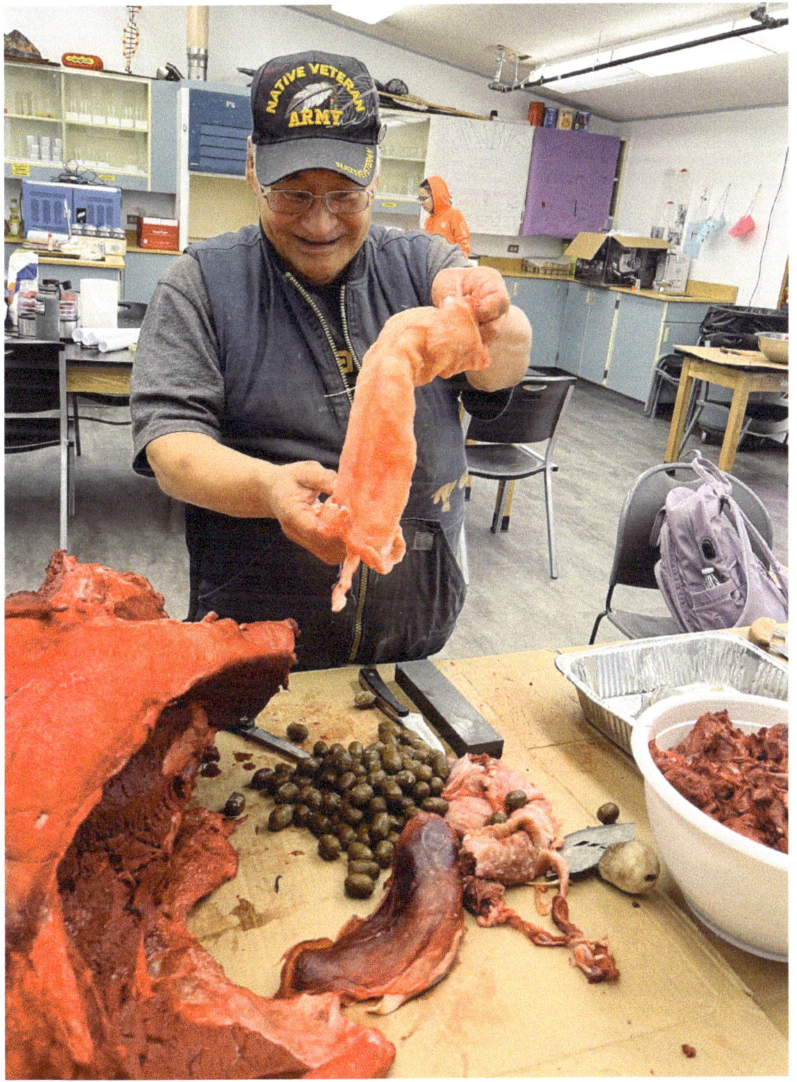

Wassily holding the colon removed from a moose, ready to clean and stuff with ground meat, March 2025. *AFR*

> home, Mom would take care of it. First, she cut up meat. No grinder them days. She cut up meat and whatever vegetables we pick from outside, from the lakes, she put 'em in there. And fill up little pieces like that with the fat part out. Like sausage. And when we go, that's what we take for lunch, you know, slice it up.
>
> Everything cooked, even the colon is cooked. You fill it up long, and you cut it so long. Then bake it or boil it.

Men dug cellars in the banks to store food in a cool place. Wassily explained: "And then, we had cellars inside the trees they called cold storage. They dig, maybe about four-by-four or eight-by-eight. Put wood in the bottom. And when the ice is going, take big chunk of ice, put 'em down there in the bottom to preserve food and whatever. Sometime that ice stay there all summer, nice and cool." John had observed similar storage techniques in Kwethluk: "Many years back there was permafrost below; they used to dig until they hit the permafrost. After they make a frame, after securing it, they'd fill it up, like [Wassily] said, with ice. When the hole is full, they'd cover the hole and secure it. They keep almost forever."

Jennie showing moose parts to a class of Aniak preschoolers, with the moose's stuffed colon and intestines in the foreground, ready to bake, March 2025. *AFR*

Michael reminded Wassily of how Wassily's mother used to cook everything from the moose, including the hooves. Wassily agreed:

> Nothing used to be wasted. My mom used to let us take that moose head. After you take the nose out, skin it and everything, and cut it up. And she boil it in big pot. Take the hoofs and boil 'em; start in the morning, and by evening they're pretty well cooked. And take them moose hooves, just peel 'em out; take the bone out.
>
> Same way with the head. Take all the brains and all the muscles and *yualuq* [sinew, tendon]; they take 'em out; and she throw some rice in there, cook 'em for another 20 minutes, and put 'em in pans. And that was our Jell-O.

John said his parents cooked the colon and head as well and that his family and relatives still do so:

> Boys, when they hunt we have to save them, their *yualuq* and stuff. Using pressure cooker, one hour is good enough. Stick the fork in. Gel overnight. They're almost solid....
>
> And those intestines of moose and caribou. Up above our village, those

Carrie Morgan and Lucy Simeon stuffing the moose's colon and intestines with ground moose meat and fat, March 2025. *AFR*

> who were way up there used to make, when they had a lot of fat, they'd turn then inside out; keep the fatty part inside. Then the bones; cut them up. They'd stuff their marrow inside those, with a little meat or if they hadn't added other parts. They say they were making *patruciq* [stuffed intestines].
>
> They used to try and save every part, and after they boil the bones, when they cooled off, they'd pour their fat into their stomach liners. Since they had no containers, they'd use animal parts as containers.

Wassily agreed that people used every part of moose and caribou. Bear, however, was different:

> We don't eat brown bear up there. One time I ask my stepdad, "How come?" And my uncles [said], "Brown bear eat anything, even people." They're just scavengers.
>
> "And if you catch a black bear with the stomach that's got no hair, don't eat it." I ask, "How come?" That black bear had eaten a person. That's how come the belly has no hair. Just go out there and bury it. That was the "Don't." Even brown bears are pretty good meat to eat. But upriver, they don't [eat it]. Maybe few people do, but most of the people don't.
>
> And the heads. Even the brown. They bury it, facing the east.

Black bear meat, however, was good to eat in spring. Wassily explained:

> I see lots of black bears [on the Ulukaq River]. Drunk black bears. They eat fermented blueberries. I had to laugh; bear run across [in front of] the tree; run across and [hit] the tree. And run down. The bear was drunk.
>
> Their meat tastes sweet in the fall.
>
> Springtime, they're tender. 'Cause they're sleeping. They never go nowhere. During the fall they travel all the time, their meat is tough. Same way with moose. You cut moose that's always on the go, it got tough meat.

John noted that if you leave them out for a period of time, and then cut them up, the meat gets tender.

Fish wheels on the Kuskokwim

Though our focus was on hunting and trapping, fish were a critical resource in all seasons, to fuel both dogs and their owners. Wassily began by explaining one piece of technology unique to the middle Kuskokwim where the current is fast and eddies few – the fish wheel, introduced by miners in the early 1900s and rapidly adopted by local fishermen because of its efficiency.

> When they used to fish long ago, two or three tiers of fish. Nobody had nets. Everybody make fish wheels. And in Crooked, other side where [the river] bends, there's maybe about ten fish wheels.
>
> Sam Parent would have boat and motor. And there was a missionary there. He had a boat and motor. And my uncle [had a boat]. There were three boats when I was growing up, with motors. And they know whose fish wheels are those.
>
> These guys would be pulling up; they go to their fish wheels. Sometimes they can't even put all their fish in their boat. And king salmon used to be so big. And it's swift up there because it's only one river [channel].
>
> And two or three king salmon, when they get in the basket, they just stop the wheel, and it never move. And somebody would go across, the fish would go in the basket. And nobody used to say, "Gee, I'm not gonna do that." You know, when somebody's there, and their fish wheel stop, they help 'em and let them go.
>
> There's no more up there. The only ones that have fish wheels are Fish and Game; they call 'em live fish. They catch fish, and they [let them] go in the water. When you catch a king salmon you gotta throw 'em out; you can't take them.

Michael also remembered fish wheels in Kalskag: "And I remember Sinka [Williams], when they had camp with us where we fish, and we had fish wheel. And that year there was a lot of kings. Three of us, three families at the camp. We had to stop that fish wheel because there were so many kings, and they were big. And that's the last time I see fish wheel."

While Michael's family's fish wheel fed three families, the fish wheels in Crooked Creek supplied the whole village. Wassily explained:

> Certain families had fish wheels; and people that don't have no fish wheels, or way of getting fish, sometime in the morning, they give it to them, that one family. And in evening, they keep. Or they keep them in

> the morning and in the evening, they give them to the other families. Everybody had fish. Nobody didn't say, "Gee, can I have some fish?" Nobody say that. Everybody just give it to them. They just share, helped each other....
>
> Those three boats, they check them. They had to keep this fish or give it to somebody.

Michael agreed: "They limit, they give limit and knew how much fish to each family." Wassily continued:

> And then, when they go for dog [salmon] fishing. They got one smokehouse just for dog fish and onc for eating fish. That's how it was – one for eating fish and one for their dogs. The [smokehouses] they put up for dogs were bigger. 'Cause most of the people had fifteen dogs, twenty dogs. That's what they fish for.

"Fish pond" (*segvik*) in Aniak, 1959. *William C. and Frances P. Ray Slides, Anchorage Museum B2016.006.1802*

Life in the summer, mused Wassily, was busy but good:

> You know, when we were growing up there was no TV, no phones, no cameras, nothing. And still there was a time when we play. We worked from dawn to dusk during the summer fishing, smoking, feeding the dogs, chop wood, and still had time to play. Family would have certain things to do all day.
>
> And in my family there was fourteen of us. We had three older brothers and sisters. And now I'm the oldest with only four of us left. Each one of us had something to do.

Delivering a king salmon to the fish pond, Aniak, 1959. *William C. and Frances P. Ray Slides, Anchorage Museum B2016.006.1804*

Once the fish were brought to shore, they were deposited in the "fish pond" and cut for drying at the *neqlivik* (fish camp). Below Aniak, fish camps like those of both John's and Michael's families had fish-cutting stations located up on the riverbank. Beginning at Aniak, fish were gutted and cut right by the shore, with guts thrown in the water. The "fish pond" consisted of a wooden dock with cutting tables. Built alongside the dock was a square area with netting in the water to hold the fish. Looking at a photograph of an Aniak "fish pond," Wassily explained: "They built that like a little roof so it wouldn't get the people that are cutting fish wet.... This one is smaller; they're for single [family]. Long ago they had bigger ones; they had two or three tables in a raft where one group is cutting dog fish and one group is cutting eating fish, and one group is gutting and heading."

Though the fish-cutting areas differed, all three men agreed that during the fishing season, it was the women who set the limits, telling the men how many fish were needed. Wassily explained:

> They used to tell us that when we're doing something like this, there's only one boss. And that's the mom. The mom is the boss.
>
> She tells you what to do. She'll tell you everything what to do. She want you to clean an area for putting away certain stuff, you'll do it. And then when it gets in the house, the dad is not the boss. The only place the

Woman cutting fish at a *segvik* in Aniak, 1947. *Don Horter Glass Lantern Slides, Anchorage Museum B2017.011.139*

> dad is the boss is outside, when they're doing men's work, making boats and everything. But when you're gathering food and in the house, the mom is the head person 'cause she knows everything. And I believe it. But it's changed a lot.

Michael had the same experience:

> I was the provider and always working. And I check 'em what they need [at camp]. Every time I ask my dad what he needs, [he'd tell me] to go see mom; summertime, fishing time. So I had to go see mom and see what they need.
>
> I was the provider and the wood getter; that was my job. My brother, he did all the fishing. And Martha and the girls, they cut the fish. That was my job every day after work.

Though fishing with nets rather than fish wheels miles downriver, John's experience of how fish camp life was organized resembled Wassily's and Michael's in fundamental ways. The tools might be different – nets rather than fish wheels – but John's mother was the boss, both in determining how much to harvest and how the harvest should be shared.

Summer gathering

Fish was not the only food harvested in summer. Wassily explained:

> We had garden. You don't see that no more. Very few people have gardens now. Every place had a small garden. [We grew] potatoes, cabbage. Some time I see onions, turnips, carrots. And them potatoes, after they flower, they used to keep the top of them, the plant. And when they cook fish they put 'em in. That's after the flower bloom and the potatoes are growing down there. And then they cut the top and add them to the fish soup, or meat.

In summer, people would tire of eating fresh fish, and dried smoked meat provided a tasty alternative. Wassily continued:

> Up there, like I was saying, they had cellars, and then they had cold storage that they build inside the trees. They either smoke 'em. Half-dried beaver, they cut the bones out; and inside the bones, they salt 'em, put 'em in salt. And during the summer and they want meat, they just take the bones and put 'em in the water, while they're cutting fish. And in the evening, they just bring 'em back and cook 'em.

Wassily said that wild rice was also harvested in the lakes near Crooked Creek:

> We had wild rice from the end of the lake. And we used to go back and pick 'em. They grow there, natural. They call it wild rice. They just say, "Go get rice." [*laughter*]
>
> So we go back, especially in the falltime; put 'em in the basket, pull 'em out. Top of the grass. We pick quite a bit. And they cook 'em when they [make soup]. It's just like rice. Every year we pick in that one area.

Asked if people still harvest rice, Wassily said no:

> I don't know if anybody know about them. Everything change so much. Now, the young people, they don't know nothing about how we get food from up there....
>
> We picked them in the fall. Those sugar and flour, they come in little bags, 10 lb. or 50 lb. We used to fill 50 lb. of rice, which lasts all winter. That's a lot of rice. And still they used to buy rice from Sam Parent's store.

Another well-known plant still harvested from the rocky banks of the middle river are the roots of *elagat* (alpine sweet vetch), often exposed after the ice goes out during breakup. Wassily explained:

> That's the food we had; and during the spring, like you seen that [photo of a] boat with a lot of people. They go along the beach; not one or two families; there'd be three or four families. And they would dig for roots. They call 'em *elagat*. They take 'em out. After breakup, dig 'em out, and wash 'em.
>
> They cook 'em for about 40 minutes to an hour. And they make *akutaq* with 'em, they're really sweet. And they don't use lard or tallow. They use whitefish and moose fat to make the *akutaq*. Mold 'em, put them in a pan, and they cut 'em like bread. That was our dessert.
>
> The moose fat, you know, they get hard; and then they slice 'em. And they'd have berries in 'em, or *elagat*.

John's dad had also taken him to harvest *elagat*: "My old man, when he went upriver to gather *elagat*, sometimes I'd go with him. He showed me how to recognize them with [pink] flowers. He'd use a knife and pull them, and the roots would look like a lot of ropes. He'd take 'em out and wash 'em out. Some *elagat* are long and look like ropes. He'd gather a lot of them."

In the fall, John's dad had also harvested the roots and tubers stored by tundra voles, known locally as "mouse food": "Sometimes when he found mouse food, he'd be so happy. He'd make *akutaq*. He'd melt the moose fat, and he'd add black bear oil and mix in mostly mouse food." Wassily observed that mouse foods are different downriver and upriver, depending on what plants the mice are harvesting: "Sleetmute got lots a tundra. And up there, they got them little strings with what look like little black berries." John knew them well and called them by their Yup'ik name: *qetek* (root nodules of horsetail plants). Wassily continued: "And downriver mouse food, they have goose grasses and all different plants."

Our group had shared not only resources unique to the middle Kuskokwim, but unique ways of harvesting and sharing food. Wassily remarked: "Like I was saying, each of the areas, they have different ways of gathering and putting away and getting foods."

Narrow wooden boat like those made and used on the middle Kuskokwim, 1948. *Don Horter Photographs, Anchorage Museum B2014.016.074*

Fish traps

Fish wheels were not the only tools used to bring home quantities of fish from the Kuskokwim each year. Wassily described how, in the old days, men worked together to set one giant fish trap in front of Crooked Creek to catch lush fish for both people and dogs:

> The *taluyaqs* [conical fish traps] they used to have then never had no fencing wire. They used to make an *ayakutaq* [side piece] with sticks, and tie 'em with willow bark [or willow roots]. Keep 'em wet, they're easy to tie.
>
> That [fish trap] must have been big, but it was like that [one in the photo] almost. And at the end, where they set the fish trap. The fish trap is full of lush. And then they had a hole, and they dip [fish out of the trap].
>
> Them women know how to make [dip nets]; they're expert making dip nets. And then they dip. They make [the handle] long, with willows in springtime, where they can put it on the stick and tie them. They used to dip until they can't catch more, and then pull up that fish trap.
>
> In the middle, they protect the braces so when they pull it up it wouldn't break, lift it, and then pull it out. And take the end, tip it a little bit, and everything come out.
>
> All the lush fish. There's maybe about ten or fifteen dog sleds; all of them are full. [They set the trap] for about a week, and they take it out.
>
> [They set the trap] as soon as the water drops, mainly around January, February. When [lush fish] get big, their liver gets good, their *meluk* [fish eggs] get big. Most of the people eat 'em. And most of them were fed to the dogs.

Crooked Creek was not the only middle Kuskokwim village to set fish traps in the river's main channel. Michael recalled traps set at Kalskag:

> My mom's brother used to [set a trap] during the early fall before the ice got too thick. Where he's gonna set the fish trap, he let us dig the trenches in. And when the water gets so far, like springtime, April, they say their livers taste really good. But since he passed away [in the late 1970s], nobody [does that]. I never see anybody in Kalskag make fish traps anymore.

Michael noted that the trap was set right below Kalskag, where an eddy comes out. Wassily explained:

And right below it gets deep, must be about 15, 20 feet deep. Go like that, the bottom. And then there's a hole right there. And they set [the trap] right above it. And they say when [the fish] come out of the hole, they go right to the trap.

Upriver it's just rocks and bluffs. When you set [a trap] right above Crooked, above the last house, under the bluff, that's where they used to set fish traps.

[They set the trap] where it kinda slopes down. They make it quite a ways down. And the river going this way; they put fencing like that. So when the fish is coming up, they hit. Most of them lush stay at the bottom, they follow the fence out. And some of the other fish, like grayling, they

The best fish-trap maker in Kalskag, along with his family and one of his traps, February 1940. *George Dale, ASL.P306.0407*

go high; trout, they go way up high. But the lush in the bottom, they just follow the fence out until they reach the *taluyaq* and they go in.

Every two, three days, they check it. And if they're catching lots, in three or four days, they're done. They pull everything out. Nowadays, them lush are small.

Hungry Village

Wassily told another story that brought home both the unique seasonal rounds of the different villages along the middle Kuskokwim and its tributaries, and the hardiness and persistence of those who call it home. It was 1978, after the passage of ANCSA (the Alaska Native Claims Settlement Act), and Wassily was working with the Kuskokwim Native Association (KNA), traveling to villages in the region documenting land ownership.

I signed a two-year contract with them for doing the 14C lands for the villages. And the director at that time was a non-Native that came in.

There was an old lady, [Emma Bobby]. They tell me to ask her about Hungry Village. And I didn't know nothing about the history of Lime Village. And I was doing all the villages from Lower Kalskag to Stony, and we included Lime Village 'cause they were so way out.

And, man, that lady almost chew my head off. Hungry Village. "I'm sorry, you know, that guy down there tell me to ask. I'm not trying to make fun of anything. I want to know." So, she sat me down. She made cup of tea. Man, she make the best baking powder bread.

So she sat me down. She tell me, "Lime Village is not the original place right there. They call it Hungry Village. And people travel in a circle like this. And they got one little creek down there they call Whitefish Creek. And the reason why they travel like that is for [following] the season."

And the people used to be hungry all the time. And that lady said the white man gave them the name Hungry Village. But they used to go around in a circle, every year, never change and just keep moving the whole village.

Following the seasons, they move. 'Til that one day they settle down, right there where it is now – Lime Village. And the reason they got the name Lime Village is 'cause of that one hill that got lime. And that whole area is all lime. And I tell her, "Thank you."

Almost murdered that guy when I went back to Aniak. I tell him,

> "These things are nothing to play with; they're the survival for that community. It's not funny. It may be funny to you. These things are nothing to play with." And four months later, he resign....
>
> The *kass'aqs* [white people] [had named it Hungry Village]. And then they named it Lime Village after.

Wassily continued:

> Lime Village is the last of the people that really live off the land. One of the last villages.
>
> I always think about that old man in Clint Eastwood movie: They made them civilized. When I first went up there in late 70s, where they dump their slop pails, they had nothing, just a dishwater tub. And they had a place where they dump their honey bucket, and everybody had outside toilet. And when I went there, they brought me to the school and tell me to stay there. And everybody was so nice. They feed me, even I bring food. So I give [my food] to the elders. They give me dry meat, dried pike.
>
> When I got there, there was dogs, maybe about six dog teams with about five dogs in each sled. And I started having my meeting. And I didn't think, or nothing dawned on me, for seeing those dog sleds. And then a young guy come in and talk to them old guys. And they turned around and look at me and said, "Well, you can have meeting with our women. We gotta go out; them caribou are coming."
>
> So, I had to go out with them. And there was a guy on top of that hill, that mountain, waving a flag. Caribous are coming, behind it. And these guys, they jump on their sleds and go back.
>
> About two hours later, they come back; each of them sleds was just loaded. And the women stand up, go out there, and take them dogs to wherever. And all the guys come in. The women take care of all that stuff. And we kind of finish up.
>
> And I say, "Well, I'll start again." The guys say, "No, go ahead, our wives will tell us." So I continue the meeting. Got done. And I was thinking I'm gonna eat. One of them young guys come in, "You gotta come and eat with us." They had community hall, table in the middle. All the food you wanna eat. And it was not even two hours after them guys came in. The women set up, made food. I must have gained about 20 pounds.

Wassily followed with a reflection on what he saw in Lime Village when he visited it a second time, after food stamps had been introduced and some people believed the federal government would provide all the food they needed:

> And they were getting welfare checks. "We don't have to go hunting, the government is going to feed us." What a sad thing. To me, Lime Village was one of the last people where the federal government came in....
>
> And that story [about Hungry Village] I got from that lady, Emma Bobby. I think she passed on. But she tell me that story. About two hours I sit in there and listen to her. And I didn't even have a tape recorder. I kick myself, I should've had tape recorder in all the villages I went to. Man, I would have cool stories; good ghost stories, shaman stories. But that's kind of the story from Lime Village. They're good people up there, all Athabascans. They're doing pretty good now, I guess.

Story telling in the past

Recalling the story of Lime Village reminded Wassily of how good it felt to talk about his experiences: "It sure brings back lots a good memories. And to me it had wake me up again, make you feel good." Mark commented that that's how many elders feel during our gatherings: It fills them up. Wassily observed:

> That's pretty much it. You know how Golga Sakar, Uncle Johnny John. He was 96 when he passed away. Golga Sakar was about the same age when he pass away. My auntie Annie. It's amazing, you know, how men used to talk about things that they went through and what kind of stories they had. And it was very rare that women, you know, tell their story. They might be telling story to other women, but not to men.

Mark affirmed that women did tell stories, but in their own groups. Wassily then recalled his own experience:

> I got my aunt from Crooked to sit down and talk with me. I wanted to know more about my mom, my side of the family. She finally open up to me and start telling me story. And it always have to be with one of my kids. If it's not one of my kids, you know my daughters, she wouldn't open up. If they're with me, then she would open up.
>
> That's what she was telling me, telling us what the women's place is. The men build the house for their wives. Their wife put everything together in that house. The men don't have nothing to say. But you go outside, that's where the men's place is put. That's where you teach all

> your sons; everything from the outside. And the mom teach all their daughters things inside the house. And if they're outside, cutting fish and stuff, they're putting away meat, and what they're gonna be eating, she teach them that. And all the men, they go out there and get the food and carry it home. [The women] take care of it.

Wassily noted how much he'd learned from the elders in Kalskag:

> And I listen to a lot of people. Kalskag was the one I learned the most. Even though I had my stepdad, my uncles; they teach me all this stuff for upriver.
>
> Working at the city office [in Kalskag], elders coming in every day at the city office, about six or eight of 'em. Come sit down. And I was pretty much fluent in Yup'ik, and I explain all the paperwork in Yup'ik.
>
> And when they see that I'm doing something wrong, they say, "You should try to do it this way. Or do it that way. Try it out." I don't have a piece of paper saying I could do all these things. I learn from those guys. You know, where I'm going wrong. And I try to fix it.

John also recalled listening to stories: "From the villagers, when I traveled with them, I used to listen to old people tell stories. Sometimes while they were talking, I would fall asleep. When I wake up, they'd be still talking." Wassily had experienced the same thing: "When I used to travel, especially upriver, and stop and camp with people I know; and the stories they told. And sometimes stay up all night listening to them talking about things. They call 'em *qulirat* [traditional tales]."

Speaking about storytelling brought stories to mind. Wassily recalled:

> There was one story I used to hear long ago. Quite a few people used to tell it. This guy was up at his trapping cabin, and he got sick. There was this person that come and brought him food, let him eat. And he did that morning and evening, come in and bring him food and go out. And he was getting his strength back.
>
> And one evening he decided to look when that person went out. Went out, open the door, and he turn into a camp robber. 'Cause he was getting fish and meat, all kinds of stuff for him; vegetables.
>
> 'Cause he would feed them birds. He used to let 'em eat whatever. Even leave some food outside, never hide no food from them. And they say that's how that bird repaid him when he got sick. That's just a story that I used to hear.

Wassily asked if others had heard similar stories, where an animal helped a person who had helped them in the past. Michael recalled a story of Crow helping people during starvation:

> My mom used to tell me story about the crows. Crow did that and save one village back during starvation. They all got sick, and Crow take off some place, go find blackfish, bring it to 'em one at a time. They cook, eat soup, they get healthier. And he follow that Crow all the way 'til they got to the blackfish and brought them back to the village. And they cook for the village people that were sick; show it to them. My mom used to tell us that story.

Finally Mark added the story of how a fox helped people in need:

> There's one about fox; like that, when a person needed help, it allowed him to go into its house and helped him. Then when it was getting ready to send him home, it said to the person, when he left its house and got little ways away, to look back. It told him to look at the one who helped him. As told, when he looked back, he saw a red fox. Apparently, it was the fox who had helped him to survive.

Listening to stories reminded Wassily of storytelling in Crooked Creek when he was young: "You missed the better ones in the past. They had good ones. No matter, they'd sit down and talk. There used to be like a story time in Crooked, mainly in the wintertime. Go to one house. All the boys in one house, and all the girls in another house, tell stories." Marie asked if this was organized by the church, and Wassily said no:

> It was pretty much set up by the people in the community. It was just like a class, kind of teach us. But they had stories. Some of them were happy stories, some of them were sad stories. And then, lots of dos and don'ts.
>
> I used to remember this one story 'cause I was a little boy and there was lots of young men. They used to tell us, "If you cross paths with a girl while walking, [don't walk downwind].
>
> They said if a boy walked on the windward side of the girl, the smell would go on you. And then if you go hunting you wouldn't catch nothing. So every time it was windy we used to go around, never have the wind from the woman to us. When the boys go that way, "Hey, you gonna be bum hunter! Bear always will smell you." We always go around.

When he was young, Mark had received the same advice from Nelson Island elders, as had his father before him. A man's relations with animals always depended on the attention he paid to his relations with other humans, both women and men. This was no less true on the middle Kuskokwim than along the coast of southwest Alaska.

Traveling on the middle Kuskokwim

Along with conversations about hunting and fishing, we spent time looking over maps and recording both Yup'ik and English names for places the men knew well. John, Michael, and Wassily have all traveled extensively along the middle Kuskokwim. They know the country and shared anecdotes from their travels, bringing home the unique character of each community.

Beginning with Kalskag, we worked our way upriver. Michael began: "Upper Kalskag was just a trading post. Paul Kameroff, that was his trading post there. In the '30s, I think they moved from Paimiut on the Yukon to Kalskag. Lower Kalskag is original Kalskag. All the people all lived there." Wassily continued:

> Lower Kalskag, they used to call it Ayimqeryaraq, and they still do. They got old village [Qalqaq], couple miles down on the old river right above Mud Creek. And what I've heard is that they moved up to where Lower Kalskag is now because of the epidemic, late 1940s. And all the people in Upper were from Yukon. From Holy Cross, Anvik, Grayling, Shageluk, and Paimiut; they moved to Upper.
>
> So, those two villages are just three miles apart. And if they combine the two villages, they would be the biggest village in the TKC region, over 500 people. That's what I understand.

Michael recalled the first school built in Upper Kalskag:

> In the early 1930s, I think they were gonna build a school for Lower Kalskag. And springtime they brought [the lumber for] that school in. Then everybody was gone in Lower. They were out spring camp, they all went out springtime to get subsistence food and at fish camps.
>
> And that old Paul Kameroff, the one that had a trading post, tell them to build the school in Upper Kalskag. That's how they got that school. Supposed to be for Lower. They didn't know where to unload it, so they listened to that old man. But that's the story of how Upper Kalskag started, with a trading post and then the school. 'Cause [Upper Kalskag] is closer from Kalskag to Yukon, 40 miles. You would just cross over [to the

> Yukon] to that trading post there. So people went back and forth, hunting and traveling, trade fur and get goods from there.
>
> Lower Kalskag was called Ayimqeryaraq and Upper Kalskag was Kessigliq [Kalskag Hill, from *kessik*, "close to the river"].

Michael remembered Paul Kameroff, known in Yup'ik as Kelevyaq, who had his own small barge to bring goods upriver to his trading post: "I tell the kids how lucky they are, they got store in the villages now. They just don't believe me, what we was going through. Springtime we run out of stuff; run out of groceries; flour, sugar, lard, and whatever. When I tell them that, springtime like this, we almost had nothing to eat. We survive though."

Paul Kameroff Sr. standing by the shelter cabin between Tuluksak and Kalskag, February 1940. *ASL.P306.0409*

Wassily shared a brief history of his birthplace, Chuathbaluk:

> I can tell you a little story about Chuathbaluk. It used to be called Little Russian Mission. That church on the Kuskokwim by the Russian Mountains was named after that Russian Mission on the Yukon. That's why they called it Little Russian Mission. And they keep making mistakes, so they change the name to Chuathbaluk [Curarpalek, meaning] "big blueberries," even they're small.
>
> And where I was born in Chuathbaluk, it's a little bit different. In Chuathbaluk, they followed the seasons. They had the tundra on the south side and another tundra on the north side; the Russian Mountains are there [on the north side of the Kuskokwim]. And they used to go across [the Kuskokwim] to spring camp. Springtime they come down Aniak River and then come up [to Chuathbaluk]. And same way with the other side; they did the same thing and come down, they call it Urraat [River]; come down, above Aniak.
>
> It was pretty much, people go up [the Urraat River] spring camp and then they come down, hunting muskrats and stuff. Seems to me that's pretty much where muskrat ends; Aniak and other side and goes downriver. And then Urraat. That was it.

Wassily explained that Crow Village was the ancestral home of many people in Chuathbaluk today. As with the original residents of Lower Kalskag, "Crow Village Sam" moved his family upriver following an epidemic, settling on the south side of the Kuskokwim, across from the Orthodox church:

> [The present site of] Chuathbaluk was nothing in there. I think before I was born, everybody moved from Crow Village; down there in Aniak, up on the other side where the sawmill is, that's where I was born.
>
> Because of the epidemic, they moved [to the south side of the Kuskokwim]. Same way with Lower Kalskag; and that's the history of Chuathbaluk. And there was only one house there and the Orthodox Church [on the north side of the Kuskokwim]. One person take care of the church, and everybody was on the [south] side of the river. So, they moved over to the church side, because there were times when they can't come across for Easter or Orthodox services. And the church had 40 acres there that they claimed. And everybody had to go around.

Wassily later noted that Canoe Village was also depopulated by an epidemic, with people moving upriver to Crooked Creek: "Canoe Village used to be big.

Crooked Creek used to be small, just fish camps. Everybody lived in Canoe Village on the north bank, all the way down to right about Uskuralek. And that mountain, where it looks like upside down canoe. They call the village down there Canoe Village. Same way, during that epidemic everybody moved to Crooked."

When Marie and I had visited Crooked Creek in August 2023, people had mentioned a rock outcrop just above the village called Quliraq. Wassily told us the story behind it:

> There's a bluff, and right above there, they call it Quliraq. There used to be a rock house, slab about that thick on that hill. And somebody used to live up there. They say some kind of *angalkuq* or something. And if you climb up and look down, there's a round hole. That's that Quliraq's water hole, in that *kuignayuk* [valley with a stream]. That round hole in the bottom, you can see it from up there.
>
> They say that Sam Parent's brother, Dennis, shoot that guy up there and he rolled down; he kill that guy. I don't know, there was something that person up there used to do to the people that's coming up. They used to never talk about it that much, 'cause they were scared of him.
>
> That guy was like a medicine man, *angalkuq*. Then after he shot him, Sam Parent had that store. He had to take a piece of rock from up there and put it in the basement of his roadhouse, where he had his store. He had to put it down there. Otherwise, they were cursed because his brother had killed that person.
>
> They call that [big rock] Quliraq. Them Parents don't talk about it. 'Cause Sam Parent is originally from Sleetmute. That's my wife's cousin.
>
> Even after he passed away, his daughter and her husband, they kept that rock down there. They used to put stuff in there. Next day it would be gone.
>
> Food, things. *Aviukarrluku* [giving an offering of food and water] in order for them to keep that building safe.
>
> No [it's not still there.] They [bull]doze it over; and after that, they left that stone down there. They covered and buried it. And a Catholic priest was there, I guess, he blessed that place. And they don't build, there's nothing in there where they tore that building down. That's a story I used to hear.
>
> And evening time when you're walking, especially when it's calm and getting kind of dark, you'd be walking and the rock make noise. They tell us to tell 'em, "Leave us alone, we're not bothering you." They go. I guess, still to this day it's like that. People walk by. Now there's a road, they're going [along], and rock would roll down in front of them.

Speaking of Quliraq reminded Wassily of another place, just upriver from Crooked Creek, where people never camp:

> There's a place underneath the hill below Eight Mile [Slough]. There's a big hill and a little stream in there. And people don't camp in there.
>
> But they always see *alangruq* [ghost] all the time below Eight Mile Slough, if you camp in there. They said somebody was coming down, and when they get to that place, they killed somebody and left him and went. That's the ghost of that place. I had forgot about all those stories 'til you mention it.

Continuing upriver past Red Devil and Sleetmute, our group spent time talking about the Holitna River and its tributaries. Wassily spoke of places on the river where people drown but are never found:

> You know, Holitna is pretty country, it's a very pretty country. But the stories they have about the river, it's amazing. People drown in that Holitna River. They never find 'em.
>
> Even that lady, up in Holitna. Her son drowned right around her place. And they never find him. Even they look all over. They pretty much knew where, but they never did find him....
>
> Her name is Nas. She live in Holitna [below Nuugmiut] with the Ignaty boys. Ignaty brothers were farther up.
>
> [She lived] alone after her husband died, she's originally from Aniak. She was Alexie Morris's aunt. When her husband died, she put him in a boat and paddled down to Sleetmute. Two days from that place, never stop day and night. They brought her back; she never left. She's one tough lady, that woman.

Wassily had also heard stories of shamans on the Holitna, around Nuugmiut:

> I guess there used to be lots a shamans up there. I was mentioning little bit about Golga Sakar. He was trapping with his mom and dad up in Tetno. And this one guy coming down towing a sled was farther upriver in Tetno. When he stopped they feed him, and ask him, "Do you have provisions?"
>
> No provisions; nothing. Just a little pup, little dog. And Golga Sakar said he always hear that guy is a shaman. So he said he run in the woods behind watching him [when he left]. He was pushing his little sled and start chanting some kind of tune. He can't take off, stop and look around.

[Golga was] hiding behind trees, watching him. He never see nobody, so he go. And the second time he stop and look around, [Golga] was [thinking,] "I better go back."

They were getting ready to go to Sleetmute from Tetno. So he went back and they go. They watch where that guy was going, and he was putting that sled in deep. And [the sled runners] get less and less pressure, and pretty soon there was no more [sled tracks].

They go home. And above Sleetmute before they get to see the houses or anything, they see like [sled tracks] land, deeper and deeper. And when they get to Mellick's store, he was ready to go back home. 'Cause he was

The mouth of the Holitna River, just above Sleetmute, at sunset, 1947. *Don Horter Glass Lantern Slides, Anchorage Museum B2017.011.159*

funny. I forget the tune he was singing, but he couldn't take off because somebody was watching him.

That old man [Golga] had so much stories, holy smokes. I don't remember most of 'em. That's the only one that I always remember, but he laughs like crazy when he tells it.

Continuing toward the Hoholitna, everyone recalled both the Stone Woman located there as well as the Stone Woman on the Ulukaq River. John has seen both of them. He noted that the Hoholitna Arnassagaq was called Amartuli. Speaking of the Stone Woman on the Ulukaq, John said: "When we see it, she seems to have a pack on her back. They used to say it was a baby." Wassily added: "The only thing I always hear is to give her *aviukaq* [an offering of food and water].... Every time I pass, I give an offering. I see some guys go by. I go and say, 'Help me. My children will get hungry.' And I go. Couple of hours later I see moose." John had a similar experience: "We used to stop for a while up there, taking some of their provisions, they'd take a little and bury them under a spruce tree. And after praying, we'd leave. Sometimes we'd get several black bears from that area, from below it."

Travel routes

Looking over maps reminded the men not only of particular places but of the many routes people traveled in the past, up into the mountains and then back down river valleys, searching for animals. Wassily described men traveling up the Aniak River in the fall, then portaging over to the Holitna:

They used to tell stories in Chuathbaluk, those Phillips, Ciquyaq. Golga Kelila, people from downriver come in the fall, during winter before beaver season. They go up Aniak River; they call that place Paqcetaaq [lit., "Place to look around," from *paqte-*, "to go to check"], that creek that [branches off of the Aniak River].

Above Napaimute is Ulukaq River.... One winter I see Mark [Leary]. They blaze the trail with ax. I seen some [blaze marks] way up high; pretty good size tree. 'Cause I used to do that, you know, blaze. Putting a marker on the tree.

So, I followed 'em all the way, through head of Ulukaq River. And here's Uskuralek [River]. And then they cross over on land to Holitna. And then that creek that they come down on, cross over. They call it Tan'gerlim Terr'a where they portage over. There's the Kilbuck Mountains in there.

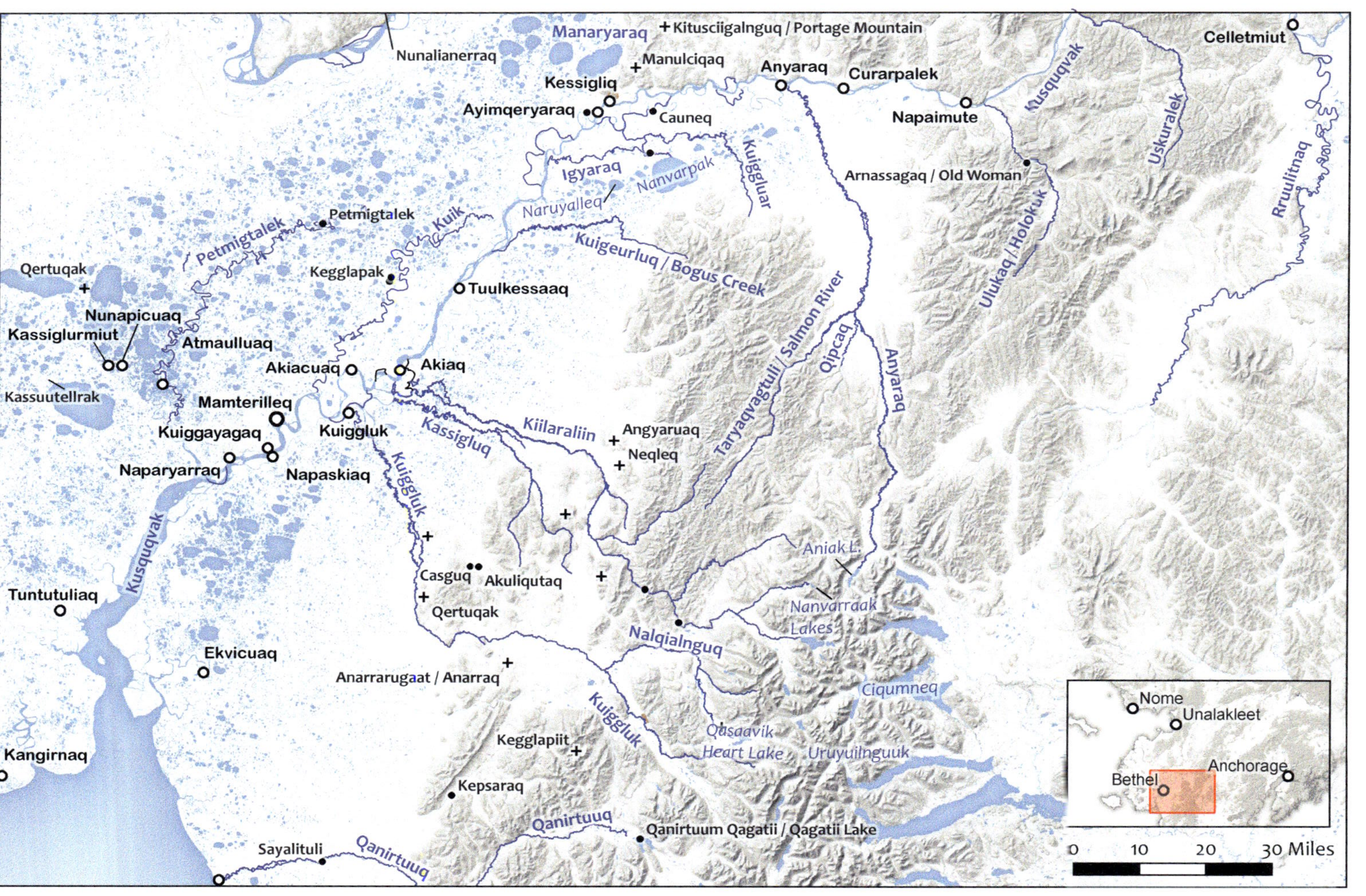

Mountains in Southwest Alaska. *Ian Moore and Jen Jolliff*

> And that's the lowest part right there where they portage over. And there's camps all the way down to [Holitna]. You can tell where they had camps.

Michael observed: "I hear about that, my dad and them go to that area." Wassily had traveled there, following the blazed trail. John commented: "Yes, I used to see some of them in that area. They used to say that upriver people hunted in that area, all the way through, from up Napaimute and down as far as Kalskag."

Wassily and John had solved the mystery of how "Buckstock" Creek, a tributary of Aniak River, got its English name. Wassily said: "Paqcetaaq [from *paqte-*, "to go to check"]. Always call it, you look over there. When those guides and services, they start going there, they changed the name to Buckstock. Long ago before them guys come in, they called it Paqcetaaq. Where they look."

John noted that Kwethluk hunters also traveled to the Holitna through the mountains:

> And those who lived with me in Kwethluk, they used to go up the Kuiggluk River to Kassigluq by dogsled, then up to Aniak Lake. My father and my brothers trapped for beaver in that area, before [beaver] became numerous downriver. Sometimes [they traveled] over to Tikchik Lake and back. Take them about two months, over and back. Trap and come back up in February and come back in March. And if some went up, they have relatives up in Chuathbaluk.... He'd go through it from somewhere in Aniak Lake, they'd portage over and go to the headwaters of Holitna. They'd come down from there....
>
> And on the way back, they said they'd trade off the skins to Chuathbaluk. They'd trade with Qiuryaar's family and get a round [bottomed] boat. They'd leave Kwethluk in the springtime, trail got bad; too much water; deep snow. They end up going upriver so they can come down to the Kuskokwim through Holitna. Then after they traded their skins for a round boat, they went home by it.

John noted that round-bottomed boats were only made by people in Chuathbaluk, Crooked Creek, and Sleetmute:

> Sometimes up there, I'd see little short, round boats. But they go pretty fast. They looked dangerous; they were too small. [*chuckling*]
>
> In Chuathbaluk the family of Qiuryaar came to our place using those kinds of boats.

Round-bottomed boats were narrow in the back and wider in the middle, and were used for shallow rivers. Wassily explained: "They made them like that so when they go into shallow water, the back end comes up." John said they were called *cauyaralget* (ones/boats with *cauyarat*, "curved ribs"). Wassily recalled: "They used young, thin birch for the ribs. They cut 'em in half. They get 'em maybe in springtime...because they bend easy.... And then during the winter, they make the frame of the boat. And they tie them. By springtime it's done."

John also described hunters traveling through the headwaters of the Aniak River:

> And those two, over around North Fork lake [on the Kiseralek River]. People from Akiak used to come through Anyaraq Lake and go down here to this area.

Round-bottomed boat pulled up alongside a float plane near Sleetmute, 1948. The man standing in the back of the boat was identified as Gusty Gusty during AFN 2014. *Don Horter Photographs, Anchorage Museum B2014.016.2004*

> They say that these rivers that start out down there [on the Kuskokwim] join together up around here [in the Kilbuck Mountains].
>
> [Aniak River] goes up, and it ends at its lake source. On the upper end there's narrow and shallow streams.
>
> People from Akiak have said that they traveled through that way to come [to Cikumneq Lake] to go hunting, they used to cross Aniak Lake and continue traveling and get to Cikumneq.
>
> They said they used to go up that way to meet up with hunters from Kwethluk, because it was easier to travel.

People also traveled from the Bristol Bay area to the Holitna. John continued:

> I've heard stories, too, that they used to travel through Tikchik Lake and cross over to reach Holitna River....

Round-bottomed boat on the Kuskokwim, 1948. *Don Horter Glass Lantern Slides, Anchorage Museum B2017.011.158*

> People from New Stuyahok have said that their ancestors are from Akiak and Tuluksak....
>
> The headwaters of these rivers are joined together up inside these high hills, like behind Chuathbaluk.

Pellat / *Places where one gets lost*

Talk of traveling led into stories of places where people need to take special care, lest they circle around and come back to where they began. Such places, called *pellat*, are found throughout southwest Alaska. Over the years, elders have shared many stories, to help their young people recognize potential danger. Wassily gave an example: "There's a place in Holitna. They always tell us not to go back into the trees, just go on top of the bank. If you go in the trees, you start hearing somebody, and you'll go and go and go and get lost. And you'll try to come, and you can't. If you do come back, you'll be way down below, where you had gone in. Or way above."

John was also carefully admonished about traveling in wooded areas and the dangers of places where one could get lost:

> Also, in the lakes where one can get disoriented and lose direction. They told us not to go inside wooded areas and wander around. They'd say in certain areas inside, you can get disoriented and get lost. When we go across some of the lakes, especially during a ground blizzard, we sometimes can't see what's up ahead. While going we'd lose direction and find ourselves in the same spot where we had been and see our tracks.
>
> When that happens, we were told to stop moving. Then I'd tell my traveling companions to stay put while I continue forward and tell them to continue on behind me if I don't return to the same spot again.
>
> When we all traveled together forward, we'd make a circle and find ourselves back at the spot we had started. But, if I go across alone, I'd make it. As I moved forward, I'd look back and see them because I had told them to keep their snowmachine lights on. When I get to the other side, since I had a little flashlight, I'd turn it on and signal them to come forward. Some lakes aren't big, but they have those "dark spots," *pellat* [places where one gets lost].

John's father told him what to do when they became disoriented and lost in a *pellat*, wandering into another dimension:

> The lakes do have beginning and ending markers, but sometimes when

The Holitna seen from the air, May 2024. *AFR*

there's a blizzard, we can't see the markers. The same thing can happen to you when you wander in the woods.

A little farther up, one time in the late fall while hunting moose, at the time when there weren't a lot of moose, we followed the tracks of a moose. While going, we'd come to a little river and continue across wading. Soon, the river got very narrow, and we could just step over it. While going I'd recognize this one tree, and when I see it I'd tie [something] on it to mark it.

Then, I think it was on the fourth time, we stopped and my late father said this, "We are lost. Stop." And when we stopped he told me to take off my *qaspeq* and turn it inside out. He also turned his *qaspeq* inside out. Then he said, "Climb up that tree there and look and tell me where the mountains are." I climbed up and looked. I saw mountains that I couldn't recognize. I turned and looked towards Kwethluk, a little ways down. When I came down from the tree, I said, "Our boat is way down there. We evidently traveled way up here."

> And yet, we had kept going and finding ourselves back at the spot where we had started in the beginning. Somehow, so many miles upriver, we had gotten out into a different dimension. That happened to us more than once. When we got lost and came out of that abyss, we'd be far away from where we had started. It took us all day long to walk back.
>
> And the little rivers we had waded across as we went. On the way back, they were wide rivers and quite deep, but we managed to cross them. It's no fun. It burn you out, especially if you go with other guys. Some get tired, and they'd get angry. I'd tell them, "If you go alone, you'll forever get lost in the woods. Got to stay right behind us." We have to stick together. Those spots were called *pellat*. Upriver in your area, you probably have *pellat*, too.

Wassily remarked that *pellat* were numerous in the flat country surrounding the Holitna. He said that the hills around Crooked Creek were easier to navigate: "Where I grew up there's nothing but hills. You can recognize places. But some people say they get lost. Knock on wood, I never get lost."

Language on the Middle Kuskokwim

Earlier in our conversations, Marie recalled that Pete Mellick's mother was from Nuugmiut, on the Holitna. Wassily noted that in Sleetmute, the older people called it Naagmiut, but as years went by it changed to Nuugmiut.

Contemplating changes over the years in the words people use, Wassily was reminded of linguistic differences along the length of the Kuskokwim. He commented that how fast you talk depends on the flow of the river:

> It makes it interesting, even the words are changing. How you talk, it change.
>
> And I've never really understand until not too long ago. When I was working in Donlin, people used to tell us how people talk, from the headwaters of the Kuskokwim to the mouth of the Kuskokwim. The farther up you go, they're Athabascan. They talk fast. And as you go down they get slower; they get Yup'ik and Athabascan, Yup'ik and English.
>
> And as you go farther down, you know the tides go in and out from maybe Akiachak or Akiak. And when you listen to everybody, when you go farther downriver, they start slurring words. Just like the water, go back and forth.
>
> And you go farther up that way, everybody talk fast. Come down. I don't know if you guys ever notice it. People in Kalskag used to tell me

when I first move over; people in Crooked used to tell me, "Listen." And I was just thinking about it, and it's true. Everywhere you go, maybe even in the Yukon how it is upriver, how they talk.

Mark also recognized different villages as having their own unique ways of talking:

> Back when I used to listen to elders, they used to say that back before people began moving from here to there, when you hear someone talking, you'd quickly know where they were from. Back in those days, people didn't travel to other places much, they kept their way and style of speaking.
>
> On Nelson Island it is that way, too. Those villages are close to each other, [but] their words are different. Newtok and Tununak, since they were always together, they use the same words. And Newtok speakers are slow. People from Tununak speak a little faster, but they share the same words. And Toksook and Nightmute, since they are also one, they are like that, too.
>
> And back when I was little, the mother of the Shavings family [from Nunivak Island] used to stay at my grandmother's house when she came. Cuukaq's son would bring her every year. And after listening to them talking, I asked my grandmother why they speak like they are singing. She told me that their voice goes up and down like waves in the ocean. And back then, listening to people from Nunivak Island, many of their words were different.
>
> And now, since they are moving around more, people from there are more adapted to mainland language. That's how people talk today and the difference. These clusters of villages, their words are similar, with some differences.
>
> Fred Augustine from Alakanuk said one time when we were meeting that even though villages are not far from each other, they have their own way of talking, and how they do things. Though they don't live far apart, they have their own ways. He mentioned that and said to be aware of that when we work with people, to respect their ways and how they do things.

Changing times

Our conversations over two days had focused on life along the middle Kuskokwim when John, Wassily, and Michael were young. They often reflected on the changes they had seen over the decades. While each village still retains its special character, they felt that the social fabric that held villages together in the past has weakened. Wassily observed:

> Each village is so different, no matter how close they are. They're so different in culture and how they do things. And when I was growing up, each village had certain families that do things. Like in Kalskag, my uncles used to be carpenters. So they build boats or houses.... Same way with Crooked Creek. They had people that build boats.
>
> It's not like that anymore. I don't know how to explain it. You guys can help me. It's so different on what used to be. Everybody is for their self. They're not for anybody else in the village.

Wassily had shared many examples of people harvesting animals and sharing with each other, "helping somebody that needs help":

> And they told us, in the future it's not going to happen anymore like that. No matter, your blood relative or brother or sister or cousins wouldn't be helping each other. They're going to be helping their selves only. And I wondered why they used to tell us that. But now I'm understanding why they told us that. It's happening right now out in the villages. And everywhere you go, it's for individual only.
>
> And something I always tell my kids, "You have to stay together and work together in order to make things happen." But everything is on paper. If you don't have piece of paper, you're nothing. You can't make the money that they're offering you. Even though you have everything in [your mind] or in [your heart]....
>
> When the Federal Government came in with welfare and food stamps, everything changed. Nothing was the same.
>
> And you can see the people in the villages kind of split. There's no more group. They never sit down and talk to you. They started splitting up.
>
> And it's a shame, you know, hard to see that. And older people that was alive then were telling us like that. They say, "*Kass'at* [white people], when they come, they'll separate you." Families will start thinking about only themselves, and pretty soon that one person only. And I seen that happen. And you can't help but feel bad.

On a lighter note, Wassily commented on how tall young people are today:

> Right now they comment, "How come the kids today are so tall?" They eat so much spaghetti. When you think about it, when we were

> growing up, we never ate much. We always work and work, and we never had much in our stomach. And that's how come we never grow. We stop at a certain point.
>
> I don't know if it's true or not. The work that we used to do with very little food. Kind of slow us down at a certain age. Nowadays, they don't do very much. We make sure they have food all the time.

John added with a smile: "And they sleep longer, too."

Thanks for sharing

Our conversations had been wide ranging, including detailed observations about growing up on the middle Kuskokwim. At the end of the day, we thanked everyone for coming, and all expressed gratitude for the opportunity both to share and to listen to each other's stories. I said with feeling: "This has been really fun. I've learned so much. My mind is full." Wassily remarked: "I really enjoyed it. It just bring out something that was held back." And John added: "You had held back and let it come out again." Mark said with a smile: "We are very happy you came. All of you; we are grateful you all came."

John captured what Mark, Marie, and I were all feeling: "I enjoy upriver people because in most of our meetings we hardly have people from upriver with us. I'm happy you two are here." Mark added: "Me too; when I listen, I have fun when I hear people from upriver talking. The villages down on the coast, they are different. The things we do down in the ocean are different." I observed, "It's so different, but there are a lot of similarities." These similarities included the importance of sharing food with everyone; the rule not to talk about animals one is hunting, as they hear through the ground; the view that if animals eluded a hunter he should return to the village, share what he had, and spend the night; the belief that the gratitude of elders will bring success; that men and women had different responsibilities and that a woman's "aura" could negatively influence a man; that there are places people tend to get lost, and turning one's garments inside out is one way to find your way back; that *aviuqaq* (giving an offering of food and water) will bring the hunter luck; and the deep respect people have for each other and their different ways. I summed it up: "It's fun to get together with people from different parts of the same river." John captured what we all knew well – no one could better tell the stories of the middle river than the people who were born and raised there: "Our forefathers used to share their hunting areas with their neighbors. But if they go to behind their place, you need to go to the village and go with someone that lives there." We had all been learning, together.

Circular beaded collar made by Bedusa Derendy and later sold to the Museum of the North by her daughter, Elena. *UA Museum of the North UA64-065-005, Micki LeClair Sievers*

Chapter 4

Visiting the Museum of the North: Exploring Middle Kuskokwim Collections

While our gatherings had taught us a great deal, we tried to think of new ways to work with middle Kuskokwim elders that would be of special interest to them. Our hope was that bringing elders from different villages together for a museum visit might evoke memories of past practices. It would also be fun to explore museum collections again, as all three of us – Mark John, Marie Meade, and I – had enjoyed our museum visits in the past. Our last museum visit had been in 2010 – more than a decade ago. How had times changed?

In fall 2023, I started writing to museums in Alaska – the Anchorage Museum, the Alaska State Museum in Juneau, the Sheldon Jackson Museum in Sitka, and the University of Alaska Museum of the North in Fairbanks – to find out what they had from the middle Kuskokwim, including both photographs and objects. The Anchorage Museum had several dozen photos, and they provided us copies. The University of Alaska museum in Fairbanks had a small but exciting collection of more than forty pieces from Sleetmute, Canoe Village (just below Crooked Creek), Aniak, and Kalskag. I worked with Angela Linn, the Museum's Senior Collections Manager of Ethnology and History, who generously sent us photos of the Kuskokwim material, and we scheduled two days in April to visit the UA Museum of the North.

Although it would be a short visit, planning took time – arranging housing, food, and transportation. We invited four knowledgeable elders we knew from past gatherings – Sophie Sakar from Chuathbaluk, Angie Kameroff from Sleetmute, Wassily Kameroff from Crooked Creek and Kalskag, and Jennie Zaukar from Crooked Creek and Sleetmute, with both Wassily and Jennie now living in Anchorage. Two weeks before the trip Sophie let us know that her health was not good and she couldn't join us. Her replacement, Agnes Andreanoff, also had health problems that prevented her from traveling. We were grateful that three elders would be able to make the trip. Angie was the only one flying into Anchorage, and we hoped that the spring weather would make traveling easy.

With Lake and Penn flights only on weekdays, we planned a week of activities, with Angie flying in on Monday, followed by a one-day gathering in Anchorage on Tuesday to give us time to meet before traveling, then up to Fairbanks on Wednesday morning. We would come home Thursday afternoon, with Angie flying home Friday. I'd originally hoped for a day at the Anchorage Museum, which also has a handful of pieces from the middle Kuskokwim, but that seemed like too much. Our plan worked.

Angie arrived safe and sound Monday afternoon, and I brought her home to be my guest for the night. We were all up bright and early Tuesday, and by 9 AM Mark arrived with Wassily Kameroff, Marie bringing Jennie soon after. We made ourselves comfortable in the living room, and Mark opened with a prayer: "We are praying that you give us a good mind as we work about our culture that our descendants will use. As we compile things, help us in our minds and show us something you know and feel important to pass on to the next generations."

We followed with the Lord's Prayer, then settled down to talk. Though all three elders are fluent in the Yup'ik language, they use it less today than in years past. As a result, most of our conversation was in English, combined with many Yup'ik names and terms, which we have rendered here as they were spoken, followed by an English translation. All three elders ended Yup'ik nouns in "s" (as in English) to form the plural, calling fish traps *taluyaqs* rather than *taluyat*, and snowshoes *tangluqs* rather than *tanglut* or *tangluk* (two snowshoes). This is standard on the middle Kuskokwim, and we respect their choices here.

Camping in spring

In keeping with the season, we started with a discussion of spring camping in the past. Wassily noted that upriver few people went spring camping, but that when he moved down to Kalskag in 1974 after he married, everyone went camping in the spring. Then he described his experience trapping muskrats south of Kalskag toward Whitefish Lake.

> There used to be lotsa muskrat. That's what they used to hunt. I went out couple times, and my friend showed me a *taluyaq* [conical wooden fish trap] on a tree. I pull it out, fix it up. And I find a cone, I fix that up.
>
> I didn't know which way to set it. I never set a *taluyaq* before for muskrat. Then I set that in a little narrow creek. And then somebody come by and say, "There's supposed to be another cone on that side." I said, "Oh yeah?"
>
> So we look around, and we found the other cone; fix it so that there'll be two when they come in on both sides. Man, it was so interesting, you

> know; go check traps and getting goose and duck eggs, swan eggs. And I check that trap every day for maybe four or five days....
>
> And that [trap] used to catch 50 muskrats a day; never catch pike. About fourth or fifth day, start catching pike. So, I took it out and put the *taluyaq* back in the tree, cones on the side.
>
> Then [that fall] I went berry picking, and I was telling my wife and them kids, "This is where I went spring camping, and over here there's a *taluyaq* on the tree, with cones." We look all over; there was no tree, no *taluyaq*. Everybody was sitting there and talking. And that one old guy come.
>
> You remember Nickoli Sergie? He was telling me that there used to be lots of people around here and down below Whitefish Creek, toward Tuluksak. And then on the other side, Johnson River. Most of the people from the villages used to go [spring camping]....
>
> Now I always feel funny that somebody gave me that *taluyaq* and them cones, and told me where to set 'em and how to set 'em. I never did see that guy again. Crazy, eh? But I had over 200 muskrats. They weren't bad, you know, five dollars a skin.

Angie noted, "That was our money maker – muskrat. There used to be lots right around Sleetmute." Jennie asked Wassily if they had skinned and dried all those muskrats, and he said that they did: "And the meat. Boy, everybody was happy when we go home. They get to eat muskrat." Jennie noted that upriver they called muskrat *ilegvak*, which was also the Yup'ik name given to her great-granddaughter.

Mark turned the conversation from muskrats to bears, noting that during this time of year bears start waking up and coming out of their dens. Angie commented: "Some of them gonna get up quick, 'cause their home get flooded, and they're gonna come out, whether they want to or not. Too wet, the house." Jennie noted: "We upriver people don't eat brown bears. We eat black bears, springtime up in George River." Wassily noted that on the George River, bear holes belonged to particular families, and that a father would pass them on to his sons. He agreed with Jennie that they were hunted in spring: "They come out about this time of the year. But they've been coming out earlier, I noticed. Last month they saw brown bear between Marshall and Russian Mission." Jennie added that not long ago a bear had been seen below Uskuralek. Wassily continued: "Back then Crooked Creek, Napaimute, Sleetmute, Stony – when they see brown bear that's close to the village, the people would go after it. They never let it come close to the village. Or wolves. When somebody say they see brown bear or bears close by, they all go get it. For the protection of the people, especially the kids."

Wassily then retold the story he'd shared in February of how when he was young, Joe Sakar bragged that he would kill a bear with his bare hands. That fall, a black bear grabbed him and held him until his companions finally killed the bear and freed him. Joe never faced a bear again:

> 'Cause they used to tell us, when we go out *yuilqumun* [to the wilderness] to go hunting, not to talk about what we're going after. When we talk, it go in the ground, it go and they hear us.
>
> Any animal, they hear us when we talk. And otherwise, we wouldn't see 'em. And then what happened to Joe. That bear hear 'em 'cause he was talking about it. After that, even we see bear and he's in the boat, he turns his back on them; *takaryugluniggug* [they say he was intimidated, feeling so much respect]. Embarrassed from him talking about doing what he was gonna do. Never eat bear meat no more. Never look. When he see bear, he turn away.

Jennie agreed: "They say those bears, animals have ground for ears. They know when we talk about them. We have to respect any kind of animals, even if they are small, 'cause they can hear us."

Speaking of respecting animals, Wassily recalled how when he was young, men spoke to the boys, while women spoke to the girls separately, at special times. He remembered being admonished never to walk downwind of a woman, or animals would smell him when he went hunting:

> We always wonder, "How come they smell us?"
>
> "And when they smell you 'cause you go downwind from that woman, that woman's scent go to you. No animals will go to you. You'll be bum hunter or bum trapper. Animals wouldn't go to you."
>
> And I watch them; uncle Johnny John, Ignaty, Golga. They'd be chuckling, but not laughing.... And I believe some of 'em, what they talk about.... They never explain why, they just tell us.

Angie then noted that animals talk:

> You know, them animals when they talk, when you're not watching them; you're inside the house or inside a tent. But you know they're outside. And if you listen, they talk like regular people.
>
> There were a bunch of wolves when we went moose hunting. And

> getting kind of cold in the evening. So them boys set a tent.
>
> While we're in there, just starting to eat, all of a sudden the tent collapsed. Boy, those two boys run out, and I go to the gas stove, and I put the tent up like that so it wouldn't burn. "Grandma, are you watching the fire?" "Yep. Hurry up, I'm getting tired." They reset it. And then after that we went to bed.
>
> And I woke up in the middle of the night, and I was gonna get up and go outside. And I hear this voice, "It's okay. You can go back to sleep. Nobody will bother you." And I turn around and go back to sleep. And at the time it didn't dawn on me to be afraid. But next morning when we got up, so many wolf tracks. They were all around us, and they never even bother us. But they were talking, like us, you know; regular talk.

Jennie asked for confirmation, "You heard them?" Angie replied: "Yeah. Maybe fourth or fifth time I hear them talking. I never did hear a bear talk. I hear 'em grumble. But I never did hear 'em talk. Only wolves, only wolves are the talkers."

Marie then asked if there were many wolves near Sleetmute. Angie replied: "They are starting to come into the village now, right around the edge; tied up dogs, they kill 'em right there where they're tied up. And they only kill the females. They don't kill the males."

Returning to the topic of springtime, Angie described her family's movements in spring:

> We used to always go up to our winter camp [at Cotton Village] because we know there's lots of animals there. So we'd always go up there.
>
> But from the time the snow melt and you can get logs together, we used to gather them. And when we think it's safe enough to go down, then we'd start drifting with the raft. And all our food, it was covered up with tarps on different places in the raft.

Years later, Angie's father moved his winter camp and built a cabin downstream below a horseshoe bend in the Hoholitna that kept bringing them back to the same place:

> Why they made it there was 'cause every time we left that place, there was horseshoe. And we always come back to the same place; no matter if we go down, we come back to the same place. So my dad said, "If it wants to bring us here, we're gonna build right here." So that's what we did.

> But Cotton Village was a good place, but now I think it's all underwater. 'Cause I can't find it.

Village life

Angie noted that there were at least seven cabins at Cotton Village, but that the bank had eroded since they moved away. She mentioned again the Slaaviq that seven families spent there one year when deep, powdery snow prevented them from traveling to Sleetmute.

> There was how many of 'em. Ap'a [Grandfather], and Golga and Big Boy in one house. Ap'a Peter in another one. Ap'a Miska in another one. Us in one. Mambo's family in another one.
>
> They used to always like to be around us, I don't know how come. You know how some people, they like to adopt people, and then they want to stay with that family. She was like that. I forget who else. Oh, Ap'a Chief.

Ap'a Chief, Miska Simeon, was the chief of the village, but as Jennie noted, everybody used to call him Ap'a Chief. Angie's dad, Steve Derendy became second chief to Ap'a Chief, becoming chief when Miska passed away. Ap'a Jack followed Steve Derendy, and Jennie's husband, Peter Zaukar, followed Ap'a Jack. There was no other chief after Ap'a Pete. Angie described the relationship between her family and Jennie's:

> [Jennie's] husband was my mom's mom's brother. So my mom called him uncle. But I always called him Ap'a because that's what they taught me when I was small. There was four of them. My grandma, Balassa Zaukar, Miska Zaukar, and Peter Zaukar. Four of them in one family.

Jennie explained that the men were chiefs in the church, *tuyuq* (lay pastor, village chief). Wassily added detail:

> Most of the villages, from Chuathbaluk up[river], the [Russian Orthodox] church used to be the main center. And whoever is the chief from the church is the main person. He's like the mayor, you know; work for the community. And that's what the chiefs used to do. Just like Uncle Johnny John [at Crooked Creek], Ignaty; they were brothers.
>
> And in Chuathbaluk, there was Ap'a Sam, that Crow Village Sam. After the church was built, he was the one that was staying there by the church to take care of it. But they're originally from Crow Village, down below Aniak. And they were too far from the church, so they moved up to

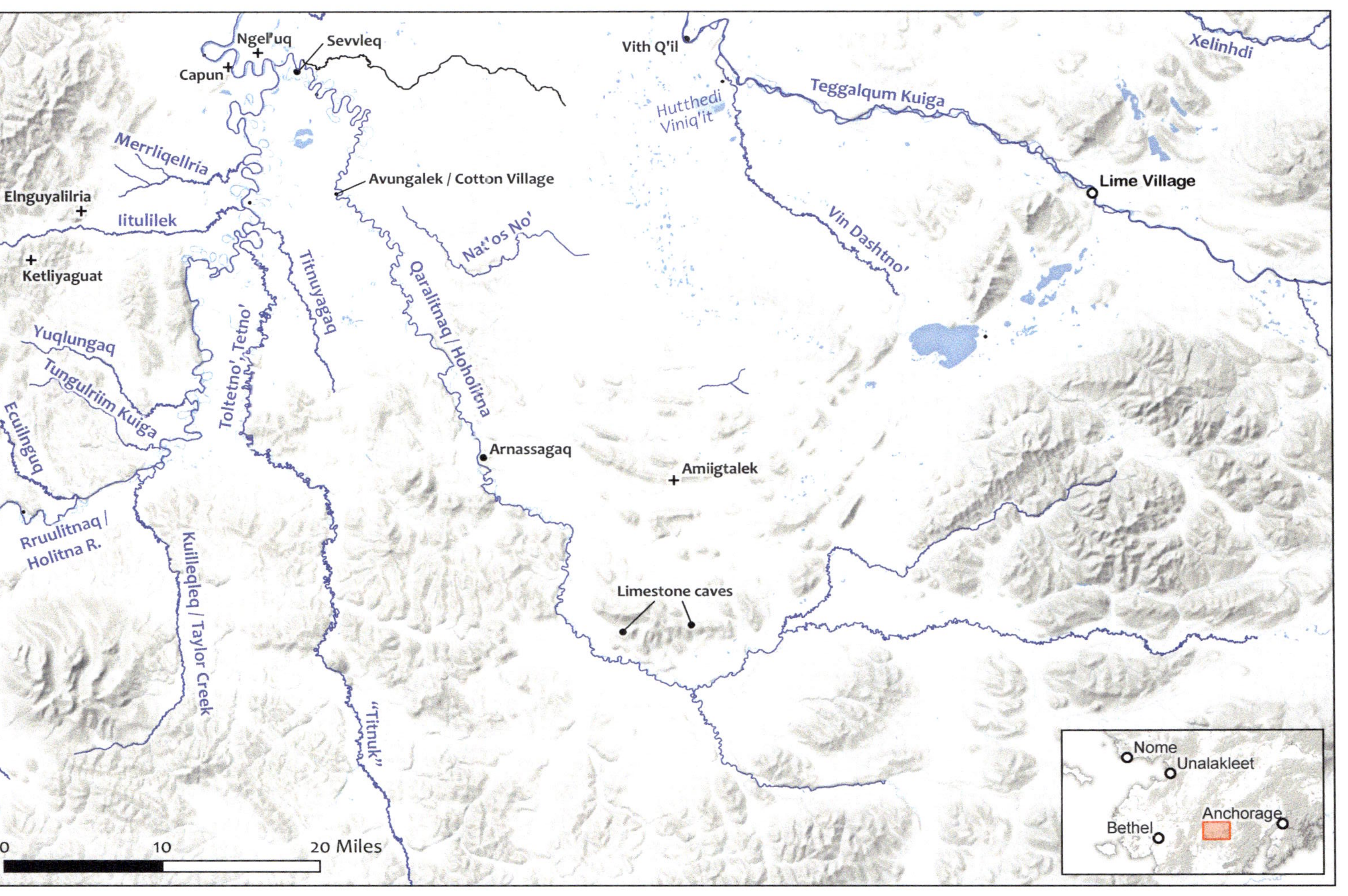

Holitna and Hoholitna Rivers south of Sleetmute. *Ian Moore and Jen Jolliff*

Johnny John of Crooked Creek. *ASA.SR55.VS947*

> other side of Chuathbaluk where the church had 40 acres of land that they claimed.
>
> And the chiefs of the village, the church, were the ones that took care of the village, and the problems, the discipline, and talking to families. And then they have that sisterhood. The brotherhood take care of all the boys and men, and the sisterhood take care of all the women and children. That's how it was run.

Wassily noted that this was true in Chuathbaluk, Crooked Creek, Sleetmute, and Stony River. Marie asked how they decided who would be chief, and Jennie replied: "They appoint. They would have meetings. And they would appoint a person for the community." Since Land Claims, however, everything has changed, with land ownership codified. Wassily reiterated how hunting territories were known in the past:

> When we went trapping, there was all these places all the way down, and on the other side of George River. And everybody go to certain area, and they trap on both sides of the river. Sometime they meet in there, and they have lunch. Nobody used to lock up their cabins. Everybody stays. You know, if it get dark and they stop in somebody's cabin, they stay there. And before they leave, they put back the wood that they were using, and then they go. And everybody respected each other. There was no "I," "mine." It was all ours, 'cause we take care of each other. And families used to help each other.

Wassily continued: "Let's use Kameroffs [as an example]. Kameroffs take care of themselves, with their families and stuff. And then when they have leftover, they help other families. And that's how it happened." Wassily remembered Angie's family's camp well, as Angie's dad was the only one who had a cache with only one leg. Angie described her family's camp on the Hoholitna:

> Up at our place we used to have the house, bath house, and a cache. But before we leave this place, all the edibles, everything we wanted to save, we bring it up to the cache.
>
> And then when we leave, my dad would take the ladder off and hang it on a nearby tree. And if somebody wanted something from our cache, it was okay for them to take it. But in return, they would leave something else. You know, if they take something, they put something there. Every

> time we got to the cabin long ago, my dad used to always go check the cache first. And then he'd holler at mom, "We had visitors when we were gone."

Angie mused: "All those places that we used to go long time ago, you can barely recognize them anymore because of the growth, you know, everything growing. They say, 'It get *umcik* [closed up, from *umcig*, 'to be airtight'].'"

I asked Wassily if the cabins on the George River were still standing, and he said most had collapsed as the river changed course and its banks eroded. River changes led to a brief discussion of rivers silting up and getting shallower. Angie noted that the mouth of the Hoholitna is now so shallow, if you get stuck you'll have to wait for rain forever. No tides upriver to help you off. Wassily then told a story of an older woman from downriver visiting in Kalskag: "She had chair, sitting down and had stick along the water. Aggie and I and the kids were going down. 'What are you doing?' 'I'm waiting for high tide.'"

Angie commented on the constant water levels upriver, varying only with rain and snow melt: "When you're from way upriver and you go somewhere where there's tide, you are really amazed, you know, 'cause the water keeps going up and down. And at home the water just stay in one [place]. It's right here, it's gonna stay right here. It wouldn't mess around and go up and down." Mark followed with a story of Willie Pete coming down to Bethel from upriver: "And he got to Bethel at high tide, and then he went to the store. And when he came back, the tide had gone down. And he was angry because he thought someone pulled up his boat."

Moose hunting

Our conversation turned to moose hunting, and Wassily told a story about what to do when one of your family members is sick:

> I hear that, too. When your family members are sick and don't have very much longer, when you go hunting with people, you don't shoot. Let them guys shoot. But if you gonna shoot, you tell them, "Don't shoot it if I'm gonna shoot."
>
> And it happened to me. Them guys never see nothing. I stayed behind. And we stopped. They tell me, "You go ahead, we never see nothing." And I tell them, "If I see moose and I shoot it, don't shoot." Go around the bend, moose stand up, in wintertime, I shoot it and it's just dropping. Somebody shoot it, and man, it just get up, it took off, run after it, and I shoot it up close and it fall. [I asked them,] "Who shoot?" This young kid

> said, "Me." "I tell you guys not to shoot, 'cause my uncle is sick, don't have very much longer." We skin it out, we go.

Wassily and his companions stayed at Crooked for the night, then headed back to Kalskag early the next day, arriving around 10 PM. His wife told him his uncle wanted to see him: "I get dressed and I walk over, and I go in. Them guys were around him. He tell me, 'Ah, you got one.' I tell him, 'Yeah.' Take his hand, he tell me, 'Good, you catch moose.' I tell him, 'Yeah.' He turn his head and pass away. He had wait for me to get home."

Speaking of moose reminded Angie and Wassily of stuffing and cooking moose colon. Wassily explained:

> They call it *anautii* [its colon]. It had the fat inside, and you have your grinder. Fill it up with raw moose meat, ground moose meat. Bake it in the oven.... I use bread pan. I cooked them one time for Slaaviq. Everybody look at it. But I slice 'em, [at an] angle. When them old people grab 'em, man they eat. Stuff it with peppers and stuff. Sam Savage and my auntie, "You have some more?" "No."
>
> Man, that's what they used to do long ago. They'd fill up the whole moose colon, and they cook it like that.

Wassily noted that moose stomach was also good: "It's kind of rubbery, but they taste pretty good. That's [called] the towel." Jennie said that it looks just like a *kaapaq* (beaded hairnet). Angie added: "They used to call it *erurciigalnguq* [lit., "one that can't be washed"], can't wash 'em." Jennie continued: "When you get it, wash it very well so you won't taste the willow, and freeze it. Then boil it with fat or meat. You always see those beef tripe. They look like that." Mark noted that Qaillukayak at Toksook had always asked him to bring home the *qecaruaq* (stomach lining, tripe) when he went moose hunting: "You'd take out the contents and turn it inside out and bring it down to the river to wash it. Pack it, and when we get home, we'd bring it to him. And one time when he shared it with me, it was good."

Speaking of moose led to comments about buying meat at Red Apple in Anchorage, where Mark buys beef heart and pig tongue to mix with moose meat for soup for his crew in Bristol Bay: "Those beef tongues are so expensive. So, I just get pork tongue. They're okay." Wassily added: "Moose tongue is the best." Jennie asked if Mark ever takes the moose nose, and he replied: "No. We don't know moose, 'cause we never had moose [on the coast].... *Kanartut-gguq* [They say they are going down to the water]. Going down from higher to lower level. And once they reach the lower region, they would disappear." In fact, today, moose are moving to the coast, while the population upriver has declined, due to both wolves and brown bears.

Respect

Continuing our conversation about women affecting a man's ability to hunt, Jennie observed: "You have to respect and take good care of it instead of just letting it lay around and rot. You have to respect any kind of animal including fish." Wassily observed:

> The thing that they used to say to us is that the family is affected by how the man take care of them. When we were growing up we were taught. I remember Big Feller, when we're over on village side, telling stories, "When you boys are growing up and you guys get married and have children, you gonna take care of the family; outside of the house, that's your responsibility. You build that house up for your wife and your kids. Inside the house, she's the boss. You can't say nothing." You catch meat; you hang 'em up outside. She wants this one, you gotta go get it and bring it in. And she'll take care of it.
>
> Everything you take care of, everything you do for your family, it's up to you. It's not nobody's business but yours. And when other families need help, you help them. But you gotta ask, tell your wife first, "These people over here, they have nothing." And she'll be the one that take that portion and say, "Okay. Give them this one."
>
> That was the thing we were taught. 'Cause it's always two groups when we were growing up – there was the young women and girls and women, and them young boys and men. And they talk to us, they tell us.
>
> But if you go and catch something, but you never take everything, you leave some, never help nobody, then you'll affect your family. That's how we were told all the time.

I summarized, "What a man does really affects his family." Wassily added: "It affects the village, too. Especially the head of the village we call a chief. That person is the most respected person in the village. And they're the ones that give directions. And if he know there's a family that is having hard time, when they get together, they say to give a portion to the family to help 'em out."

As an example of sharing within the village, Wassily described how one person had a large *taluyaq* (conical fish trap) at Crooked Creek: "And everybody used to help out, the whole community. Call the men, and they go and do the ice picking, and all the women come back, and in the back, they cook up things. The whole village help out." Angie recalled the same thing at Sleetmute:

> They used to have three *taluyaqs* in Sleetmute long time ago. When I used to stay with my Ap'a, my Ap'a would look out the window and he say, "Oh, they gonna go check their trap. I gotta go." Get ready and start walking across.
>
> By them traps, they used to have big pile of lush fish. Anybody could go and take what they want. Some people only like fresh lush. And others would like older ones; you know, they've been there a while. Maybe they were starting to smell a little bit, but some people used to like those.

Life along the middle Kuskokwim

Wassily recalled how, when he was growing up in the 1950s, people were spread out all along the middle river:

> And it wasn't a very big village, Crooked Creek. 'Cause most of the people were living down at Canoe Village, below Uskuralek, and Island Village. And down by Napaimute, above that Little Mountain Village. And then you go up. And there was maybe one house in Georgetown. And then Eight Mile used to be pretty good size, maybe four, five families living in there on the north side of the river above Eight Mile Creek, that flat area in there.
>
> And then you go up; there was nothing all the way 'til below Sleetmute, on the left side. I remember your dad [Steve Derendy] was telling me that used to be pretty good size place before Sleetmute and before even Nick Mellick come. That area used to be almost nothing at [present-day] Sleetmute, but they were mainly down below. They call them the Bluffs now, that bend below Sleetmute.
>
> Now there's fish camps right around that birch area. And that other place was above Sleetmute, Iinruaq. They call that lake Iinruaq.

Angie agreed: "Yaa. Iinruaq is between Sleetmute and Stony. We used to go inside that lake and go up the creek until you see them hills. You know, they got sides all the way down. We used to climb up in there and go *uyangteq* [look out on] them lakes." Wassily noted that it's not open anymore: "Used to be no trees around there, not much. Now, it's so *umcik* [closed up]."

Trying to recall places farther upriver, neither Wassily nor Angie could remember their names. Angie said: "We never used to hardly go to Stony. We only used to stay around our places. 'Cause we had fish camp, winter camp." Wassily reiterated: "The villages had both sides, on each side, where they do all their berry picking and subsistence. And the next village do the same thing. They never overlap that much. They respect each other's imaginary boundary lines, like up in George River."

One location north of Crooked Creek, away from the river, stood out for Wassily:

> You know, at Crooked Creek it was kind of a center to get together; not much in the village, but back at what they called Bonanza Flats. They had nomads long ago that herd reindeer. And they used to trade and barter fur and meat. And people from upriver would go to Crooked and then go back towards Flat.
>
> And there's a place in there, looked like a corral, tree lined like this. There's places where they had campfires. And they used to barter with the nomads. It's about 30 miles back, north of Crooked.
>
> Bonanza Flats. That's where herders would come up, and they'd stay there with their reindeer in that corral. People from down this area and other side of Flat and Innoko, they'd come there and have a big gathering, dances and all that stuff. I used to hear bits and pieces of the stories.

I was impressed that there was an area between the rivers where people from the Yukon and middle Kuskokwim got together: "I've heard that Crooked and up toward Sleetmute really were centers, where people moved back and forth. Today it feels isolated, but you were the center of a really big [area], with lotsa people moving north, south, east, west." Wassily agreed: "They used to bring their fur and whatever, meats and stuff, and barter with the nomads."

The star-box story

During AFN's Youth and Elders Conference in October 2023, Marie and I had taken Angie to the Anchorage Museum, where we had spent several hours looking at their small collection of middle Kuskokwim pieces. Angie had recognized a circular wooden calendar like the one her grandmother had used in the past. But the piece that most excited her was a large, carved box that we passed on our way in and out of collections. It reminded Angie of a star story her grandmother had told her years before. We had no recorder at the time, and Marie asked Angie to retell the story, which she did:

> It was one of the old stories that if you went from one house to another house, sometime you'll hear the same story in different houses. This is

Wooden calendar, where a peg is moved to change and mark the date. *Gift of the Huffman Family, Anchorage Museum collection 2002.25.233*

how I remembered it.

I used to always want to hang around people who told stories. Mrs. Moxie was one of them. Poor. [*chuckle*] She's my grandma. Poor woman. I used to be so mischief. Sometime I used to mix her up so bad, she didn't know what to say. Too mischief I was.

But the story was that there was some kind of evil man. He go to the sun, and he ask the sun, "Could I please marry your daughter, the moon?" Sun tell him, "No, you can't. You can't." So evil man said, "I'm gonna gather all the lights and put 'em away!"

So the first thing he pick was the stars, and he put them in that little box, smallest box. They used to have 'em by the door, I guess, those boxes. And he go again next day, ask the sun if he could marry that woman, and the sun said, "No." So he took the moon, and he put her in the middle-size box.

And then he went to the sun again and said, "Could I marry your daughter?" And she said, "No." And he took the sun, and he put her in that big box, the biggest box. Here, all this time, these animals are looking out, "When is it gonna get bright? It should be getting bright by now." No light.

So, the Raven, he decided he's gonna go check. They used to have magic snowshoes. I don't know what was wrong with his wings, but he used to have magic snowshoes. So he went from that village, he walk up with his snowshoes, bring 'em up in the air. And when he get up there, he look around. No light to be seen. And just as that evil man was talking to the sun again, he saw that light.

Raven see it. And all of a sudden it disappear again. So he walk down there. And he take off his snowshoes. And he put 'em behind the house; you know, the door was on one side, the back is just wall. He put his snowshoes there, and he walk over.

And long time ago them men used to carry purses, you know, with big pockets. He had that kind, and he got in the porch, and he heard that man telling that sun.

Tlingit bentwood box, which inspired Angie to tell a "star-box" story. *Anchorage Museum collection 1980.22.1ab*

> So when that evil man went out from the house, Raven's inside the porch. But he had heard the evil man and the sun talking. So when that evil man left the house, Raven went into the house and he opened that little box. And he see all the stars in there. So he hurry up and grab some and put 'em in his pocket. He put 'em in his pocket, and he covered that box back up. He tell the sun, "I'll be back for you."
>
> And he started going. And as he was walking up the air, he heard that evil man behind him. And you know that Raven always walked [pigeon-toed] like his feet.
>
> He was walking in his snowshoes like that. And that guy had stepped on the back of his snowshoe. Make that Raven fall. But instead of falling down all the way, he fell on his snowshoes. And that evil man come and he fell over him, and he fall down. That's how he got killed.
>
> And then they come back and let the sun and moon out of the box. But before that happened, that Raven was taking them stars and threw them. He threw them all over. And when he heard that man coming... You know, that Milky Way, this is where that Raven had fall down. When he fall down, all his stars spilled in there; they say that's the Milky Way. When he fell, his purse had opened and all the stars rolled out. That's how that evil guy find 'em and he tried to chase 'em....
>
> After he fall down to his death, [Raven] went back and go let 'em out. That's how I heard it.

Angie apologized. She knew the story had embellishments that she couldn't remember. She also noted that this story was told in other areas: "And if you compare the stories, like this one, star stories, if you go down by the Panhandle, they got the same story, but it's little bit different. But it's the same, they were put in boxes." Marie remembered that the boxes we'd seen in the Anchorage Museum were, in fact, Tlingit from Southeast Alaska. Chuckling, Angie said:

> Yaa, that's how come I told you; even those guys have the same stories.
>
> Sometime my grandkids, they come out, "Grandma, tell me scary story."
>
> "Gee. I don't like scary stories."
>
> "How come?"
>
> "Look, it's getting dark; it might get me."

Traveling in spring

After Angie's story, we stopped for lunch. When we started up again that afternoon, I asked a question about *nayuryarluni* (lying concealed, watching for animals or birds to come) in spring. Angie was reminded of traveling from Sleetmute with her own children in the spring:

> When my dad was alive, right after breakup, we'd go up Holitna and then Hoho[litna], just to go see the baby animals. We would never go hunting in the springtime; only ducks. But we left everybody else alone, 'cause they had babies. We saw beaver; I swear its tail was about [two fingers] wide and [two inches] long; baby beaver.
>
> Yaa, itty bitty. My dad, he catch 'em for BA, you know, my oldest boy. And BA had that beaver all day. He was holding it. He kiss and everything, just loving that little beaver.... So cute little tail.
>
> In the evening we let 'em put it back.

Later, Angie mentioned the duck decoy her mother once made: "My mom used to make duck decoys. Her first duck decoy was because Kriska Evan ask her to make him one, so we don't have to travel too far away. Wherever he was, we can get that decoy to stay there, and then he watch it. And then they'll come toward it. Then after that they start showing up with them plastic ducks."

We briefly discussed bird hunting in spring, and Wassily noted that upriver people just shot what they need at the time: "When they catch more than what they need, they gut 'em and split in half; cut wings like that and then smoke 'em. Man, delicious. Ducks, geese." Jennie agreed: "Kind of dry, but pretty good."

Wassily spoke about hunting and the instructions he was given when young:

> The eyes and the ears are the most soft spot of any animals. When I was growing up they always used to tell us that. Teach us gun safety and safety outside. They never used to just let us go. They made sure we were trained for the elements. I think they even did that, too, on girls. The girls, when they're married they go hunting and trapping together. Nowadays, it's so different. Jump in the boat and go and then come back the same evening.

I commented on the high ridges they climbed near Crooked Creek when young, and Jennie replied, "We didn't realize it was that hard until now." Laughing, Wassily commented, "Right now they have to have helicopter to climb up." Angie quipped, "It was so funny; when you're young you can go anywhere. Now that I'm older, everybody else is faster than I am. It just makes me mad."

Traveling on the Holitna

We touched briefly on animal spirits and beings of another dimension. Angie recalled Maqivik, a place near the mouth of the Holitna where people can get lost: "The one place can have so many dimensions.... There's gotta be holes somewhere to let them go in and out. Like in Maqivik.... That's a bum place to get lost because something will take you. You'll get turned around." Jennie had experienced getting turned around at Maqivik:

> Falltime we always like to pick red berries, cranberries. Then it's mostly on the bottom end of the little cut bank. And on top of those banks, there's so much cranberries. If you don't want to pick there on top of the bank, you could go back and pick inside of the spruce trees.
>
> And it's thick there. And you can get turned around there real easy. I always use the sun, 'cause the sun comes from that way, and cut bank comes from that way, and then go that way is the river. One time I almost got turned around, too. I wasn't paying attention.
>
> I heard somebody calling and calling. Sound like it was calling me from that way. So I just kept going. And I realized, "It doesn't sound like that from that way." So I hurry up and look at the sun. I say, "I think I'm going upriver." So I turned myself around and start walking. Not very far, I find those guys who were calling. Boy, I almost got turned around.

Angie remarked on places where the world "rips":

> You know, my mom and them were picking berries over here. And there was a tiny little creek, and my auntie went over here. During the time they were picking berries, one of them had a gun. And there was a flock of chicken [spruce grouse] that got startled and flew away. Those guys can cause a rip in the world. Because my mom and them were picking over here, and my auntie was on this side.
>
> After that happened, it had moved her way on top the hill. When she look up, she couldn't find anybody. So she listened after she holler. And then the women started shooting their gun. She heard it and went toward that noise. Both her and Mom, when they came to see me, they were just amazed. Mom said, "How could this happen?" There was a rip that made 'em like that.

Angie added: "Spruce hens [grouse] – every time I see those guys in a flock and they fly away, I always get lost."

Jennie noted that others experience getting lost at Maqivik: "Olga and her kids got lost, spend the night, how many days, falltime." Angie said: "You can't holler 'Hoh.' When you're picking berries, when you try to find your party, you holler, 'Oh hoh.' And if you do that in Maqivik, they'll come from you everywhere. And that makes you get lost, lose it." Jennie agreed: "Scary. Really watch where you are. Pay attention." Wassily noted other places farther up the Holitna where that happens. Once just below Iitulilek, men were found ten miles below their boat after they got turned around in the woods.

Talking about the Holitna, Wassily recalled the two brothers, Ignaty and Evan Ignaty, who lived on their own up the river.

> Nicky Sakar's dad was their neighbor. And I was talking with them guys. They tell me they had a little cabin they let us stay in. We was sitting down, their cabin is small, small little table. And window. They see a bear; they were drinking coffee. They said they tell that bear, "Go away. I don't want you. Go away!" Bear go, and he go by the door 'cause the door is open. "Get away. I don't want you. Get away. I got gun. I'll let you have it." That bear stick his one arm inside, so he shoot 'em. "I'll let him have it." He just shot that bear right there in the doorway.
>
> But they were so unique from living out there in the wilderness, like all the animals respected them. 'Cause they never bother them. When they tell 'em to go, they go – bear, wolves, everything.
>
> It's amazing when they tell stories about how this woman always come by; they call that cow moose "woman." Every day she come by. In the morning she go up with her calf; in the evening, go back down. And it do that every day. Before we got there, they just went. We were sitting down, drinking coffee and talking. Ignaty say, "Well, it's about time that woman's gonna come by." I was kinda looking at 'em. And, "Oh, right there." I look up. That cow moose, calf, come walking down. [*laughter*]

Wassily noted that the brothers were truly bushmen, living off the land: "These two can talk to them animals and they talk back to them.... They had some [store bought things], you know, rice and macaroni and sugar, salt, whiskey." The rest of their food was from the country.

Middle Kuskokwim history

Thinking back reminded Angie and Wassily of unanswered questions, things that they wished they had asked about in the past. Angie recalled: "At the time that I was seeing these things, it never dawned on me to ask questions about it." Wassily added: "Well, we never did. We never ask until we're told. And they'd say, 'Do you have a question?'" Angie agreed: "After they talk to you, if you have any questions, now is the time to get 'em out. And I couldn't think of any questions."

Wassily had watched Nick Mellick Jr., known as Nixie, recording stories from many elders:

> I think most of these stories that we hear in bits and pieces. Like Nixie Mellick flew around and talking to them older people – Johnny John, Golga Sakar, Jack Ignaty, Tim Kameroff, Paul Kameroff, Levis. And he was smart and had tape recorder and talk to them. And he was bilingual.
>
> And the stories that the guys told him. Not only the guys, he talk to the women, too.
>
> The best one; we were talking, Nixie and I, I forget who else. He said he was recording Maxie Alexie's mom, Nastasia. And she had this one song that she used to sing. And Nixie ask her to sing that song. She sang it. And then he told her, "I don't understand you. Sing again." [She replied,] "Ah, bullshit, you already heard it."
>
> I couldn't stop laughing. And she was old. She tell Nixie that, in perfect English. Sing it only one time, and no more after that.

Jennie agreed: "They used to tell us, you hear it one time, get it right."

The subject of Nixie Mellick and his recordings of middle Kuskokwim history brought different reactions. At present, the National Park Service has copies of Nixie's tapes, but since Nixie passed away, they lack permission from the Mellick family to share them. Marie felt that upriver people should demand that the stories be shared, as it is their history. Wassily disagreed: "We can't demand something like that to family. I think they understand, but it was Nixie's wishes. Nixie make that wish, you know, 'I make wish that all these things that I'm saying be erased or not be heard.'"

I shared what I'd recently learned – that Nixie's original intention was that the stories be shared, but that the family – his children – disagree on how that should be done. Wassily nodded: "Yeah. This generation might be little different. And the next one never heard it, and then they'll want it." Angie added with feeling: "'Cause it seems like everybody wants a connection, need a connection to something." We ended the day on a hopeful note. What we were sharing together would reach younger ears, continuing down the generations.

Sleetmute recipes

Our time together in Anchorage held one more surprise. Speaking of the younger generation, I brought out a copy of a recipe book, put together by students at the Sleetmute School in 1955, typed up by their teachers, and eventually deposited in the University of Alaska Archives in Fairbanks. I had found the book online while preparing for our trip to the Museum of the North, and I shared it with the group now. Opening the slim volume, they found a list of "cooks," all of whom they recognized, including then-4th graders Massa Gregory and Anella Johnson; 5th graders Annie Alexie, Peggy Egnaty, Pete Mellick, and Katherine Mellick; and 8th graders Barbara Torresin, Mary Margie Egnaty, and Nadesta Alexie. The students had shared close to two dozen recipes, including everything from *akutaq* to moose nose. Most recipes were illustrated as well. Some of the students – like Pete Mellick and Mary Margie Egnaty – were now elders themselves. Others had passed away, leaving a record of Kuskokwim delicacies they enjoyed when they were young, and many still enjoy to this day.

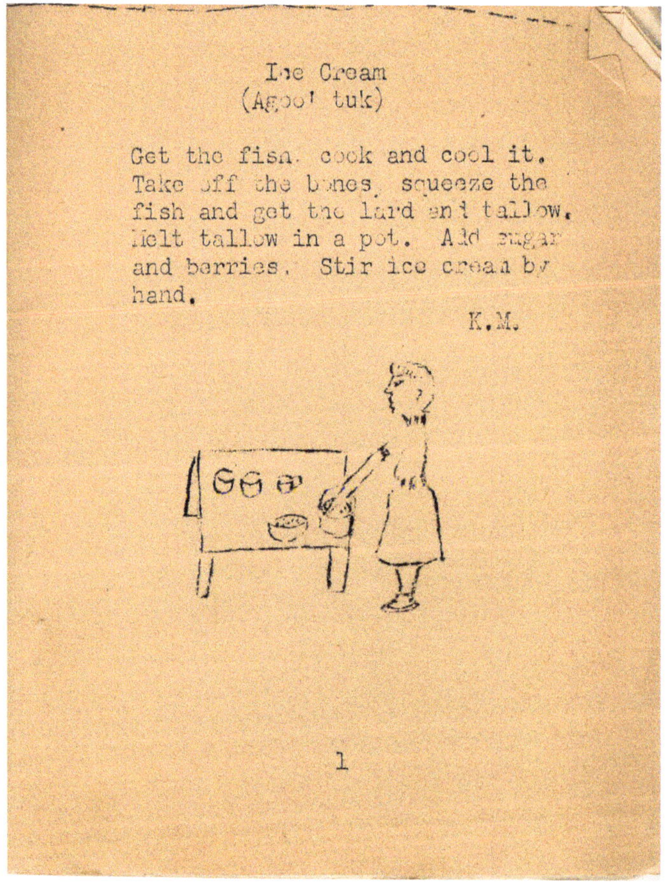

Ice Cream
(Agoo' tuk)

Get the fish, cook and cool it. Take off the bones, squeeze the fish and get the lard and tallow. Melt tallow in a pot. Add sugar and berries. Stir ice cream by hand.

K.M.

1

Ice Cream (Agoo' tuk, *akutaq*) by Katherine Mellick

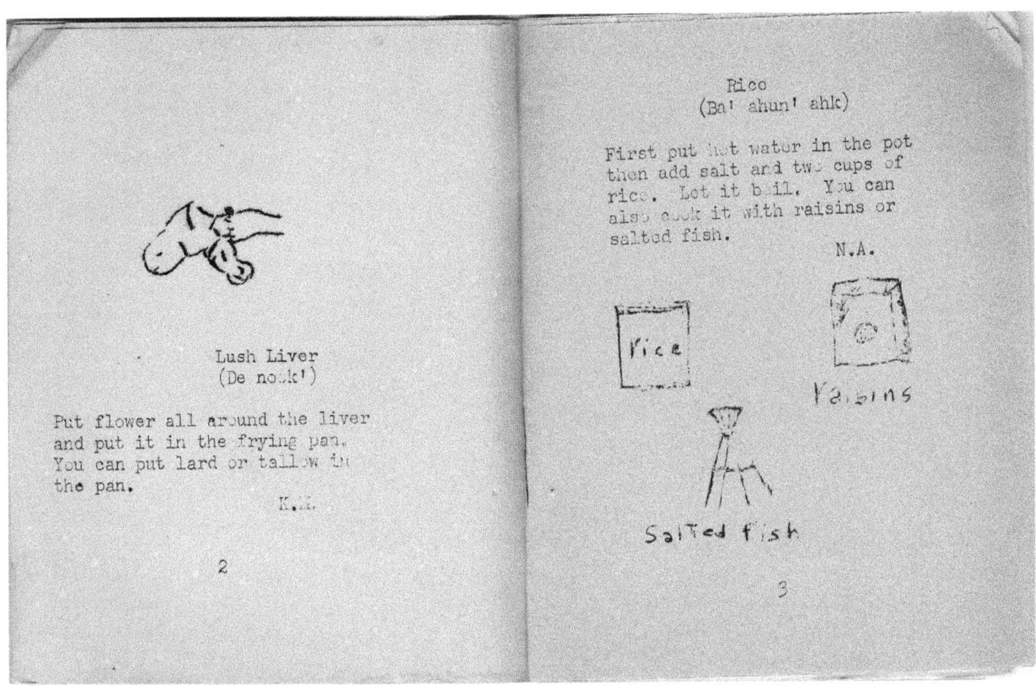

Lush Liver
(De nook')

Put flower all around the liver
and put it in the frying pan.
You can put lard or tallow in
the pan.

K.M.

2

Rice
(Ba' ahun' ahk)

First put hot water in the pot
then add salt and two cups of
rice. Let it boil. You can
also cook it with raisins or
salted fish.

N.A.

3

Lush Liver (De nook', *tenguk*) by Katherine Mellick; and Rice (Ba' ahun' ahk, *paraluruaq*) by Nadesta Alexie

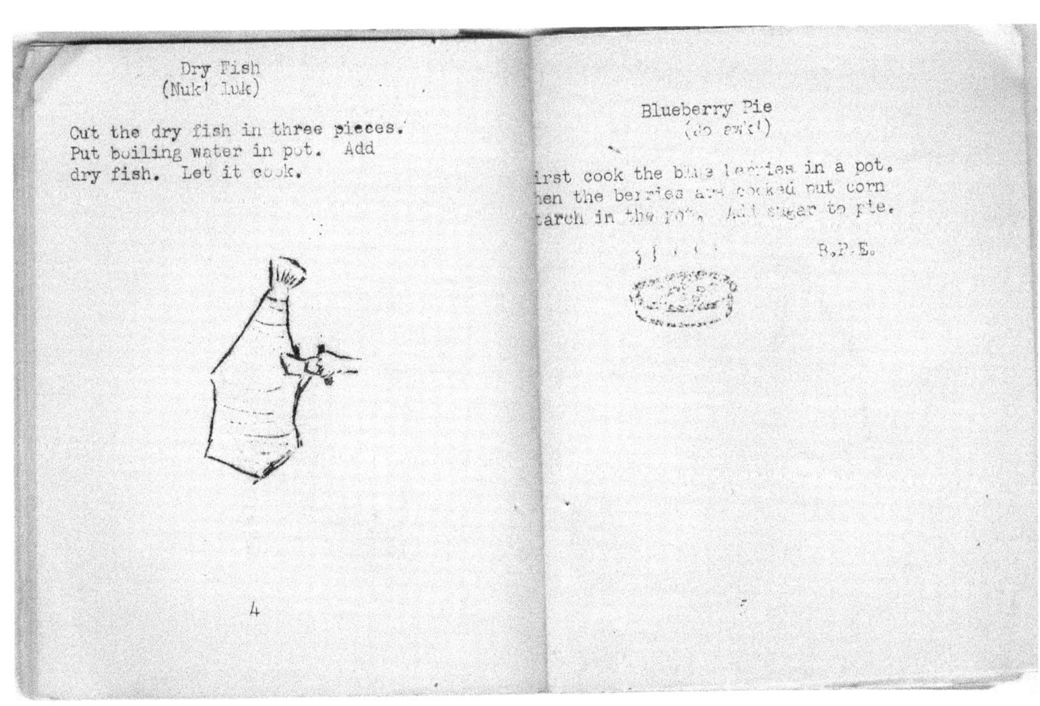

Dry Fish
(Nuk' luk)

Cut the dry fish in three pieces.
Put boiling water in pot. Add
dry fish. Let it cook.

4

Blueberry Pie
(Je awk')

irst cook the blue berries in a pot.
hen the berries are cooked put corn
tarch in the pot. Add sugar to pie.

B.P.E.

Dry Fish (Nuk' luk, *neqerrluk*); and Blueberry Pie (Je awk, *curaq*) by Peggy Egnaty

Rabbit Soup
(Ma gow' uk)

Boil hot water, add rabbit,
rice, onions, potatoes
and salt.

N.A.

6

Rabbit in snare

7

Rabbit Soup (Ma gow' uk, *maqaruaq*) by Nadesta Alexie

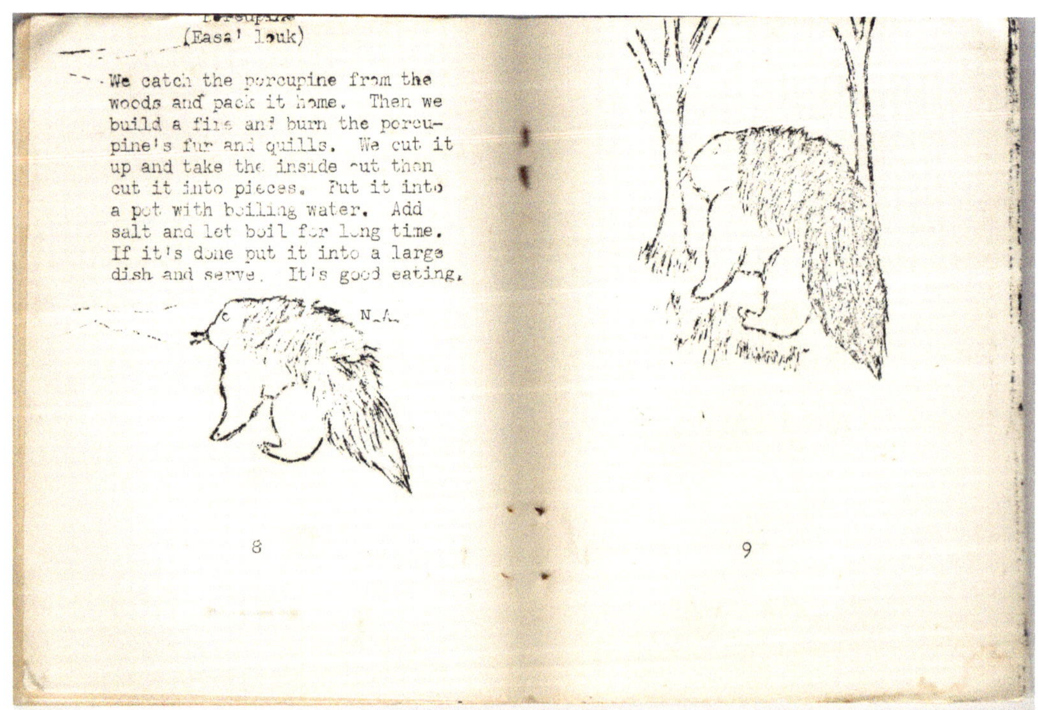

(Easa' louk)

We catch the porcupine from the woods and pack it home. Then we build a fire and burn the porcupine's fur and quills. We cut it up and take the inside out then cut it into pieces. Put it into a pot with boiling water. Add salt and let boil for long time. If it's done put it into a large dish and serve. It's good eating.

N.A.

8

9

Porcupine (Easa' louk, *issaluuq*) by Nadesta Alexie

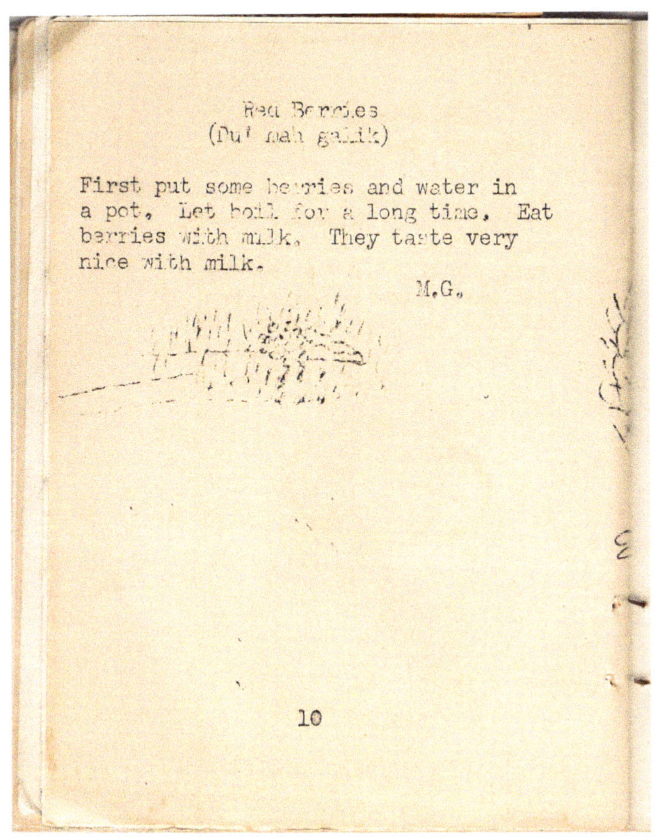

Red Berries
(Tu' mah galik)

First put some berries and water in a pot. Let boil for a long time. Eat berries with milk. They taste very nice with milk.

M.G.

10

Red Berries (Tu' mah galik, *tumaqliq*) by Massa Gregory

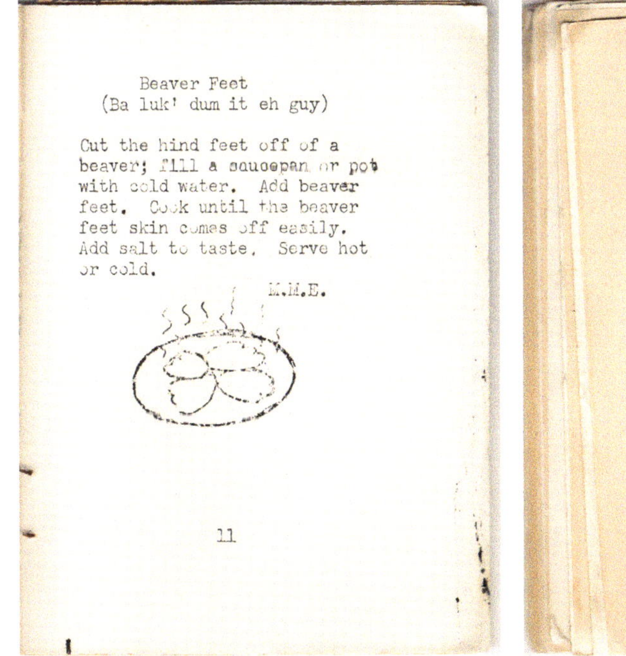

Beaver Feet
(Ba luk' dum it eh guy)

Cut the hind feet off of a beaver; fill a saucepan or pot with cold water. Add beaver feet. Cook until the beaver feet skin comes off easily. Add salt to taste. Serve hot or cold.

M.M.E.

11

Beaver in snare
12

Beaver Feet (Ba luk' dum it eh guy, *palugtem it'gai*) Mary Margie Egnaty

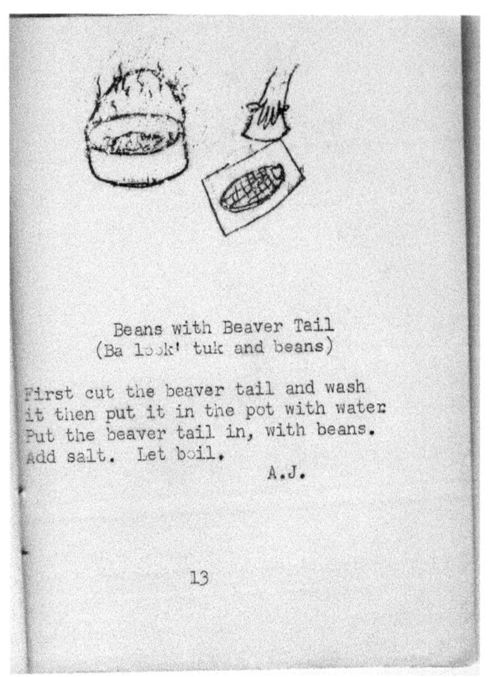

Beans with Beaver Tail
(Ba look' tuk and beans)

First cut the beaver tail and wash it then put it in the pot with water Put the beaver tail in, with beans. Add salt. Let boil.

A.J.

13

Beans with Beaver Tail (Ba look' tuk and beans, *palugtaq* and beans) by Anella Johnson

Pancakes
(Asal' ack)

Put frying pan on hot stove. Add about one or two inches of lard. Put flour in a bowl. Add salt and water. Make it watery and smooth. Then fry it.

K.M.

16

Pancakes (Asal' ack, *assaliaq*) by Katherine Mellick

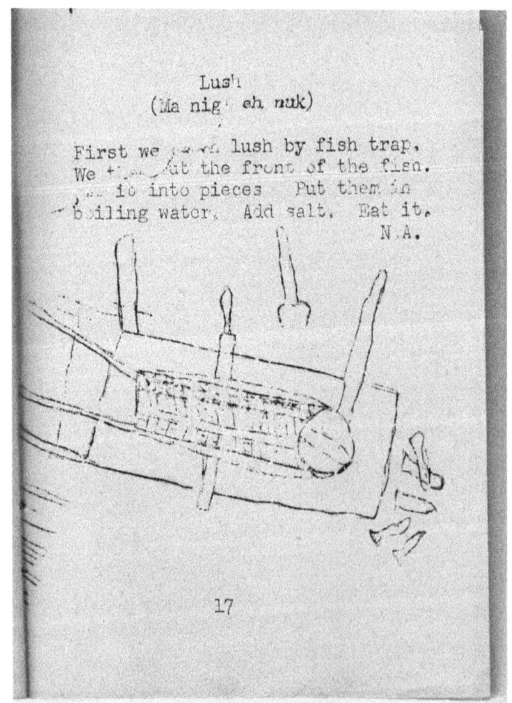

Lush
(Ma nig' ah nuk)

First we [illegible] lush by fish trap. We [illegible] the front of the fish. [illegible] it into pieces Put them in boiling water. Add salt. Eat it.

N.A.

17

Lush (Ma nig' ah nuk, *manignaq*) by Nadesta Alexie

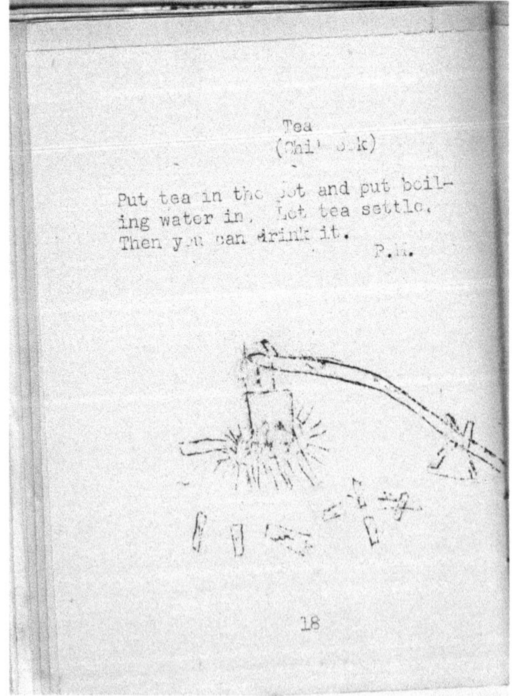

Tea
(Chi' ook)

Put tea in the pot and put boiling water in. Let tea settle. Then you can drink it.

P.M.

18

Tea (Chi' ook, *caayuq*) by Pete Mellick

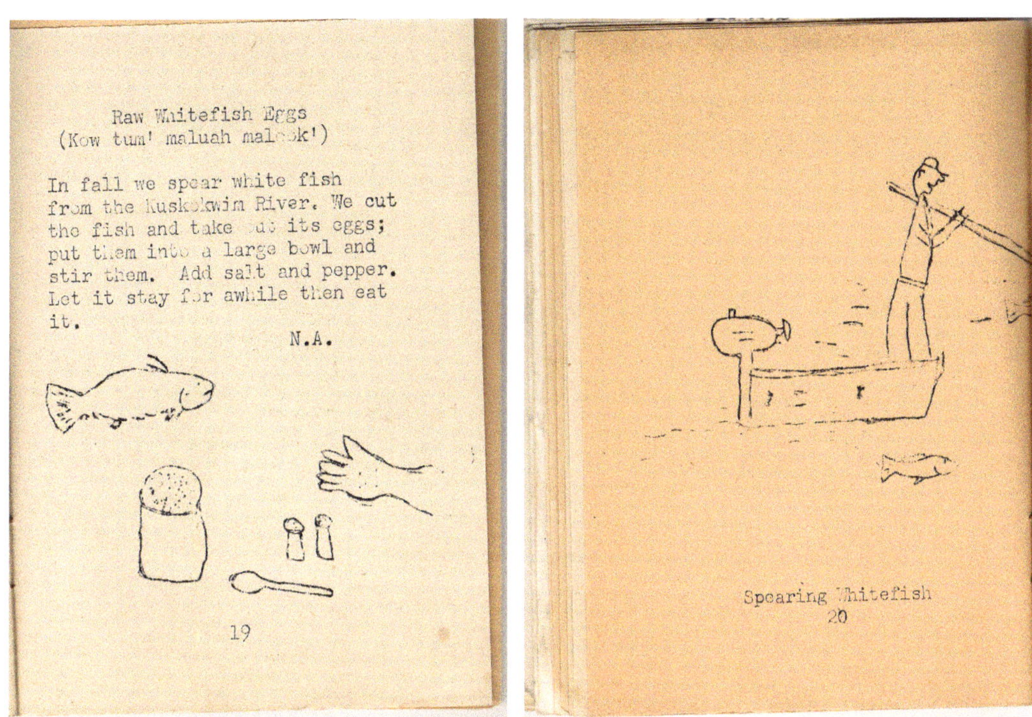

Raw Whitefish Eggs
(Kow tum' maluah malook')

In fall we spear white fish from the Kuskokwim River. We cut the fish and take out its eggs; put them into a large bowl and stir them. Add salt and pepper. Let it stay for awhile then eat it.

N.A.

19

Spearing Whitefish
20

Raw Whitefish Eggs (Kaw tum' maluah malook', *qaurtum melua*) by Nadesta Alexie

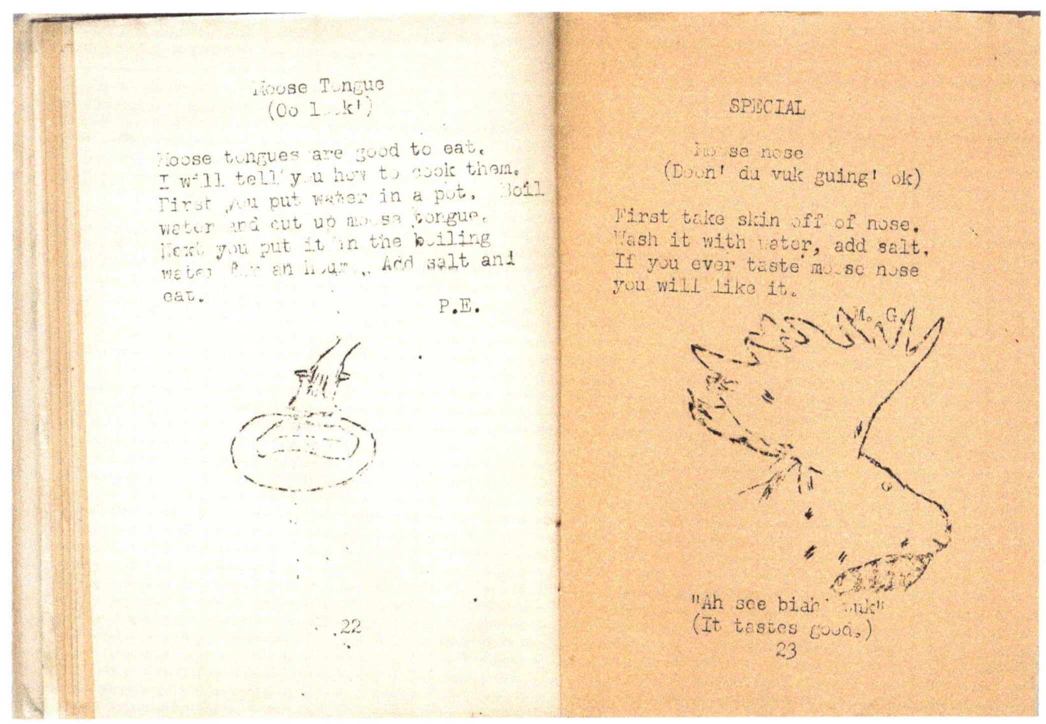

Moose Tongue
(Oo look')

Moose tongues are good to eat. I will tell you how to cook them. First you put water in a pot. Boil water and cut up moose tongue. Next you put it in the boiling water for an hour. Add salt and eat.

P.E.

22

SPECIAL

Moose nose
(Doon' du vuk guing' ok)

First take skin off of nose. Wash it with water, add salt. If you ever taste moose nose you will like it.

M. G.

"Ah see biah' tuk"
(It tastes good.)
23

Moose Tongue (oo look', *uluq*) by Peggy Egnaty; and Special Moose Nose (Doon'du vuk guing' uk, *tuntuvak qengaq*) by Massa Gregory

At the museum

Our time together in Anchorage had prepared us well for what was to come. Wednesday's weather was clear, and the flight to Fairbanks was smooth. A cab took us from the airport to the Museum of the North, an elegant, curved building perched on a high ridge overlooking the Chena River Valley, with mountain ranges rising to the south and more University buildings on either side. Angela Linn greeted us at the door and welcomed us into the Museum's airy atrium. We left coats and overnight bags behind the front desk, then followed her down a long corridor, past exhibits, and into a large comfortable classroom on the right where Angela had laid out most of the Museum's middle Kuskokwim collection on six long tables. She had coffee and snacks off to one side, but at the time no one was hungry. Their attention was focused on the objects spread before them. Everyone wandered for a few moments, taking things in. Then we settled in chairs around the table closest to the door. I introduced Angela, thanking her for the work she had done getting things ready for our visit. She in turn welcomed the group, saying how happy she was to have us: "This is why we're here."

Nillarcuun / *Skin stretching frame*

I took a moment to set up my tape recorder, and Marie began, noting the date and our group of six: Wassily, Jennie, and Angie, along with Mark, Marie, and me. We began with a large wooden skin stretcher collected by Wendell Oswalt in the 1970s from Nunapitchuk, Marie's hometown. I let them know that along with things from Sleetmute, Crooked Creek, and Canoe Village, I'd asked Angela to bring a variety of familiar things from nearby villages that I thought would spark memories. They did, indeed.

Wassily noted that a stretcher like this was called a *nillarcuun* upriver, and that

Skin stretcher (*nillarcuun*). *UA Museum of the North UA70-053-02210, Micki LeClair Sievers*

the larger one would have been for river otter, known as *cuignilnguq* (one Yup'ik name for the George River). Wassily continued: "We used to make these ones with spruce trees, them small ones. And then put these [cross pieces] in with pegs to widen it. And they had pegs like this. They drill. I don't know how they used to use nail, that little drill. They drill hole and make pegs."

Angie said that another smaller stretcher would have been used for mink or marten. Jennie noted that it depended on the animal's size. Wassily agreed, adding: "Recently they want 'em skinny like that, marten. Like that big stretcher. They used to like 'em kind a wide when we were trapping. Now they want 'em skinner and longer. I don't know why."

I asked Wassily how many stretchers he had in the days when he and his family trapped along the George River, and he replied:

> It really depends on how much traps you have. And over the years lots of people collect traps. And they never bring 'em back. They just hang 'em up in the trees. My stepdad had over 300 traps over the years up the George River.
>
> Hang 'em in the trees where rain wouldn't get to it. And falltime when he's setting them up, take 'em up and set 'em.

Wassily explained how the stretchers were hung at camp, inside the cabin. Angie remarked:

> We used to have beaver stretchers on the ceiling; maybe four. Two on this side, and two on that side. But you would stretch two beavers in one stretcher, because you can split them.
>
> You had to keep 'em up so they can dry. And once they dry they take 'em down and put 'em in cache or someplace dry. I remember one time [their pelts] stacked up, all the way from the floor up [three feet high].

Wassily explained that there were certain seasons when different animals were available:

> There's seasons that they hunt and trap. Like in September when we go fall camp. We don't set traps until late September when the marten fur starting to get good. And that's when we hunt mink, too.
>
> But once it gets lotsa snow, you can't catch mink anymore, where they go under the snow. And the only time you can catch otter is when they make a hole on the side of a creek or lake or river.
>
> Other than that, you have certain seasons to trap different animals.

> Like mink and otter are right after freeze-up, and there's a little bit of snow, where they can't hide. So you set traps for them.
>
> And once it get deeper snow, then you start trapping marten, weasels. It used to take me day-and-a-half to set traps at George River, where we go trapping. Go over the hill and go along the valley and then go again; come down the valley and up the creek.

Marie asked about muskrats, and Wassily noted that they were available around Sleetmute and down in flat tundra in spring, but not in the George River area. Marie recalled her father having lots of *nillat* (skin stretchers) for muskrat: "In the spring when it's sunny you can take 'em out; they dry fast."

Wassily added that lynx were also available in winter, between September and February:

> And after February they sit down; getting worn, you know. And they lose their hair around their hips. Even wolves do that. We catch them in the winter, when their fur is more fluffy. They're thicker, instead of coming off. 'Cause springtime just like dogs, they start losing their hair.

Everyone listening as Wassily explains the use of different sized skin stretchers. The largest stretcher, with two vertical bars pegged together in three places, was made by Golga Maxie of Nunapitchuk and used to stretch river otter and fox skins. It was said to have been made in two hours and would last for years. The medium-sized stretcher, used for mink skins, was made by William Trader of Emmonak, and the smallest stretcher with a single vertical bar was made in Nunapitchuk in 1958, and also used to stretch mink skins. Wendell Oswalt collected all three stretchers in 1971 as part of the Modern Alaska Native Material Culture Project (MANMC). *UA Museum of the North UA70-053-0189, -0210, and -0114, Micki LeClair Sievers*

> And then falltime they lose their hair and grow them other coats....
>
> They trap 'em quite a bit, in Kalskag and Aniak, Chuathbaluk [where there's] lots of tundra and lots of rabbits.

Wolves were also hunted, as well as red foxes, cross foxes, and wolverines. Wassily noted that beavers were also available:

> We get 'em certain time of the year. When they get good is in late February, late March. That's when [both] the fur and the meat get good.
>
> The meat is tender right around late March and middle February 'cause they don't go around cutting trees, or hauling cord woods.
>
> And man, [Jennie's] mom used to tell us when they catch too much beaver and they debone the meat – take the meat out, cut up the bones, and they put 'em in barrels, salt them.
>
> 'Cause the meat, you can dry 'em and hang 'em. Bones, they keep 'em. And when they want change from fish during summer, they take those [bones] and soak 'em, and then make soup. Salted beaver bones make good soup.
>
> But I learn the fast way. Just put 'em in the river in a bag. In the water; by afternoon and evening it's good, no more salty. Soak in the morning, and make soup in the afternoon.

Wassily added that they do that with moose bones as well, but not as much.

Mark asked what mink and otter eat upriver, and Wassily said they ate a variety of fish, including grayling, little whitefish, mud suckers, and a dark, slimy fish found in shallow water known as *kapatiit* (bullheads), which Jennie said resembled blackfish. Wassily used to see bears break through thin ice in spring and go after the slimy fish before breakup, when they couldn't get any berries. Neither Wassily nor Jennie had ever eaten them, although both did eat blackfish which were found around Sleetmute and Stony River. Jennie said: "When I first saw [slimy fish], I thought: What kind of fish is this? They're so ugly. I never seen anything like that. They're not that big, but they had big heads."

Returning to the subject of trapping, Marie asked Wassily if wolverines were dangerous. Wassily replied:

> When you run after them, they run up the tree. But they're pretty dangerous. One wolverine can kill a big moose. And if you leave your meat, wolverine happen to come; he'll pee on all those other meats, take one, throw it on his back, and go. Them dogs wouldn't even eat that meat. Stink. They claim 'em.

Marie asked if the wolverine comes back to get it. Wassily continued: "They do. Not only that one; other ones come. But we always set traps around it, catch them."

Wassily noted that wolverine makes the best parka ruff:

> That's what we used to use for parkas like that. They put wolverine instead of wolves or anything 'cause the hair don't frost up. I don't know how come it never [gets frosty]. You know, you always put your parka hood small [close to your face] when it's cold. And wolf and others, they get frosty. Wolverine don't.
>
> And they don't sink in snow that much, them wolverines. Not like wolves and foxes. They got short legs, and you know how them ducks are, they got webbed paws.
>
> And they hop; and their back legs come [forward] and this one go; the back legs hit them other [legs].

Marie asked if people ate wolverine meat, and Wassily said no, as wolverines are scavengers: "They'll eat anything they can get hold of, rotten meat or anything." He described wolverines killing bears in their dens:

> They catch bear; black bear in a den, wintertime, while them bears are sleeping. They kill 'em. 'Cause when bears sleep, they sleep [with their head down] in between their legs. Usually the back of the bear is toward the hole. And its neck is showing. And when they open that bear hole, they catch 'em in the back.
>
> They bite 'em and pull 'em out.
>
> There's couple times when we're trapping we see bear holes like that, where that wolverine pull 'em out.

Mark asked if wolverines eat all of the bear, including the bones. Wassily replied: "I never see leftovers. Once they get done eating, you don't see them. Whatever they got they'd throw 'em on the back, pull it, and go. I've seen 'em do that with a moose leg like that, throw it on their back. 'Cause their backs are wide, and long. They just throw the leg on top, hold it, and go."

Marie noted that they don't see wolverines in the tundra where she grew up, and Wassily agreed: "They're mainly where there's lotsa trees and hills. I seen them in between Russian Mission and St. Mary's in the area where there's lotsa trees, [and] up Aniak River, head of Tuluksak River."

Kuvyaq / *Fishnet*

The next piece we looked at was a fishnet made of moose sinew collected from Deacons Landing, below McGrath, in 1978. The group thought that it was used for whitefish or salmon, perhaps red salmon, silvers, or "dog fish" (chum salmon). Wassily observed that moose sinew was the most popular sewing material upriver. Looking more closely, he could see that the sinew was braided: "That's how come it looks like twine."

Jennie noted that the sinew was from the moose backstrap, the thin layer of *yualuq* (sinew) running from the back of the moose's head all the way to its *kuucenak* (rump). Wassily noted: "*Yualuq* is thin like this paper." Angie added: "They get [*yualuq*] from right there against the spine. You'll see it when you butcher moose. You can take that and use 'em for thread." Wassily continued: "When you dry it, then you can go like this [separate the strands] and it'll come out to be thin. Then you braid it."

The final, critical step was waterproofing the sinew with rendered beaver fat. Wassily explained:

> And then, in order to keep 'em from getting rotten, when you put it in water and soak, they use that beaver fat. Beaver fat is better than [mink oil] you buy from the store. But beaver fat, you render it and make oil.

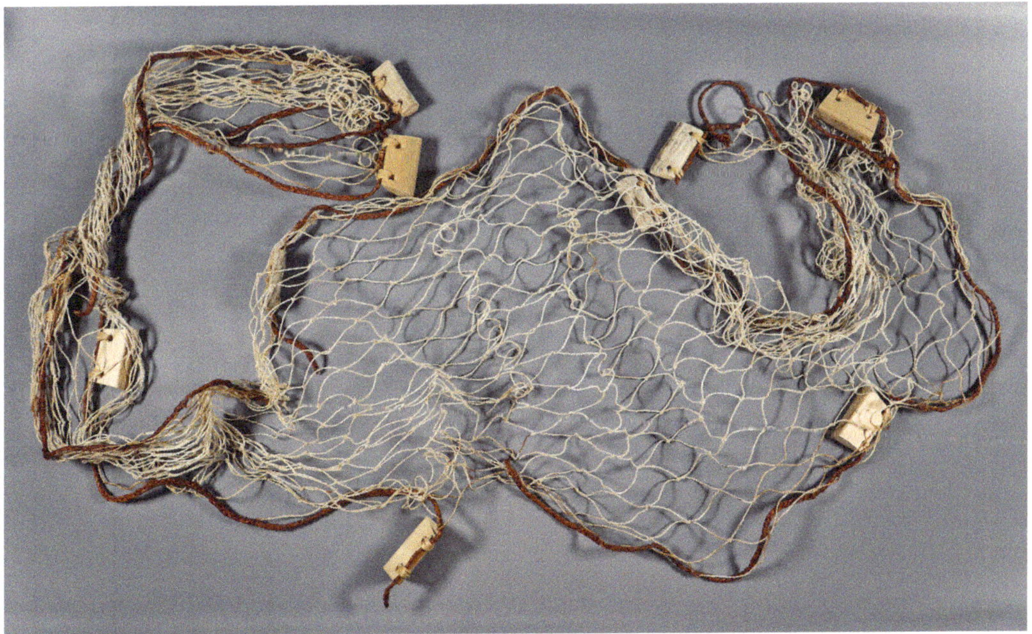

Fishnet (*kuvyaq*) made of moose sinew from Deacons Landing, below McGrath. *UA Museum of the North UA79-006-0001, Micki LeClair Sievers*

> And once it kind of cool off, that's what they used to waterproof it. Plus it stays soft. Even the rawhide, they do that, too. They use that beaver fat. That's one of the most [important things] they use to waterproof anything. *Kameksaks* [skin boots], you can use that beaver fat [to waterproof] the sole.

Wassily observed that the back of the animal is a primary target for predators:

> That's where most predators like bears, moose, wolverine; when they go after animals, they always go right there, in the back. That's where all the sinew is, and all the motor for your whole body.
>
> You know, it's just like your nerves. But it's where all the predators go after animals that they eat; right in the back of the head, always.
>
> They paralyze 'em back there. And then they get the throat. Even us, you know, if somebody hold us hard enough here, we'll get paralyzed.

Wassily then pointed out the *kic'arat* (sinkers) on the bottom and *pugtaqutat* (floats) attached to the top of the net. Angie observed: "There's wood [on the top], and in the bottom bone." Looking at the net, Wassily remarked: "And net about that size, when you set 'em where there's an eddy, that thing can catch about 50 or 60 grayling." "Or those little whitefish," Jennie added.

All bemoaned the way beavers have multiplied today, often getting tangled in fishnets. Wassily observed: "The reason why they're doing that is 'cause very few people hunt beaver nowadays. There's not that many people like there used to be long ago. And they had limits [in the past], like twenty beaver per family or twenty beaver per person that's trapping 'em when they hunted them back then."

Marie asked who set the limits, and Wassily replied:

> [The limits were] from the people themselves mostly. 'Cause they know how much they need. They don't take more than what they need. And if they have extra beaver meat, then they give other people. Twenty is good enough usually.
>
> But after that Fish and Game came in, and you start selling them pelts, then you'd be trapping. And then you'll say, "Okay, I have this many boys in my family, and each one of 'em can catch twenty for the money, for selling the pelts."
>
> But before, what they used to do was they catch enough for the family to sew and everything for food and clothing. 'Cause one beaver can feed a family for one week, just one beaver. And that's what they used to tell us long ago.

Talking about beavers reminded Wassily of porcupines, which were also an important food source:

> Same way with porcupine. When you see a porcupine, you catch it and it'll feed you and your family for a week. And they used to tell us, "They say porcupines are very jealous." If you see porcupine, and you keep going, you wouldn't see nothing because they are very jealous.
>
> And if you catch 'em, then you'll see lots – other animals, bear, moose. I know that's the tradition.

Mark commented that he had never heard the instruction about porcupines, and Jennie replied: "We upriver people talk about porcupines being jealous, when you're hunting."

Wassily observed that their quills were not only painful but dangerous:

> And them quills, when they go into your skin; as long as you're moving they go in, they keep traveling.
>
> That's why we used to watch our dogs. Them porcupine [quills] go in

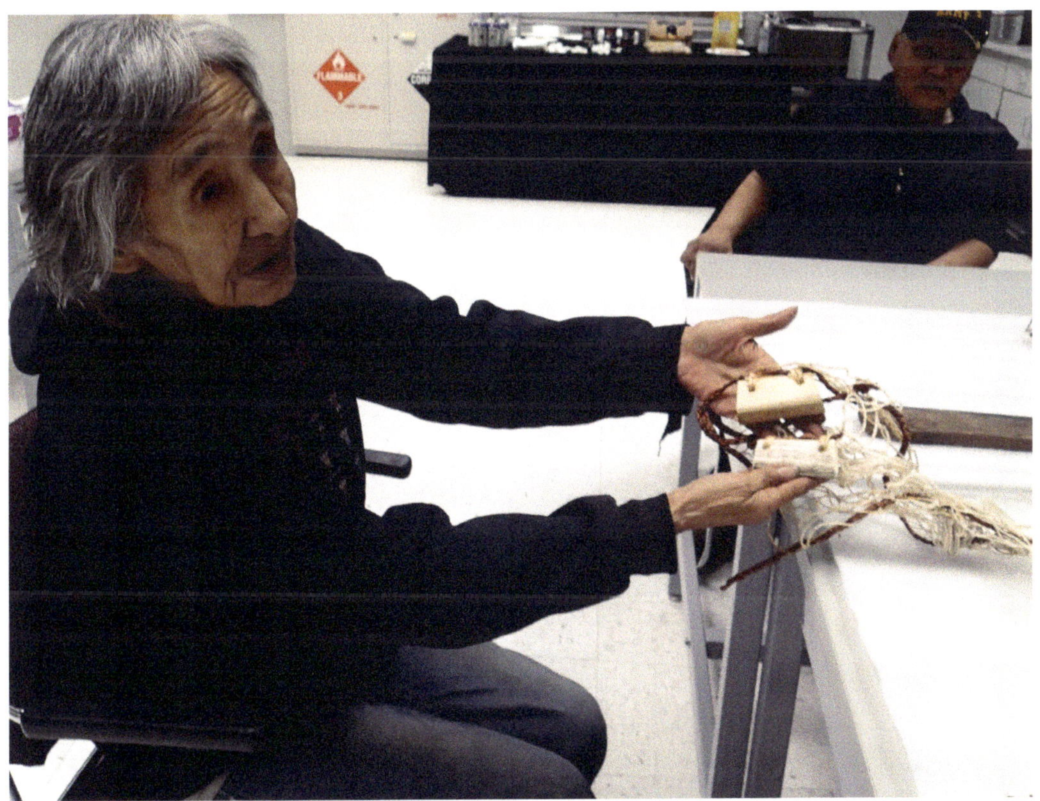

Angie examining the fishnet's wooden floats and bone sinkers, April 2024. *AFR*

them. We had couple a dogs that died because of quills. Them quills move when your muscles move, they move in. 'Cause they got little barbs.

When [porcupines] go, they go inside the trees with their head hid and their back [out]; and they always get fluffy in the back. And they go inside the willows, cover their head. They got long nails and hold the ground. 'Cause they got [no quills] down there [on the belly].

And if animals are trying to catch [porcupines], they'll try to flip them over and catch 'em in the belly, around the neck.

Angie noted that both porcupines and squirrels are bad omens:

If you gonna lose somebody in your family, you'll see that porcupine right there. And you turn around little bit, then you go toward it, you can't find it. It's nowhere to be found. They say that somebody in your family is gonna die, 'cause you can't find it. They're jealous, and they're bum.

Like squirrels, they're bum when they get into your stuff.

You know, like how that porcupine do that. Somebody in your family is gonna die, that squirrel will come, mess around your place. Can't catch 'em, but it'll mess around your place.

Returning to the moose-sinew net, I commented on the net made of braided spruce roots that elders had examined at the Berlin Ethnographic Museum in 1997, asking if people along the middle Kuskokwim made nets of other materials. Angie said spruce roots were used for *piicikat* (birch-bark baskets) but not nets. And Wassily noted that some made nets of twine. Wassily then commented on how different it was along different parts of the river:

Just like in our area, if you look at and talk to people, and as you travel upriver or downriver, the things that they used to help them survive are so different from each area.

Let's take Nikolai and Medfra; that's a little, small area. And they used different things than we did in between Stony River and Crooked. And then in between McGrath and Stony River, it's another thing, different; we're not the same. When you see things like this, mainly in your area, but if you look at other areas, then you'll understand why it's so different.

Wassily then mentioned old Gusty Mikael from Stony River:

I sat down with him, and I kick myself all the time – the stories he tells about different areas, how they take care of themselves. You know, we have all these things that come from all over the area. He knew seven

> languages. And they used to tell us that he was a shaman. He used to travel, and he spoke Iñupiaq and Athabascan, Yup'ik. And he speak perfect English.

Angie added: "He could talk to anybody in their language. People come from Lime Village. He used to sit down, have tea or coffee. Then he ask them about the news up there. And he'd tell about the news down here."

Urluveq pitegcaun-llu / *Bow and arrow*

The next piece we looked at was a bow from Kanakanak in Bristol Bay and collected in 1927 by Otto William Geist. I asked if people were still making and using bows when they were young. Wassily noted that spears were used more than bows and that bows and arrows were used mainly for hunting ducks. Angie remarked: "They used to make us bow and arrows when I was a kid. I remember that. But when they gave me my arrows, they had put a spent .22 bullet, where the point is, so we wouldn't hurt them animals, us girls. The boys had pointed [arrows], really sharp." Mark also had arrows tipped with a .22 shell when he was young: "They were worried that I might hit one of the boys hunting with me. They were good for little birds."

Wassily remembered attaching string to his small arrows, to retrieve them after shooting:

> And some people use 'em for fish. And what they do with arrows – they make a little hole, and they use that sinew and wrap it. Like, long ago, they had them wooden thread holders. They used to make one where you spin it up and you shoot. Arrow don't go too far, and you don't lose

Bow (*urluveq*) made of driftwood, nocked at both ends. The bow was collected at Kanakanak in Bristol Bay by archaeologist Otto William Geist in 1927. *UA Museum of the North UA66-002-0013, Micki LeClair Sievers*

> it. If that string end, and you don't hit, it'll drop. [Use it for] fish or ducks that are close.

Wassily added detail on how the string was wound: "The thread had a little stick in the middle, and you roll it up. You just twine that string, and in the middle of the stick it's got a little hole. And it attached to your arrow. And when you shoot it, this thing spins out, and then you spin it back. After you get done pulling whatever you catch in, you wind it back up." Marie remarked: "Roll it back up. Oh, like rod and reel." Wassily replied: "Yaa. I think that's where that fishing thing came. Learning from us."

Wassily added that the arrow points for fish had a little barb, to keep the fish from getting off. Fish spears, however, could have two or three prongs, made from moose bone: "When you cut up moose, the hind leg got one long, skinny bone [beside the leg bone]. And that's what they used to spear fish. Mainly whitefish, in the falltime. They make little barbs on 'em. When you catch a fish, you use three [prongs]."

Months later, cooking a moose leg in Anchorage, Wassily pointed out these bones, one on each side of the hind leg, leading from the hock down to the dew claw: "And those bones, they're about [eight inches] long in the back of the leg, when you cut it off. And that little bone is used for a lot of things." Angie mentioned crochet hooks and hair pieces, even a *canassuun* (carving knife). Wassily explained: "On the end, where it's fat, they file that one end, and they put a little piece of metal and rivet it on. That metal, they bend it and use it for carving."

Moose leg bones used to make a variety of things, including arrow and fish spear points, carving knives, and crochet hooks. *AFR*

Bear spear

While we had been discussing bows and arrows, Angela had been searching collections for the steel-tipped bear spear, collected by Jack McGuire in the McGrath area, that she knew was there: "It was hiding from me. I opened the drawer and it wasn't there. And I had to look again. And then it showed itself to me." As she brought it in, heads turned, and Angie exclaimed, "Whoa!"

Wassily remembered a similar spear he had seen when he was young:

> [My Ap'a] Big Feller [Sakar] used to have one. It was made out of tamarack with nothing, no metal, no rock [at the tip]. It was all [wood]. Because tamarack is one of the hardest woods in the state when they dry.
>
> The one I caught [that] my Ap'a had, it was all wood. But that thing was speared out to where it was just a point. And I thought he painted it, in about halfway it was red. But it was blood stain.
>
> What they used to do was tease the bear and run away. And that [butt] end was at an angle, where they stick it in the ground. And it wasn't metal. It was all wood made out of tamarack tree; about that size [seven-and-a-half feet long].

Angie agreed: "They used to make stuff with what was available. They couldn't look at catalog to order what they needed. They used whatever they had."

Wassily then explained how the spear was used:

> So the other end was at an angle...and goes in the ground, and the point is up there. And when you catch, it come up with the [movement] of that bear. And then you push it.
>
> [My dad] would be by the end. And the bear is coming.
>
> What you do is you run away after you tease it. And when it's getting close, you just stick this one in the ground, and the bear would be so close that it can't move it. It will get stuck around the chest.
>
> You know all your cartilage are in there. And the heart is close by, and the main vessel. And that thing will poke in, and you'll come up, and you push it this way and you roll the other way.

Continuing his explanation, Wassily added:

> When [the bear] is coming, you help [the spear] come up. Soon as [the bear] is coming, you just lift this one up and then push it away from you.
>
> You roll away from it. You push it that way and roll this way. You

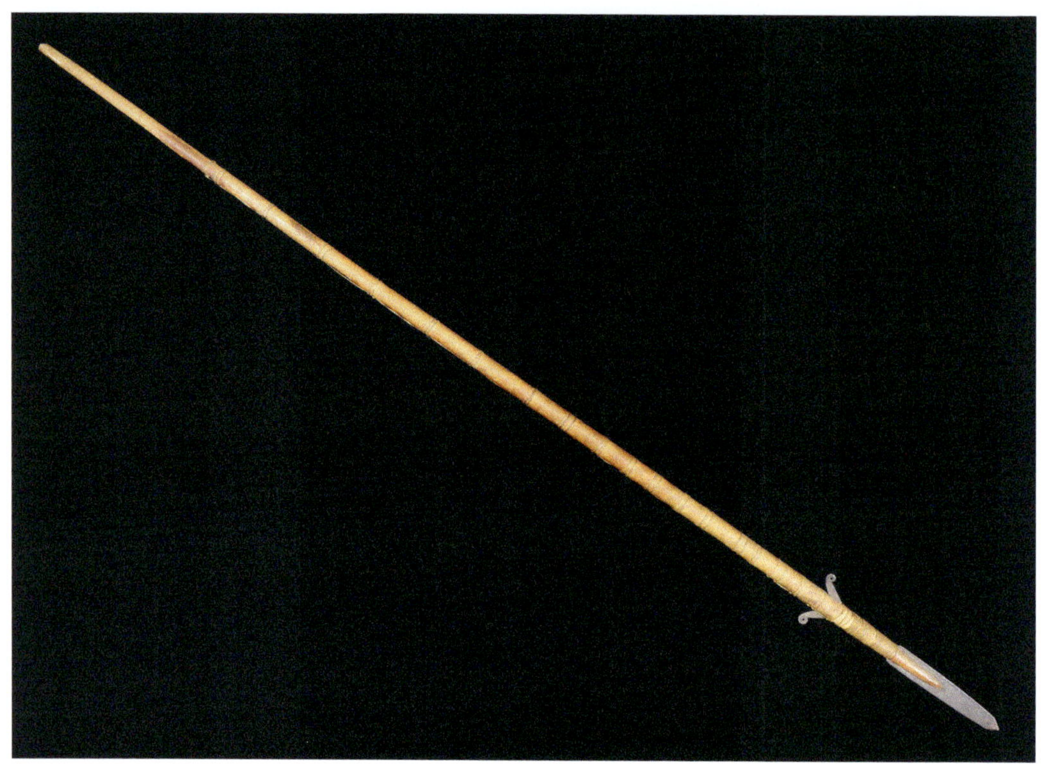

Metal-tipped bear spear collected in the McGrath area in the mid-1900s. *UA Museum of the North UA69-080-0040, Micki LeClair Sievers*

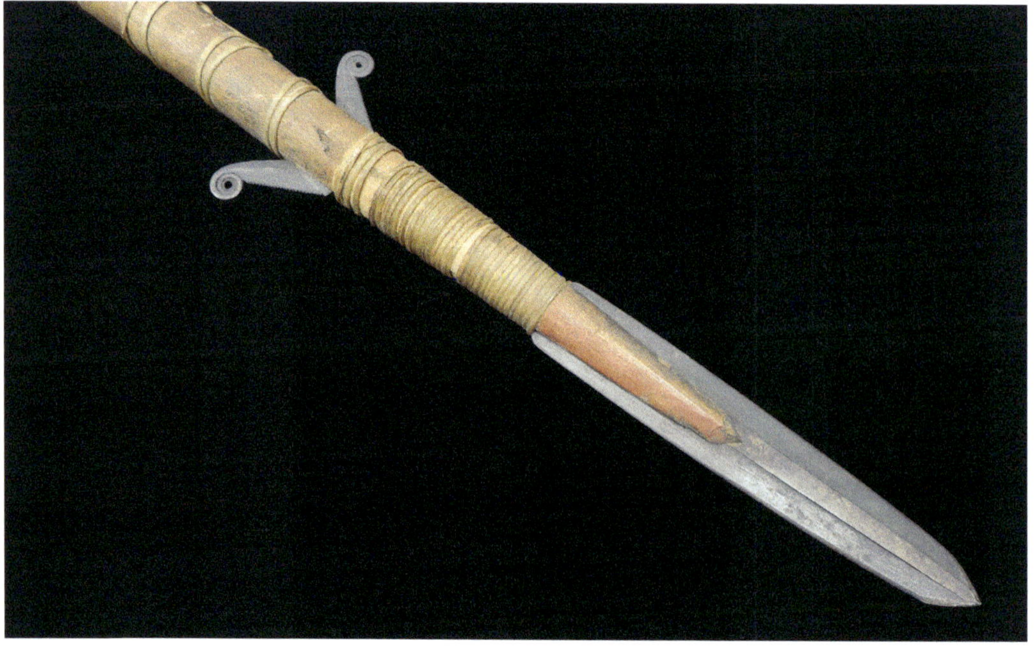

Close-up of the bear spear point. *UA Museum of the North UA69-080-0040, Micki LeClair Sievers*

don't roll with the bear. Otherwise, it'll eat you. You roll away to get away from it.

He's already poked, he can't move; can't do anything. He falls down. And you have a hatchet, they call it *kaputaq* [poker]. And hit it. And that's how you kill the bear.

Wassily added that this technique was never used on moose:

They say that's one of the most dangerous animals. You think they're very gentle animals, but they're not. When they get mad, they run over anything. And they're the most dangerous animals, they used to tell us. Bear, when they stand up, you just stay away from their left 'cause they're left-handed. You always move to the right of a bear.

Wassily holding up a skin stretcher to demonstrate the spear's angle before being raised when a bear charged, April 2024. *AFR*

Tangluqs / *Snowshoes*

We looked at one more piece before we stopped for lunch – a pair of snowshoes collected in Kwethluk in 1968, curved up at the front. Angie's eyes immediately took them in: "My dad used to make that kind." Wassily explained: "They're flat. Then when you put that rawhide in the front like that and you start working up, they turn up like that. You gotta have the wood wet, and it turn up like that when you tighten it up."

Wassily explained the choice of wood: "When they're making *tangluqs* [snowshoes] like that, they always tell us, 'Look for birch.' You know some of them birch have limbs like that, going down. Those are straight and easy to bend. Birch that have limbs that are curved. And that's what they [use to] make these wood parts."

Wassily then described the use of moose hide for the webbing:

> And the rawhide part, that's from moose skin. Man, you gotta have patience, especially working on these little ones. What they do, they get these birch and they soak 'em in water; keep 'em in water until the rawhide is ready.

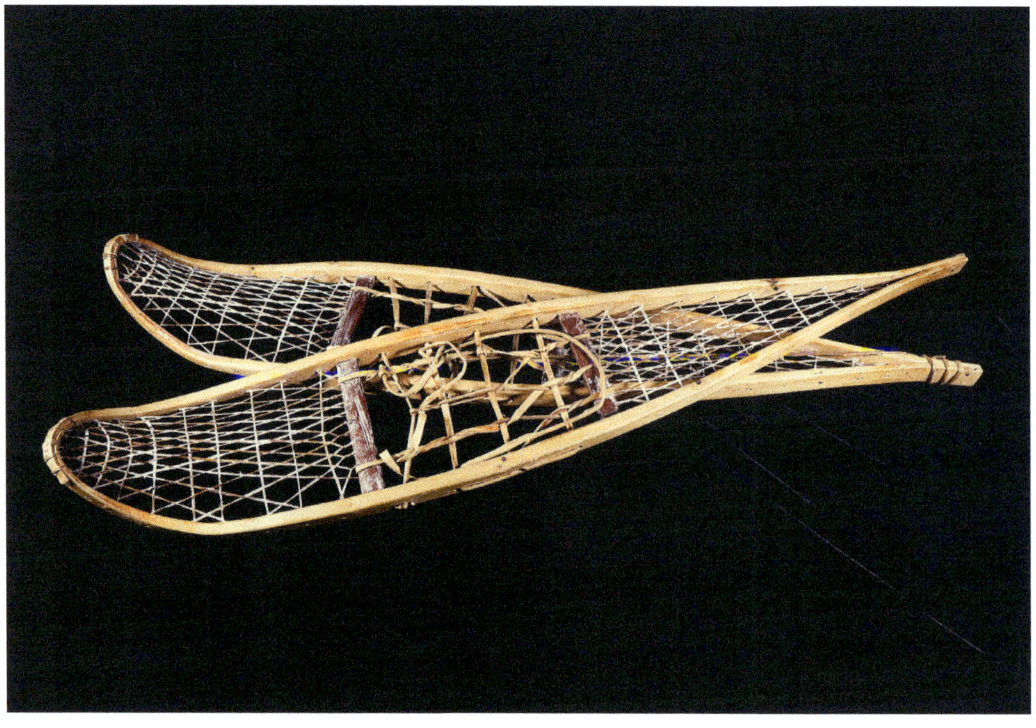

Snowshoes collected in Kwethluk in 1968. *UA Museum of the North UA68-015-0010AB, Micki LeClair Sievers*

> And I'm pretty sure Jennie and Angie has seen them before. They put that moose hide in a tub or barrel [of water] and, man, they get stink. And every now and then you grab it, and you pull the hair. And if it don't come out, you just keep it in there. Man, that's some powerful smell.
>
> And once the hair start coming off, take [the hide] out and pluck all the hair out, all of it. And then you take the hide, and you stretch it as tight as you can, just like beaver skin, and let it dry. Then they have those little curved knives.
>
> The [smaller front and back mesh of the snowshoes] are from the soft part of the moose, the stomach part, 'cause they're thin, easy [to cut]. And these ones are thicker. They get it from the back part, 'cause it's thicker.
>
> And once you get them all cut out, and you soak 'em again, maybe three [or] four days, up to a week, when it gets soft. Tie the end to a little tree and start pulling, stretching it out.

Once the webbing is prepared, work on the wood continues. Wassily explained:

> Once you get it all done stretching, you start on the wood and make holes and put these cross pieces in. And then, this [birch wood] is already soaked. And they start from up here; you tie it in on the end and go like that, and they drill holes.

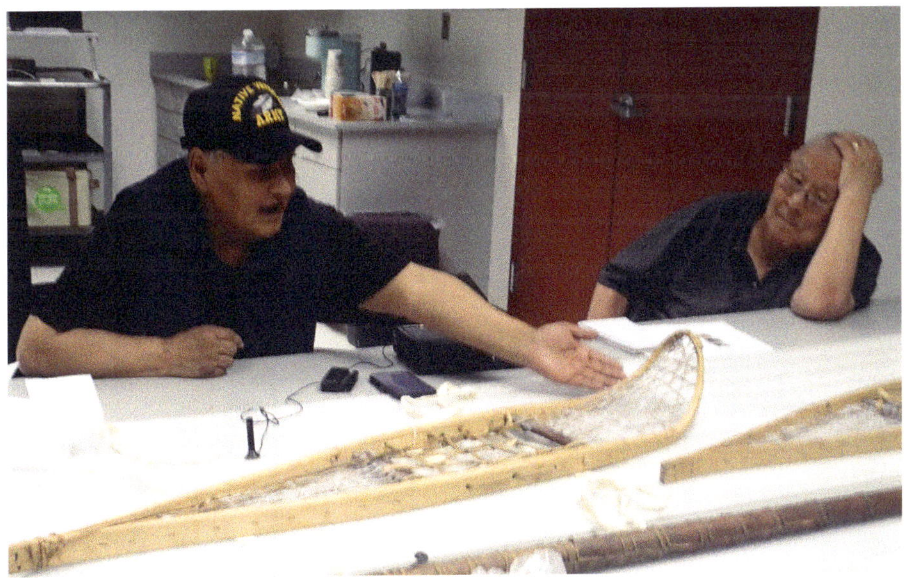

Wassily explaining how snowshoes are constructed so that they curve up at the tip, April 2024. *AFR*

> They had a little thing with little [point], they call it blue nails. When I made it, we had blue nails, and we sharpen and drill holes, and we put those things. And this rawhide [for the front and back] is wet.
>
> And when you start on it, it's tighter up here [at the front], and it bends up the wood naturally, like it's made to bend. It's thin, so it bends easy and get thicker. And where you stand [on the snowshoe], it's thicker to keep you floating in the snow.
>
> And each [snowshoe], it's got that [place] where you put your feet in. And most of 'em use 'em with *kameksaks* [skin boots]; they didn't have no winter boots. They stick their feet in there, put 'em back and then cross the [tie strings].

Finally, Wassily noted that the webbing and frame were rubbed with beaver fat to help them hold their shape:

> Like I was saying, they used beaver fat to keep it from stretching or anything once it get molded like this. And waterproof it. That beaver fat used to be used for many things, for skins, hides. I seen 'em used on canvas canoes. They didn't have paint, so they used those for waterproofing.
>
> And then the back is tied like this. These things are just like this, molded in or carved in.

Wassily had made and used snowshoes like this, and he explained again how the snowshoe got its curved toe: "When you start it, it's straight [flat]. And when you put the mesh, [then it bends]. 'Cause when you put these in, they're wet, so it'll be easier. And when they dry up, they just mold and come up naturally."

Wassily pointed out that the wooden frame was made in two overlapping pieces, attached just in front of the foot: "The reason why they do that is to help make this [front] right here, help it curve. 'Cause if you don't do that, and you make it all [one piece], it'll stay down. It'll have like a straight bear claw [bear paw]." He chuckled, recalling the wide, flat snowshoes non-Natives made when they came into the country:

> When the white man came, they make that round bear [paw] or bear feet. They're wide snowshoes like that.... When the white man came, that's when they start making that.... They call it bear feet or bear [paw].
>
> I've noticed that after Red Devil and Aniak become mainly white, then you start seeing those wide ones, round, short, they're not long. But ones like these are the ones that keep you up, even it's soft [snow]. You don't

Wassily talking about the process of using moose hide for snowshoe webbing, April 2024. *AFR*

sink, maybe about that much in the snow.

Marie asked if snowshoes were used often, and Wassily answered: "Lots." Angie agreed: "Every day. I had snowshoes. They were made skinner and shorter than regular size. But they used to make me snowshoes when I was a kid. And they were only mine, nobody else. See, I grew up being spoiled rotten." Laughing, Wassily quipped, "Only child," and Angie continued: "But I learned by watching everybody else. I had no interest in the house. I had lots of interest in the outside, what the boys were doing. I didn't really like to cook. There was girls who love to cook. I wasn't one of them."

Wassily noted that snowshoes were well cared for, kept out of reach of animals: "We always hang them up; in the house or outside. Same way with sleds, made with rawhide. Everything was all carved in. There was no ropes." Jennie added: "Only reason they put them up was 'cause there were so many mice." If well cared for, snowshoes lasted for years. Wassily had his until he went to school:

> In 1964 when I froze my feet; that's when I go to ANMC [Alaska Native Medical Center] hospital, that old hospital. That's the last time I used snowshoes.
>
> I didn't have the right shoes; plus I got wet, more then 50 below. Family was up George River. We run out of food. Was going to Vanderpools to go get food. We had sled load of fur. Too cold. He couldn't fly.
>
> So they send my brother and I down. But I got unlucky, I froze my feet.

Treasures from Canoe Village

After looking at the snowshoes, we stopped for lunch in the Museum cafe – a bright space with huge windows facing south and letting in the spring light. Settling at small tables, we chatted companionably, then headed back into collections to see what Angela had in store for us.

The very first thing we looked at was a dance belt. Angela read the record, letting us know that the belt had been made by Bedusa Derendy from Canoe Village. Angie looked up, amazed: "That's my Ap'a's mom, my great-grandma. It could've been my Ap'a's mom, on my dad's side. My dad is Derendy. And my mom's side is Effemka." Angie continued, sharing that her dad was born in Canoe Village, before the Derendy family moved farther upriver, to Sleetmute, settling just below Mellick's trading post, where Angie's dad, Steve Derendy, later built his own home.

Angela Linn then shared details from the museum records that confirmed Angie's first impression – that the belt was, in fact, made by her great grandmother, Bedusa. Records said that Bedusa Derendy (originally Bedusa Gregory before she married Stephan Derendy) had made the belt, as well as a beautiful beaded collar and decorative hair ornament, for her daughter, Elena Peters, when she was a girl in the early 1900s. In 1954, after Bedusa had passed away, Elena (then a married woman with children of her own) sold the pieces to the Museum of the North, where they are today.

When asked about the pieces, Angie said that although they were made by her *ciuliaq* (ancestor), she couldn't say anything about them, as they were made long before she was born in 1948, as well as before her father was born in 1921. Looking at the belt, I could see ties where it connected around the waist: "It looks like other dance belts we've seen [worn to this day in southwest Alaska] that would hook around the waist. Maybe she was getting ready for a first dance or something special, so her mom made this for her. Special things." The dentalia shells – the shells of large scaphopods indigenous to the north Pacific coast – decorating the "hair pretty" are, indeed, indications of significant wealth. Historically, they were important trade items and only well-to-do families could own them (Osgood 1958:63).

Angie examined the belt: "Moose hide. Lots of buttons. They used to have lotsa buttons." She added: "This Elena Peters that they're talking about; she was the one who had the calendar." This was the small, circular wooden calendar we had seen at the Anchorage Museum in fall 2023, with pegs that were moved to count the days. Angie had told us then that when she visited her grandmother, she had asked to move the pegs but was firmly denied: "Only she was allowed to touch the calendar. And I used to beg her if I could please move it. And she would say, no, I can't touch it." Chuckling, Angie also recalled that Elena was the one who made her eat too much bear fat: "They gave me too much bear fat, and I couldn't handle it. And I was trying to tell my mom, 'Mom, I can't eat this.' And then Elena Peters turn around and gave me the dirtiest look you ever see, so I tried to take another bite." I asked Angie: "So Elena Peters was an old woman when you were young?" She answered in the affirmative: "That was Ap'a Moxie's second wife."

Angela returned with a map, showing Canoe Village on the south side of the Kuskokwim. Wassily observed: "Right there Canoe Village. It used to be a big place. It's supposed to be on the north side, 'cause I remember there used to be lotsa houses in here. And there was nothing on the other side, by that creek." Angie added: "Growing up, the only time that I ever heard my dad talking about Canoe Village was when we went down there. And he told me that he was born there. And this was the first time I had ever heard of Canoe Village. They didn't tell me too much of my ancestry." Wassily agreed: "They used to hardly ever talk about ancestry long ago. Bits and pieces here and there, mainly relatives and family."

Reading from the museum records, Angela shared more of the belt's history:

> So Ivar Skarland was the director of the Museum at that time; an

Angie examining the "hair pretty" made by her great-grandmother Bedusa Derendy, April 2024. *AFR*

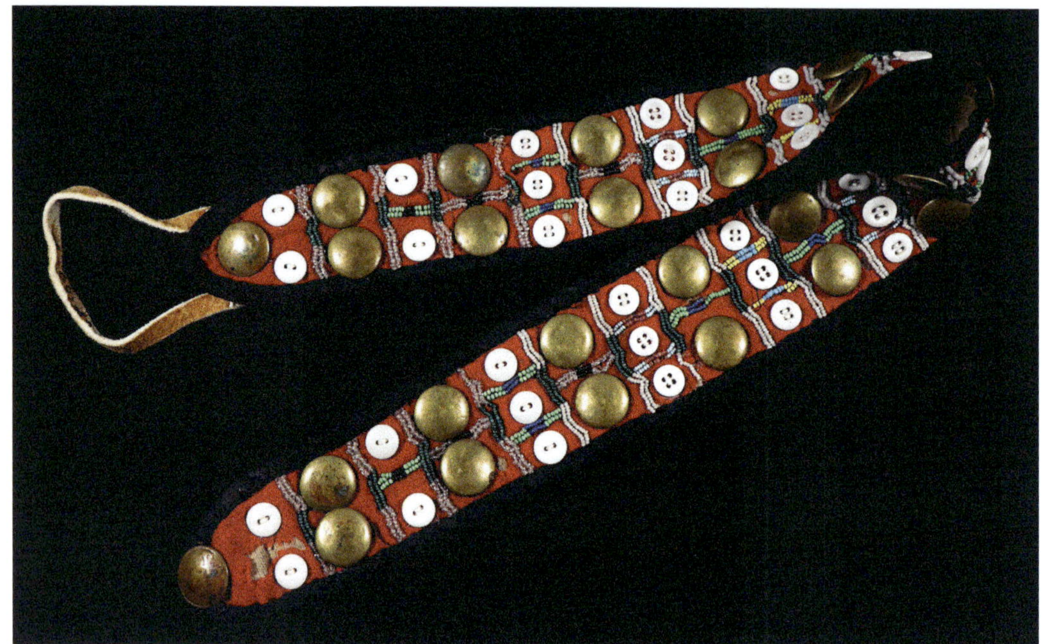

Belt made by Bedusa Derendy for her daughter, Elena, in the early 1900s. Bedusa created the design using shell shirt buttons, brass buttons, and glass seed beads. *UA Museum of the North UA64-065-0007, Micki LeClair Sievers*

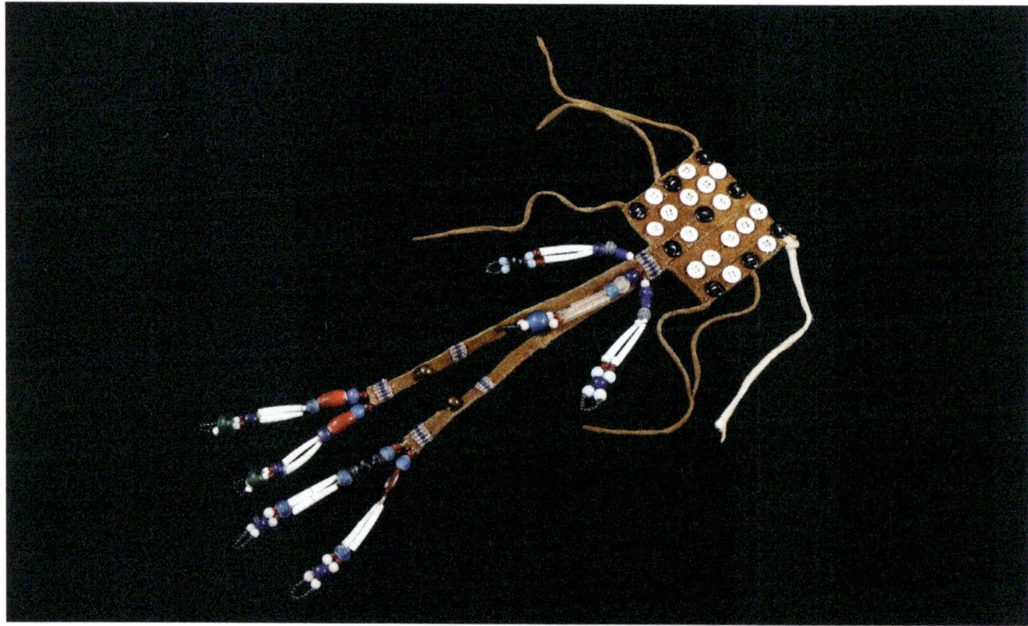

"Hair Pretty" also made by Bedusa Derendy for her daughter, consisting of a square piece of moose hide with a long, slit piece of hide sewn on. The square is decorated with black and white buttons, and fringed on each side, with longer strands decorated with trade beads and dentalium shells. *UA Museum of the North UA64-065-0006, Micki LeClair Sievers*

> anthropologist. So I think they sold these items. And it said in his letter [from F. L. McConkey, the BIA teacher in Sleetmute and one of Skarland's former students at the University]: "They were made by Bedusa Derendy, now deceased. Bedusa lived at what the local Natives called Canoe Village, a now abandoned village located below Crooked Creek. Bedusa made them for her daughter, Elena, when the girl was about six years old. Elena is now around 48. The neck piece was enlarged as Elena grew older. Elena says the beads were removed from the belt and the hair piece, but she could replace them if she had the beads. If you are interested and care to suggest a price, I'll pass the information along to Elena Peters and ask if that would be acceptable."
>
> So that was in November 1954. And then in December it says that the family sold it to the Museum.

Discussing names, Angie noted that although they called Elena's husband Peters, he was known as Moxie Pete, whose younger brother was Tony Pete. Written records noted that Bedusa's Yup'ik name was Nasaurluq. Also, the 1954 date of the letter suggests that F.L. McConkey was probably the teacher who sent the Sleetmute recipe book to the Museum of the North in 1955. We have a lot to thank him for.

Bedusa had made a beaded collar, on display upstairs in the Museum's art gallery. Angela shared: "My absolute favorite piece [in the Museum]. I remember when I first opened the drawer, my breath was just taken away."

While Angela shared details of the belt's acquisition, Angie sat touching the piece, looking closely at what her great-grandmother had made more than one hundred years before. "So amazing!" she whispered, and Jennie kindly added, "Something good to remember." It was an emotional moment, so unexpected, with Angie close to tears. Jennie continued, "So lucky you are, Angie. You are very lucky." And Angie replied: "And people can see it and touch it. Yaa. So good!"

Marie asked if Angie wanted to put it on for a picture for her family, but Angie hesitated – "So ugly my clothes" – before gently lifting the belt up and putting it around her waist. Everyone was watching. Chuckling, Angie exclaimed: "So cool! Made by my family.... I am so proud! I knew that they were very creative and talented, because of all that stuff that I've seen, what they've made. But I had no clue." Wassily agreed: "Yep. Just wondering what I was missing out." Angie responded: "No kidding. And Bertha, too; I don't think she even knows any of this. My cousin Bertha from Elena's side. But she never had interest in long ago, just here and now. Oh, man!"

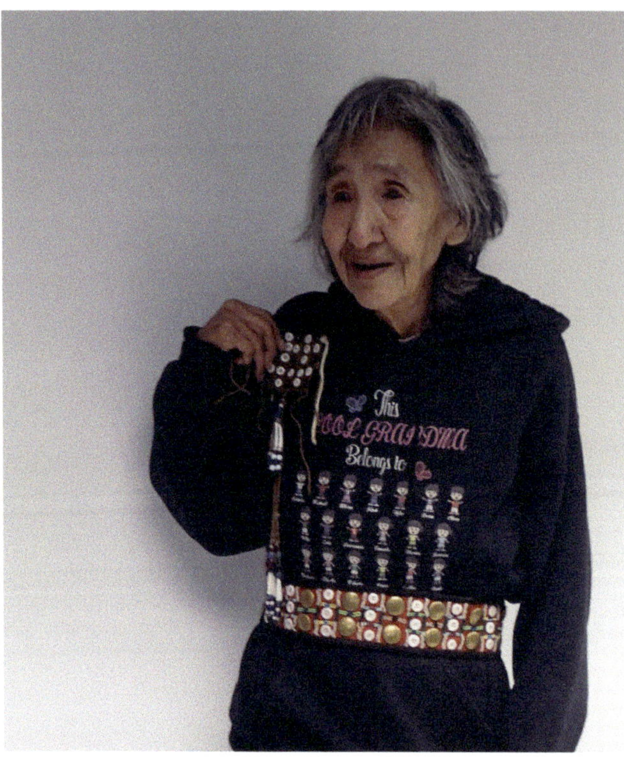

Angie trying on the belt and "hair pretty," April 2024.
AFR

Angela had been sitting off to one side as we talked, and Wassily invited her over: "That's so funny. You sitting way over there." Angie agreed: "You can come join us. So amazing! Man!" From the beginning, the atmosphere at the Museum had been welcoming, but this discovery of close relations sealed the deal. I told the group briefly how this reminded me of our visit to the Berlin Ethnographic Museum, more than 30 years before, when Marie's uncle, Wassilie Berlin, had thanked the museum staff for the good care of the Yup'ik treasures in their collection. Angela was part of the group, too: "We couldn't do this without you."

Wassily and Angie continued to examine the belt's workmanship. Wassily said: "I was trying to see the sewing, and it doesn't look like regular sewing, like it's got little creases and goes through them buttons going up." Angie added: "You can see the moose hide goes all the way. 'Cause those buttons have that loop on the back side of them." Jennie observed: "No artificial glue or anything. Imagine how long it would take."

Wassily noted that Canoe Village was one of the largest communities in the past, before people moved to Crooked Creek:

> Big Feller was the first one [to move to Crooked Creek]. And then after, they make the church there.... And then Sam Parent came down from Sleetmute and built that store. He's related to [Angie].
>
> When he built that store everybody from Canoe Village move up. They moved right there, above the store, and then up around Golga's. And our place used to be last house by that island.
>
> Lower village and upper village. And there used to be Shurp, the [BIA]

Elena Peters and her husband, Moxie. According to Nixie Mellick: "Moxie and Elena used to love to dance and were a pleasure to watch when I was a young laddie. Moxie had only one lung from TB but that never slowed him down. Elena used to handle a rifle just as good as any man" (Cussack-McVeigh 2002). *UA Museum of the North*

Mary Macar (Moxie) wearing her beautiful parka. Mary was the last one to wear "virgin beads." *UA Museum of the North*

> teacher. And Sam Parent had his own runway down there. And then Shurp had his runway. And that's where the mail, post office was. And where that TC [Traditional Council] office is now, there was the old BIA school, where I went to school.
>
> So, most of Canoe Village moved to Crooked Creek. [Angie's] dad and them moved to Sleetmute.

Angie added detail on her family's ties to Crooked Creek: "My mom's dad was Sam Parent's uncle. Sam Parent's mom and mom's dad are brother and sister. My mom was born in Crooked. Even my Ap'a moved up to Sleetmute. But Sam had a store in Sleetmute, too. Then he moved to Crooked. And then he went down to Kalskag and started one down there." Wassily recalled: "After that [store] in Crooked started. 'Cause those guys made their own barge, and they haul their [freight], they get their food in the spring. And then [they] made their fall orders and pick them up in Bethel and come up. Same way with Paul Kameroff [who ran a store] in Kalskag." Wassily shared that Paul Kameroff was his uncle: "My ancestors are originally from Emmonak, on my dad's side. They migrated up and over to the Kuskokwim. That's what Mom told me. They have relatives in Emmonak; his dad's dad and mom moved over."

Russian Orthodox Church, Sleetmute, 1956. Showing Stephan Derendy and his second wife, Olinka Derendy. Stephen is the tall man standing behind and to the left of Bishop Amvrossy (in the front row). *UA Museum of the North*

Elena Peters (Macar) (Derendy). According to Nixie Mellick: "Elena was very masculine oriented. She never took a back seat to no man. She was a good trapper and hunter. She had excellent memory. She was an outstanding citizen of Sleetmute" (Cussack-McVeigh 2002). *UA Museum of the North*

Cuukiit / *Burlap socks*

Next was a pair of socks, crocheted using thread carefully unraveled from a burlap bag and decorated with yarn designs, in different colors, extending across the top and sides. Angie picked them up with enthusiasm, "This is so cool." Wassily noted: "I used to wear this kind all the time. Mine were never this pretty. They were just plain." Angie had used burlap as well: "And mine were just little squares of gunny sack that they used to put on feet, and then they wrap them. Sometimes they put grass inside."

Jennie added their name: "*Nemerqutaq* [also *nemenglluk*, 'foot wrapping used in place of socks']." Marie mentioned *piineq* (grass insole, boot liner) used on the coast, but Jennie observed, "I don't think we ever seen grass ones in our lives." Angie noted that this pair was well-used, and Wassily joked, "Try smell 'em."

Burlap socks. A card attached to one sock reads “2.50 Anna Phillips.” Although the material was new, Anna employed the same technique used in the past to make grass socks. *UA Museum of the North UA2002-001-0101AB, Micki LeClair Sievers*

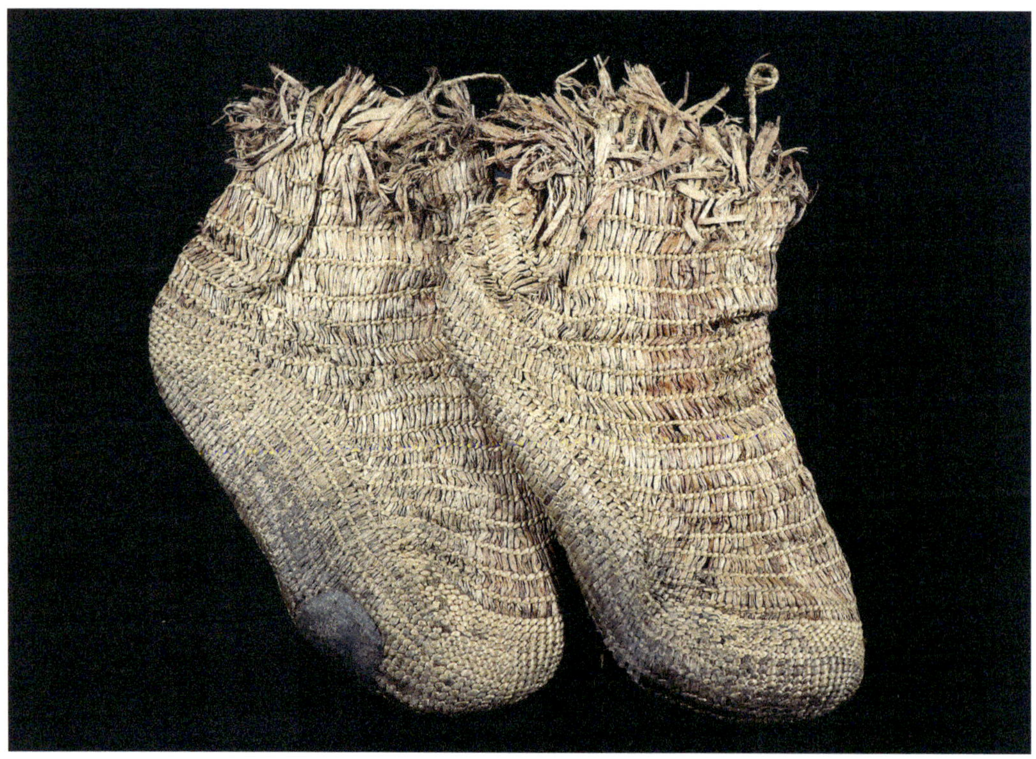

Twined grass socks collected by Otto Geist on Nelson Island in 1927. Each sock has a short strand of braided grass for fastening the pair together. *UA Museum of the North UA93-001-0003AB, Micki LeClair Sievers*

Angela showed us a pair of grass socks made in 1927 and collected on Nelson Island by Otto Geist. The burlap socks were more recent, made by Anna Phillips sometime before 1959 and collected from Aniak. Wassily noted: "The Phillips are originally from Crow Village. Descendants of Sam Phillips, that Crow Village Sam." Looking at the socks from Aniak reminded Wassily of passing by Aniak when he was young: "I remember when I was a kid, we were passing there; everybody was covered with tarp. I had to peek." Wassily's comment reminded Angie of her own father driving in the rain:

> I remember those, when it was bum weather, my dad used to use string, and he'd stay inside the tent with us, and he'd drive the motor; speed it up with string. And he had string in this hand, this hand, and he'd tie string on his feet, and he'd go like this.
>
> I used to think my dad was so much fun. He did lots of things that you never would've thought possible. Like driving through that rain, inside of a *qilakutaq* [canopy] in your boat. They used to tie everything up.

Angie and Jennie examining the burlap socks along with the grass socks, smiling while recalling what they used in the past, April 2024. *AFR*

Aliimatek / *Beaver mittens*

Jennie looking at the beaver mitts collected by Wayne House in the Aniak area. *UA Museum of the North UA2006-006-0024AB, Micki LeClair Sievers*

Our next piece was a pair of beaver-skin mittens collected by Wayne House, then living in Aniak, from Sam Phillips of Crow Village sometime before 1956. Jennie shared: "We call them *aliimatek*. These are really good for driving dog team." A standard piece of cold-weather clothing to this day, the mittens excited little comment. They did, however, remind Wassily of the skin clothing his mother made to keep him warm in winter. He recalled: "My mom make us some *ciuqaleks* [fancy skin boots, made with a piece of dark fur over the shin]; *kameksaks* [ankle-high skin boots, mukluks], and parka was like this [curved in the front and back]. Them caribou skins, they're easy to tan and easy to sew."

Piicikat / *Birch-bark baskets*

We turned to examine a group of birch-bark baskets. Angie commented: "Some of them used to have wood handle. We used to always use them to pick berries. Nice and big. You can use both hands, instead of one by one."

As soon as they began to examine them, they commented on the pieces of cigarette foil folded into the top edges for decoration. Angie remarked: "They used to make everything. And these, you know when you open pack cigarettes you have that little foil. Some of 'em they used to use for decoration. I remember they used to always make these... See how close you have to be on top. But they used to use anything." Wassily added: "My mom had two different kinds. One kind of big one for these edges, corners. And the smaller one for the top. They used to say that cigarettes [had different kinds of foil].... You know, they had red ones and you look in the back, Camels or Lucky Strike."

Jennie recalled the homemade berry pickers she had used when she was young: "When I first saw those, we would go over and ask, 'Auntie, can I use it?' Sometimes we always fight over the berry picker."

Angie remembered carrying berries home: "It was always the youngest ones that carried the berries home in the backpack. Me and Mary Dooley, we used to get stuck carrying them five-gallon buckets.... Dooley was her married name. She was Mary Effemka." Jennie recalled: "I never did carry; I had older sisters." Angie remembered picking with her mother: "I was the only child, so I had to help with everything. Bigger families would get more stuff when we went out. They would get more berries, because there was lots of them. And with us most of the time it was only me and mom. But mom was a fast picker. Me, I was more into looking around, where's all the animals."

Angie examined the four nesting baskets. Wassily teased: "They call them Native Tupperware." He commented on the roots used to stitch the birch bark

Birch-bark baskets collected by Wayne House during his years living in Aniak before 1956. The folded birch bark is lashed together with spruce roots, with willow reinforcing the outside and decorated with a checkerboard design on the rim, using strips of colored plastic and foil, some from packs of cigarettes. *UA Museum of the North UA2006-005-0031, -0032, -0033, and -0034, Micki LeClair Sievers*

together: "The roots, they mainly get them from creeks, during springtime. Any kind of little roots, from the creek, where they pick all the small ones." Jennie noted that they used mainly spruce roots to make *piicikat*. She agreed with Wassily: "Springtime is the best time 'cause they're nice and soft." Wassily continued, noting that birch bark was also harvested in spring:

> When they cut 'em, they never go all the way [through the bark]. They just go right on top. And the tree still alive. If you cut 'em all, they have what look like a membrane inside.
>
> And then they got that inside where the sap goes. And they tried to get ones where the limbs aren't hard so they wouldn't have all them little holes.

Angie added detail: "Hunters or trappers, when they get stuck out in wilderness; when they make hot water, they used to get birch bark and put snow in it and light a fire. And it never burned. They were expert at it. They had to survive."

Angie examining one of the birch-bark baskets collected by Wayne House, April 2024. *AFR*

Looking at the baskets reminded Wassily of the birch-bark canoes used on the middle river in the past. Angela noted that although they didn't have a birch-bark canoe from the Kuskokwim, the Museum did have one from Minto on exhibit in the gallery. Wassily recalled canoes used in Crooked Creek and Sleetmute: "They used spruce sap to seal them. Best tree gum in the world." Jennie asked: "Do you chew *angeryuk* [spruce sap, tree pitch]? Every time we get wood, that's the first thing we do, is chew it like gum."

Wassily agreed: "Got to suck on it for a while and make it soft."

Angela said that was one of the questions they had for boat builders: "They talk about using the pitch to seal the seams. But we couldn't figure out, long time ago, how they would've melted it." Wassily shared: "If you look around and you see them shale rocks, you can find shale rocks that are like a bowl. That's what they used to use; heat up that rock and put that in the fire.... There's lots in Crooked." Jennie added: "There's all kinds of shapes; those are the best kinds you find. And when it rains so hard, they have rockslide, and you can find more."

Speaking of stones, Marie recalled the words *ellin* and *sellin*, words for whetstone used to sharpen knives, found around both Crooked Creek and Sleetmute. Laughing, Angie recalled: "That's where Sleetmute got its name; from the rocks. I used to like to pick them from the beach, and I show 'em to my Ap'a. And my Ap'a would look at them and he'll tell me, 'I need more this size.' So I go down, go look some more. When they're too big, I bust them, to make them smaller, the size he needed." Marie asked, "How come he wanted them that size?" Wassily replied: "Just to get her off him. She was too mischief." Angie admitted: "There had to be something to entertain me. I was so spoiled. I still am."

Wassily also recalled the poles used to move canoes upriver:

> We had open canoe. When we go someplace, we never come back right away. You know you had those two little poles. That stick is long. You use that stick to go upriver.
>
> One on each side. When you want to turn right, you use one side. Boy, some people used to go fast, experts. They go up, like Holitna or George River. They used them sticks.

Jennie added their Yup'ik name: "We called them *ayaurutet* [boat poles]. Wassily continued: "And on the top [of the canoe], they have little groove in the front of the canoe and rib, they make ridges. When they're not gonna use 'em, they put them in there. And they take their paddle and cross the river or coming down. Those sticks were used mainly for going upriver, against the current. Man, some people used to go fast."

Anguarun / *Bone propeller blade*

The next piece we looked at was unique – a propeller blade for a boat engine, made of bone in Sleetmute sometime before 1938, when it was collected by Bill Park. We had included it in our Yup'ik science exhibit, *Yuungnaqpiallerput / The Way We Genuinely Live*, in 2008 as a prime example of Yup'ik ingenuity. Mark noted: "Early on when motors broke, they made parts; 'cause there were no parts

A. G. Maddren, who took this photograph, wrote: "Indian propelling birch canoe upstream [on the Kuskokwim] by means of light hand poles, August 4, 1914." Russian explorer Lieutenant Zagoskin had observed poling in the 1840s and wrote: "We skirted a small island near the fort, crossed over to the right bank, and proceeded by poling; this means that the paddlers sit in their places and each grasps in both hands a light pole about 4 feet long with which he pushes against the stony bottom and thus propels the boat. This is fairly difficult work but the natives prefer this method of going upstream to paddling. Their paddles are single-bladed; fast water can at any moment thrust [the boat] to one side or the other; switching the paddles from side to side is laborious, while with poles the man in the bow can direct the kayak in a straight line and to the desired depth of water" (Michael, ed. 1967:264, from Wooley 2008:24). *UA-hmc-0166-apu-b2-f5-27*

around. Whatever they could find, every little metal; whatever was available. They never threw [things away]; they kept cans.... And metal containers of Crisco, lard, whatever, they kept all those and used 'em when they make sleds or boats."

Wassily recognized it as moose bone:

> This one was made out of a moose, that shoulder blade. 'Cause it got that thick part, close to the back. Or the *kuucenak* [rump], the pelvic. Back here, and right here it got those two bones.
>
> Yaa, I remember making something. I broke a prop once, and we had those old frying pans that had a metal handle. We measure 'em, cut 'em, make hole in there with nail, and then change our file; then bend it and go home. We have to put lots of washers in the back and front. I think what it did was, this block, make a hole and put 'em back; so that metal would go all the way to the lower unit housing. But we made it home, it wasn't fast, but it was good. Better than oaring.

Angie said that nowadays, when people break down, they just get stuck, and Wassily observed that this generation doesn't listen. Angie then shared advice she'd given her own children: "I used to tell my kids, 'When I tell you something, I'm gonna close one ear; so everything I tell you will bounce around in there

Bone propeller blade collected in Sleetmute, and used in place of a broken commercially-made prop. *UA Museum of the North UA0140-1080, Micki LeClair Sievers*

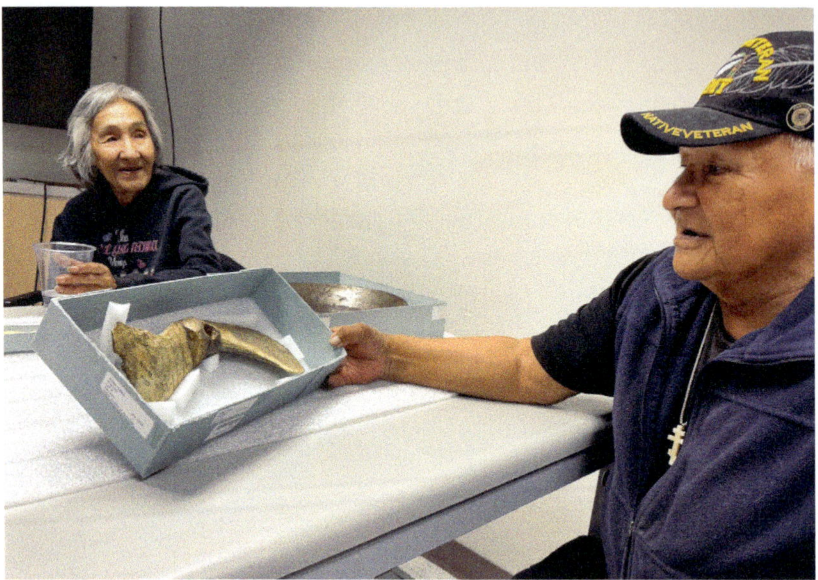

Wassily was impressed by the ingenuity and skill needed to use bone to make a replacement part for a motor, April 2024. *AFR*

before it come out.' And they used to laugh at me. But I used to tell 'em, 'Cover one ear. I'm gonna tell you something.' So, they used to cover one ear and listen."

Wassily was impressed: "It's pretty amazing for somebody to think about this, break down, and then fix it." Mark noted: "And there's even a hole for the pin." Wassily agreed: "Yaa. Right there. Very interesting. I never thought, never in my life I would see something like this again." Wassily remembered Johnny Boy in Crooked Creek making a propeller out of a frying pan: "They used handles from them frying pans, bend 'em, make a hole and put 'em on." Mark recalled watching a group of men fixing an outboard motor when he was young:

> So they took the mount of another old motor that was broken and took that piece; cut a piece off, and file it so that it fits; made it the same way. Put it back together. And there was a whole bunch of men, and they were telling stories, joking around. And when they were done, they put it together and tried it; it worked.
>
> And when they ran out of motor oil, in those old aluminum gas can up on top. And motor would come up, and we'd see it smoking, but when they pass by it smells like fried bread. Seal oil for oil. It worked!

Kepun / *Adze*

We looked briefly at a stone adze, which Nixie Mellick had donated to the museum in the 1940s. Angie commented on how heavy it was and how the stone was perfectly tied to the wooden handle with root lashing. Mark said that men used them all the time in the past when working with wood. Today they use axe blades. Angie noted: "They used to use the same kind [to make a wood fish fence]. If they gonna use wood fence, they used to tie together all them pieces of wood, with willow bark. I remember doing that."

Adze donated to the museum by Nixie Mellick of Sleetmute. The heavy stone blade is attached to a wood handle with root lashing, with thin slices of wood set on either side of the stone for a firmer connection. *UA Museum of the North EH0337-0001, Micki LeClair Sievers*

Angie examining the adze, April 2024. *AFR*

Ipuutet / *Wooden ladles*

We spent time with another group of objects – wooden ladles made in various sizes. Angie observed: "Some of these wood spoons, they used to make them so fancy. There was a guy in Kalskag, Aataq. He had made me *ipuun* [ladle]. And you could see on the *ipuun*, on the handle, he had put this [drawing] in pencil. He was gonna make some kind of design. This is the kind we used to use long time ago."

Wassily commented on the wood used to make ladles: "Most of the people use them old stumps, the driftwood in the river, and the stump [bends near the roots] like this; cut 'em [and use the curved wood]."

Angela shared the ladles' history: "All four of them were donated by a lady [Jean Burand] who worked for the Cooperative Extension Service. She was out in those communities. So those are all from Sleetmute. Her husband was a pilot, and he'd fly her around. She said those were made to be models of traditional utensils."

Wooden ladles and spoon collected by Jean Burand from villages in the Sleetmute area and donated to the Museum in 2002, said to be models of those used in the past. All but the small spoon have holes at the end of the handle for hanging on the wall. The surface of the large ladle is stained with ocher, as is the handle of one of the smaller ladles. The smallest is a spoon. *UA Museum of the North UA2002-001-0077, -0078, -0079, and -0080, Micki LeClair Sievers*

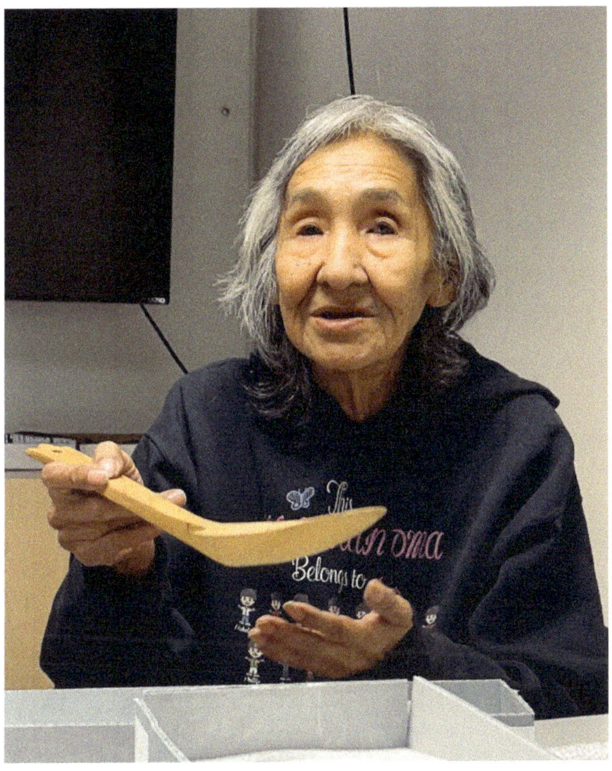

Angie holding one of the large ladles and describing how it was used, April 2024. *AFR*

Wassily observed: "Long time ago they used to make 'em so fancy. And for every kind of meal that the wife prepares, they have *ipuun* like this one they use for *egamaarrluk* [half-dried and boiled fish] or just plain boil. And then they use deeper ones like this, but bigger, for soup. This [small] one is just like you eat with it."

Looking at the spoon reminded Angie of one she'd made years ago for her granddaughter: "I had to make a spoon for Doke when she was a baby, three months old. We had to camp out on the river, and we didn't have any silverware in the boat. And she had baby food, but we needed a spoon. So I went and look for soft wood, and I make her spoon; give it to her mom. And soon as she feed that baby, when she get done, she threw the spoon." We all laughed, but Wassily added, "Makes you mad." Angie agreed:

> I was a little bit disgusted, but I didn't really care then. They just kind of made me think, "What's wrong with her?"
>
> That's what we used to do. Everything we used, we saved. Her, she just feed her baby and throw it.

Talking about spoons led to talking about knives. Angie continued: "You know how long time ago we used to always have pocketknife in our coats or pockets. We always carried pocketknife. I don't know what happened, I quit carrying them." Wassily knew the reason: "You know why you quit carrying them – you get on the plane all the time. I still have pocketknife. I was gonna leave it, I forgot, 'Oh Man.' 'Cause I lose how many." Mark lost a knife the same way: "Pocketknife that I really liked, and I had it for a long time, and it was starting to have a shine. And I lost that when I was going to get on the plane. I really felt bad about losing it. And after that I never have pocketknives in my pocket anymore."

Wassily said that he still carries an old-fashioned pocketknife: "Maybe it's a habit. It never goes away. Carry them all the time." Both men keep knives in their trucks and at home, in case of emergency. Wassily noted: "And when one of my kids move it one day, 'Where's my knife?!'" Angie noted: "Things change so fast. I know lots of my mom's relatives; all the girls had pocketknives. And some of them were so cute. They always had 'em in their pockets."

Qantat / *Bowls*

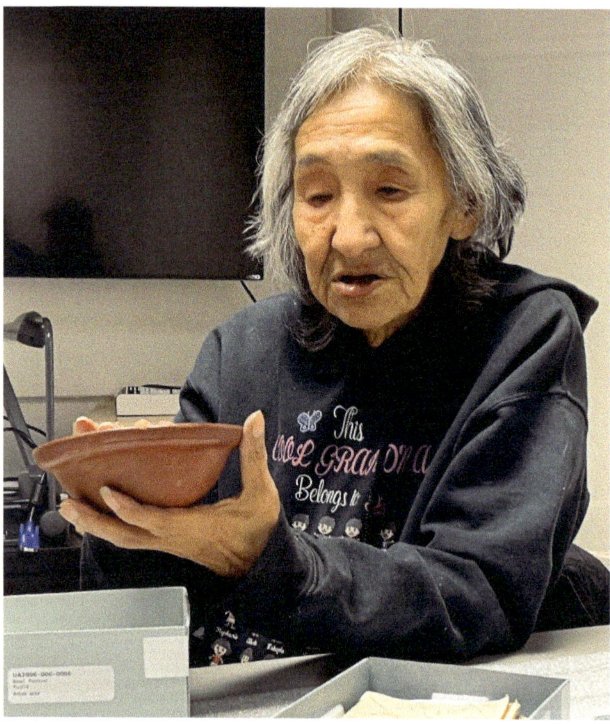
Angie recalling the plain wood bowl she used when she was young, April 2024. *AFR*

Next we examined a set of three bowls donated to the Museum by the family of Wayne House, who both Angie and Wassily remembered as the magistrate in Aniak before Mrs. Arlene Clay. Angie recalled: "The only way I know of Wayne House being a magistrate, his signature is on my birth certificate." Angela explained: "Their kids donated them, and they said he lived in Alaska between 1936 and 1956. During that time he was a trapper, prospector, a US Deputy Marshall, and owner and operator of a trading post in Aniak."

In the past, each person had their own bowl, often decorated with a family design. The bowls we were examining had never been used; looking at the freshly painted designs inside each bowl, both Angie and Wassily thought they were made as decorations. Looking at the larger wooden bowl, Wassily observed, "We used to call it *taassiq*." Angie noted, "We still do." Wassily added that large metal bowls are also called *taassiqs*: "We still call 'em the same thing."

Mark remembered the large wooden bowl his grandmother used to serve food:

When we ate plain boiled fish, all of 'em used to be in that bowl, and we ate from that big bowl, outside in the summer. And the last time I ate that way, we were in Cakcaaq. There were a whole bunch of tents with people fishing for whitefish. When we got there Mrs. Cimiugaq invited us to eat. We went there, and there was a metal rectangular one. All of the food was in there. And we all ate from that. That was the last time we ate like that. That was a few years ago, before 1989.

Wooden bowls collected in the Aniak area by Wayne House sometime before 1956 and donated to the Museum by his family. Each bowl has an old-style design painted on the inside bottom: one with a circle representing a bird's body, with its head, wings, feet, and tail facing inward; another with an x-ray image of a seal or sea lion inside a circle; and a third showing the x-ray of a sea mammal figure. *UA Museum of the North UA2006-006-0005, -0006, and -0007, Micki LeClair Sievers*

Uluaq / *Woman's semilunar knife*

The Museum's collection included a selection of semilunar women's knives from the Aniak area. To this day women throughout southwest Alaska use knives such as these for all manner of work – cutting fish, cutting cloth, skinning animals. Marie asked if the knives their mother's used were made in the same way – with two small metal bars separating the blade from its wooden handle. She noted that downriver, the handle of an *uluaq* usually rested directly on the blade. Today, some women prefer the upriver style. Angie noted:

> My grandma's *uluaq* was like that... It wasn't that tall, but when my grandma died, my mom took the *uluaq*. And from sharpening every year it's gotten smaller. And after my mom died, it's supposed to come to me, right? It skipped me and went to my oldest son 'cause he was the one who was always using it anyway. But every time you sharpen it, it gets smaller. But it's got the same kinda handle.

Jennie holding a large steel-bladed *uluaq* (woman's knife) with a wooden handle attached with two steel rods. Unlike semilunar knives used on the coast, where the handle is attached directly to the blade, upriver knives often have handles that are raised and riveted onto the blade. *UA Museum of the North UA2006-006-0001, Micki LeClair Sievers*

Marie asked if boys used *uluaqs* upriver. Angie replied: "My son did." Wassily added: "Just recently, men start using it. I never used 'em till after I got married. To me it was getting easier to cut."

Jennie said: "Some don't have this kind. And then they get little bit bigger, and they attach [the blade] to this right here [on the handle]."

Again, Wassily added detail: "They rivet it on. When you cut king salmon, you use different knife. Now that king salmon are so small, you can use that little one." Angie agreed on the need for a larger knife in the past: "Long time ago them king salmon used to be so huge. Holy cow!"

Women's semilunar knives collected before 1956 by Wayne House and, like the painted bowls, donated to the Museum by his family. All of the knives were made from steel saw blades, with handles attached in different ways – one with brass rods and another with two screws set into the metal and wood. *UA Museum of the North UA2006-006-0001, -0002, -0003, -0004, Micki LeClair Sievers*

Sami-style fur boots

Angela had set out a pair of Sami-style fur boots made by Lapp reindeer herders in Alaska and, like so many things we had looked at, collected by Wayne House. The boots were made of caribou fur overall, including the soles. Comments were brief but significant. Looking at the soles, Wassily said: "Those shoes with that hair on the outside [on the bottom], the reindeer herders use. 'Cause when you're walking on glare ice, you don't slip. Even with moose [hide, fur side out], you don't slip on glare ice." Wassily remembered the reindeer herders living below Aniak:

> Mainly in Kalskag there's Kvammes. And then they moved to Aniak. They were called Laplanders, Laapaat. They herded reindeer.
>
> They used to go up toward Crooked. And they call that place back

Jennie examining the stitching on the Sami-style boots, April 2024. *AFR*

> there Bonanza Flats. And there's a place in there where it's got pretty good size trees, where the fence [corral] used to be. Herd those reindeer in there.
>
> Mainly the Kvamme [family] were the ones that were herding reindeer.

Angie added: "And they know how to make corned moose meat. They know how to make corned bear meat, too. They say it takes long time. Boy, it tastes so good. Like corned beef." Wassily agreed: "But better."

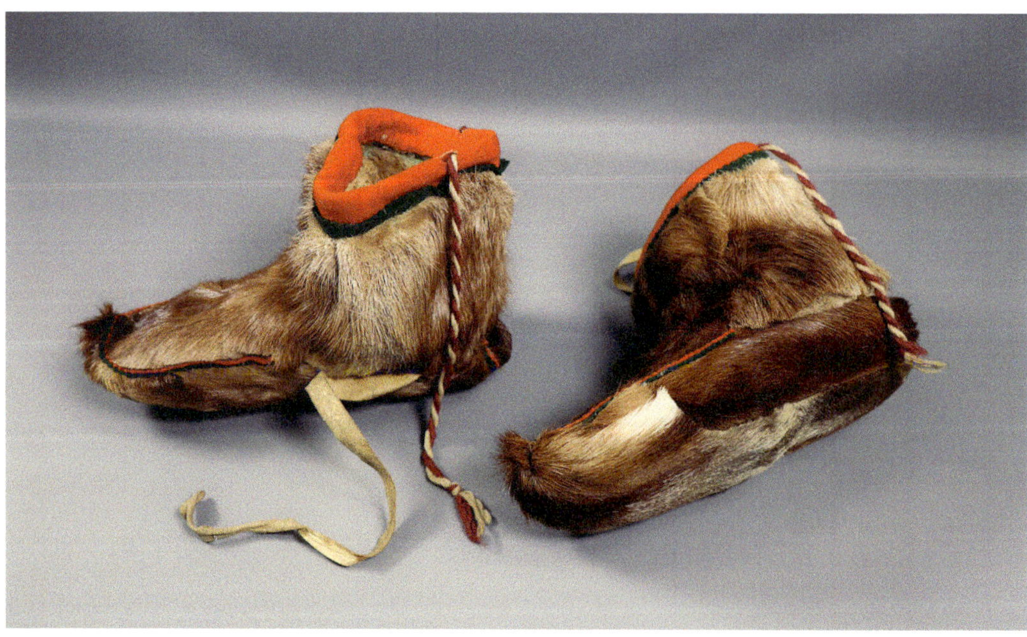

Sami-style boots made of caribou fur and collected by Wayne House. The boots are trimmed with pinked red and green felt, and the drawstrings are of twisted wool, with hide ties around the middle. *UA Museum of the North UA2006-006-0040AB, Micki LeClair Sievers*

Atkuk / *Parka*

We finished the afternoon looking at a fur parka, expertly made by Mary Valka of Kalskag in 1987. Wassily commented, "I know her. She was one of the best fur sewers." Angie added: "That is so much work. The trim is so much work." Wassily noted that the ruff was wolf. Angie agreed: "*Atkuk*. Otter coat. Those are warm." Wassily told a story about Mary:

> That one guy in Bethel, he wanted a parka like that. He gave Mary Valka $7,000, even before she make it.
>
> Just to make him parka like that. He show a picture of a parka he wanted, here's $7,000, you can make it. And you know what she did? She took half of the $7,000 for her, and she took the other half and gave it to church. And everything that she sewed, when she sell 'em, take half to herself and half to the church. And she had a longer one. Somebody bought it. He gave her $2,000 before she made it, saying this is how I want it.

Angie admiring Mary Valka's workmanship, April 2024. *AFR*

Jennie enthused: "She was so *munaq* [dexterous]." Wassily noted she passed down her ability: "She was one of them *munaq* women. Her granddaughters, there's one living in Palmer... And that Kvamme girl, Linda Kvamme in Aniak."

Looking at her database, Angela told us that Dr. Sean Stitham had donated the coat to the Museum. Wassily commented, "I'm glad he did." Angie agreed, adding, "She was known for her coats." Joking around, Wassily added: "Now, there's a gal from Holy Cross, Shirley Clarke.

Man's otter-fur parka made by Mary Valka of lower Kalskag and purchased, and later donated to the Museum, by Dr. Sean Stitham. The river otter pelts are sewn vertically, with pockets sewn through slits in the otter skin. The hood has a large sunshine ruff with three layers of fur: the inner layer of beaver closest to the face, wolverine in the middle, and the outermost layer of wolf. *UA Museum of the North UA2006-021-0001, Micki LeClair Sievers*

She's starting to do the same. She made all of Steven Seagal's underwear for [the 1994 film] *On Deadly Ground*. Steven Seagal had beaver underwear. That was the joke." So ended our day at the Museum.

The Russian Blockhouse

Jennie, Wassily, and Angie standing outside the Kolmakovsky blockhouse, near the Museum on the University's campus, April 2024. *AFR*

Our evening in Fairbanks included a festive meal with friends Uma and David Bhatt and Uma's student Amy Hendricks, and a good night's sleep at the Seven Gables. We woke early and were back at the doors of the Museum by 9 AM. Angela was there to meet us and walk us down to the Kolmakovsky blockhouse nestled in the trees one hundred yards away. It was an impressive piece of Kuskokwim River history, especially on such a beautiful spring morning, and once again we took photos for Facebook.

When the Russian American Company established Kolmakovsky Redoubt just upriver from Chuathbaluk in 1841, as a trading station and fort, the blockhouse was the first building constructed, followed by eight other structures. The Russians came eager to trade for the high-quality furs the middle Kuskokwim was known for, supplying trade goods such as tea, tobacco, and glass beads in return. When Alaska became a territory of the United States in 1867, ownership of the redoubt eventually transferred to the Alaska Commercial Company and from there to various owners. Kolmakovsky ceased to be an active trading post in 1917, and in 1929 the blockhouse was taken apart and shipped to the University of Alaska Fairbanks, where it continues to be viewed by people from all over the world as evidence of early Russian settlement in Alaska (Oswalt 1980a:48).

Wassily examining the blockhouse, showing the log construction and distinctive corner style used by the Russians and requiring no nails, April 2024. *AFR*

Wassily and Angie examined the structure, explaining how the double-lapped locking joints had been cut at an angle to keep the water out. And Angela told us the story of how the blockhouse had first come to Fairbanks and its several moves before settling at its current location in 2011 (Linn 2013). The hill above the blockhouse will soon be the home of the new Troth Yeddha' Indigenous Studies Center. A perfect spot for both the blockhouse and the Center – right beside the museum housing so many treasured heritage pieces.

The buildings at Kolmakovsky Redoubt, as seen from the river in July 1912. The blockhouse can be seen in the middle. *Robert Acheson Collection. Anchorage Museum B2009.061.1*

The Ethnology and History Lab

The five of us walked back to the museum. Mark and Marie joined us, and we went back to the classroom to stow our gear. Angela then led us down the hall to the elevator, and one flight down to the museum's storage area, including their ethnology lab. Angela's husband, archaeology curator Josh Reuther, met us at the door and showed us archaeological collections from the 2012 excavation at Canoe Village, plus objects archaeologists had found at Kolmakovsky in 1966 and 1967 (Oswalt 1980b).

Wassily identified one heavy stone as a wedge, used to split wood. Everyone was impressed by a large slate blade, which Wassily noted was used to clean beaver skins: "They put wood [handle] in the back, and they make one side [of the stone] sharp; flip it over and then they tan beaver. They call it *ellumerrun* [skin scraper]." Angie added: "We used to find [similar stones] upriver, too. Some of them were nicely worked. But we used to find them all over."

Wassily added thoughts on future archaeology in the region:

A slate skin scraper from Sleetmute (donated to the museum by Nixie Mellick in 1949) with Josh Reuther in the background, April 2024. *AFR*

> You know, when we were talking about reindeer herders going to Bonanza Flats, I was thinking about it. If somebody look around that place where they had the tents, I bet you'll find something. They used to barter with people that come. People from around there that come in to get that reindeer, and what they trade with them. I bet you there's something like [these things] in there, too.

Josh pointed out one tiny stone piece, originating 200 miles north on the Yukon River:

> So we assume it traveled across the portage [from the Innoko River].... So that's how we assume this stuff got here, and there's a lot of it. There's these little ones; they're really finely detailed. And these are made of a different material, kind of a bone point. We X-rayed one of them to see how they fit them in. We assume that these might've been traded down, or people went up and traded for them and brought them back down.

Angie and Jennie recognized an oval tin for Prince Albert tobacco found at Kolmakovsky, as well as fragments of birch-bark baskets. They also admired a fancy ivory story knife found at Kolmakovsky. A fragment from a china saucer led the group to discuss the different words for saucer – *acliq* on the coast, and *pelutsiaq* upriver. Finally, Wassily playfully pointed to a large black binder clip in the corner of one tray, asking where it had been collected.

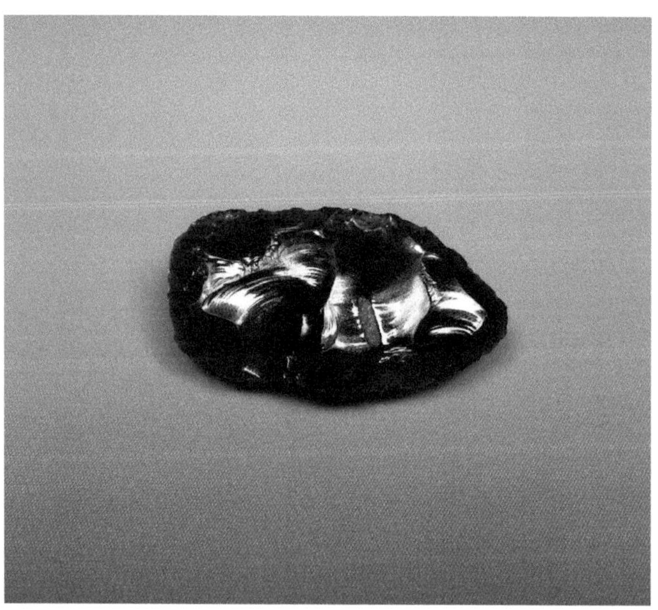

Obsidian biface found at the prehistoric site just downriver from Canoe Village (Angyaruaq). Archaeologists estimate that the material came from 450 km miles north of the Kuskokwim, likely as a trade item. *UA Museum of the North, Micki LeClair Sievers*

Our time in the archaeology lab was particularly fun for Wassily, as he recognized Josh from his work with Chris Wooley on the 2007 Cultural Resources Survey for the Donlin Creek Project. Josh has worked as an

Angie fingering a story knife found at Kolmakovsky, April 2024. *AFR*

archaeologist in the region on and off for a long time, surveying (and hiking) the route of the proposed road connecting the Kuskokwim and Yukon rivers twenty years before. He was also part of the Canoe Village dig Chris Wooley led, including young people from Crooked Creek. He and Wassily had lots to share, and toward the end of the discussion they were off on their own, catching up on friends they had in common.

Angie also made a special connection in the lab. As we talked, two people were listening from their desks against the back wall – one a Chukchi anthropologist from Chukotka, Eduard Zdor, the other a young

The Museum's archaeology lab, with Wassily playfully asking where they had discovered the binder clip included in a tray of artifacts, April 2024. *AFR*

woman, Sophie Xiaofei Zhang. Angie was drawn to the Chukotkan, and asked him who he was: "You ever hear that no matter where you go, you'll recognize your relatives? You look so familiar." When he told her where he was from, she said he must be her relative, as the original Derendy family came from the north. Angie noted that this explains why her family members are taller than other middle Kuskokwim residents. We took Angie and Eduard's picture together.

Finally, the young woman introduced herself. She turned out to be one of Marie's former Yup'ik students, who came to Fairbanks after a year at UAA. The museum was home to lots of connections.

Imarnin / *Gut rain parka*

After our lab visit, we returned to the classroom for a quick cup of coffee and a look at two more pieces of clothing which I'd chosen to spark conversation. The first was a seal-gut rain parka collected by Wendell Oswalt in 1970 from Johnny Berlin at Nunapitchuk, which Marie surmised must have been made by his stepmother Aanaller (Anna Sheppard). Jennie and Angie recognized the garment but had no experience making or wearing one. Angie recalled: "They used to always make these. Not this kind, but I remember them getting [intestines] for windows and stuff like that. And, like I said, one time I woke up and there were [beaver] guts hanging all over, all blown up. And then they cut one side and roll it like a spool of thread. And then when they need it, they just cut whatever they need." Full of remembrances, Angie remarked: "So cool. This is so fantastic. Now my grandkids want to come up and come see that piece we see. And they ask if they could take pictures. And I tell them you probably could."

Mark had used an *imarnin* and knew their properties:

> They were warm. And they kept you dry. Light. Dry. But before you put 'em on, you used to get 'em wet, flexible, and then put 'em on.... I used to be reminded to sit on them or lay on them when I'm hunting geese....
>
> And I remember the older men used to use theirs with a belt. Because they were light, they like to come up when you're going fast. So, that belt helped keep it down. And when they used kayak, they made them long enough, wide enough, near the bottom so they could put theirs around the hole [in the cockpit]. Then tie it tight. And even though the water sprays it doesn't go in.

Mark still recalls the gut parka his grandmother made for him, that blew out of his boat while traveling: "I wonder how my grandmother felt. She didn't say

Seal-gut rain parka. *UA Museum of the North UA70-053-0127, Tamara Martz*

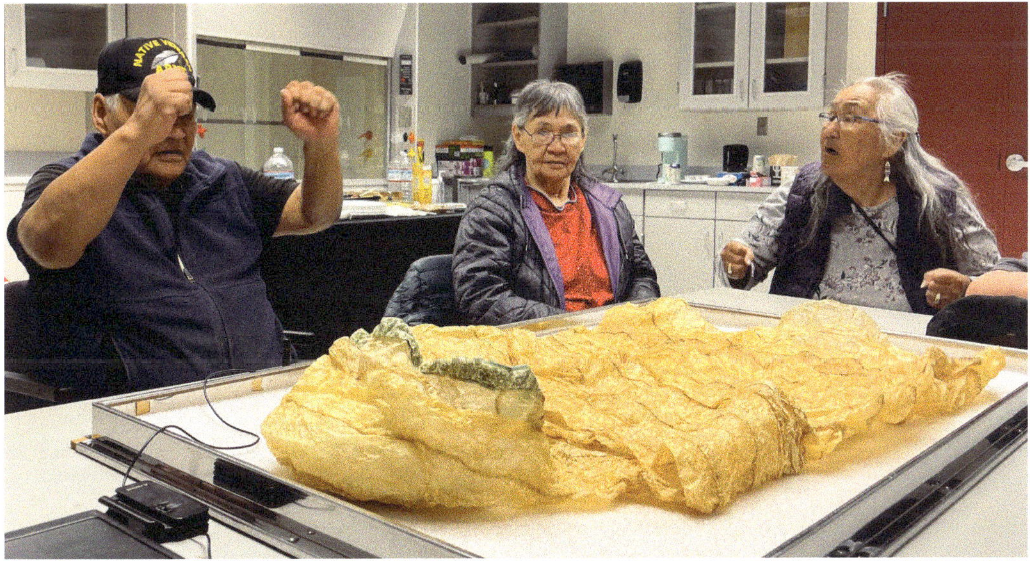

Wassily gesturing while discussing gut parkas, April 2024. *AFR*

anything. Never got another one after that. By that time, that's when raincoats were available." Angie sympathized: "Yaa, it seems like when you spent so much time making something, when you give it to another person, and they wear it for couple of days, and then the third day it's gone. Where is it? I forgot where I put it. No more. Don't take care of it."

Qaliq atkuk / *Woman's qaliq-style parka*

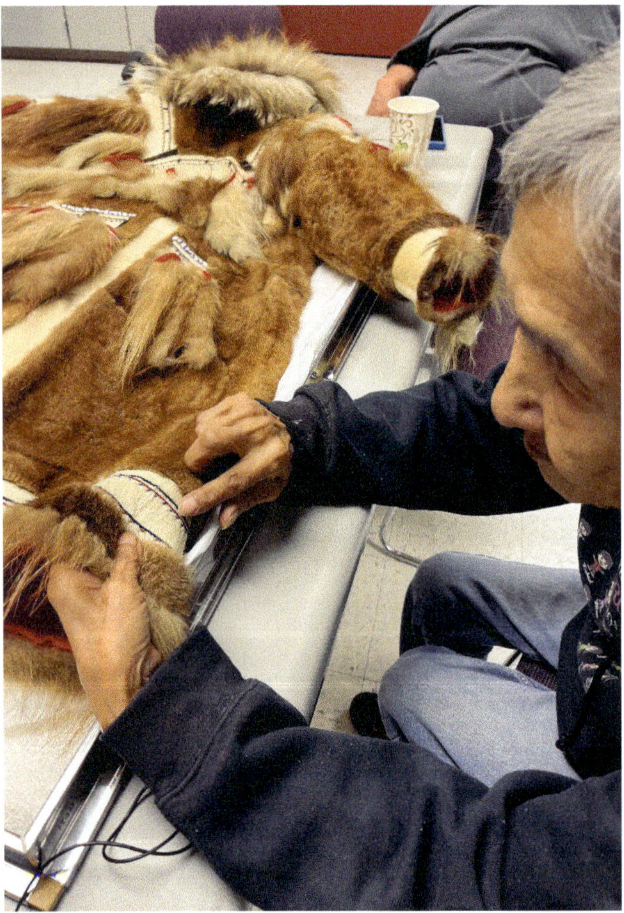

Angie examining the fine beadwork on the *qaliq* parka, April 2024. *AFR*

The last piece we looked at in collections was a fancy *qaliq*-style fur parka made for Elizabeth Nicolai of Kwethluk by her mother and purchased in 1959 by a BIA teacher who later donated it to the Museum. Angie admired the bead work and noted the variety of furs used in the parka's construction. She described her own caribou parka with a bib of white caribou at the neck, a hanging decoration on the back of the hood, and lots of tassels, which she called *ceterat*, not *alngat* as they do on the coast: "They were all over; decoration, maybe. You know like how those Indians down south when they're dancing, they bounce. Maybe that's what they were used for."

I asked Angie if her parka had a hood, and she said it did: "I remember because when it was really cold, my mom used to put my ruff down and tell me to put my head inside like this." I asked if there was a photo of the parka, and Angie replied that the BIA teacher, Mr. McConkey, took lots of pictures of her family as well as of his own daughter, Mary Alice. Angie recalled another picture she had seen, taken by Nixie Mellick:

Woman's *qaliq*-style parka made for Elizabeth Nicolai of Kwethluk in the 1950s. The body of the parka is mink, trimmed in calfskin, wolverine, and wolf. The beadwork design on the central panel signifies a blackfish. *UA Museum of the North UA68-008-0001, Chris Arend*

> There was a picture of them in front of the Sleetmute church. There was a whole bunch of women; they were standing on the first step. All same size, until you come to my grandma, standing in the end. She was on the ground. And she was same size as all them women.
>
> And the men were behind on the second step, and they were all same size. My Ap'a was behind my grandma on the floor. And he was same size as those standing on the steps. Nixie got that one. And you could see the parka that my grandma had, you could see that white all the way.

Uyamik wallu aamak / *Beaded collar*

We talked about this and that for a bit, with Wassily elaborating on using poles to push a canoe upriver, against the current. It had already been an eventful day. After another short break, we left the classroom and headed back to the elevator, which took us to the Museum's art gallery on the third floor to view one last piece. This beautiful space had much to admire, including an elaborate *camataq* (dance headdress) from Nunapitchuk. Toward the middle of the room, in a high case, was the beaded collar from Canoe Village that Angie's great-grandmother had made. It was indeed stunning – Angela's favorite piece in the museum.

Angela explained: "It's really heavy, all on moose hide. It's connected in the back, and two or three sections on the upper part were added on, as [Elena] got bigger. So there's a hook on this side, and an eye on the other, and hooks behind." Jennie was still amazed: "It's so unbelievable, those days they had beads."

After our visit, Angela shared museum records that added details on the collar's history and use. A similar collar had been collected in another Kuskokwim community, as well as a Tahltan "puberty collar" collected from people living along the Stikine River in 1907 and said to have been worn for about a year by young girls following their first menses. Athabascan women in Alaska recognize the Tahltan collar (which is on display at the Arctic Studies Center in the Anchorage Museum) as similar to beaded collars worn by young girls in their own communities, and recent Facebook posts show beaded collars gifted to high school girls in Yukon River communities to this day.

In written records, the collar's name was unclear. Nixie and Margie Mellick spoke with Sleetmute elders in 2002 and suggested to Holly Cussack-McVeigh, who was researching the piece, that people called them "yamuks" but that they didn't know what the name meant. It is likely that the Yup'ik name for the collar was *uyamik* (necklace or neck piece). Another suggestion was "aah-mock" or "ah-mok" which indicates that another Yup'ik name for the collar may have been *aamaq* (female breast) or *aamak* (two breasts), signifying (perhaps encouraging) the physical changes the young woman was going through at puberty. Perhaps a better English name for the piece would be "breast plate" rather than collar, as the heavy beads would have hung low over the chest of a young girl.

Continuing to admire the collar, Angela noted that all three things were purchased together by the Museum – the beaded collar, the belt, and the hair piece. Later I read McConkey's last letter to Skarland where he wrote: "Had it not been for their financial bankruptcy these items would have remained in the confines of their cabin. Am wondering how many other museum pieces might be awaiting similar pressure to be brought to light." I couldn't help noting that the collar provided a great example for the Mellick family: "If you share it with the museum, everyone can see it." We all took pictures, as friends and relatives on Facebook were following our adventures.

Tahltan Puberty Collar from the Stikine River, British Columbia, collected by George Emmons in 1907: "Horseshoe frame covered with tanned skin decorated with rows of beads and dentalium and fringed with worsted strung with beads and dentalium, worn for about a year by young girls released from confinement." *National Museum of Natural History E248388-0*

Angie wanted her picture taken standing below the beaded collar. She asked Wassily: "You took pictures too? You can show your kids. That's part of them, too." Wassily said he had taken photos, noting that his family hoped to come up to Fairbanks that summer.

After visiting the art gallery, Mark and Wassily went downstairs to the small cafe, while the rest of us browsed the exhibit. Angela showed us a beautifully sewn, contemporary Athabascan moose-hide dress with elaborate beadwork, as

Angie standing proudly in the Museum's art gallery below the case holding her great-grandmother's spectacular collar, April 2024. The collar was made of panels of glass seed beads stitched to a smoked moose hide backing. Tassels of glass and metal trade beads are strung along the edge. The collar fastens with metal hooks and eyes attached to the underside at each end. According to Sleetmute elders, collars come in one size and are worn when a young girl becomes eligible for marriage, and are not used again after marriage, only to be given and worn by the next generation (Cussack-McVeigh 2002). *AFR*

Mary Margie Egnaty of Sleetmute holding up the elaborate beaded collar that she made, using her own design, March 2025. *AFR*

well as a fish skin basket made by the late artist Fran Reed.

Returning to the first floor, Angela said good-bye, leaving us to browse the downstairs gallery and eat a quick lunch on our own. Angie wandered into the much older Alaska exhibit. When she returned, she told us she'd seen a dress made of fish spine bones. Indeed she had – a contemporary art piece made of thousands of tiny round salmon spine bones. A remarkable piece, which Jennie and I had to find and admire.

Once again, we were at the airport in plenty of time. The flight was full, but happily both Angie and Jennie had window seats on the Denali side with glorious views. When we arrived in Anchorage we went separate ways – Marie driving home, Mark's wife Sharon waiting outside, and Wassily picked up by his granddaughter, excited to hear his stories. I drove Jennie back to her small apartment just off Muldoon Road, and after a bit of shopping, Angie and I headed back to my house for dinner and bed.

Contemporary art piece by Cynthia Gibon of Sitka, made of thousands of salmon spine bones and on display at the UA Museum of the North, April 2024. *AFR*

Angie was up early again, and so was I. Just before leaving for the airport, she spotted a magpie outside our window. She then told me the story of how magpies began. A mother and her child were picking berries. But the child went to pick from a bush, and the mother called out in alarm. Her cry scared the child, and it flew away as a magpie.

We headed up to Lake and Penn at 8:30, checked in, and waited for the 10 AM departure. Chatting together, Angie described her boarding school experience when she was sent to Wrangell at age seven and didn't know when she would see home again or if her parents didn't want her anymore. She made friends with kids from the Pribilofs, who first teased her about her hair, then comforted her and protected her from the bigger kids. They told her she wasn't Eskimo, because they didn't like Eskimos but they liked her. There were older boys there from around Sleetmute, but Angie was so much younger they didn't pay much attention to her. At school, Angie was rapped on the knuckles and not allowed to play sports because she was always in trouble. "Trouble followed me," she mused. In May her parents met her at the plane when it landed back in Sleetmute. In the fall, they sent her off again with fish and a box of blueberries, and she arrived with blue clothes. She said her experiences toughened her up.

Angie also mentioned eating "cooked sugar" as a kid. Her mom would melt sugar in a pot, then pour it over a pan to cool. A little bit of sugar was also browned and mixed with the melted sugar, which was eaten as candy once it cooled and hardened. So childhood experiences had both toughened and sweetened her. Angie's stories always made me think and left me smiling. All three – Jennie, Wassily, and Angie – had spoken repeatedly about the importance of sharing, both food and stories of life when they were young. During our time together they had done just that, sharing memories that would enrich us all.

Angie visiting with Chuathbaluk elders Sophie Sakar and Lucy Simeon as they wait for the morning flight home on Lake and Penn, April 2024. *AFR*

Crooked Creek. *Andrea Gusty*

Chapter 5

Protecting A Living Land

Teggalquurtellret / *Those who turned to stone*

Among the most impressive elements of middle Kuskokwim oral tradition are the stories elders still share of the stone figures that inhabit their homeland, including the Stone Woman on the banks of the Hoholitna, Arnassagaq (Old Woman) on the Ulukaq River, and the stone family on a hilltop above Sts'a, near Lime Village. Place names also recall legendary battles with a giant beaver on the Holitna and a cannibal giant near present-day Crooked Creek. Altogether, this tangible evidence of past encounters, often during times of food scarcity and hardship, continues to hold lessons for the present day.

During a 2006 elders' gathering in Bethel, Golga Effemka (January 2006:194) shared the story of the Stone Woman standing along the banks of the Hoholitna River on the west flank of Amiigtalek (the Door Mountains). According to Golga, a woman and her husband were starving and traveled to the river in search of food.

> They say that woman was starving and came from somewhere. She ran out of food and went down to the river. They were hungry. She lost her poor husband somewhere on the mountain, and he sat down and is situated there. We don't see her husband, but his wife is holding a small child along the riverbank.
>
> When we travel, our elders instruct us to give her some of our provisions, anything, to place it right below her, or if we were having some tea right beyond her. Sometimes, she makes animals available to catch. It is because the poor thing is grateful for what we have given her.

The logs floating downriver are said to the bones leftover from what the woman has eaten: "We gather animal bones; they say those are wood." Also across from her is a small lake inhabited by a beaver that cannot be caught: "They call it *qimaguyuukaaq* [one who flees]." Inland is a high point where the woman goes to pack water: "They refer to it as Mertarvia [lit., "Place where she packs water"].... They say those who went there to look from a high point would pack water from there, but it's dry today."

Golga continued, describing how the Stone Woman is venerated to this day: "They say when she sat, that poor woman desired to turn into stone, as the poor thing was hungry, so the descendants who are going upriver would give her an offering. You can see it from the river. They say even white people, when going upriver, take out their wallets and throw money in the water there when told about it. How desirable, money!"

Pete Mellick (August 2023) also told a story about his experience years before when he guided the producer of Miami Vice on a moose hunt upriver. Pete told his client about the Stone Woman, instructing him to get something ready to give, as the river was too shallow for him to stop the boat: "He had nothing to give, so he got his wallet out and threw a bunch of money in the river. I was going to turn around!" Jack Egnaty (1987) recalled another instance of non-Native enterprise in giving to the Stone Woman: "You know that *kass'aq*, that white guy. So he opened that grub box and he threw Spam in [the river]. He tell them not that way, just little bit. We wanna have good luck. But that one, he overdo it.... You know what? Round the bend...they see three moose standing in the sandbar. Lucky!" Golga (January 2006) agreed that giving to the Stone Woman was important, and that she had made animals available to him more than once:

> Some of the white people actually comply as the poor things want to catch animals; she makes [animals] available to some people. And when it's nearly impossible to catch anything, when giving an offering by going up to land right in front of her and digging in the ground and placing it inside, wanting to catch an animal, she makes animals available. She made animals available to me a number of times. Then before night, she allowed me to catch.... That stone is true. They say when she and her husband were starving and traveling from somewhere, the poor thing lost her husband. He became stone.

Aviukaqsaraq (the practice of giving an offering) is not only reserved for stone figures. Sophie Sakar (January 2023) explained:

> The way I learned about that was from my mom and dad. I watch them when they're doing something. Especially when someone dies, you have 20- or 40-day feast, and they take all the food, little bit of food from the table, put them in a bowl, paper plate, something. They think of those people who passed away.
>
> And then when you go hunting, everything you eat, you put some in the ground and cover it, and say, "Those who've gone hunting, let

them catch something."... And that's how I learned from my parents, *aviukaqsaraq*.

Another stone woman known as Arnassagaq (lit., "Old Woman") stands along the banks of the Ulukaq River. Mark Leary shared a detailed account with students who were planning to visit the site during TKC's annual Spirit Camp in summer 2023, and again in 2024. Mark had heard the story years before from Willie Pitka, noting that stories like this are rarely told today and that camp was a good place to listen. He began by telling the students that in the past, young people did not chose their partners as they do today. Instead their parents arranged marriages for their children. Long ago, a family living in the old village of Little Mountain Village (Ingricuar) arranged for their daughter to marry a man from the Nushagak River area. When she was old enough, the man came to get her, and she had to leave her family and travel over the mountains to his home in Bristol Bay. Her in-laws, however, were not kind to her and treated her like a servant, ordering her to pack water, get wood, take care of meat, and other tasks.

Little Mountain Village (Ingricuar) just upriver from Napaimute on the north bank of the Kuskokwim, May 2024. *AFR*

Wassily standing on the high ground at Little Mountain Village, looking over the Kuskokwim River, May 2024. *AFR*

The woman was unhappy and missed her family, and so she decided to run away. She began to get ready by secretly hiding what she would need for traveling, including dry fish and a small sewing kit, in the trees outside their village. By then she also had a baby from her husband. She waited for the right time to leave. Then one day a caribou herd was sighted, and all the men left to hunt. Soon they sent word for the women to join them to cut up and pack home the meat. When the others left, the woman made an excuse and stayed behind. Then at night she quietly packed up her baby, gathered what she had hidden in the woods, and started her journey across the mountains.

Her husband was furious when he returned and discovered that she had fled, and he followed behind her. Although she had a head start, he knew the country better than she did and traveled directly to the mountain pass he knew she would have to cross. Traveling slowly but steadily without rest, the woman beat him to the pass, arriving on the banks of the Ulukaq River. Looking down the valley, she was filled with joy, knowing that if she could reach the river her people would find her and bring her home. But just as she started going down toward the river, her husband came over the hill behind her. Mark continued: "And he hollered her name down the valley, echoing, hollered at her. And her heart beat, afraid he would catch her. She turned around, with the baby on her back, and saw him up there in the high mountains. And when their eyes met, somehow they both turned to stone."

Finishing his story, Mark told the students that these were the stone figures they would see the next day. He added that during the devastating epidemics that accompanied the arrival of the Russians in the 1840s, killing half the people living along the Kuskokwim River, it was such a bad time with so much sorrow that the stone man cracked, and half of him fell into the valley. Mark concluded: "They say that if that stone woman ever cracks and falls it will be another really bad time. I hope we don't see that day."

Chuathbaluk elder John Avakumoff (1987) shared another version of the story of Arnassagaq. According to John, the family was living within the Aniak River drainage but famine forced them to move in search of food. Traveling east in the Buckstock Mountains separating the Aniak River from the Ulukaq River drainage, they crested the Buckstock divide and saw an area promising abundant food. In her enthusiasm, the woman ran down the mountain toward the river, while her husband remained behind. As he watched, she and the child were transformed into stone, and soon afterward he turned to stone as well. According to John, years later the child fell off the mother's back, foretelling a period of "great sickness" which decimated the area's population (Bartolini 1991:7). Thirty years later,

Ulukaq (Holokuk) River flowing out of the mountains with the Stone Woman standing on the ridge, August 2023. *Megan Leary*

Kalskag elder Steven Gregory (February 2023:90) shared a similar view: "There were two stones [at Arnassagaq]. One already rolled, and the other is still there. And they said if that other one roll down, *cella piunrirciquq* [the world will no longer be]."

John Avakumoff (1987:2) also noted that people have always left food offerings there, and do so to this day to secure good luck in hunting, both when going hunting upriver and when returning. John never saw them up close, but talked to them from the river:

> We never sing to it, but we talk to him.... Anything what you think. Tell them, "We come to see you, and give us good luck." He give us good luck sometime....
>
> And we always put something coming down and going up. Never miss them, even winter. When we going up by dogs, when we would...make lunch, and we put something. All we got in sleigh, little bit. Never pass them.

Students from the Jacob Wise Spirit Camp visiting the Stone Woman, August 2024. *AFR*

John Andrew (July 1988) of Kwethluk told a slightly different version: "[Joshua Phillip of Tuluksak] told me the story about the lady with a child up in Ulukaq. The couple was coming home from their camp, from the hills, the man was rowing down in a skin boat, and his wife and child were going on the ground right through the hills here. And he lost her in the hills somewhere, couldn't find her. After he got back to where they were going, he went back to look for her. And they found her on the side of the mountain, but she had turned into a stone, too. If you see it to this day from a distance, it will be the shape of a woman with a child on the back." John later cautioned: "If you go hunting in that area, if you don't pay homage or leave something behind for the lady and child, you'll never get what you go after" (Andrew 1988; Hutchinson 1991). John (February 2023) also noted that they used to call her Atmalek (lit., "One with a backpack").

Other versions of the story of Arnassagaq recorded by Nixie Mellick in the 1980s from Old Chief Abruska and Maxie Pitka from the Napaimute area agree with Mark Leary's telling. Both note that bad treatment of the woman by her in-laws caused her to try to return to her home on the Ulukaq River. She tried to go back to Ingricuar (Little Mountain Village), but didn't make it and turned into a *yuguaq* (pretend person). All noted that to this day people visiting Arnassagaq leave food offerings, hoping for good hunting and safe travel in the future. Angie Kameroff (August 2023) also recalled the story of Arnassagaq as that of a woman running away from her "bum husband": "They say you can even see his weapon, his bow and arrow in this rock.... Because as soon as he knew it was his wife, his wife turned to rock. He kneel on one knee [and turned to rock as well]."

Arnassagaq and the Stone Woman on the banks of the Hoholitna are not the only stone figures in the middle Kuskokwim. A 1991 report by BIA archeologist Joseph Bartolini mentions other stone families described by elders who have since passed away. Pete Bobby (1987) of Lime Village identified a stone family on a hilltop above Sts'a on Tundra Lake. When a Sts'a man's grandchild was murdered by Kuskokwim people with whom the boy had shared food, his family retaliated by digging a hole through the mountain and killing many Kuskokwim people in a blood feud. After the slaughter, when the grandparents were nearing death, the grandfather instructed his family to burn their bodies (indicating that they would continue to participate in the lives of the living) and told them that they would be there to help them in the future. Their bodies were burned, as the grandfather had asked, and the next morning one of the family walked to the top of Sts'a and saw the grandparents there as stone figures. Pete Bobby noted that to this day the stone people help those in trouble: "If you gonna starve, if you need food or help, you go to the rocks and tell 'em, and they gonna help you."

Stone women are known in other parts of southwest Alaska. Listening to Golga Effemka's account, John Phillip (January 2006) of Kongiganak told the story of the stone figure of An'gaqtar, located behind the village of Togiak. Like Arnassagaq, she has a baby on her back. In front of her is a bowl where people leave offerings, including money, candy bars, bullets, and old-time matches. John recalled:

> They speak of An'gaqtar....They say that she was tired of living for five lifetimes, and stood and became stone. Her bowl is right in front of her, and I know as I went to see it twice....
>
> Still to this day, anyone who wants to can go to her. I saw her twice myself, and I followed that custom and circled her *ella maliggluku* [following *ella* (the universe), clockwise]....
>
> They say that these land animals always circle her in that direction. And some told stories and said that when they are hunting and pass by, they give her something, thinking about what they are [intending to catch], recalling her gratitude.
>
> And he talked about her bowl, that sometimes when they go to her in winter, when they look inside her bowl, fish scales are inside. They say that occurs when there will be an abundance of fish [in summer]. That indicates [what is to occur]; her bowl is filled with fish scales. That's what they say about it.

Like Arnassagaq and the Hoholitna Stone Woman, An'gaqtar has a husband. Paul John (January 2006) recalled: "They say that An'gaqtar's husband is at the upper part of the Togiak River. He, too, has a bowl. When there are going to be many fish, it is obvious through the inside of his bowl."

Traveling past Togiak in 1883, the Norwegian collector Johan Adrian Jacobsen encountered An'gaqtar and noted that the fifteen-foot figure was so lifelike it appeared as though human hands had made it. Jacobsen (1977:187) also noted that the figure was widely venerated and that no one passed without stopping to leave a gift. Arctic peoples in Greenland and Canada were also known to make offerings to stones to further their hunting success (Boas 1901-1907:149; Rasmussen 1921-1925:11; 1938:200; Soby 1969:54).

In an account translated by her grandson, Myron Blue, Togiak elder Annie Blue described other stone figures related to the time of An'gaqtar. During her travels An'gaqtar came across some children wading in water and startled them as she approached. They began to cry and scrambled toward land, stumbling and turning to stone at Ivruaq, near Quluut, where they can be seen today. An'gaqtar also molded a humanlike figure called Tarunguaq in a place of the same name. Annie Blue (September 1997) also described the stone figure of a grandmother, running along the shore, pursuing her grandsons when they were caught in the outgoing tide and washed out to sea. She finally sat down at the southernmost base of Ingricuaq Mountain, where she turned to stone. Her grandsons were pulled by the current to Nunaalukaq Bay, where they turned to stone as well. Annie also noted that at the time of the Great Death (the 1918 influenza pandemic) the grandmother lifted her chest and turned around. Annie concluded: "All of the stone figures changed positions just before the Great Death worldwide epidemic."

Stone figures in other parts of southwest Alaska are likewise described as both changeable and responsive to human action and intention, especially during periods of disease and death. Neva Rivers (April 2006) of Hooper Bay told the story of a man wearing a visor who climbed the Askinuk Mountains but, afraid to descend, died there and turned to stone where he can be seen to this day. Teddy Sundown (October 1975) added detail: "Elqialek [One with an *elqiaq* (visor)] is on this mountain. In summer long ago, just before a great coughing sickness from which many people would die, it seemed to turn its head, and the part of its head where the visor was shifted" (see Fienup-Riordan and Rearden [2012:48-58] for stories of stone figures in other parts of southwest Alaska).

Speaking of "rock ladies" generally, Pete Mellick (August 2023) dubbed them land protectors: "There are rock ladies all over. They're up at Lime Village, at Whitefish Lake. They got them all over the country. They're land protectors. Once in a while, we get lots of hunters, then everything crashes. We got to protect our land. That's why we give something, *aviukaq*. That's what I heard." Given the importance of the land, and all that it provides, it is small wonder that stone women are widely recognized and venerated.

Though some of the details of these stories have been lost over the years, stone women still hold meaning. Julie Zaukar (August 2023) of Crooked Creek not only remembered the old stories but added to them. According to Julie, the story begins with Sleeping Lady, rising above the shores of Cook Inlet on the eastern side of the Alaska Range. Though beyond the middle Kuskokwim, she connects Sleeping Lady to both the Hoholitna Stone Woman and Arnassagaq. Today, anyone taking the two-hour flight in a Lake and Penn Caravan from Aniak over the Alaska Range to Anchorage crosses over all three sites. Making these connections is not a sign of a loss of tradition but of a continuing tradition, carrying old stories into the present day.

Ircenrraat *and their mountain homes*

At the end of his story of the Hoholitna Stone Woman, Golga Effemka (January 2006) noted: "There are little people upriver from her. They used to hear them back when they went to spring camp back there, playing inside that mountain. It so happens that it was little people, *ircenrraat*." Later he explained in detail, sharing the story of Amiigtalek (the Door Mountains, lit., "Place with a door"). Amiigtalek is a place where little people stay. Animals also live inside it, including wolves and mink. Golga said that the doorway leading inside the mountain is on the side facing the Hoholitna River, but that the ground there is too soft and moves when walked on.

Golga then told the story of a man and his partner approaching the doorway. Although his partner warned him not to enter, the man went down inside the stones. When he was inside, he saw many people. Some looked angry, while others were extremely friendly. Apparently they were animals, and the angry ones were wolves. They would hand him food as well as animal figures; the man didn't eat them but put them inside his clothing. He kept going far into the mountain, exiting at a different place. Although it seemed to him as though he had been gone only a short time, when he left the mountain it was already winter. When he went outside, the figures he brought with him turned out to be animals wearing warm clothing, and he was glad he hadn't eaten them but had brought them home: "Those ones had given him images of themselves, telling him to eat them [at home]."

Angie Kameroff (September 2023) told a similar story about a man searching for food for his family. He encountered a bear who told him not to fear him but to follow him to his home in the mountain, Amiigtalek. Once inside, the bear took off his hood and revealed itself as a person. Inside he was allowed to drink but not to eat the food. When it was time to leave, his hosts filled his sled with pieces of wood that transformed into different kinds of meat and fish, including king salmon, when he returned home (see Chapter 2). This transformation echoes Golga Effemka's observation above that the logs floating downriver are the bones leftover from what the Stone Woman has eaten.

Golga then told of Sleetmute moose hunters who had camped near Amiigtalek several years ago. At night they heard something outside their tent, and when they called out "Who's there?" they heard the reply "Who's there?" though no one could be seen: "The animals were replying to them by mimicking what they said." The hunters were scared, as this had never happened in the past. Golga noted that since the land has now changed, occurrences like this will be more frequent.

Jack Egnaty (1987) also spoke of the deep hole in Amiigtalek: "Some people tell me there's a hole in there. Way down deep. Take some rocks....Throw them in there, and you could see, bang, bang, bang. And pretty soon no more [sound]. And pretty soon them little bats come out." Angie Kameroff's dad had shown her the hole when visiting Teggalqingayak (from *teggalquq*, "stone"), the Stone Woman:

> We take a walk, with my dad. On the way back we found a well.... And we all stand around it, you know. We look inside, you could see water down there. And my dad goes, "Watch this." And he reach down, and he pick up a rock and go like this [dropped it], let it go. And you could hear that rock, "Tem. Tem. Tem. Tem." All the way.
>
> And when you couldn't hear it no more, my dad goes, "Now watch this." He pick up another rock and he let it go. Nothing. No noise at all.

Pete Bobby (1987) shared another longer account which his grandfather had told him years before. He said there used to be fog in the mountains, even in good weather. One could hear children playing up there, although they didn't answer when called. Once a hunter made a winter camp at Amiigtalek with his family, and when he climbed up the mountain, he saw lots of children's tracks. There he found a cave that looked just like a door. He entered, leaving his snowshoes outside. He went farther inside, but when he turned to go back, he couldn't find his way out.

Continuing along, the man found people inside. One of them invited him to sit down and gave him food to eat. Although the man never spoke, his host told him not to worry, that they would send him back. Wondering how they read his mind, the man stayed there. Soon they told him that it was morning and time for him to go home. Again, they gave him food – grease ice cream with berries and good meat. Although they told him to eat the food there and not to save any, he put small pieces of the food in his pocket.

When he left, his path opened right away. He looked down at his camp, and the snow had already melted and it was spring. Checking the food in his pocket, he found that it was inedible – the meat was wolf meat and the ice cream was sour. When he returned, his family said that they'd followed his tracks and thought he'd drowned in the creek. When they asked where he had been, he told them he'd stayed in a village in the mountain. Later that spring, the family returned to Sleetmute.

More recently, Angie Kameroff (August 2023) told the story of another encounter at Amiigtalek. Once when a group of hunters traveled there and were settling down getting ready to spend the night, they heard the sounds of music and people laughing from the top of the mountain. One of the hunters wanted to visit them. While the other men slept, that man's spirit left his body and went up into the mountain. While he was there, his host told him that he had to remember which door to go through to get home. His host also told him that he could eat but should not drink while he was there. While his spirit was inside the mountain, his body was back at camp in a deep sleep for three days. On the third day, the man woke up just before his body got cold. His companions thought he had died, but he lived to tell the story.

Angie noted that if you aren't wanted up there, the door closes on you. In her telling, she identified the mountain's inhabitants as *ircenrraat*, small other-than-human persons said to inhabit hilly areas throughout southwest Alaska. She was careful to note that in the past, *ircenrraat* used to take people to their world and that you have to respect them. Pete Mellick (August 2023) had also heard of the "little people" living in the limestone caves in the vicinity of the Door Mountains and noted that he gets prickles on his neck when he gets close to those mountains. Pete said that the *ircenrraat* liked to tease and entice travelers. He told of one man who went in one of the limestone caves. There he pretended to eat what he was given, but threw away the food and came back out. Pete compared this encounter to sleeping in a bear den: "If you sleep in there, you sleep for one year and don't come back until next spring."

Another abode of *ircenrraat* along the middle Kuskokwim are the Taassaatulit (Russian Mountains), just upriver from Aniak. Frank Andrew (October 2001) of Kwigillingok told a story he had likely heard from close relatives in Tuluksak of these *ircenrraat* inviting the residents of the old villages of Qalqarmiut and Urraarmiut to a dance festival. As the human guests approached, they saw the *ircenrraat* village hovering in the air, and their hosts opened it to them. The guests requested a heavy log bed for their *qasgiq*, which they received as a gift after the dance. Before they left for home, an old man lay on the bed and rolled down its length, falling off the other end as a beardless young man. The *ircenrraat* told their human guests that this would continue to happen when they got home. As they traveled back toward their village, however, the log bed was so heavy that the people left it beside the trail, planning to retrieve it later. When they returned, however, it had disappeared.

Stories of encounters with *ircenrraat* are told throughout southwest Alaska, and these middle Kuskokwim stories have much in common with those told downriver. Nelson Island elder Brentina Chanar (February 1991:5) reported that *ircenrraat* are seen as ordinary people, but clean and radiant, surrounded by a bright light. Others say they are small people, two to three feet high, and as early as 1899, the Smithsonian naturalist Edward Nelson (1899:480-81) described them

Taassaatulit (the Russian Mountains) as seen from Aniak, March 2025. *AFR*

as dwarves. Occasionally a person encounters *ircenrraat* as *yuut* (people) and later sees them as wolves, foxes, or other small mammals. At other times, humans encounter wolves or foxes who later reveal themselves as *ircenrraat*. Frank Andrew (September 2000:12) noted: "They are people like us, but they transform into animals and are seen like that, and sometimes they let people, real people, see them in human form...by those who they aren't afraid of." When people encounter an *ircenrraq*, they may at first perceive it as a normal person. Encounters with extraordinary persons generally are not remembered until days later, as the experience affects one's perception of time.

Quliraq

Stories of *ircenrraat* and stone women recall Yup'ik oral traditions familiar to those living downriver. As we move away from the coast and into the middle Kuskokwim, however, it is perhaps no surprise that the upriver stories recount unique experiences. Along with her observations of stone women, Julie Zaukar of Crooked Creek shared what she recalled of the cannibal giant who lived in the area in the distant past, blocking people traveling upriver and eating those who defied him. He was said to have hair all over his body and to have used a human scapula for a club and a skull for a cup. Finally an orphan, trained by his uncle, killed the giant and cut off the giant's wife's head. After that, people from downriver were able to move into the area. Perhaps the cannibal giant was a stand-in for conflict with Athabascans and others as Yup'ik people migrated upriver.

Sites associated with the story include Quliraq (lit., "Legendary Tale or Place"), an open area on the hillside above the upper village of Crooked Creek which was said to be the giant's home. This was the place where the orphan decapitated the giant's wife, and to this day nothing grows there. The ridge just downriver from Crooked Creek is known as Ukurritaq (lit., "Woman from another village residing in her husband's village"). Another downriver site, Angyaruaq (Canoe Mountain, lit., "Model or pretend *angyaq*, boat") is said to be the giant's canoe, turned upside down.

Jennie Zaukar and Agnes Andreanoff knew parts of the story of Quliraq. Jennie said that they were advised never to go there: "If you go [to Quliraq], you'll not come back." Agnes said that it was a true story and that her husband used to tell her about it:

> He used to tell me [that] when he was a boy he was told by the elders not to go there. And he used to tell me, "Don't ever go there." I said, "Oh. Okay."
>
> He used to tell me stories. He tell me [that] one time, there was a man named Sam Parent and [his wife] Theresa Parent; they had a son named Joe Parent. The first one, I guess. They keep telling him not to go bother that Quliraq. But he never listened....
>
> Nope, that boy never listened to nobody. So he go up there and go bother that Quliraq. And that summer he drowned, not long after he bothered that Quliraq. I said, "Oh no." ... And he said, "That summer they found him. Oh, he was in bad shape."... 'Cause that Quliraq maybe let 'em drown. That's what he tell me.

Ukurritaq also has a story. It was the place where an *ukurraq* (daughter-in-law) rolled down. Jennie explained: "She was pregnant. She was way up there, and she rolled down." Ciissiq (lit., "Insect, cold-blooded crawling thing") is the name of a creek below Ukurritaq, and Jennie said they were told not to go in there as it was the place where the *ciissirpak* (snake, legendary "great worm") slid down to the river.

A second origin story tells how the Holitna River was created. According to Jack Egnaty, what today is the Holitna River drainage was once a huge lake held in place by the dam of a giant beaver. Once a man and his family were traveling across the lake when the beaver's tail splashed down and upset the canoe they were riding in. Although he tried to save them, the man's wife and child drowned. Reaching the shore, the man vowed to kill the giant beaver. He worked to make a spear strong enough to pierce its side, and eventually he was successful in killing it. In its death throes, the beaver gave a mighty splash that broke the dam. The lake water drained, and the Holitna River was born. Today, near the mouth of the Holitna, is a low hill called Capun (lit., "Weir"), the site of the beaver's dam, and another nearby hill known as Nel'uq or Enluaq (lit., "House or den"), the site of the beaver's lodge.

Both of these upriver stories involve conflicts between extraordinary beings and a lone human hunter who succeeds in overpowering them. This seems very different from the stories associated with the stone women, all of which originate in experiences of food shortage or distress caused by distance from family and friends. The stone women were created from human suffering and are responsive to human distress in times of epidemic disease or other disasters. *Ircenrraat* stories also typically involve encounters between curious humans who enter the non-human world where appearances are often deceiving. Animals that people normally hunt for food appear as human hosts offering their guests foods

Ukurritaq ridge, just below Crooked Creek, August 2023. *AFR*

which, when they return home, are inedible or, alternately, inedible wood which transforms into food. Whereas food shortage and the proper treatment of foods are front and center in stories of stone women and *ircenrraat*, both the killing of the giant beaver and the battle with the cannibal giant focus on social conflicts – the first motivated by revenge and the second by repeated murders. It should be no surprise that middle Kuskokwim oral tradition, drawing as it does on different people moving up and down river, as well as over mountain passes to the north and south, should display such diversity. Although some stories have been lost over the years, those that remain continue to animate the landscape in rich and meaningful ways.

Chapter 6

All One River: King Salmon Fishing on the Kuskokwim, Past and Present

In November 2018, Calista Education and Culture (CEC) held a three-day gathering in Bethel to discuss the condition of salmon runs along the Kuskokwim River. Over the last decade, CEC has had many similar gatherings – meetings with small groups of elders over two or three days with conversation focused on a particular topic. This was one of our best, as we worked together to understand the role of king salmon in the lives of people living along the Kuskokwim River, a 700-mile thoroughfare originating in the glacially fed streams of the Alaska Range and eventually reaching a wide, silty estuary with many channels where it flows into the Bering Sea.

We met in the USFWS Yukon Delta National Wildlife Refuge conference room in Bethel, sleeping and eating meals of seal meat and salmon in the adjacent bunkhouse. CEC cultural advisor Mark John had invited elders from up and down the river, including James Charles from Tuntutuliak, Jacob Black from Napakiak, John Andrew from Kwethluk, and Michael Savage from Lower Kalskag. Marie Meade, originally from Nunapitchuk, also attended to help lead the gathering, and she added her experiences spending summers at fish camp along the Kuskokwim. I was there as well, to help guide discussion and to run the tape recorder that would document our conversations, which were primarily in Yup'ik with a sprinkling of English.

After an opening prayer, we began with brief introductions. Most in our group already knew one another, although during the gathering they got to know each other much better.

Introductions: Our Kuskokwim fishermen

Although physically one river, the Kuskokwim is experienced differently depending on where fishermen live. Those fishing at the mouth of the Kuskokwim set their nets according to the tides in murky water that limits their ability to see their quarry. Above Kalskag, the water is less silty and has a steady downstream current. Eddies are few, and fish wheels, introduced by non-Native prospectors in the early 1900s, have proved the most effective way to harvest salmon.

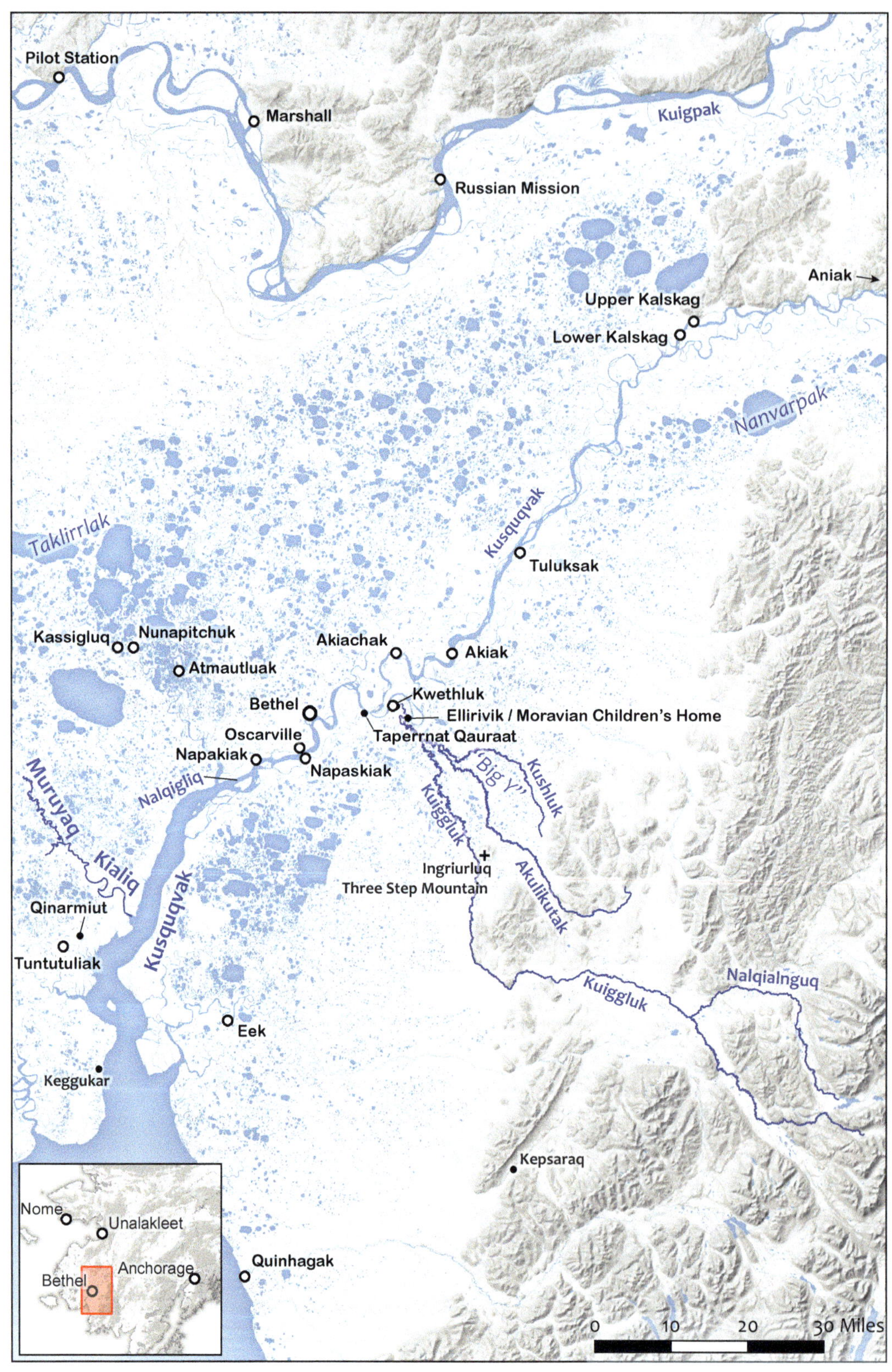

The Lower Kuskokwim River. *Ian Moore and Jen Jolliff*

Fishermen's experiences have also changed dramatically over time, as both human and fish populations have fluctuated. In the 1940s, relatively few people lived along the river and, along with fish wheels, handmade gillnets provided ample salmon for both families and their dogs, as well as excess that could be sold or traded to feed dog teams. In the 1950s, bigger boats and better-quality nets with nylon webbing were introduced, allowing people to harvest more and more fish, both for themselves and for a commercial king salmon fishery that emerged as important in the 1960s. From the 1960s through the 1980s, commercial salmon fishing was extremely profitable for Kuskokwim fishermen, but it became increasingly restricted in the 1990s due to declining king salmon runs, with no commercial fishery targeting king salmon since 1987 (Ikuta et al. 2013:4). Subsistence fishing for king salmon continued to meet people's needs through 2010, when low escapement resulted in unprecedented restrictions on the subsistence harvest. In 2012, managers followed a seven-day rolling closure in early June with a five-day extension in mid-June, resulting in a "Fish-In" during which more than 100 fishermen went fishing in defiance of the closure. Three years later, in 2015, the Kuskokwim River Inter-Tribal Fisheries Commission was established to promote a more robust form of co-management of this essential resource (Brelsford and Williams 2018; Runfola 2013). All our participants shared this common history, colored by unique personal experiences. Together, they provide a nuanced picture of people and salmon living along the Kuskokwim River.

John Andrew, Alegyuk, was the first to speak. He said that he was born in 1947 just upriver from the village of Eek. He then shared an early memory:

> I was four when I first became observant there in Eek. They brought me down to the school and said that they were going to inoculate me so that I would not get sick. And for half an hour, they tried to administer the shot. I would fight them and run away.
>
> When I was fatigued, they caught me and gave me the shot. And so, the first *kass'aq* [Caucasian] that I saw was a government worker. I say that by trying to help us, they hurt us. Up to this day, our [non-Native] counterparts that I first saw coming here, they were [a] pain in the ass, on account of them giving me a shot.

Before John turned five, his family moved upriver to Kwethluk where his father and grandfather had been born and raised. In those days, John's family was nomadic, moving to camp in the mountains each spring, to summer fish camp along the Kuskokwim, then back to Kwethluk for the winter:

> Our family would spend spring in the mountains. We would travel by dog team for a long time.
>
> Then when we went down to the village in spring, it wouldn't be long before we moved to the fish camps. We had a fish camp upriver in Taperrnat Qauraat. And in the fall, we would go camping up around Kepsaraq, far down from Ingriurluq [Three Step Mountain]. There used to be a sod house there.

John described hunting and fishing through the seasons, when he would "catch any living thing for food" for his family and dogs. He remembered their fish camp with seven smokehouses for the seven families who shared the camp:

> When they first started commercial fishing here early around 1957 when I was 12 years old, my father or my *ataata* [paternal uncle] lent me an old boat. I would driftnet with other boys as helpers to set the net....
>
> Sometimes we would set the net once and fill my boat. Then we would go up to shore and bring them up to land, not knowing anything of wheelbarrows, and we had no four-wheelers at all. We would just take them by hand and bring them up to the fish bins.

John remembered people helping one another at fish camp: "After driftnetting for this one [household], we would go somewhere else after lunch to help them by driftnetting for [fish] for them.... Because we grew up with close ties, it was our tradition to help each other. We tried to get enough for winter, even though the smokehouse was full." Once the fish were thoroughly dried and smoked, they moved them to *qulvarviit* (elevated fish caches): "And when we returned home to our village, we would divide what we caught to our family and those who did not have providers." John added that his family had two elevated caches – one for king salmon and the other for smaller fish.

Michael Savage from Lower Kalskag spoke next. He noted that although he could understand Yup'ik, he would speak mainly in English, which his father had taught him when he was young. Michael said that he was born in Upper Kalskag in 1954 and named Aqum'aq after his mother's grandfather. Michael's father was born in Paimiut on the Yukon River and raised in Holy Cross. Michael's mother was from Lower Kalskag, where his father moved after the couple married. Michael has lived in Kalskag all his life, and his extended family has a fish camp six miles downriver from Lower Kalskag, which they still move to each summer.

Michael's last name, Savage, comes from his father's grandfather, who the family believes was Russian, coming from the Dillingham area to McGrath and later homesteading upriver at Nikolai: "They call him a savage because he was always alone, not with people. Every time people come around, he'll move.... That's how we got our last name."

Jacob Black, Nasgauq in Yup'ik, has fished along the Kuskokwim all his life. Jacob's parents were from Qinarmiut, and he was born in the fall camp of Qaurrayagaq, below Tuntutuliak, in 1940. Jacob lost his father when he was young. Before he died, his father instructed Jacob's mother to send him to the Moravian Children's Home, an orphanage near Kwethluk, so that he could attend school and learn Western ways. Jacob spoke in Yup'ik when he was young and learned English at the orphanage. He left the orphanage when he was almost 16 years old. He then joined his mother who was living in Kwigillingok at the time. When his mother remarried the following summer, Jacob moved with her to Napakiak, where he has lived ever since.

When Jacob returned downriver in the mid-1950s, he found that their fishing gear was not sophisticated: "There were no [nylon] gillnets made to catch king salmon. But they had [gillnets] upriver [at the orphanage] where I grew up, but they weren't long.... When I went downriver to Yup'ik villages, I realized that their gillnets were twine. And the next year, when you'd just take them, they would easily snap."

James Charles from Tuntutuliak introduced himself with his Yup'ik name, Ayagiaq. He noted that Tuntutuliak was established at its present site in 1945 by people moving from Qinarmiut. James was born in 1940 in *neqlilleq* (fish camp): "The place where I was born, Kuiguyulleq, has since eroded and has now become the Kuskokwim River." James's father, uncle, and grandmother died from tuberculosis when he was eight years old, and James stopped attending school in the fourth grade to help his mother: "My mom struggled to raise us." His earliest memories were growing up at fish camp: "We used to come to fish camp here in Kuiguyulleq. We would fish there in summer, but we didn't catch a lot of fish back then." Later the family moved to another fish camp at Nalqigliq, downriver from Napakiak, where the Kuskokwim River starts to get narrow.

James recalled his mother's advice: "My mom used to tell me when I was growing up, 'Hey you, you are not alone on Kusquqvak. Remember the people upriver, to the side of you, and behind you.' She told me not to forget them because I am not living life alone, that I should also keep those people in mind." In 2018 James was still active in fisheries management on the Kuskokwim, including serving on the Alaska Fish and Game Advisory Board, and on the Kuskokwim River Inter-Tribal Fisheries Commission (KRITFC).

James described the short, handmade gillnets that he saw used as setnets in the 1950s when he was young, before Western nets became readily available:

"Parucuar had a handmade net tethered to the shore, downriver from Helmick Point [at Papegmiut]. He would only fish at high tide; then he picked those fish out when the tide went out." Marie asked James if the net was eight-inch mesh. James responded that in the past people didn't use number measurements but only used their body parts – fingers and hands for mesh size and armspan for net length – as standard measurements when making nets with store-bought materials: "They would get twine.... They never bought finished net[s]. They would make nets in the winter, then set it in the summer. Their sinkers down there were bones, and the [floats] were wood."

James said that when he was young, fishing was not regulated as it is today:

> There weren't a lot of rules and regulations. Our laws for fishing were not written into official documents.
>
> As this person said, we got as many [fish] as we wanted to back then with no limit. It was determined only by how full our fish racks were. Because I was evidently born at a fish camp, we used to go fish downriver from Helmick Point, too daunted to come upriver because we could only go upriver following the tide back then.
>
> Now, they go [fishing] any time, because their boat motors have started going fast, and [they can go] even against the tide. We used to go downriver when the tide went out, and upriver when the tide came in, because we have two tides a day.

James was a fish buyer for ten years in the late 1960s and early 1970s. After working in a cannery in Bristol Bay as a young man, he bought a plane and traveled to the mouth of the Kuskokwim each summer buying king salmon:

> We didn't know about freezer vans, so I made a houselike cold storage, and hired a *kass'aq* guy to install the compressor for me. I used to buy fish downriver.
>
> And because fish prices were not very high, I would send some to Anchorage. In Anchorage, I had two buyers. One was Fafco Fish Company, and the other was Alaska Sausage when it was small. I also sent some to Seattle.
>
> When planes started flying back then, I used to buy some like that. Only *taryaqviit* [king salmon].

James stopped buying fish in the 1970s when the number of kings began to decline.

Salmon traveling up the Kuskokwim

At the beginning of our discussion, the group noted that all of the salmon species that travel up the Kuskokwim each summer have two names in English, and one or two names in Yup'ik: King salmon (Chinook) are *taryaqviit*; chum salmon (dog salmon) are known as *iqalluut* and *kangitneret*; red salmon (sockeyes) are *sayiit*; silver salmon (cohos) are *qakiiyat*; and pink salmon (humpies) are *amaqaayiit*. John added that his mother labeled fatty king salmon *uqurlit*: "She said they refer to the king salmon from the Yukon that mistakenly enter the Kuskokwim as *uqurlit*. She said that their heads are more round, and their bodies are bloated. Then if you cut it, the areas between the meat will be marbled white, and it's fat. She said that if you dry it as a blanket [king salmon slab], it won't be able to dry; it will drip its oil for a long time. She said it's better to make that into strips or *sulunaq* [salted fish]." Michael also mentioned "silver kings" – the first run of kings heading all the way up the Kuskokwim to the Nikolai area. They were so fatty that people put containers beneath them in the smokehouse to catch the drips. Chuckling, Michael recalled: "And that old man, Zachar Levi, he ran out of oil for his engine, and he used that fish oil, mixed with gas. He passed by smelling like pancakes."

Runs of chum salmon also differ. John explained:

> Our elders talked about those that we caught upriver like that. They said that the first shiny [chums] that come that are a little fatter are going far upriver.
>
> Then these that they call *tulimararualget* [lit., "ones with *tulimararuat* (pretend ribs)"] that have few markings, they are the ones that are going to enter rivers closer to [Bethel]. But they said that the ones that come last enter any river, the ones that went upriver late.

Finally, *massret* is the term for old salmon near spawning, and *inarneret* (from *inarte-*, "to lie down") are dead fish, including the spawned-out fish found on gravel bars. Michael noted, "That's what bears eat up there, after they spawn." John said that in the past, men gathered *inarneret* just before freeze-up in the mountains, gutted them, and hung them high in the trees with their heads down:

> When it froze, they would go and get them. They're very good as *egamaarrluut* [half-dried fish] or dog food.
>
> These days, a lot of young people retch when they see them. Something they can survive on. There's all kinds of survival tricks out there they don't practice any more.

Taryaqviit (king salmon) were the first salmon to enter the Kuskokwim. John noted that his father and uncles used to fish for king salmon in May: "They mentioned that they caught their first ones around May 8, around the 19th; when we caught early, we catch [king salmon] when we try to catch sheefish. When we catch those at the same time, our parents told us that we caught *aciirturtet* [fish that swim underneath], some [king salmon] that came upriver from downriver under the ice." Michael noted that kings reached lower Kalskag at the end of May or early June. In fact, the Yup'ik name for June is Kaugun (from *kaug-*, "to strike something with an object") because of the way fishermen struck salmon, especially king salmon, on the head to kill them.

John added that when the smaller males are the first king salmon to enter, they say the ones coming after will be abundant: "They always used to tell us that upriver. They told us to be grateful if the first ones are small [males], saying that the next ones to come after them will be abundant."

Jacob wanted to know if the males enter first, do the females know the path they took. Laughing, John answered in English, "Good question," then continued:

Jenny Nicoli cutting salmon strips at the Jacob Wise Spirit Camp, August 2024. *AFR*

> They only used to say this: these fish know their origins, where they laid eggs before. That's why they say that when they are going to enter rivers, they go in circles at the mouths....
>
> They probably smell the water and know what the water in that river is like. They say that after some enter, they go out again and go up another river to do that. They said that when they are not going to back out, they go in diligently, even surfacing and diving, when they find the rivers where they grew up.

James added that all along the Kuskokwim, males enter first: "No matter where we are. There are a lot of channels downriver. Sometimes, there are three channels. Then after checking the channels, some of them have fish. And then as he said, we catch males first."

When discussing the different salmon runs, John noted that salmon spawn in different places. King salmon spawn in clean rivers with strong currents and gravel beds, including the Goodnews, Eek, Qanirtuuq, Kuiggluk (Kwethluk), Kiseralik, and Aniak Rivers, some traveling all the way upriver to Nikolai. Red salmon, however, travel up rivers to spawn in headwater lakes, not creeks. John then described the Kuiggluk River, with red salmon traveling up the south branch and king salmon the north branch toward their spawning grounds.

> On the south fork of the upper Kuiggluk River, there are two lakes called Nanvarraak [lit., "Two small lakes"]. [Red salmon] lay eggs there....
>
> Kings lay eggs in the midst of [rivers] with strong currents and large pebbles and not in low places. Far up in what they call Nalqialnguq [the north fork of the Kuiggluk River], Crooked One in English, they say there are a lot that lay eggs there.
>
> But chums and silvers mostly enter into *qecikluut* [clear creeks that do not freeze], and mainly spawn in those clean, clear creeks with gravel with slightly strong currents, and their waters are cold....
>
> These people who used to go up [into the mountains] said that mainly red salmon enter the right side, and kings that are going to go lay eggs enter Nalqialnguq on the left side.
>
> Some chums and silvers enter clear creeks in lower areas to go lay eggs.

John and Michael discussed salmon runs on other Kuskokwim tributaries. John noted that both king salmon and chum salmon travel up the Tuluksak River to spawn, but no red salmon. All species of salmon go up the Aniak River, while only whitefish and a few silver salmon enter Igyaraq River going into Whitefish

A young camper learning to jar salmon strips at the Jacob Wise Spirit Camp, August 2024. *AFR*

Lake (Nanvarpak).

Marie commented that there were few reds in the past, and James agreed, noting that when they saw a red salmon hanging in a net or on a fish rack, it stood out red compared to the paler chum salmon: "It was visible from afar." All were grateful that recently the numbers of red salmon on the Kuskokwim have increased. Jacob added that red salmon are *qaktaalriit* (jumping fish, lit., "ones that repeatedly breach") as they are the only fish that surface and dive.

Pink salmon or "humpies" swim upriver with the silver salmon starting in July, and some years they are plentiful. John said: "We mostly catch them with nets made for small fish, ones around four inches. But the bigger ones will get caught in five-inch nets." Michael added: "One old man, Zachar Levi, every time it rains, he used to always say, '*Amaqaayiitam tekitut* [Pink salmon have arrived].' Every time it's bum weather." John agreed: "They used to talk about them like that too, that when they are abundant, it will constantly rain." John remarked that humpies are good when hung to dry or when pan-fried. Jacob puts them away in the freezer and eats them with seal oil in winter. James also harvests humpies downriver, using a small four-inch mesh gillnet. Commercial fishermen often threw them away, as they brought in no money.

John was taught never to waste fish or food: "They said that in some years, they will be scarce. They said that sometimes when it's time for them to come, they don't appear." Michael shared his mother's story of a time when the salmon runs failed along the Kuskokwim: "She said long ago, [there were] no fish. They just disappeared in the Kuskokwim, upriver. She said that the people were playing with [wasting] fish upriver around Crooked Creek.... And she said there's no fish for some years. Then after that, they start taking care of their fish when them fish come back."

In the past, John explained, salmon were only scarce occasionally during extreme weather conditions, including unusually cold weather or floods and overflows that killed salmon fry in their spawning grounds:

> Even here, they used to say that some years, there were no fish from natural disasters out in the ocean or up in the rearing grounds, up in the headwaters. They said that during severe winters up there where those little fingerlings are [they died]. They call the young salmon *nutemllayagaat* [lit., "little original ones"] before they go out to the ocean....
>
> They said that sometimes in winter, when it had been very cold and snow didn't fall, they would call them *patsarutellret* [those that had suddenly been exposed to cold] when it had frozen all the way to the bottom. They said that when that happens, a lot of [salmon fry] die.
>
> They also said that when it rained a lot all fall and it froze, flooding so that there were no sandbars when the water level went over [the riverbank], when those fries that have yet to grow were flooded to the ground on the sandbars, a lot would not survive....
>
> They said that once in a great while, they would do that in the past when there had been floods during freeze-up.

Ways of knowing when salmon will arrive

We also discussed some of the signs people observed indicating the quality and quantity of salmon that will return during a given year. Some indicators are widely viewed as correlating with the arrival of king salmon.[3] For example, John recalled the *qaneryaraq* (teaching) that the arrival of birds indicated the arrival of the first king salmon: "When I first started driftnetting with my family as a little boy, they used to tell us this: We should watch the very first birds that come in. They said that if they are not abundant, if they come in sporadically, king salmon won't be abundant. They said that they would come just as the birds did."

James remarked that repeated thunder is also understood as a sign that fish will be abundant: "They say that there will be fish when there is thunder.... They don't say that there will be lots of kings or chums, but only lots of fish."

John said that tree swallows flying close to the water, and the arrival of mosquitoes are also indicators:

> They would tell us to watch *kauturyaraat* [tree swallows]. They said that if they start flying right above the water, seeming like they touch the water, fish will be abundant. They said there is about to be a large run [of salmon].
>
> And they also said, when there were suddenly a lot of mosquitos, that chum salmon are going to become abundant soon.

John detailed the order of fish arriving on the Kuskokwim before the salmon:

> In my observation, because my family always fishes with nets upriver, sheefish arrive first after *neqyagaat* [small fish or whitefish]. When *neqyagaat* and pike have entered lakes, and when the abundant fish have passed, sheefish swim [in our rivers] for a long time though they are supposed to have gone upriver.
>
> They leave at the end of April, then they swim upriver around the Y [located adjacent to Cingigmiut, upriver from Kwethluk] until the end of May. Then near the end of May, the *qusuuret* [rainbow smelt] arrive.

John noted that in the past people said that when the branch of a small tree was as big as a smelt's mouth, smelt will arrive:

> They measured and used as a gauge the branches of *qikmiruat* [pussy willow catkins], *enrilnguat* [soft willow shoots], and *kaviqsuyagaat* [little red-barked willows], the [branches] that they used to thread [the smelt through a gill and the mouth] when hanging them to dry. They said that when it fits inside its mouth, they will arrive.
>
> And they said that the first smelts will have *aciirturtet* [fish that swim under the ice] among them if they are abundant.

John concluded: "They always talked about using the branches of those to gauge the [fishing] season. They told us to watch nature. They said that it will tell you when the fish are supposed to arrive." James added that downriver at Tuntutuliak, people don't dipnet for smelt because they go under the ice. He noticed, however, that around Bethel the presence of gulls flying over the water indicated that smelt were in the river: "Those gulls stay around smelt. Sometimes they are late, and sometimes early, but because they mostly swim under the ice downriver we don't dip for them."

John continued: "The other [signs] that they used were those black birds that they call *itrat* [surf scoters], or some people call them *akacakayiit*. They said that when those black birds start flying upriver, smelts are on their way." John added that surf scoters don't nest in southwest Alaska, but after feeding on herring eggs on the coast, they start flying upriver toward Canada.

John described the abundant snow and regular flooding when he was growing up, cleaning the path for the fish:

> Back when we were young, there used to be a lot of snow and it would be very cold. The ice would be thicker than five feet. And every spring, when there used to be a lot of snow, the whole area used to get flooded out.
>
> Those old people would be grateful. They said that it's cleaning the Kuskokwim River. They said that it's clearing the path incoming fish will take. Flush all the debris. And the ice would break and bring a lot of wood to the mouth.... They said that when there would be a lot of water, there would be a lot of wood.
>
> We hear that it was the same all the way to the mouth, and [wood] would drift ashore downriver [on the coast]. And when they went out of the Kuskokwim with strong southerly winds, they said that the shore downriver would have a lot of driftwood. They would be grateful when it was like that, saying that there would be lots of fish when it had flooded....
>
> And when the rivers were full of water, they would say that the fish would come upriver quickly if the water is cold.

Our group also discussed causal indicators that fishermen use to predict the arrival of salmon (see also Moncrieff and Klein 2003). Wind direction was at the top of the list. John continued:

> They also said not to only watch birds. They said to watch where the wind is blowing from in winter. They said that in winter when the wind continually blows from the north and northwest, if the wind is cold, they said that the fish [salmon] would enter our rivers in relative abundance and would be fat.
>
> And yet, they said that if there was a lot of south wind in the winter, they scarcely and sporadically arrive. Those are some of the things that we who are not young heard. And our parents and fathers constantly talked to us, and they were also instructed by their elders.

John reiterated the role of the south wind in summer in bringing in the fish:

> And when a strong south wind blew, fifteen miles or better, they said that they would be happy, saying *taqikcarluki* [(the south wind) brings

> in the fish], saying that it let the fish at the mouth of Kuskokwim enter. Sometimes the day after the next, when the south wind had blown from downriver, up around Y [on the Kuskokwim], they arrive quite abundantly. But it's always a mystery what they will do, how they will be when they arrive.

Michael recalled his mother's advice: "When we have really strong south wind up there [near Lower Kalskag], she used to always tell us, '*Neqet, neqet* [The fish, the fish].'" Marie agreed: "During fishing season, they liked the south wind.... When the south wind is blowing, the water suddenly rises."

Mark pointed out that the direction of the wind bringing fish into a river varies depending on the direction the river mouth faces; fish come into a river when the wind blows directly against the river's mouth:

> The same for all mouths of rivers, the wind blowing toward [a river] causes *itercarneq* [lit., "(tide or fish) going in (a river)"]. When the wind blows, these fish start swimming. And on the Yukon River, the west

Dry fish hanging at Megan Leary and RJ Morgan's fish camp above Napaimute. *Andrea Gusty*

> wind, when the wind blows directly against [the mouth of the Yukon River], they enter. And around Qissunaq, the southwest wind also [causes *itercarneq*].... The wind blows directly against the river mouth, when there is *itercarneq* along the rivers, the fish start swimming upriver. After they mill around, as they say in English, going around and around.
>
> They go in, go out, go in, go out. Then when the wind blows, they go right in, and the place they left has no more fish. But when the new [salmon] are going to enter, there are fish there again. Then when the time comes and there's going to be a strong run of fish entering [the river], they don't wait for the wind. They swim upriver, going upriver when they want to.

Michael noted that he watches for high water after a wind, indicating that the fish have arrived: "Even a couple days after it gets windy, I watch [the water]. When the water level rises, fish are coming.... I watch that water all the time, especially if they're catching fish down here [in Bethel], wait a couple days, and then when it starts having high water, now we catch fish." Mark surmised that the mass of fish probably brings up the water level a little, and Michael agreed.

Water temperature is another factor. John explained: "They say when the water's low and warmer than average, they'll be slow coming in. The water has to be at a certain temperature where the fish can tolerate it. If it's too warm, they won't come up right away, or if it's too shallow. And if it's too warm, they swim in the deeper channels, where the water is cooler."

John was also admonished to pay close attention to the condition of the water:

> They said that if the water is abnormal, we will not catch too much fish [salmon]. They said that if it's too clear and shallow, we will not catch fish closer to the shore toward sandbars. But if we fish close to the main channel, we will catch more.
>
> Or, they said that if the waves are rough, the mud [at the river bottom]...mixes with the water. They said that when it's like that, fish swim close to the surface, not deep down.

John described salmon schooling up at the mouths of tributaries before heading upstream:

> When they arrive, they don't go upriver right away....
>
> They stay at the mouth and the *qamanret* [eddies, places without currents] for almost a week, then when it's time, they enter all at once....
>
> I think they try to get their bearings, try [to] recognize if that's their river of origin or not. When they sense their rivers, they diligently enter

> again and go upriver without stopping. Takes them roughly two weeks from the mouth of the tributary to the headwaters.

Marie asked if the indicators they had described were still true. John answered, "Yes, we who have been instructed still rely on those." He added that today he can also check with downriver friends to predict the arrival of salmon near his village:

> When I was curious about them, before they arrived here, I used to call that person Charlie sometimes, when he used to fish with nets. When they had caught a lot, I knew that the next day, or two days after, I would catch fish upriver....
>
> When they have been abundant in Eek Island and in the Tunt[utuliak] area, they arrive slightly abundantly in our village upriver. We catch the ones they didn't catch [lit., "their leftovers"].

John has no faith in Fish and Game predictions: "Their test fisheries are liars. They always say they are less than they are.... One of my friends asked me, 'What you think of tomorrow?' [I told him,] 'Ask the test fish. If they tell you five, you double that; today you go out there, you'll get that number.'"

Salmon fishing on the lower Kuskokwim

At the beginning of our discussion, James painted a vivid picture of what people at the mouth of the Kuskokwim were doing before they had the tools they needed to harvest king salmon. He recalled that into the 1950s the human population was low and everyone lived on the riverbanks, even in Bethel, because it was easier access to fishing. At that time, families harvested fish to feed both themselves and their dogs:

> Because there were not a lot of people, we only worked on enough fish for people to eat for the winter. Also there were other fish to supplement them, including whitefish, pike, burbot, and sheefish....
>
> We mostly caught chum salmon [at fish camp] because there were no nets made to catch king salmon back then. We only had handmade nets, where we got twine from the stores and people started making nets. Even women made nets along with the men.

James recalled that few people from Canineq (the lower Kuskokwim coastal area) fished for salmon at the mouth of the Kuskokwim in the past. Some like Parucuar worked on salmon at Papegmiut and Keggukar, but not many, as it was too far to travel in their small boats. Others from the Canineq area as well as some Akulmiut from the lake country west of Bethel traveled using *palayat* (large skin boats), some with sails, upriver to Nalqigliq, near Napakiak, to fish for salmon. Marie described people traveling from the coast to the Kuskokwim:

> Then from Cevv'arneq [Chefornak] out there, they would travel through Muruyaq River, through Kialiq River to the Kuskokwim. That man, Mancuaq, said that he grew up at Muruyaq.... He said that people would arrive from Cevv'arneq out there, and they didn't know how to eat king salmon.
>
> He said that when they ate [king salmon], they would get very sweaty. They weren't accustomed to eating king salmon.

Mark recalled how people from Kayalivik (north of Nelson Island) traveled across Baird Inlet, portaging through Taklirrlak Lake to reach the Kuskokwim:

> And the people from Newtok told stories that they would come through an inland route with one of them using a boat with an inboard engine...towing a lot of other boats.
>
> They said that they would pay that man with a boat with a square five-gallon tank of gas. And then as a group they would return through that same route.

Mark confirmed that in the past, Nelson Islanders didn't know about king salmon or chum salmon swimming north offshore on their way to the Yukon River. John said that the same thing was true in Hooper Bay: "They said that they didn't know about the fish swimming far out in the ocean from their village. But when they learned from outside [non-Yup'ik] fishers, they looked around and started finding them when their implements became more sophisticated."

James confirmed that in the past people at the mouth of the Kuskokwim never fished for king salmon:

> Some years, winters are long with summer coming late. And sometimes at the beginning of May, the ice starts to melt, it becomes dangerous. Back then, I never heard of people fishing for kings, but when one king salmon was hanging, it was conspicuous from afar like red salmon. But they mostly fished for chums.
>
> Evelyn Thomas [from Crooked Creek upriver] mentioned chums only. It was probably because the people upriver never used to fish for king salmon [before fish wheels].

James noted that fishermen could only catch salmon that had gone into tributaries of the Kuskokwim: "Evelyn said that those chums were the only fish. Those were the only fish that we saw before we found out about kings, reds, coho, and others. Even pink salmon. We lived not knowing about those back then. We knew chum as the only fish."

James continued, noting that although some people say that they grew up with kings, that's not true: "When chums arrived back then, they were dried into edible food, or they cooked it. They didn't catch king salmon too much. They didn't fish for them too much in my village [Tuntutuliak] either in the past because we didn't have nets for those kings."

It was only later, after they got better quality nets, that people started catching other salmon species. Fish wheels could not be used on the lower Kuskokwim because of the tides. James explained:

> The [gillnets] they made a long time ago, they only made them measuring them [with their bodies]. They made gillnets that could catch fish because we didn't have fish wheels down here because of the tides.
>
> Tide goes in and out, in and out. So, upriver water goes downriver all the time, day and night, so they need fish wheels to catch the salmon.

James emphasized that in the past their parents determined when they had enough fish: "Those handmade [boats] were two feet wide. They couldn't hold a lot of cargo.... But depending on how much they got, our parents had us stop [fishing]. They were the ones to decide." James said that his family was poor when he was young, with no money for gas: "That's why we rowed the boat all the time when I was young.... And we wait for incoming tide to go upriver, and we wait for outgoing tide if we were going downriver. So, it was not easy."

Fishing before gillnets

John provided a vivid account of salmon fishing along the Kuiggluk River before he was born and before better gillnets were widely available along the Kuskokwim. In those days, John's father and seven uncles, along with several other men, fished for king salmon in the clear waters upriver from Kwethluk:

> They said that there were twelve men before they scattered. They had a fish camp up in Cinginret, upriver from Ingriurluq [Three Step Mountain]. They said that what they call Magic Creek now was originally Kuiggluk River. Its next stop had its upper section upriver in the mountains before it cut through land and formed another [river] on the marshes in 1927.

> My mother said that they camped there to work on fish every year. She said that even though people along the Kuskokwim River caught few king salmon, those many men up there would catch king salmon by spearing them [at the end of June].

John noted that in the past people had to use spears to harvest king salmon, because of their size and strength:

> They said that [king salmon] used to be big a long time ago. They said that when they speared them, they aimed for their heads. When they hit them on their bodies or posterior areas, because of their strength [they would escape]. And if a person didn't quickly tether the line onto something, it would drag him down.
>
> They said that around Eek downriver, when daddy and some other people were there, a king salmon dragged one of them through water when he speared it and it twisted. [King salmon] used to be big.

John continued, noting that in the past few fishing on the Kuskokwim could bring these large king salmon to shore: "They said that the ones driftnetting with canoes, when one or two king salmon rammed into them, they would bring that canoe upriver. They would ram into it and drag that canoe along with the person inside it. They can't do that to us now because our boats have gotten bigger. Even though it wriggles, it will die in front of us."

Jacob asked John about the points used on salmon spears, and John explained that they were *cavget* (toggling harpoon points) made of caribou antler with a hole for the line at the point's base. When the point pierced the fish and came off the spear, it would twist to the side and hold the fish. John had a harpoon point when he was young but never used it. James added that people along the muddy waters of the Kuskokwim didn't spear fish: "We can see them down in the coastal area in clear waters. Then when they come here, we can't see them and can't do anything to them. Or, even if we see them, they're too fast to approach." John concurred that men speared salmon in creeks and shallow waters in the mountains, not along the Kuskokwim: "They can't do that on Kusquqvak, only up in shallow mountain streams in what we call *tevenret* [portages]. They wade and wait for them in *tevenret*. And the side where the sun is located, they tell them not to have the sun behind them. They say that when [salmon] see your shadow, they will avoid you. Only facing the sun." John's father and uncles used to spear king salmon upriver from Ingriurluq, although John never did: "They said that there would be a lot of them waiting for fish next to each other."

Before king salmon arrived, John said that people fished for smaller fish in the mountains:

> They said that before they fished for king salmon, they would close off small *qecikluut* [creeks with warm spots that do not freeze] with small handmade nets. And after they baited them, they would catch *culugpauget* [arctic grayling], *cavirrutnat* [round whitefish], and *neqyagaat* [small fish], and sometimes *luqruuyiit* [pike].
>
> They would cut a lot of those small things and eat them before these salmon started arriving.... They said that only their women would driftnet with small gillnets for those small fish. But when these king salmon started arriving, their men would spear them.

Men also used sinew to make small gillnets for use in *quutaaryaraq* (seine fishing, lit., "way of repeatedly closing in"), driving fish by pulling a net, one person from the land and the other from a kayak, along a river into a spot with no current, then closing in the net to trap the fish. John explained:

> They said that when they would seine fish, they would use small handmade gillnets that weren't very long or wide.
>
> Sometimes at the end of sandbars there are small eddies. They said that on a good river where nets wouldn't get snagged, one [person] would bring [the net] along on the river with a kayak or a canoe. The one on land would run with [the net]. And at the end of the sandbar around the eddy, there would be a pole to tether the net up on land.
>
> Because [the tether] would be ready to tie the net to, the one in the kayak or canoe would close in the net at the eddy, and they would help each other pull it to the sandbar. The men worked together so that the fish they caught wouldn't escape above the floats. They said that they would bring up a lot of fish.

Men also set *taluyat* (conical fish traps) made for rivers. John continued:

> After blocking off the area and making a path to swim downriver, they would set the fish trap facing upriver. When [the fish] arrived going downriver, they would enter the fish trap.
>
> They said that they would empty those *taluyat* twice a day. They would watch for when it filled because the water was clear, and they would drag them on the land side and bring them up to empty them when it was time.

> Up there [in the mountains], they only used [*taluyat*] when the river was not full. When it was very full and had strong currents, it would not be suitable [for *taluyat*]. They said that they would catch a lot of fish.

John noted that in the past, people fished for *massret* (old salmon near spawning) upriver in the mountains:

> They call them *tamuanat* [spawning fish hung to dry, lit., "those that require chewing"] because spawning salmon have thick skin.... They mostly get the males, the ones with big humps. The females have no humps, but they have eggs.
>
> But the humps of *amaqaayiit* [pink salmon, from *amaq*, "something carried on the back"] are good. They have fat in them. You can eat them raw after cutting them to pieces. Better than sushi.... You won't be hungry all day.

John closed by saying that his family stopped spearing king salmon and fishing in the mountains in the 1940s, moving to the Kuskokwim after they got more sophisticated nets.

Harvesting salmon with fish wheels

Before better nets were widely used, upriver fishermen employed fish wheels to harvest the salmon they needed to see them through the winter. In interior Alaska prospectors built the first fish wheels on the Tanana River in 1904, and prospectors subsequently built the first fish wheel on the Kuskokwim near Georgetown around 1910. When Moravian missionary John Henry Kilbuck traveled up the Kuskokwim by steamer in 1911, he remarked on the new technology, but remained skeptical of its merits: "A revolving affair, worked by the current...continually dipping, working like a water wheel. How successful it is, I do not know." In fact, the introduction of the fish wheel had a dramatic effect on the Kuskokwim salmon fishery above Akiak. The increased salmon harvest it made possible provided a substantial surplus which residents then sold or traded to white men living along the river. Hunters used the remainder to support bigger dog teams, with a corresponding increase in their ability to harvest and visit farther afield (Fienup-Riordan 1991:271; Oswalt 1990:112-114).

By the 1940s, there were two or three fish wheels for each village from Lower Kalskag all the way up to McGrath. The river was too shallow in the Nikolai area, and fish wheels were not used farther upriver. Michael explained how fish wheels were shared by several families around Lower Kalskag: "Three families, we had one pretty good-sized fish wheel. Sometimes 'cause the current is strong, we load it for a really strong current so that fish wheel will go. We would try to find where the fish go. And that's how they get their fish." When they were done fishing for the year, they used a log to stop the wheel, took the baskets off, and removed the wood frame, which they rebuilt the following year after breakup.

Michael described checking the holding box twice a day in normal years. He noted the abundant king salmon one fish wheel at Lower Kalskag produced in 1963: "We had to stop that fish wheel, 'cause that bucket [holding box] gets too full. Big king salmon. And one family would divide them with the families in the fish camp, three or four [families]. And when they get done, they go start [the fish wheel]. Not even two hours, that bucket [got full]. That's how much fish there was. After that [year], I start using gillnets." A few fish wheels remain in use in villages from Kalskag on upriver, but smaller than those used in the past and without the fences that Michael's father built downstream from their fish wheel to direct fish into the fish wheel's baskets.

Improvements in fishing gear

The first twine gillnets came from Bristol Bay and were thick and not very durable, only usable for one summer. John remarked: "They said that they would quickly rot and become frail the next year before there were nylon nets. Since around the 1950s, people who went to commercial fish or to canneries with barges would bring nets from over there [in Bristol Bay]. That's when they finally started catching a lot of fish here on the Kuskokwim River." John noted that there were always a lot of fish in the past, but because they didn't have good nets, many salmon passed to their spawning grounds. When their nets improved, however, they started catching too many fish: "They said that before they started catching fish to sell, all fish [salmon] were abundant in the river. Then shortly after they started commercial fishing, from the middle of the 1980s, they quickly started declining."

John agreed that today, with better equipment, people easily travel great distances to harvest salmon: "People say they've started [traveling far] since they started using fast boat motors, but they never used to do that back when their boats weren't sophisticated and their motors were small. They say that they only went to some places in small numbers, and they didn't gather a lot." John told about meeting Johnny Friend from Kwigillingok who had recently traveled from his home to Bethel in four hours using his two-hundred horsepower motor. Better nets also made a difference. John continued:

They said that when some people from Canineq started going commercial fishing and they got [gillnets] from Bristol Bay, they started bringing home a lot of cargo [salmon] in their boats. And they started to consider Quinhagak downriver closer [when they got fast motors]; so they started going downriver and going right back home.

And a few people who have large motors get [salmon] from [Bethel] because nowhere seems far to people now. When I used to travel downriver to Goodnews [Bay], I would sometimes steer for 19, 21 hours going downriver. We would travel slowly when it was windy and the waves were rough. And now, when my grandchildren or great-grandchildren steer for me, we fly along the crests of the waves.

Regional diversity in salmon fishing along the Kuskokwim

Salmon fishing played – and continues to play – a central role in the lives of all our group members. Yet particular family histories set the stage for diverse fishing experiences in different places along the river. Exploring these unique fishing histories can highlight both regional differences as well as the common threads that bring fishing families together. As everyone made clear in the personal experiences they shared, fishing is not an individual activity, but a complex operation in which extended families work together to harvest, care for, and share fish.

Fishing near Kwethluk

John is seven years younger than James and grew up 100 miles farther up the Kuskokwim. He came of age just as salmon fishing on the Kuskokwim was reaching its peak, and he described the large fish camps Kwethluk families used along the river:

When they started going to fish camps here on the Kuskokwim River, they said that Cingigmiut, that place upriver from Kwethluk that they call the Big Y in English, was a huge fish camp...with seven or more households.

And the other one was downriver from there, Taperrnat, where our fish camp is now. That place also had an average of seven households....

Around the 1950s and after, my parents lived with me separately, and we only used tents. And Tass'aq's namesake also had her separate place. And upriver from us, my paternal uncle, Quriciq and his family had their fish camp. And by us was Cialuq and their family, and over from Cialuq and family was Ayapan and their family.... Also, my older sister and her husband had their own separate place there, with their own fish camp.

John would row across the river to driftnet when fish arrived, as in those days few had motors:

> When [the salmon] first came, we didn't try to catch them too diligently when we had a lot of other small fish from lakes. They also wouldn't let us driftnet though sheefish were abundant, but they would have us go and quickly driftnet to catch enough to cook. Because it was close, we would quickly cross and set our net across there and drift.
>
> During our parents' time, a lot of people didn't have boat motors that we call *levaat*. Some of them once in a while would use a 22-horse motor. The people using those would go almost without wakes, but the small things were loud. And their boats were made out of chopped wood [before plywood became available]. They weren't very big, not wide, and weren't too long.
>
> Only once in a while, when they invited me to go with them with my uncle's boat, when I started hurrying, I would ask my cousin to go with me. "Let me help the motor, we might go faster if we row." Some would have nine-horse motors, and this one with a huge motor would use a ten-horse.
>
> Someone with a big motor would have a 22 [-horsepower motor]. To us, they would seem like huge motors. They used to be very loud. Cingik upriver is a long way off, but when a motor approached upriver from it, we started hearing it. It would be coming for a long time and eventually arrive.

John said that there were always a lot of fish in the past, and with better nets harvests increased:

> Around the 1950s, when the people who had gone to work [at canneries] arrived bringing [longer] nets they called Iilgayarmiutaat [ones from Bristol Bay], after stringing the float and lead lines, they started catching a lot of fish. But even though they caught a lot, we deferred to our women to tell us how much to catch....
>
> And I tell my relatives in the fish camps, when they want to go down [to fish] again, "Ask those women. They get tired." They would have them stop depending on [the women]. They wouldn't let us go down though there were a lot of fish.

John emphasized that fishing was still limited to how many fish a family needed:

> We wouldn't catch too much, only enough for one household. Or when we could catch enough to fill one storage bin, they would tell us to fish for that much. My late father would wake me up around three, four, [or] five to hurry up and go driftnet before [the fish] were spooked by those trying to dock going into sandbars.
>
> Sometimes when we were there at the right time, when we caught a lot of fish after setting [the net] once, because our boats weren't big, we would try not to load too much [fish] on them and pull the net in right away. When we went to land, we would take them by hand and bring them up to the storage bins.

John had two older sisters and one younger sister, and as the only boy they wouldn't let him help those working on fish. Instead, after he'd had a small meal, he returned to the river to fish for other families:

> When we had finally brought what we needed to shore, they would feed us just one pancake or with a little bit of dried fish for breakfast.
>
> And we would have a little water in our small cups to wash them down. They didn't bring out a lot of food. Then when they were finished, they would tell me to driftnet for one of the families around us.
>
> Once in a while when they had one to spare, they would let me fish with their boats, and I would go with other boys, or even girls, to row for me. We would set our nets rowing. We also rowed and driftnetted. We would pull in the net depending on how many [salmon] were hitting [the net].
>
> When we went up to land, we would let them take them all. All day, I used to go down several times like that, sometimes three times. And if I wasn't tired toward the evening, I would go driftnet a fourth time for another family.
>
> Those were our instructions; we would always try to help our family and those around us. But sometimes, when we were first, when women would process fish, when the daughters or *ilungat* [female cross-cousins of females] of those around us helped each other work on fish, they would finish right away.

John recalled that when he watched women helping each other, they made it look easy: "Before long, they would hang the fish that they worked on in the fish racks." John said that when they caught fish early, toward the end of May, they would cook them right way or share them with those around them: "Only later, when fish were more abundant, we finally started fishing for ourselves for what we would hang [to dry] after giving the first ones to our families and friends."

John described how his father darkened his nets to attract fish:

> I watched my daddy and his family around me when they darkened or made [nets] blue. The first gillnets, when they were twine, used to be too white. I used to watch my daddy chopping birch bark and taking off a lot.
>
> And then he would put them into a half drum [tank], and he would put that net inside and boil it. When he took [the nets] out, they would come out almost light purple to remove the white color....
>
> People say they also used alders, but my father used birch bark as dye.

John later noted that fish can see nets, especially in low water, if they are too dark or too light: "If you get a sandy, silty colored [net], they catch easier."

Nets were also treated with valerian roots to attract the fish. John explained:

> After their first drift, if [the nets] didn't catch anything, they would look for *teptukuyiit* [valerian, from *teptu-*, "to be odoriferous"] with small purple flowers at the top. They would dig them out; underneath, their roots smell very strong. They would [tie the valerian root] at the middle of the net, and one at the end.
>
> They said that when they would driftnet, fish would probably smell and be attracted to its odor.... They used that kind of [plant] to do what they call *iinruarturluki* [continuously apply medicine on their nets].

Jacob said that around Napakiak, they were instructed to use wormwood to freshen their nets: "After boiling [wormwood leaves] in a lot of water and after cooling it, gather the net and pour it on top. That works, and it's evidently true."

Michael added that fish dislike dog hair and that he was taught never to let dogs go to their nets: "We don't leave our nets laying on the ground so the dogs will get on them. My dad and my Ap'a tell me that those fish could smell that dog hair, if it's in that net. And just like he said, we use *caiggluk* [wormwood] to clean [the net], wash it, and set it when we cannot catch." Michael added that people were careful to keep all animal fur away from their nets, or they would be unable to catch fish.

John noted that his extended family harvested no more than one hundred king salmon: "When they told us to stop, though fish were abundant, we stopped and waited for chum salmon and red salmon." Because his family was large with seven to nine dogs, they needed between 500 and 750 chums and reds to feed them. At the end of summer, the large mesh salmon nets were hung to dry, while they continued to use the smaller four-inch gillnets to harvest humpback whitefish and broad whitefish, rainbow trout, and pink salmon, which were not originally abundant in the Kuiggluk River: "We would mostly give those small fish to our neighbors right away. They would cut a few whitefish to dry."

John's family harvested few silver salmon: "When silvers started coming, we wouldn't get too many; we would make them into *aqlitnguat* [split fish attached at the tail with grooves to promote drying, lit., 'imitation earrings'] if it wasn't raining too much and make them into strips." If it was rainy, John was told not to driftnet for silvers as their skins were not supple: "When it rains a lot, [the skin] where the fish is draped over the rack rots easily and they fall. But at this time now, after we got freezers, some started freezing them after vacuum packing them." John's father also used to jar silver salmon, saying that they were as fat as king salmon: "I think he learned from the people of the Ellirivik [Moravian Children's Home] because he used to help them. He would jar [fish], imitating those he watched."

John said that the Kuiggluk and Kuskokwim Rivers were full of fish camps in the early days:

> They said that people from Kuiggluk and Taparrnat set up fish camps upriver in Cingigpall'er since a long time ago. Then when they got more sophisticated boat motors around 1980 and after, some started having their own separate fish camps under land claims.
>
> There are quite a few fish camps in Kuiggluk River far inside reaching the small hills and beyond. Even on the Kuskokwim, fish camps are scattered the same way. And now, the entire river is filled with fish camps.[4]

Families stayed at fish camps from June through early August. John explained:

> Sometimes when we went to fish camp when I was small, we wouldn't return home though our home village was close. We would stay for two, three weeks, and sometimes stay for a month, before returning to the village.
>
> We would work on what we caught, trying to cure them just right. Then when they were good, we brought them home. As he said, we would divide and share what we caught to our families, especially to those with no providers, elders, and widows. And they stopped [fishing] at the beginning of August to go pick berries.

John added that although they no longer fished for themselves, they continued to fish for others: "[We would fish to give] to another fish camp or another bin. We apparently used to have [a good fishing spot] without needing to travel, just run down and driftnet right on the river below our place."

John described how food was stored at fish camp:

> Though they were at fish camps, when there were no freezers, they would only store [fish] in elevated fish caches or in wooden barrels.
>
> I used to see wooden barrels, and some were big. They would fill them, pressing [the fish] down by stepping on them. And after putting something hard over them, they would weigh them down with big rocks. Same way with *sulunat* [salted fish]. They would leave them with absolutely no air.
>
> And when they finished [packing the barrels], the permafrost didn't melt back then. They would dig deep, and when they reached the frozen land before long, they would close them securely and mark the areas after putting [the barrels] inside.
>
> Right when it started freezing, they would get them and bring them to their villages and store them in their *elagyat* [caches, originally underground, from *elag-*, "to dig"]. Some had *elagyat* under their houses or under their elevated fish caches. But the dried [food] would be put up to the [elevated] caches.

Most of each king salmon was cut into strips or slabs to dry and smoke: other fish parts were also taken care of. John recalled *igyamcuut* (dried fish esophagus and stomachs, from *igyaraq*, "throat"): "You can take out the part from the throat down to the end of the stomach. When they dried, they called them *igyamcuut*. They're good to chew after smoking them. They would give them as snacks to young people with good teeth. Like jawbreakers if they're really dry."

King salmon heads were made into *sulunat*, dried and smoked to make *qamiqurrluut* (from *qamiquq*, "head"), or fermented to make *tepeq* (aged fish). John remembered seeing people cook king salmon milt to add to *akutaq*. He also recalled people preparing *cin'at*: "After removing its front lateral fin, they put the whole [king salmon] in a pit underground and made what they called *cin'at*.... Then after cutting them into pieces, people would eat *tepeq* [aged fish]." Marie concluded: "They made all of its parts into food."

John described his father's insistence that unused fish parts be buried, not thrown in the water or left around the fish processing area:

> They always buried [fish guts] in pits in the ground at our fish camp. Over from the fish storage bin, quite a distance away, they always spilled

> the parts they wouldn't eat, like the intestines and slime, in one pit. And we threw the bones and backbones in another pit. Even though they got old, we could pull them up and cook them for dog food.... If we boil them long enough, they become edible.... What we can't eat, the dogs eat.

James concluded: "They didn't have a lot to throw away back then. We used the fish, and our dogs used the fish."

All noted that today, with few dogs to feed, this careful treatment of fish waste is no longer routinely practiced. John said with regret: "I've started seeing people today [dumping guts] downriver. And even after they fish with nets, they dock somewhere and throw them on the shore. They take the ones they want home and throw the rest away."

Fishing at the Ellirivik (Moravian Children's Home)

Jacob's early fishing experiences reflect his growing up in the 1950s at the Ellirivik (Moravian Children's Home), just up the Kuiggluk River from the village of Kwethluk, where he was sent to live after his father passed away. When summer came, elders from Kwethluk instructed the boys on how to fish:

> When we became able, when the salmon arrived, even though we stayed upriver at the orphanage, these elders from Kwethluk had us prepare our implements.
>
> They would go upriver and teach us how to tie the lead and float lines on gillnets, when [Western] gillnets appeared in my time. And they talked about how low [the gillnets] should dangle. They talked about how, if they were too tight, they would not be good at catching fish [salmon].
>
> Also, [the line] along the sinkers, they told us not to make it shorter than [the float line] on top, but to make it longer....They said that when it's longer [wider] along the bottom, even if you don't use an outboard motor, it won't slack down, and it would stay open and continue to catch fish.

When fishing season arrived, men and boys from the orphanage fished in a tributary of the Kuiggluk River, where it went out to the Kuskokwim. Jacob recalled that they only fished for king salmon at the orphanage, using a small fishing boat called the *Put Put*: "[The] reason we gave it that endearing name was because it went so slowly. It didn't speed over the water though it had a motor. Maybe it had only a two- or four-horse inboard [engine]....When we went downriver, we would go faster, but not very fast. Then when we went upriver carrying five or ten kings or even less, we would slowly head upriver for a long time."

The orphanage fish camp was near their dog yard. Jacob described how they used dogs and one strong horse to carry the fish up to where they could be worked on:

> All of us men would take care of the salmon we caught. We mostly made strips. We'd hang them after soaking them in brine....
>
> Then all summer, judging [the dryness of the fish hanging], we'd bring the strips in [to the smokehouse] and smoke them right away. The men took care of them, but they periodically tested them....When they were good to eat, they took them out from [the smokehouse] and brought them down to the people who would work on them. Then the women would finally take over.

Salmon fishing on the middle Kuskokwim

Born and raised in Kalskag, our youngest group member, Michael, provided a detailed picture of king salmon fishing upriver after good-quality gillnets became available and use of fish wheels began declining. He described how his family and two others shared a fish camp six miles below Lower Kalskag on the main branch of the Kuskokwim River. Sinka William's dad and Zachar Levi's family were the camp's original occupants, and they invited Michael's family to join them in 1959, five years after Michael was born. Just as Michael's family finished harvesting their king salmon and were ready to smoke them, Pete Abruska arrived, wanting to use the smokehouse he had built there. So Michael's father offered to trade him ten gallons of gas for the smokehouse, enough for Pete to get logs for a new one. After that, Michael's family never moved from that site: "My dad stayed in there because that eddy was good. Every time my dad want to setnet in there, for years, he'd ask [Sinka William's] dad if he can set his net in there, because that was his place first. We'd go there and start setting nets." Sinka's dad and Zachar Levi later moved, but Michael's father claimed the land in 1971, and their family still fishes there.

Michael explained that his father always emphasized the importance of fishing for the first run of kings, so as to avoid the flies: "My dad was really picky about the first run...because they say, 'If we eat food, you guys wouldn't want to eat what flies lay eggs on.' And we took really good care of them, and still my kids do that." Everyone agreed on the importance of working on king salmon early in the season, before flies lay their eggs. Jacob said with feeling: "When we work on [salmon] later, there are more maggots and [our fish] gets infested.... [Flies] are pretty hard to combat.... That's why it's good if they fish earlier. We like to have number one quality subsistence salmon for our winter food."

Michael said that at Lower Kalskag they usually caught their first king salmon around May 26, depending on the weather. If it was too warm and they had a hard time catching fish, his father would lower his net:

> He'll go look at it, and then he'll make a sack with rocks, maybe about four or five of them. And then he'd tell us, "Put one out all the way back [on the bottom of the lead line]," because our net's not very long, maybe about 50 feet setnet....
>
> That place where we set our net is 13 [to] 15 feet deep. And that's where the fish come in to relax, and [then] they go on up[river]. So, we drown that net. That's what he'll say, and I always use that....
>
> About four or five days, we'd catch 35, 45 kings. And that's enough. And he'd look at the fish, and he'd tell us to pull the net out. So, we'd just do what he said, never argue with him. We fished like that, especially for kings. That's the ones he really was strict on.
>
> And we always had to bring our fish quite a ways back to dry them on the drying rack.... If we're heading in with fish, and we get slime in the bottom of the bucket, he'd tell us not to dump it back there. Bring it to the river and dump it, wash the bucket. So we'd do that.

Michael recalled asking his father why they had to dump the slime in the river rather than back by the drying racks: "He'd tell us, 'That's because bears can smell them.... When they get hungry and they smell fish, they'll go to that. They'll smell that slime first, and bears will come."

In all, the family put away one barrel of king strips to eat, saving the rest to feed their ten dogs. When snowmachines came around, Michael bought his father an Elan to save work putting up fish for dog food. "Every winter, like every two weeks on a weekend, we'd have to go hooking [fish] for the dogs. We'd go out to that Pike Lake right behind Kalskag. We'd get maybe 200 pike."

Michael said that the family had about a week after the end of the king run before they started working on chums and reds. During that week, Michael's dad let others use their eddy to catch fish:

> When we get done, those other people are starting. And if they want to use our eddy, my dad would tell them, "Go ahead," 'cause they ask his permission....

> But we'd have that good one week break of where we just relax and take care of the fish, smoke the fish, get more wood, get ready for the next run....
>
> And then when reds and dog fish [chums] are hitting, we start working on our dog food.... But we wind up eating more dog fish than king salmon because they're just as good.
>
> And then silvers again, same way. You know, we'd have so much fish. That's how he let us work.

Michael noted that his father, like John's father, never harvested many silvers, as they came during August when the weather was wet and not good for drying fish. He emphasized that his father set limits on the fish they took: "He would always limit us. But my understanding is, he'd say other people upriver need fish, too."

Michael's father and grandfather worked together, using the cash they made from trapping to buy better fishing equipment: "I remember our first engine was a 22. The gas tank was on top, loud. [*laughs*] After that was a ten-horse Johnson." To bring in additional cash for his family, Michael's father had his sons tie dried chum salmon into bundles of 50 fish each to sell: "But he'd take his dog food first. He'd say, 'This is ours, and this is for sale.'" Michael's father also sometimes sold four or five bundles of king salmon blankets, with ten fish per bundle:

> We had two caches we'd always fill up with dry fish for the dogs, maybe 12 x 12. But whatever he had left over, he'd sell them to somebody....
>
> And we'd have one [cache] at fish camp and one by our house.... Then if it's a good season, he'd let us dig a hole, fix it up and put silvers in there. Cover them. Keep them from spoiling.
>
> Then after Christmas...when he's going to go beaver trapping, he'd go get some for dogs, and we'd have some for us, too.... The ones we buried, he'd use them in the coldest part of the month for his dogs.

James asked Michael if they fished for red salmon in the past, and Michael said that although there were reds, his father didn't take many: "The important thing for my dad and us was the first run of kings...and the top of the silvers. Once they start turning red, we don't fish no more."

John added that men as well as women work on fish upriver, and that some boys are fast:

They would be done in no time, especially in late summer when they worked on dog food, making *aqlitnguat* [split fish attached at the tail with flaps cut into the flesh to promote drying].

On a sliding board, after [hammering] a nail, then split it, gut it, flip it, take the backbone off and slice it, one, two, three, four, flip it on the other side, raise it again, then they shake it out, it's done. Less than two minutes per fish. Fast ones go a little over a minute....

I was watching this guy up at George River, one of the Vanderpools. He worked on 30 fish. It didn't even take him an hour and a half. He went up, gutted them, and he didn't take long down there after washing them, hung them on his short fish rack down on the shore.

He went up to the land and I said to him, "How come you're so fast?" [He said,] "'Cause I've been doing this since I was a boy." His relatives work on and clean fish very quickly.

And I never saw women working on fish there on those floating fish racks. And his *qer'aq* [fish rack] wasn't tall. They look like [racks we use] when we hang driftnets. He said he'll dry them for two, three days, and then put them in the smokehouse.

Marie asked if he was cutting fish for dog food, and Michael said yes.

As he grew older, Michael's job at fish camp was to get wood and furnish the gas for their outboard motors, while his older brother did all the fishing: "'Cause I was the only one that was always working [for cash]. I'd go down, make sure they have enough gas, enough wood for the smokehouse. That's always all I do." After his brother died, Michael was the only one left to fish; he set the net, then reset it, and finally it caught one king salmon: "I sit down there and cry. I talk to my brother, 'How come you didn't force me to help you do this?'" Michael took the fish to his wife who cut it up and gave it all away to the oldest people in Kalskag. Not long after, his grandchild ran in saying that something was splashing in their net: "We caught three king salmon after they bring those fish up to them people. I was suddenly happy."

Michael reiterated that nowadays fish wheels are no longer widely used upriver. Instead people driftnet for fish, as there are very few good eddies to set nets in: "That drifting is very different from Kalskag on up because of the current.... They're maybe about ten minutes drift, and we have to pull out [the net]. And then when we have four, five people, we take turns...in that one good spot." Once Michael traveled upriver, looking for eddies. From Sleetmute down he found very few, including one good place at Napaimute: "When I stopped in Crooked [Creek] and talked to them, I asked, 'Where you set your net?' 'Cause

I never see eddy, and I know where their camp is. He said he set it out and let it drift down hard as they could, maybe only four, five feet out at the end.... They want fish, that's how they set their net. They always driftnet, but I was wary of the current up there."

In the past, John added that he once fished a little below Aniak: "But the water was too fast up there. That summer we went up, the water was too high, but we were catching enough to cover our gas." Michael agreed that the strong current upriver made fishing difficult: "When it's high water up there, we have hard time catching fish. You gotta hug the shoreline and watch for snags.... And if it's really high water, it's no good to even try to set a net." John said that around Bethel fishing is easier, but harder down toward the mouth of the Kuskokwim where the river is three to five miles wide: "Maybe some places, they use two or three channels. One channel could be catching fish, other two nothing. Or one tide will produce fish, the other tide won't, they come out zero. Try to figure out which tide's gonna bring in the fish."

Michael noted problems associated with more snow in the mountains on the upper Kuskokwim: "If there's lots of snow, that's when I have a hard time catching fish sometimes, 'cause the water's too high up there. And they got logs coming down. Like they say up there in the McGrath area, if logs are coming down, they don't set their nets. But if it's clear, they'll set [nets]." Michael's mother was always happy to see driftwood coming downriver: "She say, 'Good. On the coast, they'll have wood.'... At night we don't know how many logs pass down."

Today near Kalskag, men work together to clear snags from the few places available to driftnet: "There's only two [good eddies] above Upper [Kalskag], one right across Kalskag, one across from Lower Kalskag, and one by my fish camp, and then by Nicholai Sergie's [camp].... We try to clean all those stumps out." Michael added that they also share their net if someone needs more fish: "One family, they really wanted king salmon, and they had a small smokehouse in Kalskag. When the fish were running good, I told them, 'You can use [our net] if you want.' Thirty-five kings was enough for us, and we removed [our net] right away.... We help these others out, too, if they want fish. We tell them they have to come get [the net] and take care of [the fish]."

Changing patterns of commercial and subsistence fishing

Better nets allowed for greater salmon harvests beginning in the 1950s, and in 1954 commercial king salmon fishing became legal on the Kuskokwim. Few took advantage of the new fishery, however, until after Alaska became a state in 1959 when Northern Consolidated introduced turboprop aircraft and reduced its air freight rates, making it profitable for buyers like James to ship fresh salmon to Anchorage and Seattle (Oswalt 1990:156). John noted that at the time commercial fishing emerged as important on the Kuskokwim, anyone who had a state permit and paid the annual fee could fish. The state introduced limited entry permits in 1973, designed to restrict the number of fishermen. At that time, fishermen were paid by volume and there were no restrictions. John recalled: "We could driftnet all week long. If we go down on Monday, going from Monday all the way until Friday, when we fished for what we would sell. We would see how tired we were of driftnetting and stop." At that time, commercial and subsistence fishing were open at the same time, with fishermen targeting kings to sell: "They only tried to sell just king salmon [commercially] because they were worth more money, but we would bring red salmon and chum salmon up to our fish camps."

John talked about the gillnets used for commercial fishing: "When we commercial fished in the past, we only used 50 fathom nets here, 35- to 45-mesh deep. More recently, because our river doesn't have really high water anymore, even I have started only using 35-mesh deep nets. The people who use nets that are deep get snagged a lot and their nets tear, then they lose fishing time."

John described again how the Kuskokwim River was dotted with fish camps in the early days of commercial fishing:

> When they started commercial fishing back then, people occupied fish camps, and they came from the Akulmiut area [west of Bethel] inland and downriver. The people going to fish camp, starting downriver from Napakiak, filled this area [south of Bethel] with fish camps.
>
> In the 1940s, when they started getting boat motors and moving, they said they started having people [in fish camps along the Kuskokwim].
>
> But for us upriver [around Kwethluk], there had always been people in those several big fish camps, because we're close to them. But though they are close, when they moved to fish camps here at the end of May or the beginning of June, some who had nothing [no motors] would completely move to the fish camp. [They'd stay there] May, June, and then some returned [to Kwethluk] at the end of July.

In the early days of commercial fishing, processors had limited capacity, which limited the number of fish they could buy from local fishermen. John recalled: "When these processors could not accept all of the fish when they had excessively caught a lot, they would let them bring some of them home, saying that they couldn't take any more."

During the first half of the 20th century, and into the 1980s, nearly continuous effort during June and July alternated between subsistence and commercial salmon fishing – activities that were largely compatible with one another, employing the same gear, and commercial fishing providing the cash needed to support the subsistence activities (Ikuta et al. 2013:13). Everyone recalled the period in the 1970s when buyers came to fish camps purchasing king salmon and chum salmon roe. John said with feeling: "They would buy them from anybody, even people without licenses. That destroyed us. Some would catch too much, then they wouldn't keep their fish, but try to sell the roe." Michael and his brother participated in the roe fishery during its first year in the 1970s: "We were doing about 20 gallons of *meluks* [roe] per day. And that week, [my dad] bought new engine through that, but we had to take care of those fish. And then we had no place to get rid of them or sell them or anything. So [my dad] said no more hunting *meluks*. We quit after that first year.... They'd help us out alright, but he said we're wasting the fish, so we quit." It was after the roe fishery that Michael's family noticed a decline in the numbers of fish. John noted that the roe fishery was even worse on the middle Yukon River, where fish were taken by the thousands.

From that time on, numbers of fish declined and limits on fishing increased. In 1988, the Kuskokwim River Salmon Management Working Group was established by the Alaska Board of Fisheries to help guide fisheries management decisions along the river (Ikuta et al. 2013:5), and both John and James participated. John explained:

> They held meetings after the middle of the 1980s, when they realized that [fish were declining], they started limiting us and shortening the days. And because there are too many people in all of the villages, they limit us. Last year in June [2018], they only opened [subsistence salmon fishing season] for us four times, and once in July.
>
> After that, they finally lifted the restriction. Though they lifted it and there were a lot of fish, people didn't rush down [to the river]. There were no driftnetters in the river. Only some who wanted to eat fresh fish would driftnet early in the morning, because they had already caught what they needed.

John noted that fewer families go to fish camp today. Reasons for this include conflicts with wage employment – the chief source of cash present-day subsistence activities require – as well as better equipment enabling fishermen to quickly access fishing sites and bring their catch back to their home villages for processing. John explained:

> Ever since we started getting freezers, some store [salmon] right away [instead of drying them]. And only a few [families] go to fish camps now. And in my fish camp at Taperrnat Qauraat, there are only two households, me and my grandson Anguksuar.
>
> They help me, keeping the fish camp alive. But I would always get supplies for them. The last two years, that grandson of mine would accompany me and bring his family, but we go back and forth [to the village]. It's dangerous to stay at fish camp now because inebriated people going home from Bethel would arrive. And we can't leave our supplies out because we lose them.
>
> My grandson Anguksuar would always tell me that. He said that if I were not here, they wouldn't work on fish, because I get their supplies myself, and I let them use my nets. It's good to help each other.
>
> And though those two are young, when the fish they worked on are ready, they distribute them among their inlaws and their parents, and even give some to people with no providers.

Michael shared an upriver perspective on commercial fishing: "When they started commercial fishing here [in Bethel], we notice that two or three days after they commercial [fish], there's hardly any fish upriver. We'd pretty much get the leftovers.... And maybe two or three days later we start catching them again." James agreed: "I remember Bob Aloysius [from Upper Kalskag] saying that whenever we have commercial fishing down here [in Bethel], there's no fish up there, and it's hard to catch fish for a few days. And then fish runs up the river."

John also commented on the negative repercussions of rolling closures:

> After they started commercial fishing, when it had been open downriver all the way to the mouth of the Kuskokwim, [salmon] would not be abundant upriver around Cingigmiut in two days; then they would start catching some again on the third day. They would build up slowly.
>
> But it was bad, too, when they had rolling closures, letting the people downriver driftnet first, then close it for a while, open it for an area closer to here [upriver], and then the third time in front of [our village]. When one group had depleted them, people in villages going upriver from us would have nothing to catch.
>
> They would only catch their leftover fish. But when they opened [fishing season] at once though they are far apart, they would catch more. But when they leave them open for too long, the ones with good nets would catch too much. And [the gear] we use here, they cannot use them upriver.

Michael said that in the 1970s, commercial fishing in the Bethel area was not a problem upriver: "After we started having snowmachines and no more dogs, we really didn't mind. My dad was saying [that] all we want to do is get [king salmon as] eating fish. So, that's what we did. And we never did mind about dogs [chums] and silvers and when they commercial fish." Problems arose, however, when fishermen from the lower river began traveling upriver to driftnet. Michael continued: "When they have a [commercial] opening above Kalskag or in Kalskag area, we watch people drift that came from down here [near Bethel] on up, and they were drifting in any place. We're really wary, because if they get snagged, they'll have really hard time. But when some people get snagged, even we're at fish camp, we'd go out there and help them get untangled so they can go again."

Commercial fishing, initially for king salmon and chum salmon and in later years primarily for chums, continued to be important to Kalskag residents into the mid-1990s. The fishery declined dramatically in 1996, and there has been no commercial salmon fishing in the middle river since 2000 (Ikuta et al. 2013:72; Brazil et al. 2011:99).

The situation was different on the lower Kuskokwim. Through the 1970s, commercial salmon fishing was the largest single source of non-government income on the lower river; over time, however, it was gradually reduced to supplemental. Initially it focused on kings, but by the 1980s chums and cohos represented a large portion of the fishery's commercial value (Albrecht 1990:24-26). In the 1990s, commercial fishing faced increasing restrictions, and no commercial fishery targeting king salmon has occurred since 1987 (Ikuta et al. 2013:4). John declared:

> In my observation, when we commercial fished starting from the end of the 1980s, they started quickly declining from then on. Because of people catching a lot and selling the roe, it destroyed fishing....
>
> And recently, the restrictions have gotten stricter. For over eleven years, we can't [subsistence fish] in our river. They sometimes close [subsistence fishing] for us in the spring until July 25.
>
> Though they open [subsistence fishing] for us for a short time, the people who are diligent, driftnet well with good motors and nets, they catch a lot quickly when they hit the spots where they're swimming. But when there are none in front of us, because we started having fast boat motors, we chase them upriver or downriver, trying to intercept others and driftnet looking for them.

Along with negotiating changes in the commercial fishery, many people have strongly opposed closures and restrictions on subsistence salmon fishing. Beginning in 2001, following steep declines in king and chum salmon returns to the Kuskokwim, most years saw a 12-day closure from early to mid-June, implemented to protect the first pulse of king salmon. This fishing schedule was intended to spread fishing effort over mixed stocks destined for multiple tributaries. Many fishermen, however, maintain that the schedule forced them to expend more effort to harvest the same amount of salmon (Ikuta et al. 2013:65-66).

After 2010, low escapement of king salmon resulted in unprecedented restrictions on all subsistence salmon fishing on the Kuskokwim and its tributaries. In 2012, a seven-day rolling closure in early June was followed by a five-day extension, which resulted in an emotional "Fish-In" on June 21, followed by an extended court case in which fishermen defended their access to salmon as necessary for cultural survival. The hardship and frustration of the 2012 fishing season were felt all along the river. Harvest restrictions continued from 2013 to 2017, including spawning tributary closures, rolling closures in June with brief harvest windows, and selective gear to avoid kings, less than four-inch mesh gillnet, and use of dipnets. As noted above, one positive outcome of the conflict was the establishment of the Kuskokwim River Inter-tribal Fisheries Commission (KRITFC) in 2015 to provide a stronger form of co-management to the Kuskokwim salmon fishery, bridging divisions on the river and seeking unity among 33 tribes (Brelsford and Williams 2018, Runfola 2013).

Michael commented positively on the current management strategy of opening the whole river at the same time, as opposed to opening the river in sections:

> And this is the first year [2018] that Fish and Game finally use their heads because upriver people started complaining. They open the whole [river], same time. And finally, everybody start catching....
>
> We wanted extra hours because we have harder time catching fish up there. And after that, when we did that, that first opening, we never all go but one time. We catch enough fish, and then while they're working others would also come driftnet. And they were doing that. They weren't all hitting it at one time.
>
> And everybody started relaxing fishing, 'cause most of them up there, when they fish, they put it in their freezers. There's very few of us who take care of dry fish, fish to eat. You know, we're at fish camp, like this year, I had five families in my fish camp helping us all day. And then we

> work hard at it because we wanted, for two years, we never really had dry fish. 'Cause every time we catch, three, five, we try to put it in our freezer for frying or baking or soup.
>
> And this summer, we got a little bit more. We'd put maybe 30 [to] 50 kings for dry fish [during the first opening]. And then the rest were maybe about 40 [to] 50 reds for dry fish. And we're just hoping it'll last us through the winter. And if it don't take us through 'til spring, we try to add little bit more if they open it the same way next summer. And that's for five families.

Michael noted that in 2018 his family harvested kings during the first opening, in the middle of June:

> When I look at the fish good, we were catching the end of the first run.... That first run was mostly females.... And then during the second time, we caught mostly males of the second run. And then they leave us open, and everybody just start relaxing and fished. But as soon as we had enough, we stopped fishing....
>
> Even though we wanted more, but we say, "That's enough." Soon as they tell us we have this much kings in the smokehouse, so we limit.

Michael said that his family also took a few chums with the reds, drying them and caring for them like the kings to use as dog food.

Why king salmon are declining

John's parents and their generation saw the beginning of the decline in king salmon: "They used to tell me that ever since they began commercial fishing, fish have become less abundant, especially the kings." He noted the negative impact of the incidental catch associated with the Bering Sea pollack fishery: "They say that we are destroyed by the great amount that they catch, and because of people using large trawling nets to fish down in the ocean. They say that affects us. They said that when they catch the ones down there that are supposed to go to our [Kuskokwim] river and to the Yukon River, it's like they throw them away and lose them...before they grew up." James agreed: "We also hear about by-catches, those fishing down there [in the ocean] for [salmon] that will come up [our river]. Those by-catches used to be a lot a long time ago. They've decreased now, but I think they're depleting [fish], and their high by-catch numbers hurt us now."

Mark mentioned that another factor contributing to the decline of king salmon is likely the establishment of hatcheries for pink salmon to support commercial fishing in southeast Alaska: "These hatcheries release so many humpies. Those humpies eat anything. They suspect they eat small king salmon because they [release them] in high numbers.... That's why they've recently started saying that there should be a limit. Maybe the humpies are eating up the [salmon] fry that are heading out."

Changes in the environment have also contributed to the decline in king salmon. Jacob mentioned the recent lack of snow and resulting low water: "Our land here does not get snow as it used to. We need [more] snow. Back when there was a lot of snow, there were lots of [salmon] going upriver. I used to hear our elders say that these fish will not go upriver if there is no water. You see, the snow used to be very deep back then." James also spoke of the snowy winters and abundant water in the past:

> Water is the world of these fish. They only travel in water, and they are born in water. That's the life of fish. But back then, as you said, there used to be a lot of snow in winter. And when that snow melted, fresh water would go downriver from upriver. But that doesn't happen anymore.
>
> When the water level is high, they travel easily...without hindrance. Fish go spawn upriver from us where they will not come across barriers.
>
> Now the water is starting to get low, and does not get fresh water in the spring anymore.

John spoke of changes in the weather generally:

> Our elders who have passed away used to say that as we go [on in life] we would see the changing of the weather, but that never made any sense to me.
>
> They said that when the weather changes, it will no longer be cold [with no winter] in our future. That was way back in the mid-1960s. About 47 years later, we start to see it....
>
> And they say people are changing. They said that along with the weather, people and their ways of life will also change.
>
> And they said that it will be the same way with our subsistence. They said that when these things that used to be abundant in our time are no longer abundant, they will be replaced by other things. Our food sources will be replaced [by other things], even if it's not all at once. We are watching these changes now.

As an example, John mentioned the disappearance of reindeer in the 1940s, and the recent increase in the beaver population:

> When the reindeer became abundant, the weather killed them, starving them to death, and they crashed.
>
> They said that when those are depleted, other types of food for people become abundant. And these beavers are now going downriver and are too abundant, and are starting to live in areas without trees.

John concluded: "Changing world and changing food chain."

James agreed, commenting on changes in salmon run timing and run size associated with changes in the weather: "The run timing is no longer early. Everything is getting late. And these silver salmon have started coming late. Thinking that they might replace these king salmon, I am grateful. But we are still trying to get king salmon, trying to survive with kings. But reds, these sockeyes, I will be grateful if they replace [the kings], if they start coming in during their season to this river, Kusquqvak."

John's observations also rang true to both Jacob and Michael. On a hopeful note, Michael recalled his grandfather's prediction that when one fish declines, others will take its place:

> My Ap'a too, he tell me, "We won't starve here in Alaska." Because things will disappear, like these kings, others will appear, like those reds... Those replace king salmon. He say, "Always something will come."
>
> He tell me, "If moose disappear, another kind of meat animal will come."... Because all of a sudden we had hardly any moose up there, [then] these beavers have come. Same thing with the fish.

Arguing over fish and food: King salmon want us to work together

An important Yup'ik understanding pertinent to animals generally, and king salmon in particular, is the widely held belief that things that are fought over do not stay available: they will decline or disappear. Mark declared:

> These days, fish are being argued over, and how fish will be available in the future. People also fight over how they should bring [fish] populations up and enforce regulations....
>
> I think anything that is argued over truly does [decline]. Our elders instructed us about that. They told us not to argue over any kind of animal that we catch because it will stop coming to that person.

James responded: "And now, where are those king salmon that we are making a commotion over? There are no more king salmon because we are fighting over them." Jacob replied: "So, we need to make some kind of plan where we can rebuild our stock of kings, [and] admonish these people who are fighting over the fish. What language [Yup'ik or English] are we going to say to them if we do that? So, we don't need to be quiet. We need to bring it out where we can improve our resource like king salmon, what we're trying to rebuild." James agreed: "I truly like what you said. We should let everyone hear and understand." Here both stress the importance of communicating a Yup'ik understanding of how the world works.

Marie added her understanding of the late Frank Andrew's explanation of the negative impact of "making noise" (verbally quarreling) over fish and food:

> He said this: [animals] have three levels of consciousness.... I thought the first one was here in our world where they are among us on the land [on earth]....
>
> He said that when things, moose or king salmon or birds, are quarreled over, because they are aware and can [travel between them], they leave their places here in this physical world to their other world, or to the third one. And then he said they disappear from here....
>
> He was the only one I heard that from among our Yup'ik elders. And he was knowledgeable.

Marie then mused: "So it made me think: what do we need to do as humans to bring [king salmon] back?" Jacob responded: "Our elders talk about that, nothing will improve, only by love or co-operating. Have one common goal, agreement, whatever problems we bring, solve that through love."

Such a solution is already in the works. As Michael noted, 2018 saw the controversial rolling closures replaced with regulations opening the entire Kuskokwim at one time for subsistence fishing. Michael followed Jacob's comment with a heartfelt observation:

> Thinking of what he said, maybe because this past summer [2018] is the first year we were good together, upriver and downriver. And everybody from the mouth of Kuskokwim to the headwaters up there, we all get fish....
>
> The other years, I hear lots of grumbling from upriver people. Even me, I was grumbling because of how we were opening [the river] in sections instead of all at once, so everybody will have fish. Since that, I hardly hear any more grumbling up there. Maybe it's coming down to where it's going to get back to normal as we go on.
>
> Like the other year, it was just about everybody giving up fish.

> Then all at once, we go down and it seems like it's leveling off. That's my thinking now. I hope they try [opening the whole river at once for subsistence fishing] next year again, see how the fishing turns out.

Jacob agreed: "Not leaving this alone, we should go forward with it, 'cause this quarreling with each other, it's not going to work. But trying to fix things, gradually everything improves for upriver and downriver." Michael noted: "We talked about it after we had a meeting. And when we come to that solution of how to try to fix it, we tell them, us upriver, we have hard time catching fish all the time. But if we try to work it this way, maybe it will improve like this where everybody gets a share. I really liked it, what the Fish and Game did. Next year, if they do that same way, maybe we'll come to a solution."

When asked about how people's views of the river have changed, Michael said that in the past, people got along, following the seasons within their own part of the river. Michael attributes recent interregional arguments to modern equipment, which has allowed people to travel farther from home: "We have these big motors...that we use year-round, even for subsistence. And that's what I see is where [arguments] start. After we start having these good equipment, I start hearing, 'These guys have more than we do.' And that's when I start hearing all that stuff."

Mark then spoke generally about the power of people working together, in agreement:

> If families live encouraging each other, they will be a good family. Then coming out of families, if the people of a village continually encourage each other, they will also be at peace and will live in conformity. Then if different villages are in consensus, they will also work well.
>
> Something that the elders said, when we [at CEC] asked them about our books, "How much should we open them up [to people]?" Then their answer: "Open it up to everybody." They said that if others come to understand our way of life, they will start respecting us. If we take that and bring it as a tool to organizations, like the Fish and Game board, and other boards that will establish [laws and regulations] that affect us, if *kass'at* [non-Natives] understand us and we understand how *kass'at* work, and we encourage each other, I think only then will we work well [together].

At the close of the meeting, I suggested sharing the group's observations with community members as well as fisheries managers. Our discussion seemed especially valuable, as it included the views of knowledgeable fishermen from up and down the Kuskokwim and presented a unified voice. Michael's response was profound:

> You know, for years, I've always been hearing upriver, downriver, and they're always fighting. Maybe these king salmon want us to work together to solve our problem.
>
> The fish knows it, and we're living in one river. And I think that's why these king salmon dropped [declined] on us. And last summer is the first time I heard it calm down....
>
> And there weren't any complaints. I think this king salmon wants, it's going to solve the problem for all of us.

One river

Recently, Michael thinks interregional relations are improving: "[Things were bad,] but now it's starting to settle down and come back to the old ways again. Everybody's thinking about that, how we're going to get food for grandkids or our future family." Michael recalled what his grandfather told him about his own father: "He said that he traveled wherever the animals are, wherever they're going to be."

Michael described how his grandfather was not averse to hunting out of season, if he felt his family needed food: "Every time, he say, 'Just keep an eye on your freezer, food. You don't know what's going to come next year, how the winter's going to be.' Or during the winter, he'd say, 'You don't know how the summer's going to be.' He say you just got to watch mother nature. And that's what I try to do." Laughing, he added, "But I'm always afraid I'm going to get caught."

Michael also noted that few families work together upriver: "A lot of people hardly fish anymore, but my family does. My sister, my kids, we all work together. And upriver, there's very few families from Kalskag on up...working all together. But when I come down this way, it's the other way around. I see families working together." Michael explained the need to treat everyone well and not take sides: "I'm a hundred miles up the river.... And I've got a lot of friends up and down the river. I listen to them bitch and gripe, and I'm neutral on it. And it's hard to be neutral. Even I want to say something, I don't. I got to treat everybody the same. You got to treat everybody [well]. You want to be treated that way, you treat them the way you want to be treated. That's the way I was raised."

In the same way, James was taught that the people he helped would help him, wherever he was: "That's what I learned from my mom, too. If I need help, people

I helped before will be good to me and help me. Like she said, think of people upriver, side, and back because those people will help you when you need help." Michael agreed, telling of helping families traveling past his camp with gifts of food and gas for their engines when they ran low: "Sometimes, even I don't know some guys from down here, they come over and talk to me. I don't know where I've seen them. But here, I've help them out, and they'll never forget that, they're that happy."

Jacob noted that Yup'ik people have been co-operating with Fish and Game and Fish and Wildlife for many years now, and wondered why the number of kings is not increasing. James replied that they need to continue to limit the king harvest because of the rise in the human population: "Like I said, [in the past] there were only a scant few houses on the riverbank. And now, there are a lot of houses...They close fishing for us so that everyone will have a share. I finally understand that, at least now. When I didn't understand it at first, I always opposed them."

James concluded with feeling: "We're talking good things today. And because [we are] helping other people who are not against us, because we work with everybody.... We should not be secretive, but all of us should be open with them, and them with us."

Eight-year-old Aubrielle Polty showing off her dip netting catch near Pilot Station, 2024.
Mariah Polty

Elder Bolossa Michaelson cuts salmon near Kalskag, 2024.
Annie Mary K. Michaelson

Part 2
Elders' Stories

◇◇

If you hear a story three times, it's yours and you can tell it. I was "too rough" when I was young. When I wanted to hear stories, I would get in trouble, so they would tell me stories to straighten me out.

–Angie Kameroff, August 2023

Our World is Changing

told by Golga Effemka, Bethel, January 2006

◇◇

Golga Effemka: I came down from upriver in Sleetmute since they invited me. I have my father's Yup'ik name Ungagpak. I don't have a job, as jobs are scarce upriver. Although that's the case, when they are gathered like this, and they call upon me to participate, I am grateful. My maternal uncle tells me, "When they ask you to, don't decline, but participate. If you listen to the older people's instructions, pass them down right away, and to our grandchildren."

Our grandchildren upriver don't speak in Yup'ik. There are very few of us older people who speak in Yup'ik, since we only speak in Yup'ik. When I arrive here [to Bethel] to the hospital, the elderly ladies make me so happy when they speak in Yup'ik. I tell them, "I have arrived among real Yup'ik people here." They look over at me and socialize with me. They make me so happy. I am so grateful for you who are speaking. Thank you very much.

John Phillip: This person's [Golga Effemka's] logs flow out of the Kuskokwim River. This person sends those of us from the lower Kuskokwim Coast logs that we would truly use. And when they flowed out to the ocean from the breakup of the river ice in the spring, they beach along the shore. That is the process that occurred when I became aware of my surroundings [to make it possible to have wood]. Every spring, logs would flow out of the Kuskokwim River. And the people always had wood to construct things from. And we used the wood to make items for transportation back in those times; they constructed kayaks, sleds, and paddles. [The availability of wood] was made possible by the snowfall; [the logs] that had been [pushed down] from the mountains near this person's [Golga's] village and drifted down [the river]. And they probably include Nick [Andrew's] logs as he is from the Yukon River, as they are taken out [of the river]. Long ago, we were given [logs/wood] by the work of snowfall. These days, this person hardly sends us any, probably because there isn't much snow nowadays. [*laughter*]

Golga Effemka: What he said is absolutely true. And the one who spoke earlier about the cold weather, what he said is true; I heard them say that when I was a

Ellavut Cimirtuq
Qanemcilleq Ungagpak, Mamterilleq, Kanruyauciq 2006

◇◇

Ungagpak: Wiinga-wa qavaken Sleetmute *invite*-arngatnga anelralrianga. Aatama atranek atengqertua Yupiacetun Ungagpak. Caliaritlartua qavani caliat nurnalaameng. Pingraan waten quyurtaqata qayagaurqatnga quyalartua. Angama qallatelaraanga, "Piaqatgen qessavkenak maligutlaa. Qaneryarait *older people's* niicugnikuvki, kingutmun egmian' qallatekluki makunun-llu tutgaramtenun."

Tutgaraput qavani Yugtun qallacuitut. Wangkuta *older peoples very few* qallatlartukut Yugtun, imumek Yugturrlainaq qallatlaamta. Maavet tekitaqama *hospital* arnassangaat quyavkalaraatnga cakneq qallataqameng. Pilaranka, "Nutaan Yugnun tekitua maani." Takuyarluteng ilaliungartelaraatnga. Quyavkalaraatnga cakneq. Yaa, tua-i-w' quyaunga, elpecenek qallatellrianek quyapiartua cakneq. Quyana cakneq.

Ayagina'ar: Kusquqvagmek antuut uum murautai. Uum tuyularaakut muragnek Caninermiuni atu'urkamtenek, cunaw' ilumun. Unavet-llu tua-i anngameng, cupngameng up'nerkami tepluki. Tamaa-i tamana un'a tuaten tamatum aulukellrua murilkessagutlemni. Up'nerkaat tamalkuita muriit an'urluteng Kusquqvagkun. Tamakut-llu wani imkut makut caliarkaicuunateng tamakunek muragnek. Wangkuta-llu tamakut muragat ayagassuutekluki tamakut ak'a; qayiluteng, ikamriluteng, anguaruciluteng tamakut. Tamatum qanikcam caliallri; tamakut avaken ingriutainek qavaken uum wani elivvluki atertellrit. Tayima-llu Nick-am murautainek ilangqelallilriit Kuigpagmiunguan, antaqluki. Tamana tamaa-i nallunritelqa tamaaggun qanikcam caliarakun wangkuta cikiumaluta avani ciuqvaarni. Watua tang tuyuvlaangekiikut uum muragnek, qanikcairucan piyugnarqaakut. [*engel'artut*]

Ungagpak: Augkut qallatellri piciuqapiartut. Ingna-llu ciuqlirmi qallatelleq nenglemek, piciuguq, niitelaranka mikelnguullemni. Mikelnguullemni child. It used to get cold when I was a child, and we didn't have warm clothing. Our clothes, we never wore warm clothing. When we were children, our noses ran with heavy mucus. It used to get very cold, and there was a lot of snowfall, and the moose that were roaming about would drag their stomachs upriver.

And in the spring, for those of us upriver, it isn't like how it was [used to be] in the past in the spring. When the river ice is about to break up and flow downriver, these days, they announce that the river ice is about to break and flow downriver. We go down to check on it, although they say there's a lot of water, there isn't a lot of water. Back in those times, the water was level with the top of the bank before the river ice broke up. That doesn't occur these days as we no longer have [a large amount of] snow. Their teachings that I used to hear are true. I'm so glad I listened to my grandfather. It turns out that some of our elders don't forget things.

Also, our food and fish have dwindled in number as they are coming downriver. And the wolves are killing them. Things are becoming scarce for us. If something happens to the fish in the summer, those of us from upriver will starve; all of us people upriver will experience that as the water flows downriver.

White people who are exploring for oil in the Holitna River are discussing opening [drilling]. They tend to speak over us although we speak [against it]. When they open up oil drilling, if the water flows downriver, we will truly experience severe starvation.

These people who are speaking, my deceased grandfather told me, that they speak the truth. They are speaking the truth.

And these logs, they flow downriver when the ice breaks up. They no longer [flow downriver] following the breakup of the ice, and upriver the ice no longer breaks up along with logs. When I was a child back in those times, [the ice] would be very dark with logs and other debris. These days, they would say that the ice was breaking up and flowing downriver and I would go down and search for [the logs] from further up the river, waiting for them. I would ask where those are, what we call black ice. They would mention that they had already passed. They all flow down together [at once] these days.

And the blackfish that we used to eat; I also ate blackfish in the past upriver. Since my father has gone, we no longer eat those. We're always traveling with snowmachines. We are becoming lazy; we from upriver are becoming lazy.

And after staying indoors, when we're about to leave our homes, maybe we'll use a wheelchair, as we're too lazy to walk to the door. We have become lazy. We go outdoors and start our [vehicles]. We are no longer how we were in the past. We travel by boat in the summer also. When I became aware of my surroundings, nengllilallruuq, ima-ll' aklungqerrluta-llu. Akluput, makunek maqalrianek atuyuitelallruukut. Kakeggliluta cakneq mikelnguullruukut. Nengllitullruuq cakneq qanikcartuluni-llu, tuntuviit-llu makut pektellriit aqsateng qamurluki qavani pilallruut.

Up'nerkami-llu wangkuta-w' qavani up'nerkami imumicetun ayuqsuirutuq. Cupqataraqan, cupqatartuq-gguq. Paqnauraput mel'irniluku, amtall' mertaunani. Imumi meq *bank*-amun *even*-aalallruuq cupvailgan. Watua tuatnayuirutuq qanikcairucamta-w'. Ilumun piciugut ukut qaneryarait niitelallrenka. Anirta-ll' niicugnilallruunga ap'amnek. Waten cunaw' makut ciuliaput nalluyaguciyuitelartut ilait yuut.

Cali makut neqput wangkuta qavani nurnariut uatmurcameng. Cali keglunret tuqurqelluki. Ciarutukut wangkuta. Makut neqet kiagmi qaill' pikata kaigciqukut wangkuta qavani; qavani tamamta-w' yugni, uatmun ellngarngami meq uatmun.

Imkut wani uqumek pilriit Holitna-mi ikircugaat inerquangermeng kass'at. Qaingiryugaakut qallatelangramta. Camun ikireskatni uquq, mer'a uatmun pikuni kaigciqukut, kaigpagciqukut.

Ukut qallatellriit, ap'allma ing'um qalamcitellruanga, piciuqapiarluteng qallatut, picimek. Piciugut.

Makut-llu muriit, up'nerkami cuplartuq. Cupet maliggluk' piyuirutut, watua qavani-ll' tuaten muragnek avuluteng. Imumi tanglallruunga mikelnguullemni, muragnek avuluteng, canek tunguqapiggluni. Watua cup'ninauraat, atrarnaurtua, nauw' imkut qaugkumiut nutaan utaqalgirluta. Apnauranka nauw' imkut, *black ice*-anek pilaraput. Ak'a-gguq kitullruut. Malikluteng piyaurrluteng watua.

Makut-llu nerlalput can'giiret; qavani nertullruunga-ll' wiinga can'giirnek. Aataka catairutraanranek neryuirutukut tamakunek. *Skidoo*-rrlainarluta taugaam. Qessanquurtukut; qessanquurtukut wangkuta qavani.

Waten-llu uitarraarluni enemi, anqataraqamta, *maybe we'll use wheelchair, too lazy to walk to* amiigmun. Qessanquurtukut. Anluta ayagarcelluki cat; imumicetun ayuqsuirulluta. Kiagmi cali angyatgun. Cellangllemni wiinga angyat nurnallruut. Egelruterluteng, ayaurluteng carvaningraan. Tamakumek cellangellruunga there were few boats. They traveled by canoe, poling through the water although the current was strong. That's how I became aware. We faced difficulty when we grew up. Things were scarce, including jobs. There are many jobs these days. And our young people aren't interested in doing work we did in the past. And although we try to speak to the school students, they don't speak our language upriver. When I arrive here, I arrive among Yup'ik people, real Yup'ik people who speak the language. I greatly appreciate Yup'ik speakers, as I am Yup'ik myself.

I've said a lot; these people are speaking the truth. And it used to get cold; it's true, it used to get extremely cold when I was a child. It no longer gets cold these days, and snow has become scarce. I am so grateful for these speakers; I'm so very grateful that they've mentioned the things that I used to hear in the past. Thank you so much; I am very happy now. Elders are becoming scarce upriver, too. We no longer have people to speak to us. They ask us to be the speakers. I am only a child still; I'm only seventy-two, and there are elders who are older than me, but they aren't interested in speaking to others. I try to speak to them about what I used to hear in the past. And those who are older than me say that we are too bossy when we speak in Yup'ik, that we're trying to tell others what to do, that we're too bossy. We try to speak [to the young ones] about what we used to hear. I no longer am eager to speak to these young ones myself, as these older ones say we're too bossy. I'm not too pleased about it, but when they ask me to speak [to others] I speak about what I heard. These people are speaking the very truth.

Concerning these animals, I used to hear that they are going downriver to the ocean. They said when they reach the ocean and they drink the ocean waters, they will become scarce; they will die from the salt water. That's what I hear. There was one person who would speak to me; what he told me was the truth. What he said was true, and I am starting to see the things they said would occur, but here I'm actually young. And they said these young ones will no longer act shy and reserved. It is really true. When we were children, when we'd go inside someone's home, we'd sit down near the doorway, and the elderly men and women would ask, "What are you here for?" "We're visiting." And they never asked us to come inside. And after staying there for a while, we would leave.

This person here said that I would send him logs. We only use them for taking fire baths. And for building boats; we'd use them to build boats, and other things.

Thank you very much.

Alice Rearden: Your land is probably very different from here. It is much different. What is it like? I haven't been that way.

wii. Caknaarrlullruukut anglillemteni. Cat nurnallruut, caliat tuaten. Watua caliat amlleriluteng. Makut-llu kinguneput caliaput caliaqsuyuirulluki. Qallauteqtang'ermeng-llu makut elitnaurat wangkucicetun qallacuitut, qavani-w'. Maavet tekitaqama Yugnun tekitelartua, nutaan Yugnun, qallatetulrianun. Quyalartua cakneq yugnek qallatellrianek Yugtun yuungama wiinga-llu.

Amllertuq; ukut picimek qallatut. Nengllitullruuq-llu; ilumun nengllipialallruuq imumi mikelnguulua. Watua nenglliyuirutuq, qanikcaq-llu nurnariluni. Tua-i tuaten quyaunga ukunek qallatellrianek; cakneq quyapiartua niitelallemnek imumek antait waniwa, niitelallemnek. Quyana cakneq; ukut-wa wani quyaunga. Ciuliat-llu nurnariut qavani ciuliaput. Qallaucetairulluta. Wangkuta ellimernauraakut. Wiinga mikelnguuyaaqua; *I'm only seventy-two*, ciuliangerrsaaqua-ll', qallacuyuitut. Wii niitelallemnek imumek qallautengnaqlaryaaanka. Cali ciulianka, ciulirnenka-wa atanrumayiniluta, qallataqamta Yugtun, atanrumayiniluta, *we're too bossy*. Imumek niitelallemtenek qanrutengnaqlaryaaqaput. Qallacuyuirutua wiinga-ll' makunun, makut *older people* cali *too bossy* pinilaraakut. Umyuaqa nall'arcuitelaryaaqaa, pingraan ilaitni qallacesqaqatnga qallatlartua niitelallemnek. Ukut picimek qallatut, piciqapiamek.

Makut-llu ungungssiit, niitelallruunga, uatmurrnauniluki imarpigmun. Imarpigmun-gguq kanaquneng, mermek meq'uneng, ungungssit-gguq nurnariciqut; tuqualuteng taryum mer'anek. Tuaten niitelartua. Ataucim aug'um qalamcitaaralallruanga; ilumun picimek qalamcitlallrukiinga. Picimek, maa-i-ll' tangerrsaurtanka wiinga-ll' *young*-aryaaqua, tangerssaurtanka. *What they used to say*. Makut-llu mikelnguut takaryuyuirutniluki. Ilumun piciuguq. Mikelnguullemteni wangkuta, itraqamta angukara'urluut wall' [arnassagaat], aqumqalartukut amiim caniani. "Cassurceci." "Yugnaartukut." Kiavaasqessuunata-llu. Tua-i tuani uitarraarluta anluta-llu.

Una-gguq wani muragnek tuyulallrulliniaqa. Wangkuta taugaam maqitcklaraput. Canun angyanun tuaten; wangkuta-llu angyanun atulallruaput, canek-llu.

Quyana cakneq.

Cucuaq: Qagaani-wa nunaci allaullilria mat'umi. Allaunruluni. Qaillun ayuqelarta? Tamaatmurteqaqsailama-llu cali.

Golga Effemka: It has become like what these people said. And these trees are growing. That's what our land is like, like these people stated. They are speaking the truth. And these blackfish are getting scarce.

Hoholitna Stone Woman

told by Golga Effemka, January 2006

Golga Effemka: Yes, about that stone. It is said that woman was starving and came from somewhere – her husband is inland from her – she ran out of food, and went down to the river. They were hungry. That's how I heard the story. They were famished. She lost her poor husband, somewhere on the mountain. He sat on the mountain, and [he is] there. We don't see her husband. But his wife is holding a small child, along the bank of the river. When we travel, our elders instruct us, to give her some of our provisions, anything, to place it right below her, or if we were having some tea right beyond her. Sometimes she makes animals available for us to catch. It is because the dear thing is grateful for what we have given her.

And downriver from her, downriver from the child, the logs there are the food left over from what she had eaten. We gather [animal] bones; they say those are wood. They eat them. Also across from her, there is a small lake with a beaver in it. They cannot catch [that beaver], no matter what they do, although they hunt it. They call it *qimaguyuukaaq* [lit., "one who escapes"].

We also go inland from there, up to the mountain up there to survey the surroundings from a high point. The place where she packs water from is dry. They refer to it as the place where she packs water. They would pack water from there. The ones looking at the surrounding area from a high point would pack water from there; they say it's dry today.

And upriver from her is a large mountain along the river. I heard these people talking about little people yesterday. What these people said was true. I'm attending high school from these people. What they said is truly accurate, things that I heard in the past.

They say that poor woman, when she sat, desired to turn into stone, as the poor thing was hungry, so that in the future the descendants who are going upriver would give her an offering. She sat, wanting to turn into stone, holding her baby. You can see it from the river. Although they are white people, when they are going up the river, when telling them about it, they take out their wallets and

Ungagpak: Ukut-wa tua-i qaneryaraicetun ellirtuq. Makut-llu napat nauluteng. Tuaten ellirtuq nunaput wangkuta-llu ukucetun. Picimek qallatut. Tamakut-llu can'giiret nurnariut.

Arnassagaq

Qanemcilleq Ungagpak, Kanruyauciq 2006

Ungagpak: Yaa, tauna-wa teggalquq. Arnaq-gguq naken kaigluni – uinga pavantelartuq keluani – nurulluni, kuigmun. Kaiglutek. Niitelaraqa tuaten. Kaiglutek. Uiurluni katallia, ingrim natiini. Ingrimun aqumluni, tua-i tuantelartuq. Tangyuitelaraput taun' uinga. Tauna taugaam nulirra, mikelnguyagarmek tegumiarluni, kuigem ceniintuq. Ayagaqamta alerqularaakut makut-wa ciulirnemta, taquamtenek canek, *anything*, cikiisqelluku ketiini, wall'u-q yaatiini yuurqaqumta. Paivcitlaraakut ilaitni pitarkamtenek. Tua-i-wa tamatumek quyaurlurluni, camek cikillemtenek.

Ualirnerani, wani ualirnermi, mikelnguum ualirnerani, nerlallri-gguq makut muriit nerkuari. Imkut wangkuta enrit quyurtelaraput; tamakut-gguq muraugut. Nerlartut. Cali akiani nanvacuayaaq paluqtartangqertuq. Tauna pitaqesciigataat, cangraameng, pissungraatni. Qimaguyukaaruuq-gguq.

Cali keluakun pavavet ingrimun nacetlartukut. Tauna kinertuq mertarvia. Mertarvia-gguq. Tuaken-gguq mertalartut. Imumi-gguq mertalallruut nacetellriit; watua-gguq kinertuq.

Cali kiatiini ingrirpangqertuq kuigem ceniini. Akwaugaq niigartellruunga ukut qallatellratni yucuarnek. Ukut wani qallatellrat piciuguq. Wiinga *high school*-artua ukunek. Piciugut ilumun qanellrit, cat niitelallrenka imumi wii.

Tauna-gguq arnarkaaraurluq aqumqatiini teggalquurcugluni kaigurluami, maaggun asgulriit kinguliat aviukarrlarniaraat. Tua-i-w' aqumluni teggalquurcugluni, irniani tegumiaqluku. Nallunaitelartuq kuigmek. Kassaungameng asguraqameng qanrutellriani akiviutateng-gguq anlluki throw money into the water there. How desirable, some money!

Some of the white people actually comply as the poor things want to catch animals; she makes [animals] available to some people. And when it's nearly impossible to catch anything, when giving an offering by going up to land right in front of her and digging in the ground and placing it inside, wanting to catch an animal, she makes animals available. She made animals available to me a few times. Then before night, she allowed me to catch. I did that a number of times. [What they say about] that stone is true. They told that when she and her husband were starving and traveling from somewhere, the poor thing lost her husband. He became stone. But we don't see [her husband]. There are little people upriver from her. They used to hear them back when they went to spring camp, playing inside that mountain. It so happens that it was little people, *ircenrraat*, some little people.

They say they are alone there. That's what I used to hear. Their sayings are very true. And I used to hear them also. I now understand the things I used to hear; I understand them. Things I know. They were like that. Yes.

Peter Jacobs: So the one who turned into stone expects those who pass by to give her an offering? Some people probably believed in it, or did they pass by not giving it an offering. Or do they always give it an offering.

Golga Effemka: Those who want to and have something to give stop right below her, even if they just place it in the water. If you cannot catch an animal, stop there, dig into the ground and place it inside, wanting to catch an animal. They said she will give it to you.

egqaqinaurtut mermun. Ayarinar', akinek!

Tua-i niilluteng kass'at ellaita-llu picugurlurluteng; ilait paivcitlarai. Cakneq-llu pitesciigatellriani, aviukaqluku manuanun tagluten, elak'arluku nuna ekluku, piciuluteng, paivutlarai. Paivutellruanga qavcirqunek. Tua-i-ll' unugpailgani picellua. Qavcirqunek tuatnallruunga. Piciuguq tauna teggalquq. Naken-gguq uini-llu kaigurlurlutek ayallermeggni, uini kataurlullia. Teggalquurrluni. Tauna taugaam tangyuitelaraqa. Kiatiini yucuayagaat. Niitelarait imumi up'nerkiaqameng aquiluteng taum ingrim iluani. Cunaw' yucuayagaat, ircenrraat, ircenrraraat.

Tamakut-gguq tuan' kiimaararmeng. Tuaten niitelallruunga. Makut ukut qaneryarait piciupiartut. Ilumun niitelallruanka wiinga-llu. Niitelallrenka maa-i taringanka; taringluki. Wiinga-wa nallunritaraqa. Tuacetun ayuqut. Yaa.

Paniguaq: Tauna-qaa teggalqurrurtelleq aviukarqesqumaurluni kiturteminun? Kia-wam tua-i kiputellrunritlikii tua-i ukveqluku; wall'emta-qaa kitullruat, aviukarqevkenaku. Wall'u aviukarqerrlainarluku-llu pi.

Ungagpak: Egmianun tua-i piyulriim pikangqerquni arulairluni ketiinun, kiingan mermun pingraan. Pisciigalkuvet arulairluten, elak'arluku, tuavet ekluku, pic'ugluten. Cikirciqaaten-gguq.

Door Mountains
told by Golga Effemka, January 2006

◇◇

Golga Effemka: I forgot to mention that mountain earlier that they call Amiigtalek [Door Mountains, lit., "Place with a doorway"]. The little people there. They say that animals, it is the place where these animals live, like wolves, everything, minks, and others; they say they live inside it.

They mentioned that the area toward the river near the doorway is soft, it's too soft to go to it; it's soft. One really swings [when walking on it]. In the story, the one who accompanied him warned him not to go to [the doorway]. The other was unrelenting; he wanted to go. He went to it, although he pleaded with him [not to go].

He went inside the stones, going down [into the place].

Yes, that person. He went inside and saw many people there. There were people, and some looked angry, and never smiled. Some were extremely friendly. They were apparently animals. He said they would hand them food, some sort of food, including animal figures. They say that person didn't eat them, but placed them somewhere on [his clothing]. He went pretty far. He didn't exit through the place he entered. Some of the people he passed looked angry. It so happens they were wolves. [They weren't] friendly like us. Some were nice, they were friendly. They appeared friendly.

He left right away. To him, he wasn't there for long. It had already become winter while he was under there.

Peter Jacobs: *Kuuuu* [My]! When they were amazed, this is how they reacted to their stories in the past. They would try to get the speaker more excited. Did I let you forget [your story]?

Golga Effemka: When he continued on right away through the doorway, he came up on the south side, on the north side.

When he went outside, there were some things there that were wearing warm clothing; some were wearing warm clothing. It turns out they were animals. He was glad that he hadn't eaten them. When he went outside, he looked at what they were. They were different kinds of animals. Yes.

Amiigtalek

Qanemcilleq Ungagpak, Kanruyauciq 2006

◇◇

Ungagpak: Watua nalluyagutelliaqa ingna ingriq Amiigtalegmek pilaraat. Taukut yucuayagaat. Ungungssit-gguq, ungungssit makut nunakaat, *like wolves and everything, minks*; cat nunakaat-gguq ilua.

Qetutuq-gguq *river*-aam tunglirnera amiik, qetutuq, *too soft* ullallra; qetunani. Aaluuyaaqapiggluni tuaten. Pingraan, qanemciungan taun', inerquayaaqellia malian, ullaasqevkenaku. Aipaa ciumurayugluni, *he want to go*, ayagyugluni. Tua-i ullallia, cangraan.

Itliuq, teggalqugnun, acitmun-gguq.

Yaa, yuk tauna. Itertuq-gguq anagpaa-ll' yugni-gguq makuni. Yuut, ilait-gguq qenerrnganateng, quuyurniyuunateng-llu. Ilait-gguq ilaliuqapiggluteng. Cunawa-gguq makut ungungssiit. Cikirnaurait-gguq neqkaitnek, canek, ungungssinguanek tuaten. Taum-gguq egmian' caminun nerevkenani elliqarnaurai. Yaaqsigiluni. Tuaggun-gguq anenrituq itlermikun. Tamakut kitullri ilait qenerrnganateng-gguq. Cunawa-gguq keglunret. Ilaliuqetaan wangkucicetun. Ilait-gguq assiqapiggluteng, unganaqluteng. Tuarpiaq-gguq ilaliuryunqeggluteng.

Egmian' ayagluni tuani. Elliini-gguq ak'anivkenani pekluni tamaani. Ak'a-gguq uksulliuq-llu camanelnginanrani.

Paniguaq: Kuuuu! Waten tua-i ucuryuka'arqameng-llu pitullruut augkut, waten qanemciitnek-llu. Tua-i ilungcara'arturluk' un' qanemci. Nalluyagutevkalliamken?

Ungagpak: Tuani egmian' ayagnginanermini amiigkun tekitelliuq nutaan ungalalirnermi, imna neglirnermi.

Tamakut-gguq imkut anngami cat-gguq makut maqarqelluteng, ilait maqarqelluteng. Cunawa-gguq ungungssiit. Anirta-llu-gguq nerenritai. Anngami nutaan yuvrialuki. Ungungssiit ayuqevkenateng. Yaa.

How many years now, about two years now, when they went moose hunting downriver from our village, a number of them slept there in a tent. When they heard something outside at nighttime, they said, "Who's that?" Those ones outside replied in the same way, "Who's that?" The animals were replying to them by mimicking what they said. They became afraid, they were very afraid, as this was the first time they heard anything like that out in the wilderness. They were apparently animals who mimicked those people. That never occurred back when we used to travel. Since our land has now changed, they will begin to hear things like that. They said they were extremely afraid. They looked outside, but there was nothing there.

Since I didn't want to tell him lies, I'm telling the story to this extent.

Peter Jacobs: Thank you. In this way, when they were telling stories, they always looked over at them, and they were entertaining. And when constantly replying to the one telling the story, they seemed to become eager. Thank you.

Alice Rearden: What did he do with the ones that he hadn't eaten?

Golga Effemka: I don't know what he did with them; he must have left them behind.

Alice Rearden: No, those small animals, not eating them.

Golga Effemka: I don't really know the ending of the story too well. I think he left them as they were animals.

Those ones had given him images of themselves, telling him to eat them. These people here are speaking of the many things I heard in the past; I'm glad that I used to listen to the elderly men. They were apparently telling truthful things. Listening to the elders like this, indeed, what they have to say is truthful, they are very true. They ask me to speak at our church also, although I'm not a worker there. When they don't want to listen, I become sorrowful thinking of those who spoke to us in the past. Our descendants will not be like us. These ones are teaching them. It's like teachers. These ones who are speaking here are like teachers.

I'm so grateful that I used to listen in the past. When a person is speaking, when [a listener] is fiddling around, doing something, not listening, they don't last, those people don't last; they don't want to listen. That is how one person was in our village; whenever they spoke, he would start to move around. He died some

Watua qavcirqunek, *how many years now, about two years now*, uatiini nunamtenek tuntuvagcullermeggni qavartalliuq qavciuluteng pelatekami. Unugmi-am niicameng, qagaaken, "*Who's that*?" Akiat-gguq qamkut, "*Who's that*?" Tamakut ungungssit akiurluki. Alingurtut tayim', alingqapiggluteng, niipailuameng yuilqumi. Cunaw' tamakut ungungssiit akiurluki taukut. Tuatnayuitelallruyaaquq imumi ayagalallemteni. Watua allayuurcami nunaput man'a tuaten niicaurteqatartut. Alingqapiggluteng-gguq. Uyangcaaqut-llu-gguq cakartaunani.

Tua-i iqluquyunrilamku-am tua-i tuaten pitaunga.

Paniguaq: Quyana. Tua-i waten qanemciurarqata takuyarviku'urluku iciw' tua-i anglanaqluteng. Una-ll' qanemcilria kiuqaquuralriani cumigtengatetullruuq. Quyana tua-i.

Cucuaq: Tua-llu-q' augkut nerenritellni qaill' piaqluki?

Ungagpak: Qaillun-am piaki taum; unicugnarqai.

Cucuaq: Nuu, iciw' augkut iciw' ungungssiyagaat, nerevkenaki.

Ungagpak: Iqua nallurrlularaqa. Unicugnarqai ungungssiungata.

Tamakut-wa tarenrameggnek cikiryaaqelliat, neresqelluki. Imumi amlleq niitelalqa maa-i ukut-llu qallautekellrit; angukara'urluut anirta-ll' niicugnilallruanka. Picinek cunaw' qallalluteng. Waten niicugniluki ciulirneret ilumun piciugut, piciupiartut. Wiinga-llu agayuvimteni qallatesqelaryaaqaatnga castengunrilngerma. Niicunritaqata qiaculgulartua imumi qanrutesteput umyuaqluki. Makut kinguliaput wangkucicetun ayuqngaitut. Ukut elitnaurait. *It's like teachers*. Ukut wani qallatellriit, elitnauristetun ayuqut.

Wiinga-llu anirta niicugnilallruunga imumi. Qallataqan yuk caaksuggluni, *do something*, niicugnivkenani, *they don't last, those people don't last, they don't want to listen*. Nunamni tuaten ayuqellruuq *one*; camek qallatellriani pekengnaurtuq. Yuunrillruuq qangvaq. Qallataqan yuk niicugniuraasqelallruat time ago. They told them to listen intently when a person spoke, and not to make any movement. And they told us not to do things; they told us to listen intently to them, to swallow what they said, not to forget them. That's what I used to hear when I was a child back then. And they told us not to forget the customary foods we eat.

Yes, I want to thank these people for allowing us to come here and listen. These ones are speaking of true things. They are very true, things I used to hear in the past. Yes. This person is a teacher. That's our high school teacher. And this person too. I will graduate when he's done [speaking]. [*laughter*] It's true that it's good to listen like this. If you want to speak, do so.

When I return home, I will speak of what they said. I'm so grateful that you have allowed me to participate. It seems that I have learned a little. I'm so grateful to our elders. I am so grateful. I will speak of what I heard when I go to church. I have learned a little from our elders. They have mentioned the teachings we were told in the past. I'm so glad that I used to listen. I would have not known them if I had not listened. That's why when the older people speak, I listen to them. That's what they asked us to do. Yes, thank you.

pek'arcesqevkenaki-llu. Cat-llu qaill' pinguaraasqevkenata; niicugniurluki, igluki qallatellrit, nalluyagucesqevkenaki. Tuaten-am niitelallrulrianga imumi mikelnguullemni. Makut-llu neryaraput nalluyagucesqevkenaki.

Yaa, ukunun quyaunga taivkarluta, niicugniluki. Picinek qallatut ukut. Piciqapiarnek, niitelallrenka imumi. Yaa. Una-w' wani *teacher*-auguq. *That's our high school teacher*. Una-llu. *Graduate*-arciqua taqkan. [*engel'artut*] Ilumun niicugnilleq assirlartuq, waten *good*. Tua-i qaneryukuvci, qanerluci.

Kinguniskuma agayuyaquma qanrutekciqaqa qallatellrat. Quyaunga cakneq waten ilagaucellua. Tuarpiaq elitecuaralrianga. Quyaunga cakneq ukunek ciulirnemtenek. Quyapiartua. Qanrutekciqanka agayuyaquma. Nutaan elitecuartua ukunek ciulirnemtenek. Imumi qaneryaralput maa-i qanrutkait niitelallrenka. Anirta niicugnilallrulliniunga. Nalluyaranka niicugniyuitellrukuma. Taumek waten *older people* qallataqata *I listen to them*. Pisqelaraakut. Yaa quyana.

Chuathbaluk — falltime at the Russian Mountains. *Megan Leary*

Ircenrraat of Taassaatulit [The Russian Mountains]

told by Frank Andrew, Anchorage, October 2001

◇◇

Frank Andrew: Those mountains called Taassaatulit [the Russian Mountains] are upriver from Aniak. The snow on top [of the mountains] does not melt, even though it is summer. Those are the lands of the *ircenrraat*. A village downriver from them, I'm not sure which one, Qalqermiut [Kalskag] or when Urraarmiut was a village, they invited them when they were going to have a dance festival, the *ircenrraat* invited these Yupiit who lived out in the world.

While they were singing *yuarukaraat* [dance songs requesting specific gifts], one of the people wanted a bed, they wanted a bed for the *qasgiq* from the *ircenrraat* of Taassaatulirmiut. When it was time, when the *ircenrraat* came to get them, they went with them to go and attend the dance festival. That village came into view, and it was in the air, they were visible like this, and there was nothing around the village. They saw it with their eyes; those Taasaatulirmiut opened [their village] to them.

They danced there. When they were done dancing, they loaded and carried back home the bed of the *qasgiq* that they had requested during the dance. They have huge, thick wooden boards for beds, long and thick.

When they were going to bring it home, they had them try it, having them watch. They brought in an elderly man who was walking with a cane. They had him lie down on the end of the bed on his back, on the end of the bed of a *qasgiq*. They helped him roll like this to the other end. Before he got to the middle, when he started to roll on his own, they let go of him. He started to roll faster. When he got to the end and fell, he got up and he was extremely young. And he had no beard, no beard at all, he was very young. They told them that they would do that when they returned home, when they reached home with it.

Since they were having a hard time, because there was too much snow and they had a hard time, they left it behind. When they got to their village, after waiting for some time, they went to get it. When they reached it, it was gone. It returned to its home. It is now the end [of the story].

Arnassagaq / Stone Woman

from Willie Pitka, told by Mark Leary, August 2023

◇◇◇

Mark Leary: I heard this from Willie Pitka. I haven't told this story for so long. It's getting harder and harder to find young people who want to listen and want to sit still for a long time. This [Culture Camp] is a good place to do this. You guys might have to help me out if you remember.

Boy: There's one about that boy and kayak in a big lake.

Mark Leary: They want to hear about the stone woman first.

You know what *aka tamani* means? You know in English they start stories, *kass'aq* stories, "Once upon a time." Well, *aka tamani* means a long time ago. If you hear that, it means a long time ago.

They used to arrange marriages. They didn't have dating, and all this stuff, where you fall in love, go on dates, and stuff like that. Your parents arranged your marriage. Sometimes it started when you were very small. They would pick with another family that you and him were gonna get married when you were old enough. Not today, but when you become old enough, you two are gonna become man and wife, and you didn't have a choice. You had to do what you were told by your parents. Because you respected your parents. Nas and Annie might probably know more about this, too.

There's a family... Have you guys been to Little Mountain Village yet?

Megan Leary: No.

Mark Leary: There's an old village, just up[river], you can see it from here. There's an old village there. That's something also to be aware of. That there were many many more villages than there are today. And anywhere you go, up and down the river, people were there before you. And you have to be respectful.

There was a village right up there called Little Mountain Village. And a family of a woman there made an arrangement with a family from way over there on the Nushagak River side, the Bristol Bay area. There used to be lots of connections back and forth, with people moving back and forth, lot of it was by walking.

They made an arrangement for her to get married with a man from over there. And she had to do what her parents told her. So he came, maybe his parents came with him, to get her, when it was time for them to be married. And in there way, the woman had to go live in the man's village. So she had to leave her family, leave her village over there, travel many days back over to his side of the mountains, the Nushagak River side. The Nushagak comes very close to the Holitna. They're very close together. And she went with him.

All the men and the boys lived in the *qasgiq*, a big sod house, half underground, half out of the ground. And the women and small children lived in smaller ones. Her in-laws weren't very good to her, they treated her like a servant, almost like a slave. Gotta do this, gotta do that. Go get water, go get wood, take care of this meat, take care of this skin. So she wasn't very happy over there. She missed her family. In the meantime she had a baby from her husband, small baby.

But she was secretly planning to go home, to go all the way back to Little Mountain Village from way, way over there. So she got ready. She would secretly, outside of their village, someplace in the trees, hide what she needed to travel. Maybe dry meat, dry fish, little sewing kit, things she'd need for her journey. She had them hiding. And she waited and waited for the right time to run away. Remember she had a small baby, too, but she's gonna go. She'd made up her mind. They don't treat her good. She misses her family. She's gonna run away.

So she waited for the right time. And the day finally came. A herd of caribou was seen. All the men were out hunting. They came across a herd of caribou, quite a few miles from the village. And they caught as many as they could. That's the way it worked. When the food's there, you gotta get as much as you can, 'cause it's gonna go away.

So they caught I don't know how many caribou. Then they sent somebody back to the village to tell the people to come out and help. To tell the women to come out and help take care of cutting all those caribou up and packing them back to the village. So pretty near the whole village emptied out, except for the old people, the small children. All the adults were pretty much out of the village.

She made an excuse, her baby's sick, she can't leave him. So they left her behind. She knew this is the time, this is the time for me to go. So during the night, she quietly packed up her baby. Probably had him or her on her back, inside her *atkuk* [parka], went out in the woods and got what she needed, that she'd been hiding. And she started her journey home across the mountains and across the rivers.

And her husband, after a couple of days they got back to the village. And when her husband found out that she had left, ran away, he was so angry, he's gonna go get her and make her pay for running away. And the other men offered to go with him, but he said, "No, I'll do this myself. When I get her, she's gonna pay for it." So he took off.

She had a few days ahead of him. But she was traveling slow. She had a baby to take care of. For the first few days, she traveled day and night, only stopping to take care of her baby, feed him, change him, kept going. Slow but steady. She was a ways ahead of him, but he knew the country better. He knew that instead of following the tracks – and she was being very careful not to break branches or bend grasses or flip over any rocks. What happens when you flip over a rock on the beach? Dry on top, and you flip it over. How does it look underneath? It's wet. She was very careful.

So he knew he'd be slow if he were trying to track her. But he knows there's a pass in the mountains. She has to go that way. She has to go through there – you know what's a pass, a lower place – she's gonna go through there to get to the other side. So instead of trying to track her, he went straight for that pass and wait for her.

Well, she was moving along slow and steady, slow and steady. But she was very tired. And I don't know how many days this went on. I just know the way it was told to me. But I imagine it took couple of weeks to walk over.

He went to that pass to wait, but she had already made it through that pass. The reason he found out was she was getting tired and she wasn't being as careful,

Stone Woman from a distance. *Megan Leary*

she accidently flipped over rocks, did step in the moss. He knows she's already made it through there, but she's not far. He's gonna catch her. Meanwhile she's going, going, and she got over, the Ulukaq River, 18 miles up. She came over the hill and she saw the Ulukaq River down there, she recognized it, she's almost home. Her heart lifted up. She's gonna make it. 'Cause when she goes down to that river, she's probably gonna run into some of her people up there, hunting, fishing, and they'll bring her home. She was so happy, telling her baby, singing to her baby, "We're gonna go home, we're gonna see our family."

She started down the last hill, towards the river. She didn't know that all this time her husband was getting closer and closer. He was young and strong, running, closer, closer. She started going down toward the river. He came over the higher hill behind and saw her down there. And he hollered her name down the valley, echoing, hollered at her. And her heart beat, afraid he was gonna catch her. She turned around, with the baby on her back, and saw him up there in the high mountains. And when their eyes met, somehow they both turned to stone. And that might be a hard thing to believe. But even in the Bible there's a story about two people that turned to pillars of salt. You don't know about things that used to happen.

But those two stones up there. You're gonna go see the Stone Woman. If you look all around these hills up there, and I've flown in airplanes and helicopters, you will not see a stone like that on another mountain, that just sticks out the side of a mountain.

The way they talk about it, when the Russians came here to the Kuskokwim, something like 1840s. There used to be a Russian fort down there at Kolmakovsky. When the Russians came they brought a sickness with them, a sickness called smallpox. And it killed very quickly over half the people on the Kuskokwim River. They weren't used to this sickness, they didn't have no immunity, they got sick. And during that time, a time of very great sorrow in our region. Can you imagine if half of Aniak died in a couple of weeks, you lose all your family and friends in just a few days, a few weeks, from that sickness. That's part of why people are so afraid of COVID, stories handed down about past sicknesses. During that time when the Russians brought smallpox, it was such a bad time in our region, so much sorrow, that that man cracked. He fell down. There's a little bit of him still up there. You'll see it if you go up. Half of him is still up there. The rest fell down the valley. And then they say that if that stone woman ever cracks and falls it will be another really bad time. I hope we don't see that day.

How the Holitna River Came to Be

told by Jack Egnaty of Sleetmute, 1972, and written down by Carrie Longpre, 1986

◇◇◇

Long ago when most of the land was covered with water, the Holitna Valley was a huge lake, 90 miles wide. The east end was narrow, and the people who lived in those days, the ancestors of the Sleetmute people, used it as a lake crossing. One early summer day, an Indian man, his wife, and their baby were crossing at this place. Their birch-bark canoe was filled with the whitefish they had dried that spring; they were on their way to join the woman's people for summer fish camp. The couple had to paddle very carefully to avoid splashing water into the heavily laden boat. They were intent on this task and did not notice a beaver swimming near them.

In those days, beavers were the size of black bears and were both prized as a source of large quantities of meat, and feared as a hazard to water travel. The couple did not see the beaver until it was thirty feet from them. Then the beaver slapped its tail and disappeared into the water's depths. The slap of the giant tail caused many large waves that rocked the canoe wildly and finally swamped it. Neither the man or the woman were good swimmers and the woman, who held the baby, soon succumbed to the water's pull – the man did not see his wife and child again.

The man did not allow himself to despair. As he alternated between floating on his back and paddling like a dog, he chanted over and over in his mind, "I will live, I will live, I will live to kill you, Beaver!"

At last the man reached the shore and lay shivering on the sandy beach. Finally, he regained some of this strength and stood shakily. Facing the lake, the man shouted in a voice that echoed across the lake, "Beaver! I will kill you, Beaver!"

The man spent several weeks on the lake's shore. He found a tall white birch with few branches and with birch bark, some split spruce roots, and tree pitch, and he began making another canoe. It took him many days to build the boat, and when it was done he turned his attention to carving a paddle and a spear. The man worked on the beach, always watching the beaver at its work. At night, the beaver felled huge cottonwood trees and floated them to the beaver dam on the north side of the lake. The beaver swam as easily with these trees as today's beavers swim with willows. Each day the man watched the beaver, but he never yelled at him again. Instead he thought of his lost wife and child, and worked even harder.

Finally the man was done, but stormy weather kept him on the beach – he knew he must wait for calm weather to ensure the success of his mission.

At last, one morning the man awoke to a hushed stillness; the storm had ended. All day the man waited in the tall spruce, looking out for the beaver. Finally, in the early evening, he spotted the beaver's vee in the water. The animal had a large birch in tow and was headed for the dam. Stealthily, the man climbed down from the tree and made his way to his canoe on the beach. The canoe glided easily into the water and hardly dipped with the man's weight. The man dipped his paddle into the water with the blade parallel to the canoe, in the water he twisted it to take full advantage of the blade, then he swiveled it to parallel the canoe again as he removed it. In this way, the man paddled noiselessly and was able to approach quite close to the beaver.

After the many days of stormy weather, the beaver had much mending to do on the dam and was intent on this task. The beaver looked up when he heard a

On the Holitna River. *Jonathan Samuelson*

sharp intake of breath – the man hurled the spear towards the glistening chest of the animal. The sharpened point penetrated deeply and the water turned cloudy pink around the beaver. The beaver thrashed in the water, making waves that crashed over the dam. Blood continued to spurt into the water, but the beaver did not slow its effort to dislodge the spear.

While the animal struggled, the man retreated to shore and watched from the beach. He saw the beaver raise its tail one last time and again SLAP it upon the water. The waves hit the dam with unprecedented force. The dam broke and the water gushed out, carrying with it the whole trees that made up the dam. The water drained out of the lake for many days, but finally the northward flow stabilized to a trickle and became the Holitna River. If you travel 25 miles above the mouth of the Holitna River, you can still see the remnant of the giant beaver's dam. Look for a 400-foot hill that stretches for several miles to the southwest, eventually merging with the Chuilinuk [Ecuilnguq] Mountains. The Sleetmute people call the hill "Capun" and even the white men call it "Beaver" on their maps. Five more miles up the Holitna, you will find the beaver's house, a sandy bluff which to this day is called "Beaverhouse Hill," or "Niiluq [Ngel'uq]."

They Called [that Shaman] Tairtaq

told by Frank Andrew, February 2003

Frank Andrew: Out in the Yukon, about a child who had just grown. Aqumgaciq told about that shaman who he watched.

One who raised a person from the dead. From a village of Kassurpagmiut. They called him Tairtaq. He walked in a crawling position. His legs were bent in [from being crippled].

His name was Tairtaq.

They said a *yugaq* [nonhuman being] of the wilderness made his legs shrivel. He threw a rock at him. He was sitting on a tree. It was at a time when they were fighting each other through their shaman powers.

His staff had five designs on it. That *yugaq* was young, a person of the wilderness.

Tairtaq had a regular person from his village sit back-to-back with him [in his kayak]. Because he could not walk, he took that person with him to help him.

The other would [attack him] with his shaman powers. That shaman would retaliate.

That *yugaq* [would retaliate against] Tairtaq. This was when he used to walk, his legs had not shriveled.

Peter John: They were fighting each other.

Frank Andrew: They did that the whole day. I'm not sure what time of day they came upon that [*yugaq*]. Then night came, and they [fought using their powers] all night, too. They did not run out [of spirit powers].

When daylight came, his companion there, Tairtaq, started to stop for a bit, trying to recall [what he could use]. But his opponent there would counter him right away when he was done. But that Tairtaq started to hesitate and try to recall [what he could counter with].

Just when daylight came, [Tairtaq] ran out of [ways to counter him].

Tairtaq. That person [of the wilderness] told them that they both were going to die. He said he's actually not the one [who would kill them]. But the things that he had used earlier were going to [kill them].

My, because they were about to die, his companion, the regular person had him sit behind him. They were across from each other. He scattered them from his armpits, saying to get out of his way. "I have warned you repeatedly knowing what will happen to you. But you go right ahead and do those things anyway!"

When he was trying to see those things, he took him along. Those [*yugat*], that kind [of being].

A *yugaq*. And he threw a rock at him. The rock grazed him on this side and did not hit him directly. He immediately buckled.

Then he told him, "As long as you live, you will never stand again!" Just as he stated, he never walked again.

So his companion changed [their fate]. They kept retaliating to one another all day long. As you know, the summer day is long.

Just before sunset, that *yugaq* started to hesitate. Before too long he said that he had run out and said that he could not recall [what to use] anymore. He got sad and said that he could not recall anything now.

That young man told him not to worry and that they would not do anything to him.

He got happy because he was not going to die.

Marie Meade: Yes.

Frank Andrew: After he was told that, he asked, "Which one of you wants to be a shaman?"

The regular person answered him that where he comes from he was not called a shaman.

But he said that person [Tairtaq] was their shaman at their village. He told him to make that one [a shaman].

He said to him, "Now you are going to become a shaman!" He said to Tairtaq, "Give him half of all material things given to you for your services without fail!"

"He has given you life!"

He told him he was finally going to become a shaman.

So they went home, they went their separate ways. After that he became a shaman.

Aqumgaciq started hearing about Tairtaq, a shaman who lived upriver from them somewhere around Urraarmiut; he was revered.

In winter, when [Aqumgaciq's] father was going to go to the Yukon, since he wanted him to take him along, they went to the Yukon.

When they arrived at Iqugmiut [Russian Mission], when they arrived there they saw that the *curukat* [guests invited to a dance festival, lit., "attackers"] had already arrived. They were going to have a Kassiyuq [Dance Festival].

So they went to the *qasgiq*. When a person who was his age made a motion to come to him, he went to him and sat down beside him. And his father there probably sat with his age group.

So that one also got him some food.

After they ate, after he ate, they took his bowl out. So he became his host.

In a little while, one of them said, "Gee, those who are getting people, when are they arriving!"

Because he was curious, he asked his fellow boy what person they had gone to fetch.

He told him that they had gone to fetch a shaman from the Kuskokwim area, and his name was Tairtaq. So he started to anticipate seeing how Tairtaq looked since he had heard so much about him.

They had installed seating in that *qasgiq*. When they were going to dance, they put in seating.

They said that there was a sick person in the village, the daughter of their elder. And she had not acquired a husband yet. She was getting critically ill.

Later on that night, when [someone] came in, he announced that the [elder] over there told them to go ahead and dance because those guests had already been there a long time.

They answered him that they would not dance while he was not there.

They said that they would not dance well while he was not there and not with them. So they decided not to dance because their guest there had said the same thing.

Later on that evening before dark, one of the people who had entered said that they had just arrived outside, those people who had gone to fetch a shaman.

As they were waiting, from outside of the log frame entrance to the underground tunnel, the top of a head appeared with hands pulling back the covers. Two people quickly went out and opened it and took and pulled him up on each side of his arms, and when he came up, he looked just like a boy, he was a small man!

When they released him, he crawled to this side of the wall, and there was the door out there. He sat at the edge of the floorboards. He crawled up to it. He sat on the edge of the floorboards on the head rest and began to take his clothes off. He was a small, skinny man.

His flesh was white. His head was full of gray hair.

When he got through taking off his clothes and putting them down, the person who had gone to fetch his food came in. He placed his food in front of him. When he set them down, [Tairtaq] asked, "That person who you fetched me for, have I gotten to her in time?"

They said to him that she had [moved] earlier that day. But she hadn't done that since.

Pushing his bowl away, he said, "So now is not a time to eat!"

He told them to go and fetch her. They answered him that they could no longer walk her over.

He repeated that if he tried to cure her in the house, he would not cure her properly. But if he [doctored] her by standing up, there would be a 50/50 chance of success.

They answered him, "She is in such a state that we can't walk her over." They said it was too risky.

Peter John: Yes.

Frank Andrew: They said that she would die [if she was moved]. He answered that even though that might happen, they should get her right away. He said that even if she dies in there, that he had gotten to her in time, and that he wanted to [doctor] her by standing up. He said that she might as well die inside the *qasgiq*.

So they finally went to fetch her. Carrying her on the sides, they brought her in.

When they brought her in, he knelt down behind her and got into a prone position, covering himself with a seal-gut parka.

After he had been down in a prone position for a long time, when he got up he told them to get a grass mat and a young bearded-seal skin for her to lie on. So they went to get those things.

He told both of her parents to come to the *qasgiq*.

So they made a mattress for her at the end of the floorboards toward the inner wall and let her parents sit by her side.

So then he let them beat the drums and started [his ceremony].

Because he could not walk, he stayed crouched down there. But he kept swaying his head to the drumbeats. While he was doing that, his entire body started to [do something].

After a number of *yuarulluut* [songs of incantation] had been sung, he suddenly stood up on his legs. When he stood up, he put on a seal-gut parka. His legs stretched. Then he circled the one he was healing when he stood up.

Before too long, he raised his arms and told them to stop. When they suddenly stopped, he got down by bending his legs.

As soon as he crouched, from the corner across there, from the edge of the people, a man suddenly got up. When he got up, he said that if anything happened to [the girl], he would put her in the coffin along with the person doctoring her. He was not cordial at all.

Without saying anything, [Tairtuq] told them to start again.

After he [did that], he circled her.

So the second time, he told them to stop. When they stopped, before he could say anything, that person retorted like before, that if anything happened to her, he would put her in the coffin along with the person who was doctoring her.

Again, without saying a word, [Tairtaq] continued a second time.

Then he told them to stop for the third time. Before he told them to stop, that same person said the same thing again.

Peter John: He kept saying one thing?

Frank Andrew: Yes. So again without saying a thing, he started again.

Marie Meade: He circled the one he was healing?

Frank Andrew: He circled the one he was healing. After the fourth time, he told them to stop.

Oh, just before he told them to stop, when he circled her, he went around in a circle and when he got to that man, he put his arms up and told them to stop. Then he went down on bent knees right away.

When he stood up, that person back there said the same thing, that if anything happened to that girl, he would put her in a coffin along with the person doctoring her.

Kneeling down he said to him up there, "You are too much! Ever since I have come down here you have been the only one making noise! This person who you plan to bury with me once she dies, there was too little compensation given to cure her! There are not enough places for her to walk on!"

That person who had been bad-mouthing retorted, "Listen! He randomly wants more compensation! Those of you who have things to give, you must give him some!"

The people started to go out. This was at the time when they used to give material things to ask a favor [of a shaman]. They came in holding things and placed them down there in front of him. When all the things were put there, instead of having them take them away, he continued.

Before too long, when he told them to stop, he said that they had gone beyond what was necessary!

That person said to him, even though they had given too much, to go on because they would not take them back.

[Tairtaq] told him that if they did not take some away, this person would not live for long. He told them to take some away.

He started to take some of his compensation away. When they were just right, he added them on to the ones that were not enough. And since they were not going to take those back, he said along with the guests, they told them to make songs for him and that he would have gifts to give during the dance.

He finally continued. That person who kept retorting never said anything again.

Peter John: Because he now understood.

Frank Andrew: When he stopped, he asked those two. They answered him that she was no longer breathing.

He said to them, "It's okay, because I got here in time while she was breathing, even though she is not breathing [now], it is okay!"

Then finally after he stayed awhile, he said to them that they should separate her parents and have them settle along the lamp posts behind the people and cover them with their goods. They should cover them with the goods of the people of that village who were in the *qasgiq*.

He told them not to cry sorrowfully, he told them not to be down-hearted because they would [cut off his ability]. If they were sad, they would cause him to fail.

And he told those people in the *qasgiq* that if he left, they should appoint a person to check on him whenever the fifth song was sung. This was a time when the moon was full, and it was bright outside at night.

If [the one checking] saw something, he told him to quit going out. And if something should appear to them, he told them to stay quietly in the *qasgiq*. Even though they were scared, he told them to be quiet and stay still.

After he instructed them to do that, he went down into the floor door. As soon as he went down, they started singing a song. On the fifth *yuarulluk* [song of incantation], he would go outside [and check].

Peter John: That checker there?

Frank Andrew: Yes. Just the way he was instructed, he checked for something on the moon. When the *yuarulluut* were done being sung, they would stop. He would check [the moon].

One of the times when he went out, when he came back in he said the moon, when it [had no shadow?], when he looked again [when it appeared], he said it looked like a dog, he said it looked like a dog. When he saw the moon as it was shining. When he came in, he told about that, and he never went back outside again.

So they waited without drumming.

After they had been like that for quite a while, vapor burped from the door! It suddenly filled the floor up to the seating section. And going up and down, [the vapor] went down. When it retreated out to the door...

Peter John: It went down.

Frank Andrew: He had told them to cover the opening with a grass mat by elevating it from the ground. He didn't cover the *pall'itaak* [log frame entrance to the underground tunnel passageway into the *qasgiq*] with the real covering.

As soon as that vapor was gone, a nose started to come out from under the grass mat out there. It was a huge nose! It started to come up. When it appeared, it was a huge dog! It was a giant dog!

When it came out, its body had no fur at all! But along it's spine back there there was a small amount of fur. And the tip of its tail had a small amount of fur. And its paws had a little bit of fur. And the tip of its ears.

It kept sniffing.

It sat down out there facing the inside [of the *qasgiq*].

That dead person, this was after her parents had gone back there. I forgot to mention, he had also let them take the clothes off that [sick girl] before he went out. They put that person on top of a young bearded seal skin and a caribou hide, too.

Marie Meade: They took the clothing off the dead [girl]?

Frank Andrew: He had them take her clothes off, yes. And he let them put her clothes just on this side of her.

It got in a prone position. Moving like this, it went around this way. It was sniffing around.

So those people in the *qasgiq* never made a sound.

When it got to the place where the mother was, I'm not sure which of the parents, when it got to his/her location, [the dog] stood taller. When it stood taller, it sniffed up toward where he/she was.

After it did that, it went around again and went past that [dead person].

When it got to the location of the [other parent] across, it stretched up once again and after it sniffed, it went toward the door, it then faced the inside [of the *qasgiq*] where that naked body was.

It approached her [twitching its ears?]. And when he reached her, sniffing her, it circled her.

When it had gone all the way around her and stopped at her legs, it began to put her lower body into its mouth up to her waist. Chewing on her, it cut her in half. Then it put its head up and began to chew on her. It was making crunching noises! And blood ran down [the sides of its mouth]. On top of those.

While it was chewing, when it stopped chewing, its ears started to twitch. After it did that, it started to chew again.

So it would do that, it would stop chewing and twitch its ears. It so happened it did that when her mother would feel sad.

After it swallowed her, going around her, it put her head completely into its mouth. So like before, it would stop chewing and listen from time to time.

After doing that, it continued on. When it had eaten all of her, it started to lick all the specks of her blood. So it thoroughly licked every speck of blood.

When it was done [eating her], it went to her clothes. Then starting from her boots, it began to eat all her clothes. When it was finished, after sniffing, it went toward the door in front of the *pall'itaak*.

Sitting down on its haunches and facing the door, after it was like that for awhile, it gave out a small howl. When it howled, inside of the *qasgiq*, it started to go down into the tunnel entrance.

After it did that a second time, it went down the floor door.

Beating the drum, they started singing the song.

Because Aqumgaciq was curious about that shaman, he stood up below those sitting down and watched him, Tairtuq who he had only heard of with his ears.

But at that time when [the dog] circled, he was terrified, even though it wasn't going to do anything to him. He would hear his own breathing, too. Whenever he thought he heard something, he would realize that it was his breathing. And when he thought he heard something pounding, he realized that it was his heart. [*laughs*]

It was because that dog was so terrifying!

He had instructed them when he went out, to watch him closely. If they should see something along the *pall'itaak*, he told them to stop drumming and singing.

And he told them to bring down her parents. So then he really concentrated on the door out there.

Just like before, the door burped with vapor. So the singers immediately stopped singing. But this time the vapor wasn't as dense as the first one. Right away, it went down, and it went toward the door.

And those two people, like they had been told, swiftly went toward the door across from one another. But they didn't remove the covering. As soon as they did that, those hands down there patted the underside of the *pall'itaak*.

So opening it more, situated across from each other they took [the person]. When they pulled that person up, it was that person who had died! She had been real skinny, but now she was fat, and she looked healthy and fleshy.

So they took her inside [the *qasgiq*] and gave her to her parents. So they let her sit between them. Just as they did that, a sound came from just outside the door. Rushing out [to the door], when they pulled him up, it was the shaman who had doctored her.

When they pulled him up, he said, "Because I was rushing her, she left me behind!"

He said that there was no doctoring to do; they were finished. But he told them to take that child to their house, holding her arms and making sure she did not slip at all. When they brought her into the house, after letting her sit on her bed, they should let her go outside and play with her peers. She would be fine.

So after they did that, they finally got ready to dance.

So he watched him at that time.

When they pulled him up from the door that time, his legs had shriveled. When he doctored people, his legs would stretch out; he was able to walk when he was using his spirit powers to doctor people.

Peter John: Probably because his *tuunrat* [spirit helpers] walked [he was able to].

One Who Drowned and Was Brought Back to Life at Urraarmiut

told by Frank Andrew, February 2003

◇◇

Frank Andrew: There at the village of Urraarmiut, a child drowned right at winter, when it was about to be winter. It was at Upper Ayimqeryararmiut. Though winter came, the place where he drowned never froze over.

Those Urraarmiut didn't know what was going on.

One time [Tairtaq] had them take him up there. He probably had children, probably visiting his child. They went by sled. When he arrived, he went to the *qasgiq*. They went and got him food, and having eaten, he stayed there.

While they were there, his father, I think they said it was the father of the child who had drowned, he came into the *qasgiq*.

When [the father] saw [Tairtaq], he went to him and sat by his side. After he did that, he told him quietly but loud enough for him to understand, that since he knew who he was, he had thought of him last fall [when his son drowned]. But since he did not have any messenger, he did not have them get him. And he wondered why that spot where his son drowned never froze. That it doesn't usually occur.

That Tairtaq said to him, "I was the one who didn't let it freeze! In case you might want me to do you a favor! I'm going to try [bringing back that child] who drowned now! It is I who have kept the water from freezing!"

He told them to get [that child's] parents. He also told them to get him a seal-gut parka. And he asked him [to get him] a skin line, too.

When they entered, his drummers made preparations for him.

Then he said that he also needed a helper, to get one boy for him.

And he told the parents there not to touch [their child] in case he retrieved him. He told them not to touch him. If they touched him, he would break his incantation, and the parents themselves would never see [their son] again.

And he also had a second helper get ready. In case he retrieved [the drowned boy], the two would hold his arms on each side and bring him up. He told them not to force him to take more steps as he walked forward. If he stopped, they should stop. The only time they should let go of his arms was when he was inside the porch of the *qasgiq*.

So he did an incantation.

When he started, when he was done after a while, he had them lay out the skin line and put a loop on the end. And he let them take it outside, and he told them to dip one end into the hole in the ice, and the other end inside the *qasgiq*.

And he also got someone to hold onto the other end. In case there was a tug on the rope, [he would] make it taut. He told them not to suddenly pull on it, but seeing how fast it came, he told them to pull it in steadily. Just like those who would hold his arms, when [the skin line] stopped, [the puller] should stop. But let it be as taut as it should be.

So he instructed those two to pull the skin line by letting it stay taut, to stop when it could no longer be pulled.

And they also let the one in the *qasgiq* know. When he [would stop], he should stop pulling the skin line in the *qasgiq* that he was rolling up. When he signaled them again, they would resume pulling.

So they kept doing that to him.

Soon the top of [the drowned boy's] head appeared. When his face appeared, his eyes would blink. And here he had drowned quite a while before that. When he would stop, they would stop.

When he got out of the water, that small loop at the end of the line, it was *?ekiumaluku* on the center.

Those two held his arms on each side of him. So whenever he went a little faster, they brought him farther up.

He had also appointed people to watch his parents there. Even though she had been warned not to, his mother there tried to go to [her son].

But they were holding onto her. Her husband didn't do that, but the wife there tried to [go to him].

So they slowly brought him up. Soon they got to the *qasgiq* with him.

So just like that, they brought him into the *qasgiq*. After they brought him in, they also took him to their house. After he had been with his things in their house, he said to them that he would no longer doctor him. That's what they did to him.

They say he brought that person to life.

When he tried the second time, the mother broke his incantation by not following his guidelines.

At that time he said that, even though there was someone in a similar situation, not to ask him, that he would never do that again. He would not perform that [incantation] anymore. Even though he did it again, he would never again bring anyone back to life.

He said that [she] had broken [that ability].

Peter John: He would never bring a person to life again.

Frank Andrew: If they hadn't caused him to [break his incantation], he would have brought that [other] person back to life like that [first] one.

So about that person he used to be curious about, Tairtaq, when Aqumgaciq told about him, I was one of the ones who was listening. About one named Tairtaq.

Marie Meade: Where was Aqumgaciq from?

Frank Andrew: He was from Kwethluk. His mother was that person by the name of Qucillgaq. She was a large, tall old woman.

She was alone, her husband had died. Her husband's name was Qugyulek. He was not the real father of Aqumgaciq.

Marie Meade: Qucillgaq [Crane] and Qugyulek [One with a swan].

Frank Andrew: They both had the name of a bird. Qucillgaq [Crane] and, Qugyuk [Swan], Qugyulek [One with a Swan].

I saw her when they were at fish camp. She was their mother, Qucillgaq. She was a big old woman, she was tall.

Marie Meade: And there was a *yugaq*, a person of the forest?

Frank Andrew: That *yugaq* was a being of the wilderness. They say there were those kinds of beings in those days. They are called *yugat*.

When that person ran out of [powers], he showed his staff, saying that he was not finished [acquiring them]. But if there came to be ten designs, he would have acquired all of them. He said since the five on there were few, if there had been ten designs he would not have run out of [powers]. That's the way he explained it to him.

Those *yugat* are *ircenrraat*, they are shamans, those are evidently shamans.

Battle at Maqallartuli

told by Joshua Phillip, Tuluksak, 1988

Joshua Phillip: They say that although they had Kuigpagmiut as enemies, the Kusquqvagmiut didn't decimate people [during battle].

So one day Kuigpagmiut [warriors] spoke amongst themselves, wanting to go to the Kuskokwim River area to attack in the summer, sometime around the month of August.

From north of the Kuskokwim River, they came to the Kuskokwim River to attack, saying this. They said they wanted to arrive through Maqallartuli River [Mud Creek] and go down the Kuskokwim River and kill all the people in the places they came upon. They wanted to kill every single person. They wanted to leave the area close to the mouth of the Kuskokwim with only grass growing there!

And those Kuigpagmiut [warriors] were probably thinking to travel along the coast along Canineq [the lower Kuskokwim coastal area] when they returned home.

But they say they had one who was knowledgeable to guide them in traveling, one of their captives. Those Kuigpagmiut apparently had a captive from the Kuskokwim River from a previous time when they had won [a battle], a man whom they took when he was a boy. Then as a grown man, they apparently took that one with them on a raid because he knew the route.

They apparently had a captive from the village of Kalskag, and he knew the trail, and he knew the portages, the portages to the Kuskokwim River.

It is said there were also a great many of those [warriors]. After first gathering, after inviting people to the north of them, and probably also those Malimiut to the north [of the Yukon River], they told them that they were going to raid the Kuskokwim River, to annihilate the Kusquqvagmiut.

Once they gathered together they apparently left [on a raiding trip]. And they entered the river that is across from Iquarmiut, Igevraq, since it was a portage to Kuicaraq, Johnson River. They reached the Johnson River through that portage and apparently headed up the river with their captive to show them the way. They planned to first reach [the Kuskokwim River] through Maqallartuli, planning to fight and kill all the people of Kalskag first.

During the time that they headed upriver through Kuicaraq, since our ancestors hunted young birds during the month of August and also small Canada geese and molting swans, [two men were hunting there]. Two [men], because Kuicaraq River usually has a lot of Canada geese, apparently went to Kuicaraq to hunt for young Canada geese. They left. They portaged through Maqallartuli. When they reached Kuicaraq, they apparently went down the river.

That Kuicaraq River is a winding river.

While going downriver, from their other side they heard splashing noises, the [enemies'] kayaks making a splashing noise.

Then they brought their canoes to shore along a bank and hid them up there. And they covered their tracks to make them indiscernible. And they made the grass that they had flattened upright again.

Those two evidently hid. They say one had a beautiful muskrat parka that was newly made. And the other had a nicely and newly made bird parka. Wearing really nice, new parkas, those two evidently hid, lying belly-down along the north side of Kuicaraq River.

My, it is said that when those kayaks started to pass, they made splashing noises. For a while [they passed]. Eventually the sun started setting and early evening came while the kayaks were passing.

After a while, the very last person down there evidently spoke. It was an elderly man, and they knew [he was elderly] when he spoke because elderly men can be distinguished by the way they speak. That one down there said, "Where is this human scent coming from?"

He smelled him. When he passed those two lying belly-down on their lee side, he smelled him. [He said,] "Where is this human scent coming from?"

Then they say he said, "And it seems to smell of nice, newly caught muskrats." He smelled that one who had on a nice, new muskrat parka.

And after smelling around some more, he apparently said, "And it seems to smell of nice, newly caught birds."

He apparently smelled both of their newly made garments exactly as they were!

The one next to him down there, since they were apparently the very last [kayakers].... Their fellow [warriors] had gone on ahead. The one next to him said, and probably since it wasn't the first time that he had smelled something, "Gee, this person is always smelling something! You are probably smelling yourself!"

Then they heard [the younger warrior] start to row with his paddle down there and he left. He paddled and chased after his comrades.

Since that [elderly man] wouldn't stay there alone, when he also left by paddling after him down there, when he left and their sound became inaudible, immediately, leaving one of their canoes behind, [the two men] brought one down and evidently traveled through the lakes across there that they knew, taking a straight route inland.

When they went inside small lakes, they paddled as fast as they could. When they reached the other side, they grabbed their canoe on the two ends and ran and portaged it. That's what they did. Eventually when they reached Maqallartuli, they once again went downriver.

As soon as they arrived at Qalqarmiut [Old Kalskag] they told them that Yukon warriors who were going on a raid were approaching.

Then immediately the people of Qalqarmiut sent two of their villagers upriver to a village. Two people in the place where they arrived also took off paddling fast once again upriver to alert people.

And when they arrived at that village, they told them that Kuigpagmiut warriors going on a raid were approaching in great numbers!

The people of the village where they arrived also sent two among their people upriver to alert people.

They say that as soon as those alerting people would arrive at their destination, another two from that village would head upriver. I'm not sure up to which village they alerted people. Based on my own calculation, they alerted people up to the village of Uskuralegmiut during that time. Villages were populated during that time; they evidently grew and their population went up.

But they say when they alerted people coming downriver this way, they went as far as the old village of Siimartulirmiut. Upriver from the old village of Uuraavigmiut was another large old village, a village called Siimartulirmiut that also had a large population. I think they went as far as that village when they alerted people downriver from them.

Then that captive lied to them, pretending to forget the portage to Maqallartuli River and had them pass it. Pretending to have forgotten about the trail with the excuse that he hadn't traveled through there for a long time, he wanted to bring them up to Kessiglit, to the mountains, to look at their surroundings from a high spot.

Since long ago that village upriver was called Kessiglirmiut, not Kalskag. Those mountains up there are called Kessiglit. Those [mountains] along the north shore are called Kessiglit. They also call them Ngel'et [lit., "Borders"], Ngel'et. They are a border, they are in a line. That place where one arrives first, those over there call them Ngel'et. They also call [the mountains] up there Kessiglit.

[The captive] wanted to bring them to the Kessiglit mountains there to look at their surroundings from a high point and led them past that portage.

When they went to the [mountain's] highest point to look at their surroundings, they saw canoes down below heading down the Kuskokwim River one after the other with no end in sight! And those small boats that can hold four people, they were using those kinds of small birchbark canoes, heading downriver one after another with no end in sight!

Then their captive apparently said, he evidently told his comrades from the Yukon River area, "You are going to be fortunate! You are going to kill a great many people! You evidently have come during their time of dancing! You see those down there who have gone to attend a dance festival. You see, they aren't carrying weapons at all down there, but they are only carrying their urine containers as they are heading downriver down there!"

They were [in fact] people who were heading downriver to Qalqarmiut. They were those [Kuskokwim warriors] who had gone to wait for those attacking warriors. That captive apparently told [the Yukon warriors], lying to them, that they were going to surprise those who had gone to attend a dance festival, that they happened to go at a time when they were going to dance!

Then when [those in boats] had all passed, the Qalqarmiut...the mouth of Maqallartuli River is right downriver from Qalqarmiut.

Then [the Kusquqvagmiut] evidently planned the following. They told half of their [warriors] to head up inside on the downstream side of Maqallartuli, a little ways back from the river reaching the portage up there. And the other half headed up on the upstream side of the river, also reaching the portage up there.

Then they evidently gave a password to the people on the upstream side who were crouched down. This is what they told them, that when all those [Yukon] warriors going on a raid had gone inside Maqallartuli...There was one [Kuskokwim] person who was keeping guard. There was a spruce tree with a top [branch]. They told him to go on top of that and to keep watch wearing a hawk owl on his head. Those *qakurtat* [hawk owls], we also call them *eskaviat*, those that eat ptarmigan in winter. Those are *qakurtat*. They told him to put one of those on his head and to keep watch.

Then those two who had gone bird hunting apparently said that the one who had a good sense of smell was the very last in line. They told them that he was an elderly man. They told them not to kill that one with a good sense of smell if the Kusquqvagmiut happened to win. And they told those Qaugkumiut [people from the upper Kuskokwim] who were mainly Yurialnguut [Athabascans] not to kill that elderly man if they won. That's evidently what they instructed them to do.

And they evidently gave those who were on the upstream side of Maqallartuli a password. That one up there guarding them would make noise when [the warriors from the Yukon] all got inside Maqallartuli. He would make a raven noise, "Qerraq, qerraq!" He was to make that noise. If that one made noise like a raven, all the people who were crouched down on the upstream side would make raven sounds down to the mouth of Maqallartuli. And from down along the mouth of Maqallartuli, the ones who were crouched down on the downstream side planned to make swan sounds.

Finally, once again they called out their password, also as swans. The portage is quite a ways up. Once again, the sound of a swan calling echoed up the river.

And then after doing that, at the same time [from both sides of the river], they went down to those kayaks [in the river].

They surrounded the Kuigpagmiut on both sides. They came down from behind them and shot arrows at them.

And when some of them would shield themselves with their arms out of fear, they would hit them right on their armpits with arrows. They capsized [in their kayaks]. They quickly decimated them.

Before an hour was up, they quickly decimated them all! People were on both sides [of the river], and [their enemies] had no way to flee.

And they say the water of Maqallartuli rose. What was entirely blood was one foot deep. From the portage, the [river] rose one foot from the blood. It was that deep from the blood of [the slain] people!

And when they captured that elderly man, since they had planned not to kill him, they asked him, "What is your name?" They asked him. He said his name was Aaquqsaq. He told them his name was Aaquqsaq. Aaquqsaq.

Then they were going to send him home to the Yukon River so that he would be the only one left to tell the story of what happened; since he was using a canoe, they cut off its back portion. And they sat him far back and had the bow high in the air so that the water would not enter.

And when they did that to him, they cut both the tips of his ears and marked him!

And after marking him, they cut all the way around his mouth.

And after doing that to [his lips], they also removed the eyelashes of both his eyes, removing them!

Because he might lie and say that he had escaped, they made those marks on that person, on Aaquqsaq.

And after they did that to him, they pushed him away, with his bow sticking up high in the air, "Okay now, go back to your home so that you can be the only one left to tell them that we have killed all the people, that we have killed all of your comrades!"

They pushed him away. When they pushed him away, he said down there, "I wonder which way the current of this [river] is flowing?"

One of them quickly went to him and pushed him upriver, pushing him in this direction, "Head upriver this way. I am pushing you! Go and portage across through the portage so that you will be the only one to tell the story in the Yukon River and the north!" They apparently had him return home that way.

Then that blood that was this deep, the people upriver starting from Kalskag up to this time today, they paint half of their paddles red, the people upriver from us starting from Kalskag on up.

Memorializing the depth of that blood, that is marked on their paddles. Qaugkumiut have that marker on half of their paddles.

That [insignia] doesn't belong to the people of the lower Kuskokwim River because they didn't participate with those who annihilated people.

But the people upriver starting from Kalskag, probably from the old village of Siimartulirmiut on up, that is their memorial [insignia]. It was before Uuraavigmiut was established.

They apparently memorialized the time when they decimated many people. The depth of that blood is depicted on their paddles. Up to this day, Qaugkumiut from the Kuskokwim River area have that insignia.

Then that Aaquqsaq, that old man slowly headed home. And I don't know which village he came from since it is not known where he came from.

He apparently arrived at his hometown. That old man told them that he was the only one to survive. But here he was only using one end of a canoe, with its end cut off. But here the tips of his ears were also cut off, and they had healed also. And the rim around his mouth had been cut off. And the rim of his eyes had been cut off. But here he told them that he was the only one to escape. He said that he alone was telling the story.

Then the people of the village that he told the story to, those women apparently lined up! They apparently stood one after the other in a line. Then they took Aaquqsaq who had told the story and laid him down on his back! And they held his legs. And they held his arms down and held his head down also.

When they had done that, those women, starting from the first one in line, pulled their pants down and urinated on that old man one after the other! When one would get done, another would pull her pants down and quickly pee on him only on his face!

And they say the old man died with many still left to urinate. Urine killed him! They peed on Aaquqsaq. He died while many women were still left to urinate! Women from his hometown evidently peed on him and killed him.

They say while the elderly men of that village were leisurely sitting in the *qasgiq*, they would say, "If Aaquqsaq had teeth, nothing would have been done to him!" He probably would have also bitten those who urinated on him on their vaginas. Because of that those old men would say, "If Aaquqsaq had teeth, nothing would have been done to him."

They say that's how it went.

Those people up north including Malimiut up north up to this day apparently resent the people of the Kuskokwim River area who live farther downriver, thinking that they participated in the decimation of people.

It was only those Qaugkumiut starting from the old village of Siimartulirmiut up to the village of Uskuralegmiut who decimated those who had gone on a raid at Maqallartuli. Those people starting from the old village of Siimartulirmiut on up evidently won.

They also mentioned that the old village of Qalqarmiut located above the old village of Siimartulirmiut had the most residents. I think those from Siimartulirmiut had their second largest village help them.

There evidently weren't many people living downriver from those two villages during that time. And Urraavik wasn't a village yet.

Starting from that village, they apparently decimated [warriors] from the Yukon River and those to the north of them. They killed them all up at Maqallartuli. They killed them all.

[The Malimiut] apparently helped the people of the Yukon River area during that time when they were going to die in great numbers.

And the Caninermiut down the coast also evidently helped the Kusquqvagmiut when a great many of their people were going to be killed up along the east side of the Qanirtuuq River's lake source. That's evidently what happened.

It is said that the one to show them the route, after he showed them where the portage was, they killed him up at the highest point at Kessiglit, up on the mountain top.

After they killed him, one person, after taking a rock from the ground, they would place one rock on him one after the other and go on their way.

And they say that [rock pile] became a large hill!

That's how many people there were. Placing just one rock on him as they passed, that became a large hill!

I don't know his name, but the one to show those people the route, their captive. They had their captive show them their portage, the route they took to go down into the Kuskokwim River. Those apparently had that person show them [the route]. And after killing him, they weighed him down with stones, one person after another placing one stone on him as they passed. And they say it became a large hill! Jacob also saw that rock pile hill there.

Jacob Nelson said it was a large hill. During this time, the rocks have fallen and are spread out, since it happened a long time ago.

A great many of those people apparently [put rocks on him]!

The Man Who Got Killed by a Porcupine

from Phillip Gregory, Kalskag, told by Mark Leary, Jacob Wise Spirit Camp, August 2023

Mark Leary: I've come here to tell stories because I've been blessed in my life to have spent a lot of time with elders, especially Middle Kuskokwim elders. And I learned to listen, and it's important for you guys to do that, too, to be respectful and listen.

One thing they used to always tell over and over again, don't make money off of what I'm telling or what I'm teaching you. Don't make money, but pass it on. And that is why I'm here: To pass some of this on to you.

And there isn't nearly enough time to tell you everything that I've been told. But I'm going to give you a small sample, and I hope it'll help you.

When there's older people around, listen. You know, like when there's a big feed going on or something, and there's elders gathered and they're talking. Sit quietly and listen.

The way that I got tuned into this elder knowledge is when I was a kid in Kalskag. I'd be getting ready for the day, having breakfast in my Ap'a's. My Ap'a used to have a little log cabin, and it had like four additions on it. Old time log cabin built on the ground, and I'd be eating breakfast, and some old guy would come in and start talking. And I'd be in a rush, wanting to go play out. And I remember Phillip Gregory. You know Julia Dorris?

Boy: Mm-hmm.

Mark Leary: Her dad. He came in, and he started talking to my Ap'a, talked about porcupines. And Phillip started telling a story. I know you guys want to hear other stories, but I gotta tell this one first cause this is where it started with me. He started telling a story about a man who got killed by a porcupine.

I learned that any animal can kill you, any animal. There's lots of stories. I, myself, was hit in the head by a ptarmigan flying full speed ahead. Lucky thing I had a helmet on in my snow machine. If I didn't have helmet, I would've been knocked out and probably froze.

A guy in Kalskag shot a caribou, ran out of bullets, went up behind to cut its neck. And that caribou threw his head back, and the antler hit him right there. There's a story of a man who climbed inside a moose to warm after he caught it, and it's cold weather. He got stuck inside and froze there. So, any animal can kill you. How do you think a porcupine can kill you?

Boy: With his quills.

Mark Leary: That's what everybody thinks. This man got killed by a porcupine in a way you would never imagine. And the way, in my mind I'm sitting there as a kid, had some bowl of cereal or something, and I started listening and picturing it. In my mind, it took place in those lakes behind Kalskag. There's long, skinny lakes towards Marshall. He knows they're behind his Ap'a and Grandma's place, behind your old house. Those long skinny lakes.

One fall right after freeze-up, a man went out to look for something, to feed his family. And he was walking. You know the ice was thick enough to walk on but there wasn't much snow yet, maybe just a little bit of snow. And he was walking down the long lake, and he saw porcupine trails. Ever see a porcupine trail in the snow?

Boy: No, but I saw a porcupine before.

Mark Leary: It's very easy to tell a porcupine trail because they're dragging their tails, and they're low to the ground. And so he started following it. Porcupine can feed your family for a long time. You know, some porcupines are really big, you know, they're as big as black dogs, some of 'em.

Camper: Big as the black dog? A black dog?

Mark Leary: They're big, huge ones, yeah. So, he started following it into the woods. It turned off the ice and went into the woods. How do you catch a porcupine?

Camper: You kill it with a stick.

Mark Leary: You hit it. Don't waste your bullets. You don't need a gun to catch a porcupine, and I don't know how old this story is; it might've even been before guns. But even if it was after there were guns, bullets were so hard to come by. People didn't waste bullets, and a porcupine doesn't need a bullet. So he followed it, and he caught up to it in the woods, and he had a little hatchet, and he cut two poles. One heavy one for club, and one lighter just to tickle it to make it turn around. And he did that, he touched it by its head with that long, skinny one. And as soon as it flipped its head towards him, he clubbed it. And he got it.

This is why if you ever club a porcupine, and Francis Levi was with me one time over here when he clubbed a porcupine. We put it in the boat. I told him, "Man, you better club it again." He said, "It's dead." I said, "You never hear about the man who got killed by a porcupine?" A little later, that porcupine came to life in the boat.

Anyway, he clubbed it, and he grabbed it by its arm, and he dragged it out to the lake. It was a big porcupine.

So now he's trying to figure out how he's going to carry it home safely to his family. He had a piece of rawhide, like leather, like leather rope. And he folded it in half, and he cut it in two equal length pieces. And he tied one side around the back leg, and he tied the other side to the wrist. And he had like a pack sack, a porcupine pack sack.

He sat down on the ice. Later they figured this all out by following his tracks. Sat down on the ice and put those rawhide straps over his shoulders and he stood up, and he had a porcupine pack sack. Pretty good idea he must've been thinking. So, he had a big porcupine, he had enough food for his family for a while. And he turned and he started going back. What he didn't know was that porcupine wasn't dead, that porcupine was on his back, unconscious.

And it came awake. And soon as it came awake and started smelling a man, it got scared. And he starts pushing on him. Oh, I'm sorry. When he put the rawhide, he crossed it. Yeah, that's what he did. From back leg to front arm, he crossed it. And the porcupine came alive, came to life, and it was scared. When it got scared, he started pushing. You ever see a porcupine body with no skin on it? Yeah, strong, muscly little legs because they're always climbing, walking, whatever. Short, but muscly, strong.

He starts pushing on him to get away. And those two ropes right here, those two rawhides, they got tight. And all of a sudden, he couldn't breathe. He didn't know what was going on, he didn't know it was from porcupine. He got scared and that porcupine got scareder and started pushing harder. Pushing to get off this man, just pushing.

And it got tighter and tighter and tighter. And he couldn't breathe and fell down and passed out on the ice. And that porcupine was standing on top of him for I don't know how long. Pushing, pushing until he suffocated. The man suffocated; he died right there on the ice. When he didn't come home that night, of course his family started worrying. And they went to look for him.

It wasn't hard to follow his track. See where the porcupine went in, he followed it, dragged it out, started walking back. Found him laying on the ice. And there was track going away, porcupine trail, and they followed it. Looked up in the birch tree. At the bottom of that birch tree, there were the two rawhide tracks. Ate 'em off, and climbed up there.

So, that was told to me. First story I became aware of by Phillip Gregory in Kalskag. I always give credit to who told me. That's probably not the kind of story you were expecting. Sad ending, but it's true. And it makes you aware that any animal can be dangerous if you don't treat it right. If you catch a porcupine, make sure you club it hard, really hard. So, what's next?

The Man Who Drowned in Whitefish Lake

from Iftikum Evan, told by Mark Leary, Jacob Wise Spirit Camp, August 2023

◇◇

Mark Leary: How many of you have been to Whitefish Lake? Okay, good, you gotta hear this story.

If you haven't been to Whitefish Lake, Whitefish Lake is south of the Kuskokwim River, little bit up from Kalskag towards Aniak, between the tundra, it's a big lake. It is one of the biggest lakes in our region, six miles across. There's a little creek that goes out to the Kuskokwim that people go up, windy little creek. And on the other side of Whitefish Lake, on the south side, there's a mountain, big mountain. And there's a river that comes out of the mountain they call Ophir Creek now. I don't know what the Native name is.

And that Ophir Creek comes from a hot springs. Up in those hills, there's a hot springs.

And that Whitefish Lake is very important for gathering, fishing, gathering, and hunting. It's well known throughout the region, not just in the middle Kuskokwim. I've seen old stories written in a book about people coming to downriver going to Whitefish Lake once in a while. But it's very important for the people of Kalskag and Aniak for hunting and fishing and gathering.

Right now it's berry-picking time, lots of people are going out there. Now next month, it'll be time for the whitefish. Whitefish Lake has huge whitefish, like salmon-sized whitefish. They're beautiful fish.

And this story was told to me by Iftikum Evan, Ukayaq. It's about the man who drowned in Whitefish Lake. When you go out there, think about it, somebody drowned in that lake.

And the way he told it, he was out there, you know, sometimes the water is really low out there. It's hard to get into the lake, and there's mud way out.

That fall he was out there, he had a net, and he was walking out in the mud to check his net. And he saw something sticking out of the mud. And when he took it out, he knew what it was. He brought it back to his boat. It was very old. And he covered it in canvas, put it away nicely, went to check his net, went back to Kalskag, and called, "Come see, come see what I found. It's laying on the kitchen table."

It was a bow stem of a kayak. You know what a kayak is, right? It's like a canoe, but it's covered and has a hole in the middle. But you know what? People around here didn't use kayak, only coastal people did.

You know where that came from, it's a bow stem. Kayaks are made out of wood, right? It's a piece of wood like this, with a big hole in it where they grab it and drag it.

It had been covered in the mud for hundreds of years. Already, after he brought it out in the air, it was deteriorating. But he started telling the story of how that kayak got to Whitefish Lake.

What did people around here use? Canoes. What kind of canoes? Plastic? This was *ak'a tamaani*, long time ago, before any of this *kass'aq* stuff was here. What did they make a canoe, what did they cover it with? Birch bark, they covered their canoes with birch bark, believe it or not. You know you're learning about birch-bark basket making. They used birch bark for lots of things.

After canvas came around, they started covering the canoes with canvas. Easier, right? The reason we do everything now is because it's easier. Tents used to be made out of skin, now they're canvas.

Anyway, people up here used birch-bark canoes. That's why he knew where that piece of kayak came from.

The story started way, way down the coast around Quinhagak. There was a *nukalpiaq*. You know what that is? A good hunter, a good provider. There was a young *nukalpiaq*. And you know how these young guys are, when they get good at something, they get cocky, right? This guy, this young hunter, he caught everything. Anything you wanted, he'd go catch, he'd catch lots, and he was cocky. He was getting bored, hunting the same animals. He was getting bored by it.

But there's one animal in the ocean that they don't hunt. I think it was a whale, I don't know what kind of whale. But they said when they're out in their kayaks in the ocean hunting, and it got very rough, that animal would come up and block the wind, and drift with them and help them get to shore. I'm pretty sure it's some kind of large whale.

"I'm tired of hunting all the usual stuff that everybody hunts. I'm going to go hunt that thing that nobody hunts." And he told the people in his village, "I'm gonna go hunt that thing." And they said, "Nope, you cannot do that. If you do that, you're going to bring some kind of bad luck onto our village."

He didn't listen to them, he took off, and he went out there and he hunted it. And he caught it, he killed it. But it was so big he couldn't do anything with it. He couldn't handle it. So he went back to the village to get help. You know, I think that this is a whale, and they usually tow whales with a bunch of boats.

When he got back to his village, and they found out what he did, they were so upset. People were crying and pulling their hair, like there was a Great Death or something really bad was going to happen to their village.

And immediately they called a meeting in the men's house, in the *qasgiq*. All the older men went in there and discussed all night long. They made that young hunter stand outside to wait while they discussed what to do. Some wanted to kill him, some wanted to do nothing, just wait and see what happened. Some thought they should make him leave the village, what they called banishing, make him leave.

In the end, when people used to rule by consensus, everybody would have to agree. They all agreed, finally, that they'd make him leave the village. Early in the morning, they went out and told him, "You have to leave, you have to leave now."

And he tried to fight them. They brought him to his kayak, threw him his stuff, and they pushed him out. He stayed off the beach a little ways and tried to come back, tried to plead with them and cried to them to let him stay, but they were holding bow and arrow, "If you come back, we'll kill you." People had bow and arrows and spears. "We'll kill you. Go."

Sadly, he turned and left the village. This was somewhere down around Quinhagak by the ocean. And he started up Kuskokwim Bay. And as he got into the bay, into the mouth of Kuskokwim, he started checking, going to check other villages, other camps.

Every place he went, they already knew what he'd done. You know, they call it tundra telegraph. Before phones and everything were built, they had some way of communicating, I don't know. But everywhere he went, they already knew what he did, and they were waiting for him. He'd come, and they'd do same thing. A bunch of men, [with] bow and arrow, spear [would say]," "Keep going, keep going, don't stop here."

So he kept going up the river, got into the Kuskokwim River. Same thing, every place he tried to stop, same thing, they already knew. He kept going, kept going.

Finally he got up around Kalskag, and you know that's where Qaugkumiut people start, upriver, and Unegkumiut, downriver. There's kind of a gap.

When he got to Kalskag area, nobody knew what he did. All of a sudden, he was welcomed. He had gone far enough, they let him come in, they fed him. They could tell he was from the coast. What's he doing way up here. He had kayak, harpoon, everything was coastal, even the way he dressed. "Looking for a new place to live, tired of the coast," something like that.

They had an idea, they said, "There's an old man living in Whitefish Lake."

And I seen where he lived. There's a place in the tundra, little below the mouth of the creek where that old sod house was. "There's a man living out there. Maybe you could go live with him, he'd be glad to have a helper." "Okay." So, he left his kayak, and he went out to Whitefish Lake, and he met this old guy living out there, and he took him in.

And it was a good relationship. The young guy hunted and fished for the old guy, and the old guy took care of what he caught and kept them fed.

So, this went on for a while, it was working good. One day, Whitefish Lake gets very rough because it's so wide and, in the tundra, it gets very wet.

What can you tell me about Whitefish Lake, is it deep or shallow? Shallow. So, it can get big waves, but in between the waves, it's not very deep.

This young *nukalpiaq* wanted to go across to Ophir [Creek] to go hunt something or fish something. And the old man told him no, not today.

"How come?"

"It's too rough, look at it."

He started laughing, "That's not rough."

"Yeah, that's rough. It's dangerous, don't go today."

He started laughing harder, "It's not rough." The old man was getting mad, and the young hunter was laughing harder. Finally, he fell on the ground laughing, holding his stomach, "It's not rough, it's not rough."

The old man was getting frustrated and told him, "Why you laughing so hard? I'm trying to tell you."

"I'm from the coast, this is like a mud puddle."

And the old man said, "No, no, no. It's not like the coast. It's not a mud puddle, it's dangerous."

"I'm going anyway." He got up and pushed his kayak out and started going. And the old guy was trying to hold him to the beach. He pushed off with his paddle, got away from the old guy, and he paddled off into the waves.

Looked like he was alright for a while, he was going along. You know how they paddle kayaks, going up on the waves, come down. He got way out there, but every time he went down, he just took longer for him to come up. But he kept going. Taking longer and longer. But guess what happened? When he came down in between the waves, where it was very shallow, his kayak was hitting bottom, over and over.

How was the kayak put together? Tied together, they didn't have screws and nails and glue, welding, and all that. It was all tied; they drilled holes and put pegs. So, every time he hit bottom, over and over again, it was slowly loosening up. You know the waves, I've seen the waves over six feet tall in Whitefish Lake. That time they were probably taller. Come down, hit. Boom, over and over. His kayak was getting loose, starting to come apart. Go up, come down. Boom.

Finally, his kayak came apart, and he drowned out in the middle of Whitefish Lake. His body washed ashore soon after. Pieces of his kayak were found over and over throughout the years, washed up. And when the waves are washing up, they are also covering it with mud too, you know. And that's where Ipuk came and found the bow stem of the kayak of the man who drowned in Whitefish Lake.

I don't know what became of it. It was already quickly falling apart when he took it out of the mud and into the air.

Are we running out of time? You guys probably need a break. From sitting still. Probably longest you've been sitting still in a long time.

Why You Don't Talk about Bears

from Iftikum Evan, told by Mark Leary, Jacob Wise Spirit Camp, August 2023

◇◇

Megan Leary: Yeah, tell that bear one.

Mark Leary: Oh, that's my favorite story. It was also told to me by Iftikum Evan. It's about why you don't talk about bears.

You guys ready? Why you don't talk about bears. This story took place in Kalskag area, and it ends up in the hills between Aniak and Kalskag, east of Whitefish Lake.

One fall, there was a *nukalpiaq*, a young hunter, hunting in the foothills over there. You know, people used to walk all over with nothing. Maybe he canoed up so far up Discovery [Creek] or something, and then walked.

But he was back in the valley, and he found a bear hole. But the bear wasn't in there yet. It's high up in the valley. So, he made a note, he's going to come back in the winter and look for that bear.

You know, people used to hunt bears in their holes all the time, fearless. You know that's fearless to me. We think what we do now is great. Hunting a bear with a spear, with no gun, this is long before guns, with a spear. He's going to go back and hunt it.

So, after freeze-up, not long after freeze-up, when it got good enough to start traveling, he told everybody in his village, he's gonna go hunt that bear. Kind of bragging about it, you know, "I'm going to go find that bear and kill it."

People would shake their heads and not say anything. And he left. And he traveled for I don't know how many days back to that valley, walking with nothing.

When he got to that valley... And how is it in the mountains? Is there more snow or less snow? More. Almost always more snow back in the mountains. When he got to that valley, he couldn't recognize anything. He was standing there trying to figure out where that bear hole used to be. And he walked around some more, and he then started poking with his spear in the snow, trying to find it.

All of a sudden, the snow caved in, and he fell, fell down long ways. Snow gets deep in those valleys, drifts. When he hit the bottom, it was dark, smelled bad. He knows that smell, but he couldn't quite place it. Then he started reaching around in the dark for his spear, and he felt what was on the bottom on the ground. And the hair on the back of his neck went up. It was a blueberry bush. That's what brown bears like to put inside their holes for bedding for the winter.

As soon as he realized that and his hair stood up, a brown bear came out of the darkness, an old, ugly, scarred up brown bear. Hardly any teeth in him, jumped on him, knocked him down and started killing him. Biting him, scratching him, tearing his clothes off, started scratching his chest and biting him.

And the last thing he remembered before he passed out, he saw another bear, a younger one, coming over to talk with that old bear that was killing him. And he passed out.

And sometime later, I don't know how many days, he woke up. He didn't know, he thought he was dead, and he was careful not to move, he just cracked his eyes just a little, just a crack. And he was expecting to see that bear waiting to kill him. There was no bear. There was a beautiful young woman, sitting there doing something. And an old, wrinkly, old grandma behind her. And he passed out again.

Then I don't know how much time passed, a day or two more, he became conscious again, and he woke up again. And he cracked his eyes again, same thing. There's a beautiful woman sitting with her legs straight out, sewing, and this old, mean looking grandma, lots of wrinkles, sitting in the back with her hands inside her parka, just looking at him. He passed out again.

Next time he woke up, he opened his eyes little bit wider, same thing – beautiful young woman sewing, ugly old grandma glaring at him. But this time, that woman stopped, stopped sewing. She put her sewing down and she whispered to him, "Are you thirsty?"

He could barely move, he was hurt so hard with scratches and cuts and bites. But he moved his head a little, and that woman reached behind her back, and she brought out a wooden bowl with a little wooden *ipuun*. You know what *ipuun* is, right? A spoon. Then she gave him couple drops of water on his lips. Then he fell asleep.

This went on. He'd wake up, and she'd ask him, "You want water?" She'd do the same thing, wooden bowl and *ipuun*, giving him a little more.

After a few days of giving water, when he woke up, she asked him, "Are you hungry?" He could move better, he said, "Yeah." She reached behind her back, took out a wooden bowl with an *ipuun* that had some kind of fish broth. And then she gave him a little bit of fish broth. Man, it tasted so good.

This went on and on, she'd give him more every day, and he was getting a little stronger and healing up where he was scarred up, cut up. But he was getting stronger, and she kept feeding him. Then she'd go back to her sewing.

After so many weeks, a long time, he started getting up and staying up longer, and talking to her. And that old grandma would always be back there, watching, never saying anything, just looking at him mean.

Him and that woman would stay up and talk and talk and laugh. They were starting to like each other. She was pretty, and he was young, good hunter.

And all this time she's sewing this fur together. You know what she was sewing? She was sewing his clothes back together, all the cuts and tears from the bear attacking him, and she was sewing it all back together. Day after day.

After a long time passed by, he was starting to feel pretty good, healed up pretty good, he started thinking, "Man, I've been in here a long time. I wonder if I should go home sometime."

Finally, one day, he asked that young woman, even though he was really liking her, he asked her, "When can I go home?"

She said, "Ah, I don't know. I'll have to ask my grandma. I'll tell you tomorrow."

Oh, the reason he started asking about going home is because one day, while they were talking, a drop of water fell from up there. And he thought, "Where that water come from?"

So, the next day, when he woke up, the grandma said like this, "You can go home tomorrow, but you have to follow three things."

He said, "Okay, what?"

"One: When you leave here, no matter what, don't look back. Just keep going. Once you come out of here, keep going, don't look back. We don't want to see you again. Don't look back."

"Okay."

"Two: When you leave here, don't ever eat raw fish again. You know people eat raw fish, frozen. Different ways of eating raw fish. Don't ever eat raw fish again."

He said, "That's funny. How come?"

She said, "Just listen."

He said, "Okay, I won't. What's the third one?"

"Third one is very important. When you leave here, tell the people everywhere, in your village, spread it everywhere. Don't talk about bears when you're gonna hunt them."

She said like this, "It's okay to hunt bears, they don't mind. But when you talk about it...they hear. They don't hear your words, but it's like a buzzing in their head. Like when there's one mosquito at night bothering you, *buuzzzzz*. That's what they hear. They don't like it, drives them crazy. You can hunt bears but be respectful and don't talk about it."

"Okay. Okay, I didn't know."

So, they stayed up talking, their last night together. In the morning early, she woke him before he usually gets up. "Time to go."

"Okay."

He followed her, climbing up, climbing up in the darkness until it came to snow walls. And she started digging. She made a little hole, and fresh air started coming in. He pushed her aside nicely, and he opened it. And he looked out, and he couldn't believe his eyes. Even though the sun wasn't up, it was so bright. He had been in the darkness for so long, it was so bright even though the sun wasn't even up.

Took him a little while, and then he looked, it was springtime. He had been in that hole all winter since he went down. The snow was melting in the hills, and the water running in the valley. There was still lots of snow, but it was melting and there was bare tundra showing.

He could smell. You know how spring smells? When you can start smelling the tundra again.

"I've been gone a long time, I gotta get home."

Took him a while, he never uses his legs, too, for a long time. Took him a while to stand up and get going, and she helped him. And that old grandma came out, too, really looking ugly at him, lots of wrinkles. Finally, it was time for him to start going.

He started down the valley, then he crossed little creek in the bottom, started going over the next one. After that, he's out of the hills. Man, before he crossed that last hill, he kept thinking about that beautiful young woman back there. Man, he wanted to see her one more time. He's going to break the first law, first rule.

And he turned around to wave at her, and he stopped. Over there where he came from, that hole, there's no beautiful woman, there's no old grandma. What did he see? He saw pretty young brown bear and an old, ugly brown bear standing there. They were standing up, shaking. He'd been living with the brown bears all winter long.

He took off. I don't know how many days it took him to get home, but he got to his village. Must've been, you know, before breakup, I don't know.

But then he walked towards his village, and there were people out everywhere, doing things, getting ready to go somewhere, taking care of meat, whatever. They saw him coming.

"AAHH, a ghost!" Everybody took off.

You know, they thought he was dead, he'd been gone all winter long, and they gave him up for dead. Everybody scattered into the woods to hide. He walked into his village. Empty, nobody there, everybody hiding in the woods.

He walked around talking, "Look, it's me, I'm alive. Look. I'm not dead, look, look!"

People were watching from the woods. He kept walking back and forth talking. There was a canoe, upside down canoe. He was walking by it, and there was a little boy hiding under there. The little boy reached to touch his legs. He grabbed that little boy and pulled him out, and that kid was screaming and hollering. "Look, I'm not a ghost. Look, look!"

Little by little, the people started coming out from their hiding, and pretty soon the whole village surrounded him. They were touching and hugging, crying, he was okay, he was alive. And they brought him to the men's house, the *qasgiq* where they have meeting and gatherings, *yuraqing*.

They brought him in there, put him down on the skin mat, start bringing food. Everybody, the whole village gathered in there, and they sat there quietly, waiting for him to eat. Eating whatever he wanted, whatever he never had for a long time.

Everybody was sitting there, waiting patiently. They want to hear the story, they want to hear what happened to him all winter.

When he was all done eating, he started telling it. He told everything that happened. How he lived with the bears all winter, how that beautiful woman took care of him. And then he told them... The first two rules they gave him, he didn't talk about those. Not to look at them and not to eat raw fish, he didn't tell them about those. But he told them not to talk about bears because it buzzes in their head. If you're gonna go hunting for them, don't talk about them. It bothers them, makes them mad.

"Just go hunt them quietly, don't brag about it. And spread this, spread this to the other villages, spread it to your relatives everywhere. And think straight." And a lot of people still follow it.

So, the years passed by, and he became a normal person in the village, but he was always held up high. And they whispered, "That's the guy. That's the man who lived with the brown bears all winter." So, he was kind of high status.

And years passed by. One day he was in the men's house, and then he looked over, and they were eating frozen whitefish. Probably dipping it in seal oil, made it look real good. So, he was watching them. Started thinking, "It's been so many years, it probably wouldn't hurt nothing if I had some."

He asked him, "Can I have some?"

"Oh yeah. Here!"

Give him a piece, started melting in his mouth, started tasting so good. Then all of a sudden, his clothes started ripping. Right down to his bare chest.

And those men across the room, they were watching. Right down to his bare chest. And all his scars and scratches from that bear attack started opening up. And he fell back, dead. Then they looked at him, looked like a bear attack.

The Woodsman

told by Mark Leary, Jacob Wise Spirit Camp, August 2024

◇◇

Mark Leary: This story. You wanted to hear a scary story. This isn't scary, but this is very strange. All the stories that I tell you here are true. In my mind, they're true. And this one is definitely true because it happened – I don't know how to say it. It's an example of the power of oral tradition.

I first heard this story up the Koyakuk River. That's way up the Yukon. It's a big tributary of the Yukon River. I heard it from an elder up there while we were moose hunting. And that's where the story starts. But the story ends 200 miles away around Holy Cross. And I heard the story told there, too, and it was told exactly the same way. Everything was the same, even though the story was told hundreds of miles apart. And the end of the story is in post-contact times; that means after the white man was here.

The way this story starts, there was a family. And it happened same time of year, in August. The family went to pick berries. You know people used to go to berry camp. You know, whole family, extended family, everybody goes out and camps and picks berries, and picks and picks and picks until they have enough blueberries or red berries or whatever berries they're after for the winter. They all went up for camping.

Let me back up. This story's about a woodsman. You know what's a woodsman?

Camper: Like Bigfoot.

Mark Leary: No, don't be confused with things you hear about Bigfoot, Sasquatch. It's not that, it's not an ape. Woodsmen were people, human beings, that turned wild. The reason they turned wild is because they weren't allowed to live with other humans anymore, because they did something bad. And the main two reasons people weren't allowed...

What about like you, what if all of a sudden you weren't allowed to live with any other people, what would you do?

In order to not live with people you would have had to murder another person, taken another human life, or you would have had to commit cannibalism.

Full berry buckets. *Cally Phillips*

Camper: What's that?

Mark Leary: That's when you eat a dead human being. And that has been known to happen when people would starve once in a while, they would run out of food. Especially at the end of winter. If a winter was longer than it was supposed to be, and colder, and more snow, they would run out of food. And sometimes people wouldn't survive. And sometimes the people that did survive survived by eating the people that didn't make it.

But that was bad. They weren't allowed to live among human beings anymore. They were pushed out of the village. They were made to go live by themselves in the woods, alone. And by doing that, they got wild. Can you imagine? If you had to go live out in the woods all by yourself, never talk to people again. But you'd get stronger, maybe your hair would get longer. You would adapt. That's what a woodsman is, and still are.

That's another reason to be respectful when you're out. You never know who's out there, too. You never know who might be watching you.

This family went to pick berries, whole family, little kids to A'pa and Grandma. And you know how it is when you're picking berries, you get scattered. Some are over here, some are over there, somebody wanders way off. That Kelsey back there, she likes to do that, man, she goes far, far from everybody.

There was one young girl, maybe a teenage girl. And in the evening, when everybody started coming back to the camp for the night, this one teenage girl didn't come back. Nobody thought too much about it until it start getting dark. Then they start to get worried. They started calling, walking out and calling for her. You know, like when we pick berries around here, there's trees and tundra, not just tundra. Calling for her, nothing, nobody, nobody out there. They made a big fire. They kept that fire burning all night. She's out there, so she could see them. She never came, never came.

So in the morning, still no sign of her. So they sent one of the boys down in a canoe, down to their village to get help. Everybody came up to the berry camp to help look for her. Lots of people. And they searched and searched and searched. Nothing. No sign of her.

Except for one thing. There was a lake, a long narrow lake. And they found her trail going into the grass out to the lake, into the water. Maybe she went to get a drink of water and fell in, drowned. So they started searching the lake. But it wasn't a very big lake, and it wasn't deep, maybe three, four feet deep. So they searched and searched, nothing. She wasn't in that water, she wasn't there. Why'd she go in that lake? Paddling in that lake, checking with poles, searching, but nothing.

Eventually the search was called off. They didn't know what happened to her. They never heard from her again.

So years went by, years, maybe ten. This happened way up there on the Koyakuk River. Holy Cross is way down here, not far, right across from Aniak. There was a village there before Holy Cross. Holy Cross was started as a Catholic Mission, but there was a village across the river. A family in that village had a fish camp upriver a ways, and they were getting ready for fishing season and went to their fish camp.

The picture I have in my mind. How many of you know where Sonny Kameroff's fish camp is? Halfway between Kalskag and Aniak. Some people know it as Man Man's fish camp. Or even between here and Chuathbaluk there's Jerry Peterson's. A place like that. There was a hillside right behind their fish camp, a valley, a little creek coming down, and then their fish camp was down there at the bottom. And they went there and started getting ready for fishing season.

But something started bothering them. Something from up on the hill would throw rocks and sticks down on top of their cabin roof. They'd wake up and they'd be scared, and this would go on all night. They were terrified. What was doing that? Why were they bothering them? So the man of the family, he went down, he took his family and went back down to the village. And he went to see the *angalkuq*.

You know what *angalkuq*?

Camper: Yeah, shaman.

Mark Leary: Yeah, medicine man, a shaman, spiritual man, a healer, some were good, some were bad. Well, this *angalkuq* told him, "That's a woodsman bothering you. And the only way you're going to stop him from bothering you, you have to catch him."

And they had a long talk, they talked for hours, and that *angalkuq* explained to him what he had to do to catch that woodsman. There's one thing that can take away the strength of a woodsman. They're very strong, they're wild. They're like a bear or a moose, all those animals that live in the wild are strong. There's only one thing that can take away their strength and that's rotten *meluk*, rotten fish eggs.

Camper: Why?

Mark Leary: I don't know. So after they had this long talk, and he explained everything he had to do, the man got his family. He moved his family to his brother's fish camp. They gotta fish, right? And they started getting ready to catch a woodsman.

So one of the things they did whenever they caught fish with *meluk*, put the *meluk* in birch-bark baskets and buried them in the ground to ferment. They lined a hole in the ground with grass and bark and put the baskets in there, layers and layers, and then cover it to ferment. That was one thing.

And they started making rawhide rope. They took moose skin or caribou skin. You know that skin I was sitting on? They take it and soak it and take the hair off. And they cut it in a spiral. They have a long, long piece of rope. But they had to make really strong rope. So they braid them together. They get a thick rope. The women worked on that.

The men started going out on the sandbars on the Yukon. You ever see the wood on the Yukon? There's so much wood, so much logs. The Yukon comes all the way from Canada. There's trees all along the way. There's a lot of wood on the sandbars, and they started going out on the sandbars and picking up logs. They picked the straightest logs. Just for the right size they were looking for. They cut 'em and bring 'em to that guy's fish camp.

What do you think they were doing? What did they need the logs for?

Camper: So maybe he'll trip.

Mark Leary: They got lots of them. They started building something.

Camper: Or maybe a barrier so when he tries to go, he falls in it, and the rotten eggs are in it.

Mark Leary: You're real close. You should have helped them catch it.

What they were building, they were building a woodsman cage. They built a log house. They built it as strong as they knew how to build it. They made it simple, small log house. No windows, one solid wood thick door with a way to lock it.

They built all this to catch a woodsman. They were fermenting fish eggs under the ground. They were making thick ropes, and they built a cage.

This took pretty much all of the summer to get all these preparations made. But when they were ready, there was one more thing they needed. They sent word out. Man, people could communicate. Even before all this electronic stuff, people had a way of communicating. Even today, it's still around. People know things that happen far away.

They sent word out that they need the four strongest fastest men in the area. So young men started coming, and they would give 'em tests. The *angalkuq* and the man with the fish camp and some other helpers, they would give them tests to see how strong they were and how fast they were. They pass or fail, pass or fail.

Eventually they found the four they wanted. Now they had everything they needed. Now it's time to try and catch a woodsman.

So they sent the four to the fish camp one evening. One thing they did. There was an animal trail coming down the valley following that little creek. And they went up there, and they preselected where they were gonna set that trap. There was a spot in the trail where there were two big spruce trees, one on each side, that's where they were gonna make their trap. And then farther up the trail, they gathered dry spruce branches from under the tree, the ones you make fire with. They grabbed a bunch of those and sprinkled them on the trail.

Why do you think they did that?

Camper: To trip the woodsman.

Mark Leary: So they could hear him coming. They were way up the trail before the trap, that woodsman stepped on them, they could hear, "crik, crik, crik."

So the four strongest, fastest men went up there. They went to those two trees. One guy climbed up in each tree with a birch-bark basket of *meluk*. One guy waited at the bottom of each tree with a birch-bark basket of *meluk*.

You guys still with me?

And they waited. I don't know how long they waited. But they're waiting in the dark. By this time summer's coming to an end. It gets dark at night. They're waiting and waiting. And you know how when you're waiting in the dark, your eyes get used to it, and you can see. They heard them dry branches on the trail, they heard them, "Crik, crik." Something's coming. They got ready. Guy at the bottom of the tree. Guy at the top of the tree. They watched the trail, and they saw the woodsman coming down the trail.

And there was another one. There was two. The one behind the first one was smaller. And the first one was big. When that first one got in between the two trees, the men at the bottom grabbed onto its legs, and the men on top jumped down, and they were throwing the *meluk* on it. And they were fighting it.

That first one was so strong. It just screamed, some kind of scream they never heard before. And it threw them off, just threw them off like they were nothing, and it took off screaming into the woods.

But the other one, the smaller one was just standing there, it was in shock. And they saw it, and they grabbed onto that one. And they were fighting it, rolling around in the *meluk* on the ground. And that thing was screaming and hollering and scratching and kicking and biting them. And they almost gave up. It was overpowering them. They couldn't hold it much longer. Four strong men couldn't hold it. It was screaming and scratching and pulling their hair, anything it could do to get loose.

But suddenly it lost its strength. That *meluk* they had been rolling around in got all over its body, and it lost its strength. And for a minute, those men just lay back, breathing, sweating, bloody, and they realized they might not have much time, they got to tie it up. So they grabbed their ropes and they tied its arms and legs, tied behind its back, tied its legs to its arms. And they dragged it down that trail, straight to that cage. And they opened the door and threw it in there and closed the door and locked it. And they lay down, exhausted.

And after a while, the power of the *meluk* wore off, and that woodsman started trying to get out, pounding on the walls, kicking, scratching, screaming, pounding. It was terrified. And those four men just outside, waiting for it to break that little house. But it didn't break, it held together. And eventually that woodsman quit and got quiet. And after that, it never tried to tear down that cage again.

Camper: Maybe it dug under.

Mark Leary: It could have. I always wondered about that. It could have done that. I don't know if they did something to the floor. It could have done that, but it didn't.

So word spread that they caught it. They had it, and people started coming to the fish camp and camping and waiting to watch what's gonna happen. Every day, they would get a bunch of guys to guard the door. And they would get a wooden bowl of food, fish soup or something, and a wooden bowl of water. And they would unlock the door little bit, lots of guys waiting to push it back, and they would push those bowls in, and hurry up and close the door.

But that thing never tried to run off, that woodsman never tried to come out. And then the next day, when they go to do it again, the two bowls they put there before were empty. They'd be by the door. They'd take those out and put new ones in.

I don't know how many days this went on. But, you know, what happens when you feed a wild animal?

Camper: It starts to like you?

Mark Leary: What do you call that? Tame. It was getting tame. It wasn't trying to escape. It was giving the bowls back. So they start opening the door and looking at it. They'd see it in the back. It was dark in there, but they'd see it in there, always like this, always sitting like this [hunched over]. You couldn't really see it good. It wasn't an animal, it was a human, a wild human.

And more people started coming. There were a lot of people camping around that fish camp like this, waiting to see what was gonna happen. And the *angalkuq* and the fish camp owner and other older men started talking about it. Maybe it's time to bring it out. Maybe it's time to take it out.

So they decided to bring it out. And when the word spread about that, more people came. Pretty soon there was pretty good crowd at that fish camp, waiting to see.

And they got ready. Same thing. They had a bunch of strong young guys ready in case that woodsman tried to run away. There were really lots of people watching. They opened the door, wide open, left it. Two of the men, they went in, that woodsman, they lifted it up by its arms and walked it out of the cage. That thing came out into the bright sunlight and covered its face. As soon as it did that, a group of women got up and rushed over there, and they pushed those men away. And they took that woodsman, they brought it away from everybody. How come?

Camper: Because there were so many people, and she might have been scared?

Mark Leary: Why did the women do it?

Camper: Because they know.

Mark Leary telling the story of the Woodsman, August 2024. *AFR*

Mark: Because it was a woman. It wasn't a woodsman, it was a woodswoman. They took her away from everybody to a quiet place behind the camp, and they made everybody stay away. And they gathered what they needed, and they started washing her, cleaning her up, fixing her hair, combing it, brushing it.

Pretty soon they could see the woman, just a human woman. Yeah, she was dirty. Yeah, she was hairy. And her muscles were bigger than a normal woman, but it was a woman.

And they started talking to her, slowly in their language over there. And that woodswoman stared for a long time at the ground. Her lips started moving. Sounds started coming out of her mouth.

At first the women from the village couldn't quite tell, but it was starting to sound like something. And after a long time they became words. You know who that was?

Camper: It was the one who got lost.

Mark Leary: It was the little girl, the teenaged girl that disappeared way up there on the Koyukuk River years ago. She told them what happened to her. She was taken by a woodsman to be a wife.

The only thing she could remember from her old life is that she ran out into that lake to get away from what was chasing her. She ran out into that lake, and after that she couldn't remember anything until later on when she was a woodswoman.

Camper: Maybe that one who was really strong was the guy who forced her to be his wife.

Mark Leary: Yeah, that was. And they brought her back to humanity. They brought her back. It took time, it took care and love, but they brought her back to being a regular human being again, a woman from the people.

But this was the same time that the Gold Rush was going on in Canada. And thousands of people were going up the Yukon every year from all over the world on steamboats and all kinds of boats. And at some point she met one of these guys and she left with him. And nobody knows what became of her.

[Camper asking about Bigfoot]

Mark Leary: I don't know about Bigfoot.

Camper: Are they real?

Mark Leary: Woodsmen, I believe they are.

Camper: My grandma was all alone in her camp, and she heard sounds. She heard Bigfoot.

Mark Leary: Don't call him Bigfoot though. That's not our name. Something I really don't like. I don't like it when people from somewhere else come here and tell us what we're calling things is wrong. You know, like Chinook salmon. I don't know what's a Chinook salmon. They'll always be king salmon to me.

One time I was talking to a fish biologist, and he asked, "What you use to smoke your fish?" And I said, "Cottonwood." And he said, "Oh, you mean balsam poplar?" I looked at him and I said, "No, I mean cottonwood." [*laughter*] "And when the cotton's flying, the dog salmon are running."

I don't know about Bigfoot, but I can tell you about woodsmen.

Ircenrraat

told by Mark Leary, Jacob Wise Spirit Camp, August 2024

Camper: Do you have any stories about little people?

Mark Leary: Yeah. *Ircenrraat*. But not very long stories like these stories I just told. I just have [short ones] I can tell you in Kalskag.

You know in Kalskag, there used to be no school in Lower Kalskag. The only school was in Upper Kalskag, that school right on top of the bank at Upper. All the kids from Upper and Lower Kalskag used to go to that school. So there were a lot of kids in that school.

And when my dad and uncles and them were in Junior High, one day during recess, they're all outside playing, and they saw an *ircenrraq*, a little person. And not only did they see it, they chased it around and they surrounded it. All these kids, they had it right in the middle of them. And they stood there for a while, a minute or two, long enough for them to see how it was dressed.

And then it darted toward some girls in the circle, and the girls got scared and broke the circle, and it ran through. And Paul Kameroff, he used to go up and down the river with a wooden barge and a wooden tugboat. He had his barge up on blocks off the ground for the winter. And that *ircenrraq* ran under that barge and got away.

They ran in and they told their teacher what they just saw. And the teacher made 'em all come in, sit down, and gave 'em all paper, pencil, "Draw what you saw." Everybody drew basically the same thing. The teacher gathered them all up, and I don't know what became of them. That's the best *ircenrraq* story I have.

I have bits and pieces of things we've been told growing up. For example, I always think maybe *ircenrraqs* originated when there was a war. There was a huge war in our region, like a Yup'ik civil war. Maybe they go farther back. They were people that went underground for safety. 'Cause there are other parts of the world where there were huge cultures living under the ground for awhile for some reason, to get away from something. And when you're away from the sunlight, and the air, you don't grow very much. I don't know. That's just one thing I thought of.

One night we were camping, we were in high school. Four of us boys were on our way to Kalskag to go moose hunting. September. So we were camped on an island by the bluffs. And late that night – it was a dark, rainy night – late at night, 11 or 12 at night, a boat came, a wooden boat came drifting in quietly. And there was a guy in there, an old guy. He landed at our camp, and we invited him up to the fire.

He came up, but he never came close to the fire. He stayed back, and he had a hood on, and he kept it like this [closed]. And we couldn't see his face very well. He didn't come close to the light. But he visited us for a while, and he started telling us about *ircenrraqs* in the bluffs across there.

You know, *ircenrraqs* are often associated with bluffs. He said that there's a door somewhere in the bluffs where they come in and out from the underworld, and whoever find that door, don't open it. You'll get drawn in. And when you come out, even though it seems like you're just in there for a little while, years will have passed. You'll come out and go home, and everybody will be either very old or passed away. Don't go in there.

By this time he's telling us all this, and it's like one o'clock in the morning. And we're scared, teenaged boys. "Hey you, camp with us, eh."

And [he says], "No, I'm gonna go."

"What?" I mean he's gonna go down the river in the middle of a dark, rainy night. Who is that guy? I don't know. We never found out who he was.

He did go. He pushed his boat out and started drifting down. But we were scared. We almost begged him, "Please camp with us." But to this day, I was watching for a door. And I found one one time, up here. You know that bluff, where Megan's fish camp is, at the lower end of it, where the bluff slopes down, I walked back. I walked way back there, just me and an ax. No gun. Just walked, checking out the country.

And way back there, at the slope of that ridge, there was a door, an old handmade wooden door, made out of old gray boards, laying on the tundra. And right away that story popped in my mind, and I thought, "Oh, here it is, a door. Can't open it." But you know, curiosity killed the cat. I got my ax and put it underneath that door. And I opened it! It was just tundra.

But how did that door get back there? I don't know. Couldn't be from a flood, not where it was. I don't know how that door got back there.

Camper: It could have been an *ircenrraq*, that used their magic that closed it.

Mark Leary: That's kind of what I thought. They sealed it up real quick.

Piiyuuk: Maybe they didn't want you.

Mark Leary: Good thing! [*laughter*] That's what little I know about *ircenrraqs*.

How the Willow Grouse Got White Meat

from Iftikum Evan, told by Mark Leary, Jacob Wise Spirit Camp, August 2024

◇◇

Mark Leary: You guys want any more stories?

Many campers: Yeah!

Mark Leary: Do you know what's a willow grouse? You know what's a spruce chicken, right? There's spruce chickens all over around here, and on the roads in the falltime in Aniak and Kalskag, wherever there's gravel, there's spruce chickens.

But there's also willow grouse. It's the only bird in our region that has white meat. It's white like chicken meat. How could that be? This is the story of how the willow grouse got white meat, when every other bird around here has red meat, dark meat. It looks like the spruce chicken, but they're browner, and they live in the willows. Late in the winter in the evening, they're up in the willows along the river. They're up eating buds way up high. That's not spruce grouse, that's willow grouse.[5]

Audrey Leary: Last November, Dom and I came by boat. It was November first, and there was a willow grouse living under the community building [at Napaimute]. That was my first time seeing one that close. It was like a chicken. I freaked out.

Mark Leary: They're here. You might think you're seeing a spruce grouse, but it's a willow grouse. But this is the story of how they got their white meat. This story was told to me by Iftikum Evan.

So, there was a village. And in my mind, the village was up this way somewhere. But I'm not sure. And in that village there were three sisters. An older, middle, and younger one. And they were pretty. But the younger one was beautiful. And a lot of men wanted to marry her. But she was very picky. You know, we were talking about arranged marriages.

In that village there was a mean, old *angalkuq*. You know in the woodsman story, we talked about an *angalkuq*, a medicine man, a spiritual healer. They did a lot of different things. But I also told you there were good and bad ones. This one was a bad one. He wanted that youngest sister for a wife. But she was always, "Eeeuw, get away from me." Like that. So he waited and watched for a time when he was gonna take her. He knew the people in the village were afraid of him and wouldn't stop him. He could tell them that he would make them sick or cast evil spells on them, they were scared of him.

So one day, the three sisters were down by the river. They wanted to go pick berries right across the river. And they were waiting for someone to come around and ask for a ride. This was before boats with motors. What did people up here use to get around? Canoes. What were the canoes made of?

Campers: Birch.

Mark Leary: Yeah, birch. So, the *angalkuq* saw his opportunity. He put his canoe in the water, and he came paddling along. He pretended like he didn't see them. As he was passing by, he looked at them, "You need a ride?"

"Yeah, we want to go pick berries across there."

"Okay, I can bring you over."

Those girls were kind of suspicious. "Really?"

"Yeah, I can bring you. Okay, I'll take you over one at a time, my canoe's small."

So he put one in, they rode behind him. He went across, dropped her off, came back across, next one came. He made sure that the younger one was the last one.

When it was her turn to go across the river, her two sisters were waiting over there, he turned his canoe downriver and took off. He took off down the river.

And those two sisters across there were frantic, chasing him down. He was much faster going with the current, and they ran into bushes and stuff. They fell way behind, and he disappeared around the bend. And that sister that was in the back understood what was happening. But she was also not only pretty, she was smart. And she started thinking what she should do.

She'd seen in the bottom of the canoe, in the bottom there was a piece of rawhide rope. And she took it, and she tied it to him. Right behind him is the cross piece of the canoe. And she tied it to the crosspiece. And then, after she had him all tied up, she told him.... By this time he had drifted over to the other side. She told him, "I need to go bathroom."

"No."

She kept bothering him, "I need to go bathroom."

"No."

Kept bothering him. Finally he said, "Okay." And he pulled over to the beach. He told her, "Go right here on the beach."

She told him, "No, I'm not gonna do that. I'm gonna go up in the trees."

He couldn't argue. She went up in the trees. He was sitting in his canoe, waiting.

As soon as she got in the trees, she took off upriver. Her sisters were still up there somewhere, coming down. He was sitting there waiting, starting to get mad. Started calling for her, nothing. And then it dawned on him that she took off. And he jumped up out of his canoe. He tore his *qaspeq*, he ripped out that cross piece of his canoe. He ran up the bank. Boy, he was really mad now.

He ran into the trees, dragging that cross piece, and it got stuck in the trees. He fell down, and he was getting madder and madder and madder. But the girl escaped. There's no way he's gonna catch up to her. She met her sisters, they went back up. They got somebody to pick them up.

In the meantime, the *angalkuq* was boiling mad. He got back in his canoe, fixed it back up, paddled back up to the village. By the time he got to the village, the young sister was hiding somewhere. And all the people knew that something bad was gonna happen.

The *angalkuq* came up the bank with his spear. He was so angry, he started tearing apart the village, searching for her, kicking over canoes, going into every sod house, poking everything, bundles of fur, bedding, poking, looking for her. When he found her he intended to kill her. He was so mad. She was hiding somewhere.

The people in the village, they were scared of him. They didn't do anything to try to stop him. They just watched. They knew where she was. They were hoping he wouldn't get that far. She was way at the end of the village, hiding in a cache.

Know what a cache is? It's a little log building on legs up in the air. People would keep their food and their fur and stuff high off the ground, away from animals, away from flooding. Like a little log house. Yeah, like the one in front of the Kalskag high school. She was hiding in one of those. It had a little round door, with a skin covering. Maybe a wood covering.

He worked his way through the whole village, tearing up the whole village, stabbing with his spear. He couldn't find her. He was getting exhausted. People were watching, hoping he would give up. But he looked at that one last place he never looked at, that cache down at the end of the village. He started walking down. People were getting so worried, so scared, "Oh no, he's gonna find her."

It had a ladder going up, made out of two skinny logs, and cross piece. But he was tired, he didn't feel like climbing the ladder. He walked underneath the cache. You know, the cache was made out of split logs, so there were big cracks here and there. He started poking in the cracks with his spear. Nothing. He's tired, he's gonna go home and get her later. So he started going home from under there. There was blood right in front of him. He started laughing, an evil laugh. And where the blood came from, he started spearing it more and more. And the people watching him are crying and sobbing, "Oh, oh." The blood got more and more. Lots of blood, and he was just laughing. And people were pulling their hair, screaming and crying.

Finally he got tired. There was so much blood came out. He was still laughing. He went to the ladder, he climbed up. He got up to the door of the cache, and looked at the people, laughing. He opened the door. Whoosh! Willow grouse flew out!

You know how when things surprise you. He fell off the ladder. Now he was really mad again. He hurried up and climbed up there again to get that girl. There was nothing. Lots of blood, but nothing. Somehow that girl turned into a willow grouse and escaped. She lost so much blood, that's why willow grouse meat is white to this day. The only bird around here with white meat.

Survival Skills

shared by Mark Leary at Jacob Wise Spirit Camp, August 2024

Mark Leary: I was invited here to talk to you guys about travel safety. I appreciate the invitation. I'm glad to be here. I'm not an expert though, don't consider me an expert. I just had the privilege in my life of having a lot of good teachers, a lot of

Mark Leary instructing campers in survival techniques at the Jacob Wise Spirit Camp, August 2024. *AFR*

good older people. And I wanted to dedicate the time today to some of those people, and I want to name some of them. And you'll probably recognize the names, because a lot of them were your Ap'as, and your great Ap'as, maybe your uncle. A lot of good teachers.

And I'm still learning. Everytime I get on the river, I learn. That's one of the most important things that they taught us is to always have an open mind. The guys that think they know everything are dangerous. I don't know nothing, really. Every year I look back and man, I was dumb last year. I get a little smarter every year, hopefully.

I want to dedicate this first of all to John Borowski. I learned a lot from him. When I talk to young people, I always tell them that my generation was the first total snowmachine generation. We didn't have nothing to do with dog teams. We road snowmachines all the time.

But the generation before me, like him and others, they started out in the dog team generation, and they slowly switched to snowmachines in the '60s and '70s. But that generation was my teachers. They were the people that traveled slow, observant, and was always camping. They didn't go Aniak to Kalskag in half an hour. No, they went in six or eight hours, maybe more when the trail's bum. They camped all the time. They had what they needed to take care of themselves. And you know what? They never got lost.

An elder went to one of our Search and Rescue meetings a few weeks ago, and he was talking about it. He said, "Back in the dog team days, nobody got lost, except for people in airplanes." He said, "All the searches we went on were for airplanes." Airplanes that crashed, or airplanes that landed in bad weather somewhere. Or airplanes that broke down and landed. Nobody got lost with dog teams.

But I wanted to recognize some of the people who taught me, starting with this guy right here. In my mind, he's a legend. He was the last person to use a dog team around here for something besides racing. He used it for everything. For traveling up and down to Aniak, to Kalskag. He trapped all over the country with a dog team. That's something we're probably not gonna see again. Very rare.

Starting with him. Others that I thought about, I was thinking about this on the way up today. The river's a good place to think. I start thinking of Jerry Simeon Sr., Sonny Kameroff, Iftikum Evan, Earl Morgan, my uncle Dan Ausdahl, there's so many. But I wanted to dedicate this time to them because I wouldn't be here telling you anything if I didn't spend time with them and watch what they do, and listen to what they tell you. It's really important to listen.

Oh, here's one. This was a teacher of mine, a mentor, a good friend. Especially during freeze-up and breakup, we'd always talk every day, thank goodness for these phones. And when we were making the ice road in his area, which was Tuluksak, he'd always come out and help us, guide us, give us advice to listen. This is Joe Boy Demantle, Joe Demantle, Jr.

I'll tell you who I am. I'm her dad, if you don't know. My name is Mark Leary, and I was raised here on the Kuskokwim. My parents are David and Sharon Ausdahl, and my Ap'a and Grandma are Martin and Audrey in Kalskag. So I spent a lot of time of my growing up in Kalskag, and I've lived in other villages along the river. I've traveled, and I've been in every village on the Kuskokwim River, from Nicolai to the coast. Most of them I've been to by snowmachine or boat. Not all of them, some by plane. So I've seen a lot, how people do things differently in different places. And I always pick out different things from all the places I go.

I've also been in Search and Rescue. I've been in different village Search and Rescue groups – Holy Cross, Kalskag, Tuluksak. And I've been a team leader for Bethel Search and Rescue for quite a while.

And any of you can be in Search and Rescue. It's just about carrying on what we already do in everyday life – helping, helping each other. And in Search and Rescue it's about helping get people home, home to their families, whether that's alive or not alive. It's important that they go home. You understand?

What I carry

So, I'm going to show you a little bit about what I carry. I don't expect you to carry what I carry. Every year this box gets heavier. Believe it or not, most of this stuff fits in my backpack that goes on my Sno-Go, or even goes in the truck when I'm on the ice road.

But I'll give you some ideas of what you could carry. First, where's Dom and RJ, those guys run around a lot, they could pitch in. This guy [John] can pitch in. Even if you're just going down from Aniak to Kalskag to watch a basketball game, you should carry something, something to take care of yourself. And if you're traveling long ways, to go hunting, trapping, you need to carry more.

Cell phones

Because you guys are of the cell phone generation, I want to show you something that I think will interest you, about cell phones. How many of you have iPhone? You ever push the power off button and see the SOS? That works. Anywhere. That SOS works anywhere, you don't need cell service. The reason I know this is 'cause I tried it. People who answered at the other end weren't very happy, but I told them, "I gotta know if this works, and then I can pass it along."

How many of you have been to Whitefish Lake? Do you know where Taqika'ar is, to the east side of Whitefish Lake? That creek. We were way in there. And my lower unit was sounding funny. I thought, "Man, if you break down here, it's gonna take a long time to get out of here. We'll be fine, but it will take a long time. I wonder if this works, this SOS?"

So I pushed it. And it tells you, "Point to the satellite." You just move your phone, and it will pick up a satellite. And then they'll answer you. I was amazed. You can be anywhere. Remember that. Anywhere, even you don't have cell signal. If you really need it, not if you ran out of gas. But if it's serious and you need somebody to come and help you, you can use that SOS.

I'm gonna show you one more thing. Most of your phones have a compass on them. Yeah? That compass is useful. But what's more useful is down at the bottom, it tells you where you're at on this earth, in co-ordinates, in numbers, in latitude and longitude, it tells you. And you can take that information, you can copy it, and paste it in a text. That's if you have a signal. You can text with a real low signal, right? You can take those numbers, text them to somebody, and they can go find you.

So remember that. There's two things in your phone that are very useful. There are lots more things, but this isn't supposed to be about cell phones. It's supposed to be about old-fashioned common sense travel.

Knife and a way to make fire

So, first to begin, you should always have on your body when you're traveling, I have 'em on me every day all the time, I can't go anywhere without them. You should have a way to make a fire, and a knife.

Back in the day, everybody had a pocketknife, like an old timer pocketknife. But then they came out with these Leathermans. Oh, man, they have everything on them, right? Carry one of these. It doesn't take up much more room than a pocketknife.

With these two things, you can live. You can survive. These two simple things. You get yourself in a bad situation, and with your mind and these two things, you can live, you'll be okay. It might not be so comfortable, but you'll be okay and live. What I've got in this box, you could live like a king.

But before I open the box. You guys are welcome to ask questions, and you can touch anything, it's okay. And for my grandsons, anything you see that you want to have, you can have it, okay? I know Rainer is gonna grab the candy. [*chuckling*]

It's important that you guys, especially my grandsons, follow some of this stuff that's been taught to me.

Carry an ax

So, don't leave home without it. An ax, okay? You can always tell somebody that knows what they're doing or who has experience, they have an ax with them. This ax goes in the boat, it goes on the snowmachine, it goes in the truck. I always have an ax.

I'd rather have an ax with me than a gun. Lot of times I travel up and down the river, I don't touch my gun. I have my gun, but I don't touch it. But almost every time I go somewhere, especially by snowmachine, that ax gets used. You can do so many things with that ax, so many things.

This is a trail ax. There are all kinds of different axes. This ax is not for chopping wood, it's not for chopping down a big tree. You can do it with this, but you'll work hard. This ax is more like a knife. You see how narrow it is, and not so heavy. It's very sharp, it's sharp like a knife. This is for taking care of trails.

You know, when you're on a snowmachine, and on a trail, and you come across a branch across the trail. That's what this is for. Or you need to cut a pole to make a marker. That's what this is for. It will cut through a two, two-and-a-half-inch tree in one beat, if you're using it right.

Reflectors

You'll notice that a lot of my stuff has reflectors on it. And there's a reason for that. Winter's dark, right? And we work in the dark a lot, especially during searches, we work in the dark a lot. And it's easy to lose your stuff in the snow. So reflectors.

Carry a good rope

A rope. Carry a good rope in your boat, on your snowmachine. A rope has thousands of uses. This rope right here is near and dear to me. I've had it for a long time. It's helped a lot of people. It's even saved some lives. But it's towed a lot of people, pulled out a lot of people. I've used it over and over again.

This rope here has saved lives. And if you look at it, what I have on there. It has a floater with a reflector on it, and a quick hook. What do you think that's for?

John Borowski added information to what Mark shared, including showing the safe way to hold an ax, August 2024. *AFR*

Mason: Throwing to people.

Mark: That's right. This floats, right. Throwing to people that are in the water.

Mason: Towing people.

Mark: It is. I use it for that. I towed a broken-down boat with this rope a couple weeks ago. But the main reason for having this floater is to be able to throw it to someone that's in the water, somebody who falls through the ice, somebody who falls out of a boat. I can throw it, and they've got something to grab that's floating. Then they can get this around them. And this rope has saved people in that way.

So, a good rope. Carry a good rope. This one goes on my snowmachine, around the handlebars. It's not in the way. And my gun rests on it and has a cushion. Your gun's not scratching up your snowmachine, or your gun's not getting scratched up.

You can go anywhere safely if you have an ice pick

Mark: For snowmachine travel, what's this?

Boy: A spear?

Mark: Could be a spear, but it's an ice pick. And with this, this is one of the very important lessons we learned from the older guys that we traveled with. You can go anywhere safely if you have an ice pick, and you take the time to stop and check.

Me and a couple other Search and Rescue guys are always the first guys to go on the river at Bethel. We watch, and when the ice stops, we watch the temperature, and then we figure three, four days, and if the temperature's right, we go out and we check.

Sometimes we go check, and it's too thin. We want to walk on it safely, we want like four inches. You can get by with three, but four inches is better. Ice pick in front of you, check, you can go anywhere. Some people say, "One hit, if it breaks through the ice, it's not safe. Two strong hits, safe enough to walk on." That's a rule of thumb.

John Borowski: I'll mention something that happened to me one time with an ice pick. I was trapping, checking the ice. Kind of weak, but I was carrying a bunch of traps, and I didn't want to go back. So I just kept on going. Pretty soon I went like this, then I went down! [*chuckling*]

So don't be afraid to turn around and try someplace else.

Mark: That's right. Don't be afraid to turn back. I've turned back many times, lots of different ways, in boats, in snowmachines, in trucks, sometimes it's just not worth it. Maybe you can get there. But it's not worth it, not worth the trouble.

So, this one has reflectors on it. How far apart do you think these reflectors are?

Mason: One foot.

Mark: Yeah. Why? So you can measure your shoes? [*laughing*]

Mason: So you can measure how deep the water is.

Mark: Or how thick the ice is. This is used for both things. It's just a way of measuring.

And these reflectors, also same reason as the other stuff. I use this also to guide helicopters coming in the night, to pick up people. Or when there wasn't enough room for us, we had to leave the area, I stuck this ice pick in the ground, and the helicopter come in the night, it had spotlights, saw the reflector, and came in and landed. Ice pick.

John: You know a lot of ice picks had wooden handle on it. I broke it one time trapping. To replace the handle, I had to drill a hole in there. So I just took my .22 and bang, there's a hole for the bolt.

It's about the same size, quarter inch.

Mark: Everybody used to have ice picks with wood handles, and just a little piece of metal that they found for a blade.

And before we stop talking about ice picks, what's this for?

Camper: So when you put your hand in it, it doesn't fall out in the river.

Mark: Yup. When I see an ice pick with no rope on it, I shake my head. That person must not use their ice pick very much. You gotta have this around your wrist. 'Cause when you break through, a lot of people lose their ice pick, 'cause they don't have them around them.

And it's also used to tie it. So this one stays on my Sno-Go, and I tie this rope to my backpack so this can't come out.

Shovel

Mark: Hey, before we open my secret box, one more thing that's good to carry is a...

Campers: Shovel!

Mark: Boy, good eyes. Yeah, a shovel. I don't carry it in my boat, but on a snowmachine. What do you use it for?

Camper: When the snow's too deep.

Mark: When you get stuck in deep snow. What do you call snow with water in it? Slush or...

Camper: Overflow.

Mark: Overflow. Who told you that? [*chuckling*]. Man, you don't have to get wet to get your snowmachine out. You don't have to get off your snowmachine. You can stand on your snowmachine and clean all the slush out from around it and keep going.

I see a lot of guys, especially around Bethel, where there's a lot of recreational snowmachiners. They have those plastic shovels. They're on their back. And they look like those guys in the Sno-Go magazines. You know, our snow is rarely soft. It warms up, it freezes, it gets hard. The wind blows it, it gets hard. A metal shovel.

This one has holes in it. How come? What good is a shovel with holes in it?

Camper: To let the water out.

Mark: To let the water drain out. I use this shovel for checking blackfish trap, or beaver snare. A good shovel, and it's got a rope so I don't lose it.

Okay. Any questions? Anybody want to touch the shovel?

Dry fish

Mark [opening his box]: Now, let's get to the good stuff.

Now, the first thing. Dry fish. Why dry fish?

Camper: 'Cause you get hungry.

Mark: If you want to stay warm, if you want to have energy, if you don't want to be hungry all the time, eat Native food. And dry fish is one of the main ones that you can carry with you. It doesn't spoil, it's light. Don't leave home without dry fish. We always have dry fish. If I don't have dry fish, I feel wrong. We're traveling wrong. We don't have dry fish.

One time we were doing a class with the troopers for people new to our region on how to travel. And the troopers had a little can, and it was dry, like powdered juice. And they were really proud of it: "Everything you need to survive for a month is in this can. Just add water."

We were sitting in the back, being polite. And it was our turn, Bethel Search and Rescue. Okay, this is what you carry. Bring dry fish. That thing they have is okay, but you gotta have water. It's hard to get water in the middle of winter. Dry fish will keep you alive indefinitely. And if you really don't want to be hungry, eat the skin. It will stay in you, keep your stomach happy longer.

And if you guys want some, I'll open it and you can have some. But I know you guys just had lunch. You guys want fish? Strips or dry fish?

Boys: Strips.

Mark: Strips. Okay. It always makes me glad to see kids eating fish, because that's the reason we fish. And if the younger generation don't eat dry fish, why are we gonna fish? Why we gonna have fish camps? Eat fish.

Junk food is okay. I like junk food, I love chips. But you know it never ends, you'll be good for a little while, but then you'll be hungry again. Eat dry fish before you eat your junk food.

You guys can pass them.

I always like this time of the year. The dry fish is fresh. The *akutaq* berries are fresh. It's a good time of the year.

John: I used to also carry a sack of rice. It's light, and you can eat it by itself, or you can eat it with anything. I always had a sack in my grub box, a sack of rice.

Mark: Grub box. Everybody used to have a grub box made out of a gasoline box. But I'd have to take all day to explain a gasoline box. Have any here, Audrey? Gasoline box?

Tarp

Mark: What's this? A tarp. A really simple thing that can help you in so many ways. And not a very big tarp, it don't have to be very big. Just something to cover yourself when you need cover from the wind, from the rain, from the blowing snow, a tarp. It doesn't take up any room, it doesn't weigh anything. A tarp.

The purpose of my box

Mark: Okay. The stuff I carry has three purposes. Not every purpose is gonna be for you. My box has three purposes. One, to take care of myself. It has stuff

Megan Leary practicing traditional food storage for her family by cutting and smoking salmon in her smokehouse. *Andrea Gusty*

that I need to take care of me or the people who are with me. Two, it has stuff for Search and Rescue, to take care of people who we find. And three, it has hunting stuff. Cause we're always hunting.

What's this? Good first aide kit. And you'll notice, everything I have is in a Ziplock bag. How come?

Camper: To keep it dry.

Mark: Right. Even in winter, my stuff stays in my bag and it stays outside. It doesn't go in the house. It stays outside all winter. It's always at the same climate as the weather. Whatever the weather is, my stuff is the same. And sometimes winter is as wet as summer. So everything is in a Ziplock.

These are waterproof gloves, insulated.

Trauma pack

Mark: Oh, here's a Search and Rescue thing. This is a trauma pack. If somebody is bleeding very badly, you open this and put it on them. It stops the bleeding.

Pic

Mark: Oh, Pic. In summertime, man, we don't go anywhere without Pic. And as soon as we're gonna land on the beach, we have a Pic lit in the boat. So we're ready for the bugs. I was reading it, man, it's really not good for you.

You know, we looked up the other day, they still make Buhach. That's another story I have to tell you kids. And it's not really that bad. I don't have any, but you can order it. They still sell it.

John: I was trying to get some, but I don't know where.

Mark: Buhach was a powder that you sprinkled on something, like a piece of birch bark, and you light it, and the powder starts burning and makes smoke that keeps the bugs away. It came in a cardboard can.

Trash bags

Mark: What's this? Trash bags, a roll of trash bags. Millions of uses. Use your imagination. What could you use a trash bag for right now? Raincoat! I can pass these out right now. You'd look pretty cool with a hole right here and a hole right here. You'd stay dry.

You can make hip boots with these. You can put 'em on, and you can walk in deep water. Or if your feet get wet, you can take your wet cloths off and put dry socks on, put a trash bag, and put your wet boots back on.

It's also useful when you catch things. When you catch some fish or catch some ptarmigan. But you got to make sure you don't use trash bags that have scent. They have trash bags that smell pretty. Don't use them for food.

For dividing things up and passing things out.

Safety pins

Mark: Oh, here's one you'll never guess. Safety pin. I'm proud you guys even know what these are. What could you use this for?

Boy: You could use it on your clothes.

Mark: You got it. You ever see somebody's zipper break? At forty below? Or their boot tear? That's why I carry safety pins. So you can put your coat back together to get home without freezing.

You know what? You can even make a fishhook. I hope I'm giving you guys some ideas of what you could bring. My box gets heavier and heavier 'cause I see more and more things, thinking I wish I could have this or wish I could have that.

MRE

Mark: Okay. Does anybody know what these are? MREs. How you know that?

Boy: We went camping upriver, and we ate those 'cause we didn't have any food left.

Mark: What does MRE stand for?

Boy: Meal ready to eat.

Mark: Meal ready to eat, right. See, I carry this. I'd probably use it as a last resort. But it has everything in there.

Box of memories

Mark: This box here, too, is also a box of memories for me. And a lot of them aren't good. And I'm gonna show you. These are the first pair of waterproof gloves I ever used in my life. They are from when a classmate of mine drove his car into an open hole above Akiak, and we were searching for him. This was a long time ago. He was never found. But I've been carrying these all these years, as a reminder.

Space blanket

Mark: What are these?

Boy: Like a blanket.

Mark: What kind of blanket? They're commonly known as what?

Boy: Space blanket?

Mark: Space blanket. They're invented for space men or men going to the moon. But they're very, very useful, and they're very inexpensive. They're small. We've used these over and over when we find people in winter that are cold. We just rip one open, wrap 'em up, and they get good. Very, very useful.

Gloves and socks

Mark: Okay. What are these?

Boys: Gloves.

Mark: Gloves. Why are gloves important? Some of this junk you don't need to carry. But there's some things you should always carry. Besides dry fish. You need to have a way to... If you get wet, you need to have a way to get your hands and your what warm first?

Boys: Feet.

Mark: You have to get your feet and hands warm first. Because if they quit working, you can't do anything. You gotta keep your hands warm.

Another pair of gloves. I have a lot of gloves, and a lot of socks, 'cause a lot of times I'm with other people. Like on a search, and I gotta watch out for them, too.

I love rope

Mark: Okay, we talked about rope. I can never have enough rope.

Boy: You love rope.

Mark: I love rope, too. When I had to tow that broken down boat the other day, I realized, "Man, I'm out of rope." I usually have more rope than this. My other ropes got used doing different things during fish camp. I had no rope.

And I couldn't tow that boat far enough behind me. When we were coming out of Napakiak Slough, and the water was going out low tide, I hit bottom. And my boat stopped, and that boat was too close and it hit me. Nothing happened, everything was okay, but I needed more rope. Next day, I got some more rope.

This is another space blanket, but a really good one.

VHF

Mark: You see the boys playing with this? What is this? This is VHF, these are almost becoming obsolete. But back in the day, not too long ago, everybody used these. Kalskag still uses them a lot. There are a couple in Aniak. [John] has one. Does yours still work?

John: No.

Mark: Eric Morgan used to have one. His don't work anymore. VHF marine radio. Everybody used to use these. They still have some value. Airplanes still use them a lot when they're calling a village. I'm not ready to put my VHF away yet. I have a VHF in my boat.

Candy

Cody: Can I have a candy?

Mark: Okay, let's talk about candy. There is a value in candy and junk food. What's that value?

Boy: Hyper.

Mark: You define hyper. Fast energy. It gives you fast energy, if you don't want to take the time. If you're busy doing something, you're busy on a search, you can't stop to have fish or whatever. You have piece of candy. A piece of candy will give you a little boost. It won't last very long.

Megan: One Skittle each.

Mark: Pass it around.

Traveling with an ax

John: You know, Mark, I always have a cover on my ax.

Mark: You want to stand up and show these young people the proper way to carry an ax.

Megan: Are you guys paying attention? Chopping wood and walking around carrying an ax. Look at how John Borowski carries it, the way you're supposed to carry it.

John: Like this [with the blade away from your body], so that if you fall, the blade is down. I've seen people carry them like this [with the blade pointing to your body.] Good way to cut your neck off.

Mark: You got to have [your hand] up here [below the blade] where you can control it if you fall.

John: And you always have a cover. Even if it's just made out of cardboard.

Mark: They come with covers, and mine always wear out.

John: And there's a hatchet, made to wear on your belt. And if you fall, it pops out of the case and cuts you.

It's a very dangerous tool. In warfare, it was used as a weapon.

Mark: I never seen anyone use an ax better [than John.] When he uses an ax, the chips fly.

Homemade treasures

Mark: Okay. If anybody gives you something homemade, that they made with their own hands, a *malagg'aayaq*, a neck warmer, gloves, treasure it. These things were given to me long ago, and I carry them with me. I don't use them very often, but I always carry them with me. When somebody makes something with their own hands and gives it to you, that's a treasure.

What are these? Wrist warmers. These are stuff we're not seeing as much as we used to. Man, I had a neck warmer that Mary D. Williams made me and gave me for Christmas, and I treasured that thing, I used it for twenty something years. Every spring I would wash it and put it away. Last year when it was too warm out, I had it under a bungie cord on my snowmachine right here, and it fell off somewhere, and my heart was sad, knowing I'll never be able to replace that.

But things like this, they really made a difference. Keeping your wrists warm does wonders for keeping your hands warm.

Fingerless gloves

Mark: And on a day like this, with the wind blowing, check these out.

Look at these, when you need to use your fingers, this will keep them warm.

Fingerless gloves, really useful.

But the message... Am I losing them?

Megan: Almost done.

Mark: Well, not almost done. There's lots in my box.

I have some, Bradly, that your Ap'a Earl gave me for Christmas many years ago. I still have 'em, and they stay in my parka. They're always there.

Flashlight

Mark: I also have a flashlight in my parka, that [John] gave me long time ago. And it doesn't use batteries. It's from Russia, it came in a little box with Russian writing. And you squeeze it, and it makes light. And man, when you're in a bind, and your batteries are dead, this thing will still be working. It's in the pocket of my parka, all this time, all these years since you gave it to me.

John: Helps keep your hands warm while you light it.

Make yourself visible

Mark: Okay. What's this? Spam. Good stuff, right. But I carry it not only for what's inside it. But I carry it for the can. The can is very useful. You can make lots of stuff out of a can. You can make a signal.

When you're lost, it's very important that you make yourself visible. I've been in Search and Rescue airplanes that fly right over people and don't see them.

You have to make yourself visible. You have to shine something, or make smoke, whatever you gotta do. Make a sign in the snow with your feet. Help. S.O.S. Or if you have no other options, light your snowmachine on fire. Or your snowmachine chair. Get that smoke going. That thing's worth your life.

Search and Rescue gear

Mark: This is a bag of Search and Rescue stuff. There's reflective tape. This is important to know. If you are traveling on the river and you see this, what does it mean? Water, or thin ice. This is for marking open water. If you see a reflector, attached to willows, put close together, stay away from that. That's danger, open water.

There's a thing called traveling by brain power, not horsepower. You guys have snowmachines now, they can do amazing things. But you still have to use your brains.

Using a mirror to make yourself visible

Mark: There was one other thing I was gonna tell you. We were talking about making yourself visible. This is a little survival book. It has a mirror in it. Shine it and attract attention.

Something tore up this book. You remember?

Mason: A wolf.

Mark: It was a wolf. I left my backpack laying around, and I went back to get it, and a wolf had torn up my backpack, bit this up. And I saved this, thinking it's probably a good thing to tell people. A wolf chewed this up. Darn wolf.

There's another mirror here, too. Remember that: If you get lost and people are looking for you. Make yourself visible. It's really hard to spot somebody from the air. Especially out in the tundra, where there's all kinds of little black specks, little bushes and trees and bunches of grass. Seeing one person out there is very hard.

Stay with your snowmachine

Mark: Stay with your snowmachine if you can. We always find the snowmachine, always. Unfortunately, a lot of people leave their snowmachine and start walking. And that way sometimes we don't find them.

Sometimes you have to leave your snowmachine, like when you break down, like in the middle of the big lake behind Kalskag. If you broke down in the middle of that big lake, and it was blowing 30 miles an hour from the north. Would you stay by your snowmachine? No, you would walk toward the trees, toward shelter.

If you have to do something like that, make an arrow. Make an arrow on the ice, scratch it on your snowmachine chair, [showing] I went this way.

Making a snow cave

Mark: One thing I forgot to tell you when we were talking about shovel. What else is a shovel good for in winter?

Making a snow cave. The snow is your friend. The snow will keep you warm. Most of the animals we know use the snow to stay warm. Moose lay down in it. Marten go underneath it. Mice live under it. Ptarmigan sleep in it at night. Rabbits sleep in it. Get into the snow. You need to spend the night out there, get into the snow. If you're in the open country, there's usually big snow drifts on the north side of lakes. You can dig a snow cave, you can get in there, you can live.

Especially if you have one of these. If you have a candle. And these are long burning candle, I think these go for eight hours. But if you have just a candle inside a snow cave, you'll be roasting warm, you'll be good.

But if you're in a snow cave, and it's blowing bad weather, make sure you leave a marker, a stick poking up through the snow. And also so you can get air.

Piiyuuk: In a snow cave you can poke your shovel or your ice pick and have your back to it, it will make a mound over you, and you have a hole where the stick is.

John: Me and Joe one time, I think we dug it too close to the ice. We got in a snow cave like that, and it was cold. We had to keep going outside to make a fire. I think it was too close to the ice. I think it's supposed to be dug down, and then up a little bit. Ice is cold.

Mark: Yeah, don't camp on ice. You can also put your sled on its side, or your snowmachine on its side and use it as a windbreak.

Around here, mostly there are spruce trees. You can use spruce trees to make a seat, a pad to sit on in a snow cave, and you won't get wet. You guys good, should I keep going?

Boys: Yeah.

Mark: More gloves, socks. Bring socks and gloves, way to make a fire, some dry fish, you can live pretty good.

Cracker can

Mark: But I got something, you guys remember this? Whoever opens this can have it. This can is very old. It took me a long time to find this can. This can is a very special can. Whoever opens this can have it.

Gorilla tape. Many uses, from fixing your snowmachine chair, fixing a hole in your rainpants, fixing your boots.

You know when we go to feeds, they always like to hand out things like gloves, socks, things like that. I always like to put them in. That's where these came from. I got washcloth.

Oh look! He opened it. It's crackers. Took me a long time to find something where my crackers won't break. I treasure this can. It saves my crackers. Want to have them?

Safety glasses

Mark: I got to show you this. What are these?

Camper: Sunglasses.

Mark: It's not sunny. Safety glasses. What color are they?

Campers: Yellow.

Mark: What are they good for? Pass these around and look at the river right now. Yellow glasses are good for bad weather. They make it brighter. And in winter they're real good in bad weather.

But they're also very useful when you're traveling in a boat. Why? Why would a pair of safety glasses, any color, be useful in a boat?

When you're in an open boat, it protects your eyes from what? Bugs! Man, there's some times of the day, especially in the evening, where there's bugs hitting you in the face, you're coming down Whitefish Creek, you're coming down Aniak River, and there's lots of bugs.

One time we were coming down Aniak River and one of those black gnats hit me in the eye, moose season. And I couldn't use that eye for a couple days. Good thing it wasn't my shooting eye.

Whitefish Creek cabin. *Megan Leary*

Those safety glasses protect you from bugs, they help you in bad weather. And they don't cost much.

Zip ties

Mark: What are these? Zip ties. Millions of uses. I caught a beaver with Zip ties one time. I had a beaver that didn't want to take my bait, so I got a little birch tree with lots of juicy branches, and I Zip-tied the branches close together, and I put it down in the ice. And I put snares, and I caught that beaver.

Useful string and snare wire

Mark: I got some cool stuff to show you guys. I got string. I got so many different kinds of string. [*chuckling*] Don't laugh at me. String is useful.

How about this? This is a good one for you guys, 'cause I know some of you guys are doing this already, right Rainer? What is this? Wire. What's it good for? Snare. What's a snare? You catch an animal by doing what to it? By choking it.

You know, you can catch any animal with a snare. Any animal around here. You can catch a mouse with a snare, a squirrel, a rabbit. You can catch a bear with a snare. You can catch a moose with a snare. The bigger the animal, the bigger the wire.

You don't want to snare no bear with this. But a long time ago, they used to snare everything. They used to snare ptarmigan, chickens, geese, can you believe it? You could catch a person. Snare wire.

So if you're going to the store and you want snare wire, look for picture frame wire. It's called picture frame wire.

Extra socks and knives

Mark: Extra socks. Again, these are homemade socks. Only kind of socks I use in winter is yarn, homemade socks.

The real reason I started carrying more than one knife is that I've been with too many guys that forgot their knives, or they have a Leatherman. No, no, we'll be here all day. You got a moose to cut up, or a couple of caribou to cut up, and there's only one knife, it's gonna take a long time. So I bring more than one knife.

Knife sharpener

Mark: And if you're gonna have a knife, what you gonna have? Sharpener. There's no use to have a knife if you don't keep it sharp. A dull knife is more dangerous than a sharp knife. How come?

John: You're using more force. And when you're using more force and you slip, you're gonna cut yourself bad.

Mark: You hear? You got to work hard with a dull knife. That's where accidents happen. When we're cutting up anything, fish, moose, anything, take the time to sharpen your knife.

One time Ray Peterson caught a moose down there by the lake. And me and Jacob Wise went down to cut it up for him. And I told him. Stay in the boat. Just keep the knife sharp, we'll do everything. He got the knives sharp. Man, we were fast. Knives stayed sharp.

Headlamp

Mark: Okay. Headlamp. I have a bunch of them. Headlamps are very useful, right. You have a headlamp, Rainer? And extra batteries.

Aspirin

Mark: What's this? It's aspirin. What is aspirin good for? The reason I carry it is for me or anybody I'm with, if somebody has a heart attack or a stroke. If you can get to this aspirin fast and get it in their mouth, get them to chew it, get it under their tongue, it can help them. When I have this on my snowmachine backpack, it's in the pocket on the front, where I can get it fast.

Magnesium fire starter

Mark: Here's some stuff you might like. This is fire starting stuff. You know there's all kinds of ways to start a fire. You don't have to have a lighter, you don't have to have matches. Use your imagination.

Flint and steel. Keep thinking. If you don't have any of this stuff, there's a way to make a fire.

If you have a gun you can start a fire. Gun powder.

John: If you have a snowmachine, you can get a spark.

Mark: So don't give up. Who has a piece of birch bark? Anybody know what this is? You see this? It burns very very hot.

John: You want to know something? I never go anywhere without it.

Mark: Hear that. Magnesium fire starter.

John: I have one hanging on my belt.

Mark: I got tired of getting wet. Heard enough?

Kids: No!

We don't leave people behind

Mark: And this one has coffee and sugar and tea, stuff like that in it. And I gotta show you how this works.

Remember I told you this is a box of memories? This come from a flare. Five people from two four-wheelers went through the ice. Me and Charles Guest responded to it. We saved three of 'em. Two of 'em didn't make it. We had to leave their bodies that night and get the survivors to Bethel. And we don't leave people behind. That's not our way around here. We don't leave anybody.

So we went back the next day, even though the troopers told us not to, because river conditions were deteriorating very badly, to get the body. They told us not to take 'em. They told us to wait, they're sending a helicopter. We said okay. We waited all day. They didn't tell us the helicopter was coming all the way from Anchorage.

We waited all day, and we watched the river disintegrate in front of us. The helicopter finally came in the evening. They couldn't see us, I popped the flare, they came in and took the bodies, and I asked the pilot, "Can you follow us, make sure we make it across the river?" The other side of the river was okay. "Yeah, I can follow you, but there'd be nothing I can do if you fall in." I said, "Yeah there is. You can tell 'em where to find us." So he followed us. We did make it across.

Flares

Mark: We talked about being visible. Hey boys, you boys would love these. They're flares. They shoot up in the air, like a firework. We don't play around with them, we only use them when we really need them.

Something to read

Mark: String, rope, and I got a book in here. If you get stuck and you have to wait to be found, you broke down, you ran out of gas, you have to wait for somebody to come, it's good to have something to read. Sit there with your feet up on your snowmachine, "Oh, you guys come to get me. I'm good."

Fishhooks and string

Mark: *Manaqing* string. I got fishhooks in here. Catch something to eat.

Especially downriver. That's why there's so many people downriver. You can catch a fish any time of the year down there, there's fish down there. Up here, little different in winter.

Gunny sacks. What's a gunny sack good for?

Extra glasses

Mark: Oh, this is for me. Extra glasses. I'm getting to the point now that if I don't have glasses, there's some things I can't do. That's kind of scary. I can't work on my chain saw, I can't sharpen it if I don't have glasses.

Search and Rescue stories

Mark: I got more stuff in here, it's not so exciting. But I could tell you guys a story, a Search and Rescue story.

The first one I want to tell you is not a good one. Are you ready for it? But I think it's important to tell because it will help you in the future.

Once we were hunting geese at a place called Lonely Hill. It's way downriver between Eek and Napakiak. It's a hill. By tundra standards, it's a real hill. You can see it from far. And on top of that hill, there's a little lake. And we always hunt in there in the springtime. Geese love that place.

So there were four of us. We went down. We could still go by snowmachine, and we went down to Lonely Hill. And we hunted there all day. And I remember looking at my watch – that's when we still wore watches – I looked at my watch. A young guy walked up the hill. 'Cause we parked our snowmachines at the bottom, and we walked up there to hunt.

And he walked up the hill. I didn't know him, but the other guys with me knew him. He was a nice young guy. He visited with us for a while. And then he said he was gonna go hunt farther down, farther away. And he left us. It was like one o'clock in the afternoon.

And we heard him. He got his snowmachine at the bottom of the hill, and at the bottom of the hill is a big lake. It was frozen, still. But in the springtime the ice gets pretty smooth, right? Everything melts, the snow melts, everything gets pretty smooth.

We heard him, he was going fast. You know, you could hear a snowmachine going fast, "Wow-wow-wow-wow." And then the snowmachine faded away. So we hunted there all day, and in the evening, when the sun was getting low, maybe like 10 o'clock, we packed up and got ready to go. Got all our birds that we caught, and our pack-sacks and stuff, and we had to walk down and get our Sno-Gos.

And as we were walking down, way down on the end of that lake, there was a black spot that wasn't there in the morning. And if you've been in a lot of searches, you become suspicious, or more aware: "What is that? That wasn't there."

Well, I got binoculars on my Sno-Go, I go check. We got our Sno-Gos and we drove up on the hill, and I looked. It looks like a Sno-Go. And it looks like it had a sled behind it, and there's a couple other little black things. "Huh. Let's go closer and look."

So we drove down to the end of Lonely Hill. And that thing that looked like a snowmachine wasn't so far away. "Yeah, that's a snowmachine. I don't know what that is behind it, laying on the ice. And then those other things. Let's go down there."

Me and one other guy went down the hill. There was a lot of water on the side of the lake. We were trying to find a way to get on the ice. We got on the ice finally. And as we got closer, I saw it was a snowmachine. And that thing laying on the ice, that kind of looked like a little black plastic sled was a person. "Oh no." And as we got closer, we could see that it was a gun, a backpack, a *malagg'aayaq*, a person, a snowmachine.

I went right to that person. It was that young guy who visited us in the afternoon. He was laying on the ice like this. I checked his pulse. No pulse. Already cold. Oh, my gosh. What happened. We just saw this guy. He wasn't drinking, he wasn't smoking or anything. He was just out enjoying the day hunting. Maybe going too fast. What happened?

We followed his tracks. Here he had been going very fast, on a nice smooth lake. We all do that, right? Smooth, but all of a sudden there was one snowdrift. And it wasn't even that high. He hit it, there was no snowmachine tracks for a long ways. He was in the air. When he hit the ice, his snowmachine flipped and it landed right-side up. The snowmachine looked like nothing happened to it, it was just sitting there nice. But when it flipped, he must have hit his head. He had a little bit of blood right here.

By this time it was getting dark. We got hold of the troopers with a VHF radio. We watched Earl with the trooper plane, in the dark we watched him take off from Napaskiak, go to Bethel, land, pick up a trooper, and then start coming.

And we lit up the lake with our snowmachines. We picked out a spot, and it landed. We told them what we thought happened. And they looked at the body, they lifted up his shirt. Right there on his chest, was the imprint of the kill switch on his snowmachine. The kill switch on his handlebar, that's how hard he hit.

So they took him, they brought him back to Bethel. We spent the night out there. We couldn't go home, high tide. But that showed me, every time I'm tempted to go fast, "It's smooth, man, it's smooth, go fast." Jonah Andrew's snowdrift. That was his name. Young guy, one little snowdrift, and his life was over. He passed away from hitting that one little snowdrift.

So remember that when you're tempted to go so fast, it's so smooth. There may be something out there ahead of you. Be careful.

Another Search and Rescue story

Mark: Want to hear a happier one?

Kids: Yeah! Happier one.

Mark: So, one day, the weather was really bad in Bethel, blizzard like crazy, they canceled school. Yah! Right. Then couple hours later the weather got clear. There's a Yup'ik name for that, but I don't know it. It's like it's fooling you, sucking you in.

So these two brothers, "Yeah, we got no school! The weather's good. Let's go ptarmigan hunting." So they took off. They went west of Bethel a little ways. And all of a sudden, the weather came back in, blowing and snowing.

You know the big wide place where you go pick berries, they were losing sight of it. So they called their dad. This was in cell phone times. And he told them what to do, or what he thought they should do. But when you can't see nothing, it's really easy to go the wrong way. When it's blowing so hard, and you can't see from me to you, it's really easy to start going the wrong way. And they end up turning away from Bethel and going farther and farther away from Bethel to the west, and they got lost.

Just as it was getting dark, their dad called us, Search and Rescue, to help. And three of us took off right away. We were ready. My stuff is always ready, usually on my Sno-Go.

We were out there. It was terrible. We couldn't see anything. We wandered around, wandered around, barely keeping track of ourselves. Finally we decided, "We need to go back to Bethel, get organized. We need to get more help." So we did.

By that time a lot of people had come to help. We got reorganized, got people with GPS's. You know what GPS is? You can travel with a GPS, even you can't see. You got to be careful with that. So we went back out, and we were out all night looking for them. We couldn't find them, couldn't find them.

Next day same thing. Storming, storming. We were out, six of us. Went back out early the next morning. Terrible weather. Couldn't see anything. I was thankful for those guys with GPS.

We went everywhere. We ended up going to Atmautluak, took a break in Atmautluak. Then we went to Nunap[itchuk]. Couple of us got lost at Nunap, right in front of the village. You couldn't see. You know Nunap is on a big bend, the village on one side, and [bank] other side. And we were going around that bend, trying to go to the Public Safety Building, and we couldn't see the guys in front of us. Pretty soon we didn't know where we were. We just stopped and we waited. We know they'll come back for us.

They came back. We went back out after a little break in Nunap. By this time it's getting to be life and death. These two young boys, who had nothing with them hardly, except for a gun and shells, maybe some snack, they'd been out there for two days, terrible weather. We were very worried for them.

That night, we were out 'til dark, late. We went back to Atmautluak, tired, we were frustrated. I got on the phone to the Search and Rescue representative in Bethel. And I told him, "You know, if this was some kid in the city, they would have everything out here. Everything! Planes, helicopters, everything. Scuba divers, and bomb squads and SWAT teams. But not us, we don't get that."

"Hold on. There's a plane coming."

"Oh yeah, from where?"

"From Kodiak."

"Oh yeah?"

"C130, rescue plane, they're gonna help you guys with infrared."

"Okay, all right!"

We got boosted up, we're gonna get some help.

They told us where to meet. We went out to the big lake. You know where those bluffs are? Back where we were picking berries? We waited. We got there with Nunap and Kasigluk guys, and we waited for that plane. And I had to keep going on top of the bluff to get signal.

"Okay, they're refueling."

"Where's the plane?"

"They just took off. Go!"

We went out in the tundra in the spot they told us. We were all lined up in the dark, maybe 20 snowmachines. I was in the middle. I was the guy talking to the plane. And that plane came out of the clouds. Big plane, a C130, four turbo engines, "*vroom*."

Everybody was taking pictures. And then they said they were gonna fly around first with their infrared. You know what's infrared? Infrared can see heat. So if there's a person, they can see the heat of that person, out there, in the tundra. They flew around, flew around, flew around. Nothing. Oh man, here's what they're gonna do now. And the reason they couldn't find those boys. You know why? You know why they couldn't see the body heat of those boys?

Mason: They were dead?

Mark: No, they weren't dead.

Mason: They made a shelter, in snow.

Mark: A snow what? A snow cave. They were in a snow cave! They couldn't find their body heat.

Mason: They were underneath snow.

Mark: They were under snow. Then that plane said, "We're gonna drop flares. And when we drop flares, you guys go and look." Man, they go right over, drop a flare, boom. It has a parachute, a flare on a parachute, it floats on a parachute and it floats really slow. And when that flare lit, it was like daytime!

So we all took off, twenty snowmachines. Where are they, where are they? Keep going, keep going. And that flare would float, and burn out, and they'd drop another one, boom, bright, and we go looking, looking, looking. We see rabbit, ptarmigan, we never see boys.

They did that ten times. Man, it was awesome. I got a picture somewhere. That flare going off.

At the end, they dropped ten flares, they didn't find those boys. Those boys were in the cave, and they didn't even hear the airplane, they told us later on.

So we finally went home for the night. The next morning was nice weather. The storm was over, the two boys got out of their cave and started walking. And right away, an airplane saw them. They were fine, they were okay. They didn't get frostbite. They did the right thing.

They did the wrong thing first, going ptarmigan hunting when there was a storm in the area, not checking the weather before you go. And then they went the wrong way in the bad weather.

But once they realized they were in trouble, they did the right thing. They made a cave, and they stayed there. Two days in their snow cave.

Did they have food? They had some little snacks. They're alive and well, they're good. Their parents had a big dinner for the searchers at their house. Their last name was Charlie. Ray Charlie's sons, I forget their names.

Boy: How old are they?

Mark: I don't know how old they are now. Back then they were in high school, like a sophomore and a junior.

Running out of gas on the way to Pike Lake

Mark: Are we done or do you want to hear another one?

Kids: One more!

Mark: Okay, I'll tell you another happy one. I told you this is a box of memory. There's little army men in the box. These came from a woman that I found underneath the ice. She had bought these for her sons at home. She was traveling back to her home village and didn't make it. I gathered up these army men and brought them to her sons. I kept one or two. It was scattered all over.

I'll tell you one more happy one, real quick. One year we were looking for a guy from Kalskag, who went to Pike Lake. You know what's a 12-horse? Elan, a little snowmachine people used to have, everybody had 'em, and they didn't even need snow. They had wheels instead of slides. This guy went on a 12-horse, in late November, to Pike Lake.

Who knows where is Pike Lake? Pike Lake is right across from Aniak, on the Yukon side. You go that way when you're going to Holy Cross. But you can go there from Kalskag by going behind it. And people liked to go there to *manaq* for big pike. It was famous for that.

And this man went on his 12-horse. He was the first one to go there early in the winter, and he didn't come back. That year we were having a lot of blizzardy weather, early in the winter. So we went to look for him.

His brother and another guy had already been out all night looking for him, and they couldn't find him.

Catherine Ignatti: Wasn't it Sinka? Sinka and Connector?

Mark: Yeah, you know who I'm talking about, right?

So we got organized and we went to look for him. And we spread out in a long line from Big Lake to Pike Lake, sweeping for him, looking. And it was getting late, daylight is short in November. The sun was going down. We were running out of ideas of what to do. We never find any sign of him.

So I told those guys, "Let's go up on the hill. See if we can see a light out there where he has a fire or something on the Yukon flats." The flat country going toward the Yukon.

So we all went up on the hill. And there was an airplane helping us look. And way way over there, miles away, we saw a light blinking off and on, off and on. Do we have anybody over there? No, we're all here. Who's that? We told that airplane to go check. That airplane flew over there, start circling.

"That's a guy walking, and he has a headlamp." That's why it looked like it was blinking, he was walking. He was tired. He'd been out how many days. No snowmachine, just a guy walking.

As soon as we heard that, everybody start their snow machine, twenty snow machines, and took off. And I thought to myself, "Nah, I'm gonna stay here and watch. This is gonna look cool." So I stayed up there and I watched those nineteen snowmachines go down the hill. And I thought it was far, several miles away. Slowly, slowly, all these lights going to this one dim light. And the airplane light flying above him. Man, it was cool.

Finally, finally everybody closed in on that little light. And they called me on the radio, "Yeah, he's good." The first thing we do when we find somebody that's been out, we check their feet, make sure their feet aren't frozen. Give them dry socks, cause their socks are sweaty and dirty and they're not warm. Check their hands. He was good.

"Okay, I'll come down." They waited for me. So his snowmachine, when he was lost in the bad weather, his little 12-horse snowmachine had run out of gas, so he was slowly walking home. He got a new snowmachine. And he spent the whole rest of the winter, going back, looking for his 12-horse. He kept looking and looking for it.

So years went by. And I found out what happened to his snowmachine. A guy in Aniak was out taking a ride out by Pike Lake. And he found a 12-horse. And he dragged it home. And he never told anybody. That was the end of the mystery of what happened to Jagar's 12-horse.

Catherine Ignatti: Yeah, we kept wondering what happened to that.

Camper: Why's his name Jagar?

Catherine Ignatti: Nickname, right? His real name is Andrew Wise.

Gusty Mikael, Legend of the Kuskokwim

by Cheryl Jerabek

Introduction

Gusty Mikael on a moose hunting trip, 1981.
Terry Bissonnette

When people think of Gusty Mikael, they smile. They smile because of the fond memories his name brings. Sometimes they are humorous stories; often they are stories of amazing strength, traditional knowledge, and spiritual power. His death in September of 1984 was an end of an era. Yet he died as he had lived, two caribou in the boat, traveling down a swift river in his own country.

That strength of character, that spiritual power, that joy of life, the confidence that you can handle anything that comes your way, was Gusty's legacy to his children, grandchildren, and future generations.

In 2003, Iyana Gusty, Gusty Mikael's oldest living son, asked me to "write down everything that I remember from my father before I die." He told me: "My dad have lots of good experience. I learn lot of things from him. And it's good I used to do that. You have it written down, not waste it, you got it."

From 2003-2005 I carried out a total of 22 hours of interviews with 16 relatives and friends of Gusty Mikael, Iyana Gusty being the primary informant. Included here is a small sampling of Gusty's knowledge and abilities.

Names

Tracing family names and relationships can be very confusing and fascinating at the same time. According to District Court records, compiled by a past magistrate in Aniak, the surname of the family includes variations of Mikael as well as variations of Gusty. Gusty Mikael has been referred to as: Gusty Mikael, Gusty Michael, Goestia Michael, Constantine Kosto, and Constantine Michael. Gusty is pronounced "Gooste" by many older people. Gusty's wife also was referred to by a variety of names: Agrafina Alexie, Agraphena Nagoja-mitty, Aggripina Alexie, Agraphina Alexie, Agdafenye Alexie, and Afrafena Alexie. Gusty's father is most often referred to as Mikael or Medicine Man Makile. For this publication I have used the spellings as Gusty Mikael, Medicine Man Makila and Agrafina Alexie.

The children of Gusty and Agrafina had either Gusty or Michael as a last name. In modern times the adult children and their descendants use Gusty as a last name.

Iyana explains it as follows:

> My grandfather was Makila, Michael. Supposed to be us guys too, Michael after my dad's name. My dad's name is Michael. Same thing.... Last name, probably first name again, Michael. His Native name, they called him Makila, them old people, Native name, Makila, I guess Michael, couldn't say it.
>
> My dad, they called him Goste. And we use his last name, us guys, when they write it down. Whoever that trading post, those guys. Could be my dad tell him like that, make it short. Our real name would be Constantine. Could be Gusty. And they make that name, send those papers. If we get it right it would be Michael. My dad's name was Constantine, and they called him Goste. Only his dad Makila, that's an Indian name to me, Makila.

Others also related to me how the traders simplified people's names.

> Someone told me it was either Reg White, or who was the guy before him? Was it Barnhart, that changed the names? The Bobbys all used to be Constantienoffs. They were, ya. 'Cause they'd come down to trade at Stony River with Barnhart or Reg White and the guy just got fed up with these long Nicholas names. Heck with this stuff, you're now Nick Bobby, you're Paul Bobby. Here's some easy names, and that's the way that the surnames started.... The Russian way was stepped down whatever, first name became last name.

Languages

Gusty's language ability was well known. He traveled extensively throughout the region and was able to switch between Yugtun, Athabascan, and English. Priscilla Russell Kari describes the languages of the Stony River and Gusty's ability as follows: "Stony River village is the modern contact point between Yup'ik Eskimo [Yupiit] and three distinct Athabascan languages: Kuskokwim Ingalik [more properly Deg Hit'an / Deg Xinag], Dena'ina, and Upper Kuskokwim. The 'patriarch' of Stony River, Gusty Mikhael, is one of the most polyglot Natives in Alaska, speaking Yup'ik [his mother's language], Ingalik, Dena'ina, and Upper Kuskokwim, plus English and Russian. He also is a song leader in the Orthodox church. He prefers Yup'ik [Yugtun] when telling stories, but can shift rapidly into precise conversational registers of each of the neighboring Athabascan languages. Gusty Mikael refers to the Kuskokwim Ingalik [Deg Hit'an / Deg Xinag] language as the "Yukon" language, implying a recent incursion of Ingalik from the Yukon to the Kuskokwim. Eskimo [Yugtun] and Athabascan languages share boundaries around the circumference of Alaska, but there may be no point of contact with as high a degree of Eskimo [Yupiit]-Athabascan multilingualism in modern Alaska as Stony River" (Kari 1985:5-7).

The following maps show the languages and culture of the region.

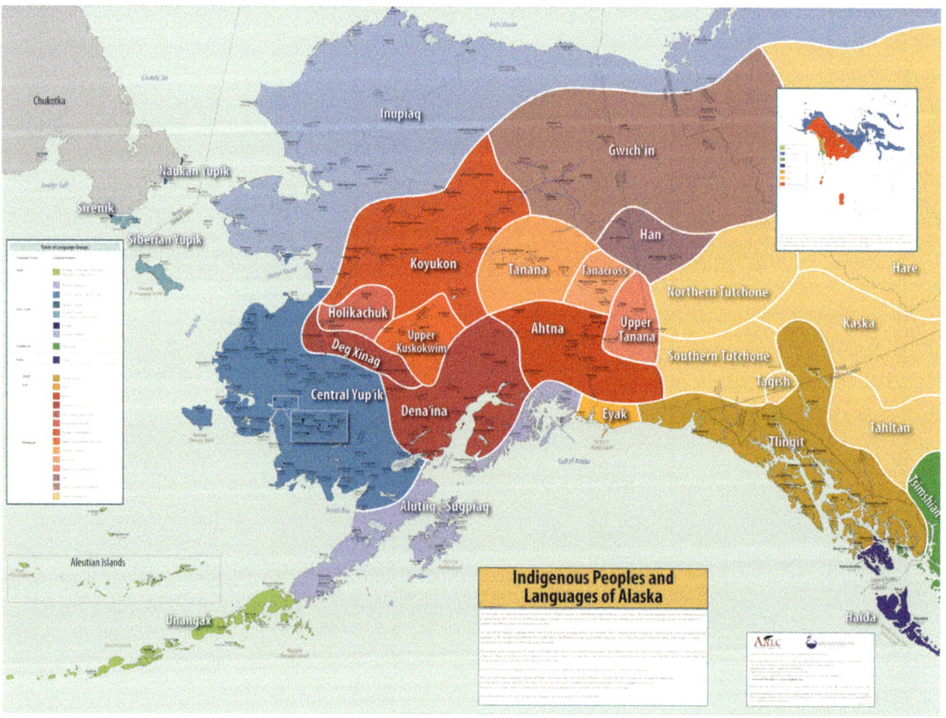

"Indigenous Peoples and Languages of Alaska." *Alaska Native Language Center*

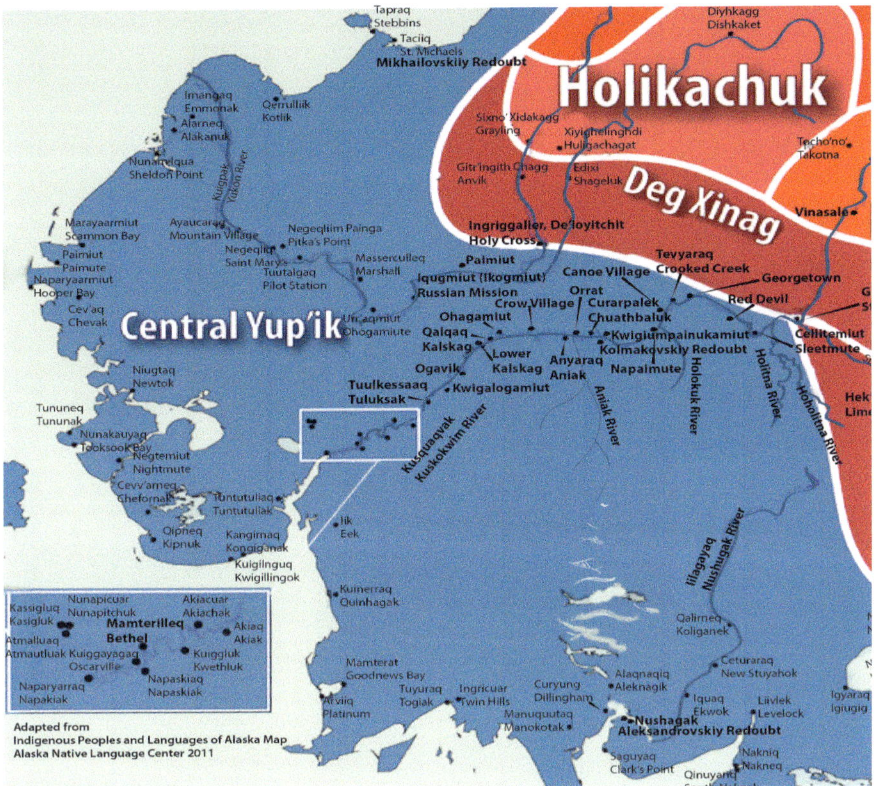

Close-up of the Middle Kuskokwim region. *Alaska Native Language Center*

Teaching and learning

Gusty passed knowledge to his children by having them participate in subsistence activities and training them to be tough and knowledgeable. Iyana states:

> My dad taught me, teach me how to hunt. He know how to do it himself. He tell us what to do. If we didn't do it right, he give us hell. From long time ago my dad give me hell. And I said to myself, my dad picking on me, I guess he don't like me. I never tell him, my dad picking on me, I say it to myself only. But he teaching us. And this days after he die, I say thanks to him, he was doing it for me. That means going to my kids and all my grandkids. Not for himself, for us, we could learn. Whatever my dad teach me and everything always come true. I always have good luck like that. Whatever I do, it turn out. That was good. That's how I learn.
>
> Constantine, my oldest brother, was grown up, young though. And he travel. My dad teach him first before me. And Constantine teach me what he learn from my dad. Sometimes I half cry, and I try to keep up with

them. And I kind of scared evening time. I must be small. I try to do best I can, try to keep up with them. They walk their selves, they used to run fast, my dad and Constantine. They were big, me, I was kind of small. They don't feel sorry for me. They watch me, they don't leave me, kind of keep eye on me. I try to keep up with them and when we stop I'm happy, take a rest.

Some day he said you guys gonna get married maybe. And I say I don't think so. And Constantine, my oldest brother, he tease me a little bit. He laugh, he kinda smiling, "You gonna get married maybe, find some woman." And I didn't like the idea. And first thing, sure enough, that's what he used to tell us, everything turn out what's gonna be happening.

Now I try to remember and I look back maybe 30 years back, 40 years, pretty close 50 years back what people used to tell me. They let us sit down on the floor, them old people used to talk to us, important, "You guys got to sit down while I'm talking. That's important for you guys." When we was younger, they let us sit down in one place, we don't move until they finish. When they finish they tell us to stand up and go ahead and go and play, go do something. They listen to the parent from long time, maybe more than a 100 years, lots of years before we were born, and my dad's dad before he born. He make that story continue on, keep it going. That's really important what you hear from older people, keep it in your mind.

Not only that, my dad, quite a while ago. Past my knee, I fold up my pants and without socks in the deep snow I run. He made us how far to run. Every morning, I get up. My dad tell me, "Time to get up and make fire." So I make fire and, "Time to run now." Without socks, no shoes, "Time to run now, in deep snow, don't go by the trees, go in deep snow." Not only that, he watch me from the window. I run as fast as I could. By the time I come back when I was young I was half crying. And sometimes my oldest brother, name is Constantine. He's the one taught me. He take his shoes off and he run too, himself, fold up his pants, past his knee. And we run through the deep snow. No matter how cold, 30, 40 below, he let us run, we run. It used to be hard for me, but that's the way I been told, that's the way he taught me. If I didn't do it right, he looking at me, so we have to let me do it right way, whatever he tell me what to do.

Sometime I complain to myself, my dad picking on me. I find out I say thanks to him, he was doing it for me, for my kids. It's really important to learn those important things. Would be good to hear. They may not pay

> attention but remember later. I go through that what my dad train me. I know how to get along with people, how to hunt, make boat, canoe, skin boat, sled too. That's how my dad train me, and I grow up and I don't forget it. I say thanks to my dad. Taught me what to do and how to get along.

Family friends also talk about how Gusty Mikael taught his sons.

> You know the boys having to do this, you probably heard this, go outside running around barefoot outside and get wood. In the morning it's the boy's job to start the fire, and part of this was to go outside barefoot and get wood and start the fire. What he was doing was training them. Iyana has such a strong vision of how to live, it's according to this book and I suppose the old man [Gusty Mikael] has his book that was given to him, and he really imprinted it on those boys. He's those boys without the rough edges. How that is I don't know. It's mysterious. He [Iyana] knows the whole picture and his dad's history and doesn't come up with negative stuff and always from a positive view that his dad was training him, that there was a purpose of how they are operating.
>
> You know how guys are when they are talking about their dads. Well, dad was good at this and good at that and then they'll get around to how the old man failed him. And you don't get that from Iyana and his dad, and it makes me think. It fits my picture of him that he was a special man. It's not that he was perfect, but he's not making serious mistakes with his boys. If he did, the boys aren't carrying that around. Blaming him for how their lives are turning out. They're never complaining about the old man, they got enough from him of the right stuff.

Gusty Mikael's teaching extended to non-Natives, but once again it was by the traditional method of watching and learning. This style is described by a former Stony River resident as follows:

> I knew how much he knew and I was always asking him questions: Well, why do you do this and how do you do this? And whenever I needed to know something, he's who I would go to, and of course that's not the Native way to ask a lot of questions. And he was doing something with a fish wheel down by the river and I asked him something about it. And he turned around and said very annoyed, "You watch, you see." "Okay, Gusty."

Making a skin boat and traveling down in the spring

Gusty Mikael was well known for his ability to make a skin boat. I was told about this from several people. Travel would be upriver in the fall and then downriver in the spring. Traveling the river with lots of meat was never a problem for Gusty. Iyana described the making of a skin boat.

> We have lots of food, moose meat. He caught anything, black bear, sometime he caught brown bear. When we go hunt moose, I remember that, we go hunt, go camping, we never see nothing. Never see anything in the river sometime. And my dad go out, my dad go walk way up in the valley. He caught moose way up there. He never say it's too far. When we camp, my dad hear the moose make noise far away. And he go to him in the morning and he caught it. And from in there we pack our meat, pack him down to the river, hang 'em up by the beach. And pretty soon, he just caught one moose, he wouldn't give up. Gotta get enough supply for all winter.
>
> We got one big boat, round bottom boat, maybe 30 foot, maybe 6 feet wide boat. We got old style Evenrude, he call them 32. We use that kind. And we run out, we got no more room. My dad said, "Time for us to stop, camp. We gonna make skin boat. I got material already. We got that moose skin. I gotta sew them together. We make boat. You guys go down with the boat, and I go down with the skin boat. You just watch me what I'm doing. You learn something. You gotta learn, you guys gotta learn, just watch me, just follow what I do. What I need you guys just go to get it."
>
> And he tell us what to get, wood roots from the trees. He used to let me get it. He tell me what he want, the bent one from inside the ground, bent like that. And he tell me to get that, how many he want. We used it again, that root from the trees. Tie it. Really strong, no nails, nothing. No bolt, nothing. By hand, everything done by hand. He know how to sew it himself. We do it. Water never get in where he sew. I watch him put the skin together, he sew it cross ways and the same other side.
>
> He cut one whole moose, he put them together, and big skin boat, that good tarp right there. And after he finish that boat, that skin boat, he gonna make that. Sharp point both ends, pointed both ends. When he finish, we take that upside down, turn it over, and put that skin over, and we tie it, put 'em inside the cache and we can go under and we put that tarp over that tent, that big skin boat, he put them together, nothing wrong. He sew. He use that skin again and sew 'em together to the wood. And bend it inside

like that, it goes in.

And we watch when he finish that, he paint it. He make some moose grease, sometime, melt it, moose grease cut it up and put it by the fire and he put it where we sew and not a drop of water. Water never go through.

Now he gonna make paddle. He tell us get two Y's. Birch is usually stronger, Y like that and kind of curve it up so he can ore both sides. He tie 'em together again. He don't use no nails again. He put them long side skin boat. Put the Y this side, same other side, put seat in the middle, and handle the boat again just like a toy.

What ever he want us to do we do it. I can do lot of things, I can't figure out how he do it. But he make it, he do it, in couple days he make skin boat. We load them up, we got two boats. Our boat is overloaded. Half and half, take half of them. Go down river. We load up we got enough supplies for all winter. Never get stuck, we don't have to make two trips, just make it one time to go down. He make skin boat in a couple of days. I watch it. I get idea pretty good. Everything done by hand. No hammer, no nothing, just tie from roots from trees. He tell me to get that kind, he tell me what he want, and I go get it. I have to do what he tell me. That way we learn.

Iyana also described traveling through shallow water.

My dad and my brother Constantine, we go hunt fall time. And some places too shallow, he don't back off, he never say it's too shallow. He never back off. He say we gonna make it. If we have to pole up, or some place we have to line up, he used to do that. In my mind I used to be lazy little bit. He use long rope. If it is bad place, we use line. Same line, you tie up the boat and you hold the boat, right now. We hold it from the beach, we walk down with it, hold the long line. We walk with the boat and himself he push the boat, sometime, one of us pole the boat, me and my brother we pull the boat up, we walk up on the beach where there is good beach, and we line up and we pull it and my dad keep pushing it. My dad push the boat, keep pushing it, past the bad place and we go again. That way you don't go in a bad place, you hold the line and walk down by the beach.

We get past that shallow place. I'll take it little bit deeper. Lots of places just like some crossing is shallow after you go over it. It's deep now and you start the motor from in there. If it get shallow he do the same thing again. Never get stuck my dad. He never say it's too hard, he not back off. Everything turn out good. We follow what he tell us to do.

The game they know they need supply for winter. Those days we didn't know about freezer, had to dry and make dry meat and put it in the cache. We don't waste it and we got it, dry fish, meat, beaver meat. Right before breakup time, we gotta get going and make spring camp. Lots of water on the river already, come to creek and can't go across already lots of water. My dad say, "Iyana, you follow me and I tell you what to do, I know the country. If we can't go across we make a raft and bring them across little bit at a time and we start all over. We not going to back off and we not turn around. I not going to turn around."

I asked him another question, how we gonna go back. "Don't worry, I kill 3-4 moose already and we make skin boat and gonna make canoe too with skin. I gonna show you how, and you make skin boat, crooked roots and cottonwood little tree and we got."

Got no string. "We got lot of string." He make spruce roots in the ground, and use babiche rawhide to tie boat together. I never see no nail. Both side and the joint he tie them together and he finally finish it, and he put two moose hide and sew them together, and he turn the skin boat turn it over and put fur side inside. And we used to hang moose skin right over skin boat, and when he's done it won't come apart in spring time.

Another thing he's important. One bird, if he tell us there is no more ice in the river he tell us, night time…walk by Native way. If there's no more noise, he won't make no noise if he start to make noise. I hear that wak...there's no more ice in the river. Let's load up the boat, make two skin boats, made big oar in the middle and one steer it. If it's bad place, we all get out, and that's how we get back to Stony River. He won't say it too hard. When he plan it, "Just follow me, I know where to go, high ground. Won't take no nails. Take rope and tie it and make spring camp."

Medicine man or angalkuq?

All of Gusty's children who were interviewed were emphatic that their father was not a medicine man, not an *angalkuq*, which is the Yugtun word for medicine man or shaman. However, their grandfather Makila was described as a medicine man, and was widely known in the area as Medicine Man Makila. Iyana explained:

No, [Gusty's] not a medicine man. He's not, only his dad, not him. My dad's dad. He sing and cover up with a shirt like this, and sing, and make a little dance and see what's going on. He said somebody get sick. He make

> medicine, he fix them. He sees what's going on and take the germs off with the medicine. Nothing wrong, he fix them.
>
> I used to watch him, my old grandpa. He dance, he sing same time, he go round, he do like this, he see what's going on, what's happened. Something going on, he say, something bothering us. Another medicine man, he see it, as soon as he come around, he start to sing and see what's going on. He used to make medicine. He help lot of people too, somebody get sick. Makila, Michael.

Gusty's daughter Marvara added: "Gusty said if you believe in Jesus you can't believe in the old ways. He wasn't a medicine man. He admitted his dad was." Her dad also told her about going to the *qasgiq* at Ohagamute and the games there, like jumping up and pulling down a greased stick. Everyone brought food.

Iyana continued:

> My dad was not medicine man. It was not true. He had nothing. People think he is but was not. He was no medicine man. Only his dad. His dad didn't want to give it to nobody before he die. He didn't like it if it didn't turn out the way he want. It might not work out good. He didn't want to give it to his son. He figure his son he got temper and it might not turn out good. So he didn't give it to nobody. When it's gone, it's gone. My grandpa said, "I don't want to leave my medicine to no one. You have a temper, better off that it is lost, disappear." He didn't give it to him, he didn't turn him over. He could, before he die, but he didn't. So nobody had no medicine. People think my dad was medicine man, but I know myself he was not. People think he did. Lots accused him, he had no medicine. People always picking on my dad. It's a medicine man, they say, but he was not a medicine man, as far as I know he's not.
>
> My Apa [grandpa] was. When something going on, somebody get sick, somebody get sick pretty bad, he make medicine and he see what's going on and he fix it by medicine. He do lot of people, do lots of favor for them, he used to do. He use his medicine and fix somebody just like that.
>
> I remember that one. I used to watch my grandpa make medicine, how he make medicine, he cover up, take shirt off. He take his shirt off and cover up and sing same time he go round and round. "If you know how, sing with me." And he go round kind of go around like that and put his head over, his own shirt and kind of shake and sing same time. I don't know what he say, I don't understand.
>
> He shake his shirt and shake it, and after he finish singing he tell us

what happened. He sing with them and he can see what's going on when people get sick, when something going on, when something bother, other medicine come along he always try to get him. I look at it and he said he done. "I saved somebody's life. He was really close, almost somebody got him. Caught him just right." He used to do it all the time. He always help somebody.

See my grandpa, and he always help them, fix them up, fast, faster than doctor. Just like that. He used to be really strong. Somebody get sick, really sick. He used to come from other village, come down and go see him. People didn't know what's going on, he gonna die. And he make medicine, go around and check on him what's going on. He sees what going on and the only way he find out, he go around and find out, look and sing same time and cover up with a shirt and he go around and he see everything what's going on, going on in the village.

And right after that, that guy he gets good, nothing wrong, and he get good, nothing wrong with him. He passed that, what was gonna be happening. He catch 'em before he die, and he help him out of that, just like a doctor. Really fast though, less than an hour. He make medicine and what's the problem he got. Another man, another medicine man, try to get after that guy like that, and he see it, he get him outta there and chase him away. Make medicine and fix it. But my grandpa didn't give it to my dad, didn't trust him.

And one time one summer, some time ago, everybody gang up on him [my grandpa, Gusty's father] by medicine way and they kill him. They got him. It was something like a beaver hole, they stay inside the ground, used to have house like that medicine, hide you know. Lot of people, he had a problem. But lot of medicine people, everybody gang up on him.

He had a problem, especially a woman. He know which woman up by Nickolai. He can't see it, he can see the man medicine, but he can't see that woman medicine. He's the one get him right away. He see only fire, red, just like that one [points to red] like that. He can't see the person, only see that, only a little fire. He can't see, women medicine is different from a man. Isn't that something. I didn't know that, there's two that one.

He could pay it back afterward, but he didn't. I think that not too long after, some of them is gone. After he died. He pay them back. Maybe all of them gone. He pay them back after. It was too late. He find out, already they gang up on him. Eat him too already, part of his body gone. He's in there but he know it himself. Us guys we got two way, our body here and

> just like our picture is different. From us, it's with us but always right there. That's the one that's really important.
>
> That's what happened, everybody gang up on him. I used to hear him, "Women medicine is different from man medicine." You can't see it. You can see only fire, only fire, just red mark. But medicine man you could see. He used to say that. But he know it himself. We don't know. He can't see, he can see the man medicine, like man, like him, he can fight with him but he can't fight with the woman, only the fire he see. He can't see the person. That's what mostly got him, he said. We didn't know nothing about it but I hear him talking to my dad, and he talk to Ignatti, too, I think.

When Iyana was asked how his Aunt Lisa (Gusty's sister) died, he replied:

> My dad was mad. Medicine man kill him. She was shacking up with Gleman. "You kill my sister with your medicine. I can kill you right now by hand," he show him. "But I let you go." Gleman had nothing to say. Told him long after it happened when we were big. She used to be hard worker. Gleman and his mom is big medicine woman. Isi Isi was Gleman's mom from Nickolai. Gleman was married to Malfa, my mom's sister, younger than my mom. After he was with Lisa. She [Gleman's mom] is the one that killed Mikila, can't see. He was telling story can't see woman medicine different from man, just see little dot, just like fire. If it was man like him, can't see woman, only the fire."

Alexie Gusty, who was raised for a time by his grandfather and grandmother, also described Makila's healing.

> He was some kind of magic, he was some kind of power, medicine some kind. He sing about, covered up by blanket, start to jump around, dance. I guess those guys, *angalkuq*. All of a sudden he stop, get just sweating, "Devil place is down there, too hot. Too hot, try to get him out, somebody, one of them. I don't know who is that, devil got him," he say, try to get him back.
>
> I don't know who is that, maybe one of his sons. He have Molga, Sam, I don't know how many he had, four, son. I don't even see them, *angalkuq*, Sam, Molga, Alexie, that's how he call me Alexie. I had another Uncle his name was Alexie. After he died, he gave me his name.
>
> Sam, those days, those guys used to have TB, that's how he passed away, my old man. Used to be no doctor those days, start to vomit, got

> TB. My uncle Sam, other one, lots of them, besides by dad, he had four brothers, all TB. That's why he gave us name. He passed away, like they do right now, same thing. Die give it to somebody else. Living in there only us I know. Stony River used to be nobody.

Andrew Gusty also described seeing his grandfather using his medicine.

> I used to stay with him. Not go to school. They used to call medicine man. Different way some kind of breath. Hardly can't eat he put them away. He used that medicine, he sick. Singing. One time he closed the windows and the icon. Devil work. Sparkle, log he got crack. I see him in a crack. Just like spark. He had lots of things. Them guys they holler at them. What's going on. Nothing he say. He fix him, boil some kind of thing then he throw up. It's pneumonia, he get some kind of plant he vomit. Homemade medicine. Helped. When we go some place he take them jars.
>
> We stay with him two weeks sometime, me and Alexie. Somebody come sick, he closed the icon inside the house, put towel. He told us to go outside. We go outside. He make some kind of song, sing, medicine. This guy pay maybe 10 marten. His parents. The next day this guy eat, he eat with us, too. Lots of stories like that I see. He close all the Jesus pictures, close the window. He stand all around him, sick guy. He told us not to peak, us can't look, too bright sometime like a tundra. Said I get spark in my eye if I watch.

People seem to agree that Gusty Mikael did not have healing medicine powers. Yet he did have a reputation in the area of having some sort of extraordinary powers, especially with animals. One former hunting/trapping partner described it: "The stuff that he does, it's not what a normal person would do. Just a few little things I seen him doing. The way he hunt, normal people just don't do it like he does. He lived with the animals, too, so he knew what they were thinking I guess. I don't know, maybe he was half animal, too, I don't know. He never go hungry though. He always get something somehow."

Another former resident of Stony River described the respect and fear that people had of Gusty Mikael.

> I could just see how much respect people had for Gusty and a little bit of fear, too, which I didn't understand at the time. But those were times when shamanism was still quite active. I don't know now, but he was considered a shaman. That's the kind of thing that I just got rumors of. It

wasn't the type of thing people would talk about. They would have if I would have just come out and asked. But I didn't feel that it was my place to do that. I just knew what his reputation was and I kind of accepted it. Well, he did have some powers, and that he could use them, and that some things happened that they thought he was behind. There was some fear there.

One long-time resident explained that there were two types of powers.

In terms of medicine power, you can use some pretty lousy stuff aimed at people. My father-in-law says there is two types of medicine power, one is for animals, one is for people. Everyone felt that to use the power to hunt, like to call in the animals was okay, to sing the song to the moose or the brown bear or whatever. But to use that power for people was considered to be pretty evil, to go there. But Gusty was said to have power for people too.

Now I've heard different stories. One story is that he got the power from his dad, his natural dad. The other is that he went downriver, that he had no power at all, that he went down to Yup'ik country and somehow purchased or acquired his power from a downriver shaman. To be honest I don't know. He spoke fluent Yup'ik, old Gusty did, but what percentage Yup'ik he was, I don't know.

There are lots of people, particularly amongst the intellectual circles, they want you to think that shamans were these nice little men and ladies walking around like beggars with somebody to heal. I've never heard a positive story of an *angalkuq*. Maybe there were out there.

He went on to explain other local beliefs.

A lot of the old gambling games weren't really gambling. It was an arena where people could test their shamanic powers, one against the other. Say for example, we are both *angalkuq*, and so we'll play some little gamble game. That's an area, let's say you beat me, than I know you have more power than I have. 'Cause if we confront each other head on in the shamantic realm, one of us is going to get hurt. But if we do a few little bones on the table or some little stick game, we've found out who has more power and nobody died in the process.

Do you know how to tell a shaman? It's really funny, at least back then, 30 years ago. You'd just ask people, and people who didn't have any power at all, they'd talk about it. People like old Gusty would say, "Oh,

> I don't know anything about that, I don't know a thing, you're talking to the wrong man." And they all did that, everybody with shamanic powers claimed to know nothing, and people who didn't have any would talk. Oh, that was another thing. He just always denied any, I didn't do anything about this.

He continued:

> It's hard to say, lots of time people would just have bum luck and they'd blame someone made bad medicine for me. You can't trace that stuff. So that people were often describing something to be a curse when it was just their own stupidity or something.
>
> Mary Nicoli, that old woman in Aniak, told me a story about when a shaman came to her house. She had some beaver mitts hanging on the wall, and the shaman said I want those. She said, "No, they are for my husband." The shaman said, "Whatever you are stingy for you will lose." Three months later Mary's dad fell into a blade at the saw mill.

Another local story of *angalkuq* was told to me.

> There was a woman named Mrs. Sergie years ago in Sleetmute. She was the adopted daughter of Old Sergie, halfway between Stony and Sleetmute, didn't have any children of their own, they adopted children. And Mrs. Sergie had some power. And in front of her house in Sleetmute was this gnarled tree, this strange tree. She died, late October maybe. About two or three weeks later I was over in Sleetmute and a strange wind blew. And the sky turned green, just as green like that 7-Up bottle. And the wind came out of the west, and it never comes out of the west in Sleetmute. It goes up or down, it's north or south. Sleetmute, that big hill like Nixie's, the wind came over that hill, and whatever trail we had, it was deep snow, total powder, it took me about 45 minutes to get home. It was strange, it was weird, green sky, I'd never seen a green sky before and that gnarled old tree that was out front of her house blew down.
>
> So I've seen strange phenomena that have been connected with people that had medicine power. So when that rock that Gusty flipped over on vanished, it didn't surprise anybody. Lot of the old shamans when they died they would vanish like Gleman Nisi. No one ever saw part of his body. And Ernie Holmberg's mom, from McGrath, just vanished. A little mystery there.

Where Gusty was concerned, a long-time resident explained his view as follows:

> So I think there were two things he was known for the most. One absolutely his ability to travel, his physical prowess. And at the same time because everybody knew that he had some medicine power. I didn't believe in that stuff. He was always friendly to me, always kind to me. I'm absolutely certain that Gusty had power with animals, and that is the lesser of the powers. If anybody got anything they've got that. In terms of that, I don't think there is any question. People would say he's *angalkuq,* which is the Yup'ik word. People drew on animals for power. I've heard it described like the northern lights song, the brown bear song, the song for ice. There's a song for different animals, and they'd all try to take. The one shaman in Sleetmute had porcupine powers. Who'd want that? But when I went to Sleetmute there were 7 people that claimed they had some new creative power. I don't know if they did. And the event would come to pass, or they'd use a song for protection like northern light songs for protection. The ice of course had lot of power. And people would use the songs as medicine for their dogs, but they claimed if you do like that, particularly the wolf song, the dog won't live long. He would be an incredible dog but it will die young, like burn up.

Although people were wary of Gusty, he did not invoke the fear that was shown to another more notorious shaman as described by a former long-time resident of the area:

> He [Gusty] was a bit feared because people knew he had medicine power. There were only two *angalkuq* upriver, one was old Gusty and one was old Gleman Nisi. People feared Gleman. He was from Nickolai, little tiny guy, five foot two, five foot three, big ears. I remember that. I saw him land in Sleetmute and grown men, Jack Egnaty and Andrew Alexie, they ran down and helped steady his boat. They were so afraid of him, they just didn't want to piss him off. They treated him, if they had a red carpet, they would have rolled it out, it was like that because they were afraid of Gleman. He was not a nice man.

Others described the comparison this way:

> To me it wasn't that he [Gusty] was a shaman, he was just really smart. I mean he could figure things out. And he was willing to embrace

> the modern culture. But he also knew a whole lot about growing up and living in the woods. Some people feared him. I was never afraid of him. Well, like with Gleman I remember my mom washing his seat when he left. Wash off his seat and wash his cup in boiling water. But I never saw anybody do that to Gusty. When I saw Gleman, he seemed just like a normal person. I didn't see anything different. 'Course I was real little then.

Another former resident stated that sometimes people would come and visit and make comments about Gusty being a shaman.

> There were those that would make comments and kind of quiver, "Oh that old Gusty, ya know." Andrew told me the fact that [Gusty's] dad was the shaman, and the way that it worked that when old Gusty died that it was inherited by him. He never explained it in any other manner other than it being straight forward, that's the way it is and that's the way it was.

A long-time resident of the area stated:

> No, he [Gusty] wasn't perceived as an evil shaman, Gleman was evil, and I think Gusty's dad was not a nice man. I've heard the term wicked used to describe him. He was described as wicked by some people who know wickedness when they see it. Somebody I respect described him that way. I don't know if Gusty had any, I never know any. I never heard of him beating anyone up. I never heard of him hurting somebody. I never heard of him abusing women. I never heard any story at all. I know that in general when a shaman would go to any village, or any visitor, people always hid the young girls. The girls were told to go hide because a shaman would say, I'll have her tonight, and then people had to choose between giving up their thirteen-year-old daughter or a curse. I'm not saying he was like that, but that was a precaution as people came.

Another elder from the area answered the question of Gusty being a shaman as follows: "I don't know. I don't think so. I know my uncle Isi from way up there Nickolai, my uncle, his brother, step-brother, Isi was a big medicine man, he and his wife."

Religion and spiritual power

A family friend told the following interesting story of Gusty's spiritual power and effect on people.

He come down here [Bethel] once, stayed over night with us. I take him to Swansons (a local store) and we walk into Swansons. And it's as if, I can't explain it to ya, my hair went up on the back of my neck. We walk into Swansons, and the next thing we're walking towards hardware. Hardware used to be back where movies and toys are now. We're walking toward that direction and in the isles in groceries, there are people clear in the back of the store, that are you could see them.

It was like they got a scent in the air, and they turn around and they see him and they light up and they got a big smile on their faces. Now all these people didn't know who he was, it wasn't like just one person, so he's going through Swansons, and he looks like the Pope and he's going, he's waving and smiling and people are turning around. They're getting these really big smiles on their faces. It was like his spirit or some kind of aura that came out of him. And he had this, something that other men don't have. Everybody would like to have it, but they don't have it, and he had it. It was some kind of mojo, or I don't know what it was.

So we go to the store and he gets his stuff, ordinary enough. He came down for some kind of medicine man meeting. He came home and he was pissed off about that. It was bastard this and he could really carry on. So he says those guys are making themselves big with talk, I don't like that. He didn't go back either. That was the end of it. They got him down here not to have him talk but to have his name associated with whatever they were doing. Not seriously looking for answers from him.

The thing at Swansons, I tell you what I saw and he had this power in him that in that occasion just came out. And I sensed that about him upon meeting him and hanging around him. The powers he had, he wasn't showing off, but it expressed itself in everyday life, like that Swansons thing. Some of those people knew him and some didn't. Something that they felt, and why they turned around in the back of the store and why they turned around in the first place, turned around looking for something, see him and he's smiling. People felt better, it wasn't just me. I see other people come in and out of his life, and they seem invigorated I guess. He had this power. You know like seeing him after he died, and scientists would trivialize this. I'm 60 and know there's stuff that's true, that the world has shifted somehow, and trivializing it with science is just that. There were some keys to the kingdom handed over there or shared.

Caribou knife story

One of the great stories told about Gusty Mikael's hunting ability is the story of killing a caribou with a knife. Iyana loved to tell this story.

> Quite a few other guys was with my dad, Moxie Sr. and Jack Egnaty, could be, hunting together. My dad was tricky, pretty tricky sometime, and he plan on it. He want to play, that's what he said. What my dad tell me story. My dad says he want to play, way up the Swift River some place. Jack Egnaty he was with him, Moxie Alexie, that Molga and Moxie Alexie Jr. dad.
>
> One time, a long time ago. He tell everybody, there's a caribou asleep in summer time, and he go to them. He said, "Hey you guys, I want to play. I want to have fun. You guys do what I tell you. Don't take any gun, don't shoot, don't take any gun. You guys stay behind, watch me from long ways. That caribou's out there sleeping, I gonna try to sneak up on him. The wind from the north. You stay behind the wind."
>
> He take his shoes off, he crawl over. When he get to about maybe 15, 25 feet, the caribou jumped up, my dad jumped up, and go after the caribou. "When I do that, I want you guys to come after me, everybody don't take any gun. We gonna do it by hand, kill him by hand, we gonna use knife only, cut him up, poke him with knife only, we wouldn't use no rifle."
>
> Sure enough those guys give him hell before he go.
>
> "What we gonna do?"
>
> "This is what I gonna do. You follow me, you guys watch me from long ways and when I holler everybody run over, don't take any gun." He get everybody to do that. And about 25 feet, maybe 20 feet, and caribou hear him. He make that noise. Soon as he jump, my dad jump, he jump on him and grab him by the horn and knock him down, twist his head. "Now you guys come on over, everybody come over right now. We use only knife. We gonna take him by the hand. I gonna hold it back. It pretty tough, you guys hurry. I gonna get tired really fast."
>
> Everybody run over to my dad, he hold the caribou, he run, he knock him down, he stand right back up. He running pretty fast, as soon as he start to run, he twist his head again, knock him down. By that time everybody come, everybody grab, some of him he flew off, he kick 'em, you know them people, that caribou is strong too, they're fast. Some grab him by the leg, he just push them by the side. Some people just cut him

with the knife, he use knife, he don't use no rifle. "Hey, we're having fun. We got it now. We get him with the knife." He pack him home. Bring him to the beach and skin him up. That's what he used to do. Fast. My dad used to be fast, run, no game can leave him. He keep up with them just like nothing.

Moose hunting

Iyana described the use of hunting dogs.

He use his dog for moose too, everything. Smart. He used to have a moose dog, he come along. He take 'em with them when he want to go. Sometimes he never see nothing in the river. And that dog, going up the river, and if he's not tied up, as soon as he smell, he jump from that boat, no matter how fast we go in that boat. And he jump off and swim to the shore, and went back. Sometime he jump off if he not tied up, and most of the time my dad used to tie and as soon as he smell.

I used to borrow them once in awhile. He tell me, "If you gonna go, take my dog. As soon as he smell something, you gotta head for shore. If you don't he'll jump in the water." One dog I used to borrow. I take him along. Sure enough I go along up the river. Swift River, all of a sudden he smell something. My dad he give me warning, "Be sure, my dog, soon as he smell, don't try to go. If he didn't land, as soon as he smell something you headed for beach and let him go and he'll bring them to you." That moose. You don't have to look for him. He go get 'em. Bring it to us. We stay right on top. "Be ready for him." He tell me, "Get your rifle ready, he'll bring it to you. Don't just think he not going to do that, he do that." He tell me, "You gotta watch really close. He come really fast that moose. He come right up to the boat. He bring it to the boat."

Sure enough. I take whatever he tell me, my dad. I kind of hold back I thought he wouldn't. Anyway soon as I going up the river and that dog listen to me good, too. I talk to him. And he listen to me really good, and we go along. And all of a sudden from the north he smell something and headed for shore. There he go. He gone. 10, 15 minutes already bark way back there. You can barely hear the bark. You hear all kinds of breaking sticks now. Sure enough, that dog he chase him from the back. He's watching both sides. If he had two dogs he guide him that side and this side, and he guide him to you. There he goes, lots of noise coming. He come right straight at me, on top the bank where I tied up the boat. Tie the

> boat to the beach, walk up the bank, and right up to me, right behind the boat, and we shoot it right there. I kill moose right there, bull moose. He just bring it to me. That's the way he used to do. That's how my dad used to do it all the time. I didn't believe he would do that, sure enough he do that. That's how he treat them. He treat them really good, he talk to them he tell them what to do, treat them really good. Treat them talk to them like a person.

A hunting partner also added:

> He had his dogs. He'd be in the boat. Boy, his dogs would go wild. They'd smell moose, three four bends down the river. We'd be trying to catch moose, cut it up, we'd have enough and his dogs would go wild again, they want some more, and he'd have to holler we already have enough. And his dogs would be pissed off at him. After he catch it, I didn't hear him. He'd be over there doing something to it, you know. He had his little things he did. I don't know what he did, I didn't pay no attention to it.

Gusty also watched the weather to determine the best time to hunt. Iyana described:

> He teach me how to hunt moose. And night time we go trap line we stay in trap line, he go bathroom, whatever he have to do and he see that tent moving, wind. He point up like this, up the ceiling and he see the tent moving, that's the wind, that's the grub. "We gonna go hungry, we don't got much meat, we gotta go hunt if there's lot of wind. Listen to grub," he tell me. He make me wonder, and after while I catch on. He meant when there is lot of wind the game wouldn't hear you, you can sneak up, he knew how to do it. He know how. He taught me. "I gonna teach you how to hunt moose some days in the future, even maybe I'll be gone you gonna do it like me. You stay and watch me, this is what I gonna do. I gonna follow that moose."
>
> And he follow from this side, wind from that way, he start from this way, he walk from that way and come back, and same way we come back kind of far, keep working that way, go all the way down and we come back again, not run all over. We come this way and you looking, and when you come back, not too far from where we was, go as far as no more track. And come back again and come back again, and no more track, see on this way, keep on going. And he taught me, "Now stop, moose is coming

closer, don't make noise, don't break any stick, just look at me, see how I hunt."

And I do what he tell me. I'm not on my own. He teach me. And I got it. I stay way back there. Don't break any stick. Another thing you do, if lots of wind, don't just cut off the trail and go any place you want. Go back this way, and where you can see where I was and come back again, and maybe pretty soon we see timber, a little island. He tell me to come. "He's on that island, middle of that island." And he keep on go and he tell me. I just follow what he tell me, I never get close to him, try not to break anything.

And pretty soon I hear him shoot. That moose, he never go no place. Where he was laying down. He just drop him same place, he never run away. He drop him one shot. Maybe 50 feet, 100 feet, maybe less than 100 feet. The way he doing it, that moose never smell him. Because he doing it, he hunting it so he wouldn't smell it. As soon as moose stand up, he just shoot one time, he just drop it right there, where he was laying down, was sleeping. And he just sneak up to it, and he start to leave when he hear my dad close by, and he just drop it right there. And he say, "Now you see, you learning." He tell me. And sure enough he turn out, turn pretty good, we cut him up. Taught me lot of things. But you can't do, you have to stay on this side, that moose gonna smell you, you come close to him he gonna run away, just waste your time. He taught me maybe two, three times like that.

Not only that when he used to go hunt moose, he used to go: "Hey I gonna go hunt moose. We don't have much meat now, we need some fresh meat I gonna go. You guys stay around here. I'll be back tonight." And he go, and towards the evening, fall time, kind of short day. He chase moose way back in the woods, chase them to the river, and keep up with him, chase him to the river, and he bring him down where our home, kinda old place, across there, about four miles from Stony, above it, around the bend, they gonna come around the corner and they shot it. And he come home and have tea.

He tell them old people, "You guys go ahead and cut that meat up. I didn't want to haul it, so I bring him back, I let him bring himself, I let him pack himself. I chase him down the river and I bring him down to our home. That way we didn't have to haul him. That save lots of work. We didn't have to make no brush any place. I just take him to the river, Kuskokwim. I gonna go hunt moose now. I don't want to haul it. I gonna let him haul himself. I gonna shoot it around the corner."

And that's what he used to do. He do that every time. Chase him to the Kuskokwim River and take off fast, that moose, and my dad watch it, which way he turn its head. When start to go away, guide it to river and keep him going so he wouldn't go in woods, land side. Moose have to turn, he guide him. Go on the other side too far, he run after him again. He run after him and let him turn. Guide him, just like gee and haw. Play with them like a toy. Keep him down the middle of the river, guide it. And close to our home, maybe half mile away, and he shoot him, and he go home and have some tea. And that's what he tell us.

He used to do, bring it home and those guys go and cut the meat. Those days they never worry about no game warden, no season, just what we have to do, just feed us what we need. "If he run away I gonna chase him to the river, I gonna let him come down himself, that way we don't have to haul it." And it just come round the corner. Sure enough he always do it.

I don't see how he do it. Us guys we can't do it. Right now that moose, just leave us, in a few seconds, good going, he just leave us right there, they're gone. He go wherever he want to go. But my dad he was not like that, he keep up with him. He used to do that. He keep up with 'em, never leave 'em, those game, those moose, he run pretty fast, not much snow. But my dad never get left off, just handle him like a little pup, just follow, guide him down the river, take him down the Kuskokwim River and shoot him above our place, just around the corner, that way I don't have to haul him. That's what he tell us before I go. Caribou, too, guide them which way to go.

My dad mentioned how they caught moose before guns. He could put some snare, moose pretty strong, he can do that alright. You got good size rope, you can hang it where moose go in there, like wolves whatever, maybe underneath the bank, kind of close to it. And you know how high that moose and kind of tie it with piece of string whatever and tie it up and moose come to him and he got caught. I think they used to do that long time ago. Tie him up. Most of the time they used to use bow and arrow for moose and caribou. They got lots of caribou skin, caribou snare, hide you know.

A family friend summarized Gusty's hunting ability as follows:

All these Native beliefs, that animals hear us when we are talking about them, that's not all nonsense. There have been reasons why that belief system has come around, people by and large have ignored that or don't have the ability to pay attention to stuff there. He was recognized even as an old man as a great hunter, particularly for moose, and that was tied to his ability to [train] dogs. In the old country, everybody had dogs, everybody's a dog man, but Iyana's talking about how they would come to a place where people didn't have any meat. They knew were the moose was, but they couldn't catch them. And his dad then would go and catch a moose and come back and say, "Well, boys, he's over here or over there." And I think those incidents were tied to dogs and using dogs to help catch moose. Iyana's stories of hunting with his dad, snowshoe stories. And what's interesting, everyone was a dog man, but what was it that he had that made him more skillful than other people? I watch and see how dog mushers are, my contemporaries, you would think that everyone would be more or less on the same page, but they are not.

He went on to add:

Iyana's winter stories on snowshoes involved, instead of having to follow the moose's track, and by following the dog and where the dog knows where he is. And then they could get the drop on the moose. And Iyana's stories are always what a good runner his dad was. He can't tell a moose hunting story without getting to that right away. And Iyana's a good runner, a young guy on snowshoes, and there's some fellow they are hunting with. I'm kind of thinking it was Marvara's husband, but I'm not sure about that. Anyway, they are bragging it up, and the next day they start running. They're with dogs, and the dogs smell a moose, and away they go. And so first thing Iyana's…let's see how it goes. The braggart, he breaks trail for a little while, doesn't last long, and then…anyway the story goes that Gusty quickly just leaves them, and by the second or third meadow, and Iyana says you can just see he's gone. It impressed Iyana. Well, he says, "My dad is getting old," and he left that guy and Iyana as well completely out of sight. He liked to kill these animals with a .22, you know it was light, he's not carrying a big gun, and he's running up along side of them with snowshoes and kill them with a .22. I don't know anybody who could do that now, and pull that off."

Gusty Mikael. *Photo taken from Facebook*

Gusty's death

Gusty died, like he had lived, traveling along the river with caribou in the boat. Just as his life was filled with spirituality and a little mystery, so was his death.

A former school teacher stated:

> I know on that whole vein of a shaman there were two things that just struck me as being almost supernatural about the way he died. The way that he was spotted when he was up above Lime Village in the canyons.... [Magistrate Terry Bissonnette and the Troopers were] in a plane up above circling looking for the boat or whatever, and there was like this golden aurora at this one spot in the river. And him and the pilot were saying, "Why is this such a strange-color whatever?" They couldn't get too low cause it was right at the start of the canyons and stuff like that, and they tried to circle and stuff. And they were able to determine, pretty sure that there was a body there. But the way he explained it was that there was this halo effect or something and they were able to mark the spot. And then they told the Lime Village people where to go, and right there on the other side of a boulder was where he [Gusty] was lying, apparently stuck in rocks, face up, and they had spotted him.
>
> And then his funeral when I went up. It was a real nice fall day, and then right as the burial started taking place, whatever, the wind just started really picking up and then blowing as he started to be buried and stuff. Ya, that made a real mark on me. It didn't start blowing trees over or anything, but it was a real noticeable change in weather.

A long-time area resident stated:

> I wasn't in Lime Village when he died, but I was very close contact. But I understand he and Chuck Elson were up the Stony River above the village. They had caught a caribou coming down just about dark, and I know coming down that river the sun is right in your eyes. Sundown, I travel that all the time. And when you are traveling downriver often times where a rock is, if the water is just coming over the top, it looks smooth, you can't read the river going down. Going up you can.
>
> Apparently they hit a rock, boat flipped and Chuck spent the night on that rock and it was cold, really cold. Usually the Stony is pretty silty, glacier water, but when the water starts to drop like that it's pretty clear. And Larry Hensley was flying, the game warden there. He was flying around and spotted the body under the water from the air. And to this

> day we still call it Gusty's island, the rock. But the interesting thing was that the rock that he ran up on, was gone the next spring. The rocks move around the river, we see them, we know them. But the rock that he ran up on no longer exists. It was a big rock, probably as big as these two beds put together. It was at the head of the island, and the next year it was gone. And other rocks that were there at that time are still there. A little mystery.

A family friend stated:

> Look at all the people that came for his funeral from all over to pay respect, and what we were there for was the spirit that he had. He visited me after he died, a little brief encounter, don't worry about a thing. I went and visited his grave and brought along some homemade little thing, I had no training in this, moose hair, cranberries and goose down. So I went to his grave to pray just to say I respect ya. So I stuck this under the leaves there, and on the way back to camp he appears to me. He and my mom were together, and just a brief little thing. The message was – there were no words – the message was that everything was okay. This would have been maybe two years after he died, I guess.

It's hard to know how old Gusty was when he died in September 1984. Court birth records list his birth anywhere from 1885 to 1897. So at his death he may have been between 87 and 99. *The Tundra Drums* newspaper listed him as 84 and stated: "Gusty's death marks the end of an era on the Kuskokwim. He was the last of the Native hunters and trappers of that region who could live completely off the land. He had hunted and trapped not only throughout the Kuskokwim region but up the Holitna and into the Nushagak drainages. No one else has the knowledge of the land that he did." He was still very spry, going out hunting and getting wood. One person described him as "one of those ageless people." An article in a local Aniak paper summed it up: "He was still rejoicing in the way he lived, when he drowned. He seemed to know that it was finally time for him, and he wanted to leave this life the way he lived it. Out hunting in a swift and dangerous river, with huge boulders, and traveling at night carrying two caribou in the boat. That was the way he probably would have wanted to leave."

Evelyn Thomas: An Appreciation
by Chris Wooley

Much of my 40-year career in Alaska was as a cultural resource management consultant. Briefly, it involved contracting with entities ranging from the largest resource development companies to the smallest tribes. The development work was driven by laws, regulations and permits pertaining to oil exploration and drilling, mining planning, emergency response, and other projects. The tribal work was driven by the need to preserve cultural heritage in a rapidly changing world. [1]

I was fortunate in my career to work with many amazing people – none more amazing than the late Evelyn Thomas of Crooked Creek.

When I first met Evelyn in 2006, I was visiting Crooked Creek to begin cultural resource surveys associated with the Donlin Gold project. Evelyn challenged me the moment I introduced myself.

I had come to Crooked Creek weeks before our project began to consult with the Traditional Council on work plans, which involved archaeological surveys of the proposed mine site and other infrastructure areas. I had only briefly worked in the Middle Kuskokwim region, and I wanted to make sure that our work involved authentic local input and involvement.

The gist of the laws, regulations and permits related to "cultural resource management," in my mind, boiled down to respect – for the sites and for the people whose history and culture they represented. Twentieth century historic preservation laws in the US were passed to account for the effects of projects on cultural and historical sites and the communities who hold those sites dear. Respectfully collaborating with local communities before starting fieldwork was important – particularly if any human remains were discovered. It was not just a box to check on a permit to-do list but an essential element of working in rural Alaska.

1. The most important initial step in the development work was identifying specific places that held – and retained – significant information about the past. This information ranged from scientific data present in buried archaeological deposits to iconic historic locations and cultural landmarks. Information contained in analyzed archaeological deposits, recorded oral traditions, historic maps, and photographs enabled us to evaluate the significance of the potentially affected sites. Once sites were identified and evaluated, we made workable plans to avoid damaging the sites and preserve the significant information and cultural values they contained.

"Are you here to steal our bones?" This was the blunt and disarming question Evelyn asked me when she interrupted my summary of our planned field work. But typical Evelyn – she asked with a twinkle in her eye.

Fortunately, I had just re-read Aleš Hrdlička's "Alaska Diary" in which he described his arrogant approach to doing fieldwork in rural Alaska. I knew that in 1930 Hrdlička had dug up the human remains of a woman from the Crooked Creek community, but I naively assumed repatriation of the remains had already occurred.

I replied no, I wasn't interested in taking bones, but I knew some had been taken from Crooked Creek years ago. Evelyn quizzically asked: "What do *you* know about her bones, and do you know where they are?" I told her that most of the remains Hrdlička had "collected" were in the Smithsonian Institution in Washington, D.C. The next day I contacted the Smithsonian and confirmed that they had her remains. From then on, Evelyn and I shared a common bond. We eventually visited the Smithsonian and got them to return the woman's remains – she was almost certainly Evelyn's relative. The woman was respectfully re-buried in Crooked Creek, and we wrote a professional paper together about the whole episode (Wooley and Thomas 2011).

The topic of racism had been the unspoken "elephant in the room" during the repatriation. It came to the fore after we left the Smithsonian and Evelyn asked me – point blank – "Why did that man [Hrdlička] think it was okay to take her?"

I responded by attempting to summarize white supremacy in general and Hrdlička's pseudoscientific approach of racial hierarchies in particular. We talked about how Hrdlička grouped Africans, Asians, Natives and other non-Europeans into graded categories and studied these races to understand how, in his mind, the white race maintained a top position on the pyramid of race.

Those racial hierarchies mirrored – and promoted – economic systems that ignored equality and social justice. Under feudalism and mercantile capitalism, European rigid class structures placed the gentry at the top, a few merchants and professionals (such as doctors, parsons, and lawyers) in the middle, and most everyone else in the lower class. During Hrdlička's time, the social construct of "race" had been used by colonial powers to enslave Africans and dispossess Indigenous Americans of their lands.

We never really discussed the issue further, and I don't think Evelyn spent a lot of time worrying about racism per se. She did ensure that those around her, especially visitors to the region, respected Alaska Native culture. Her love for her people and their unique culture was tied to the land and the resources, and her love was fierce. By her example, I experienced the beauty of the Indigenous way of life and its deep connections to the land. I will always be grateful for her example and her leadership.

Our field project progressed for several seasons. Evelyn and I spent many hours together in meetings, in the Thomas Lodge at Crooked Creek, and, later, at the Angyaruaq site. The archaeologists respected local ways, and the community members tolerated our nerdy interest in scientific archaeology. This mutual respect came to fruition when we collaborated on a two-year community archaeology project at the Angyaruaq site just downstream from Crooked Creek (Hays et al, 2012).

Evelyn was always happy to review the results of the archaeological surveys. Her cultural pride was particularly evident as she facilitated our community archaeology collaboration. The project involved Crooked Creek residents working with archaeologists to excavate a prehistoric site downstream on the banks of the Middle Kuskokwim River. It was a site which figured in the origin story of the Crooked Creek community. It was a sacred place and some of us followed

Evelyn Thomas and Sue Gamache at Angyaruaq, August 2012. *Chris Wooley*

local protocol by greeting it and tucking a small piece of food under a log when we arrived. The excavation of the site over a period of two field seasons provided some important scientific data and cultural insights into the people who lived there. It also included, for me, this exceptionally memorable and timeless moment.

It was a beautiful summer day on the river. The breeze was light, which kept the vicious mosquitos at bay. The crew members, consisting of professional archaeologists and community volunteers, were making good progress painstakingly removing the dirt, bones, rocks, small obsidian flakes, and the occasional artifacts from one-meter square units – layer by layer – from within an ancient house pit. The site was almost exactly 2,000 years old, based on 14C dating conducted during an initial test excavation the year before. Every item and sample was put into a labelled bag after its specific location had been mapped using a high-quality laser mapping device. All the hard work that so many people had put into the project was finally coming to fruition.

I was doing my best to keep from getting too excited, but it was hard not to feel a deep sense of gratification. Everyone was in a really good mood that day. I was ecstatic.

There are rare moments in life when everything just seems to come together, and this was one of those times. In sports, these moments have been termed the "flow state" or "being in the zone." The pitcher cannot miss the plate. The batter cannot miss the ball. The golfer cannot miss the putt. My experience was akin to tapping into a deep collective unconscious well, resulting in a sort of dissolving of my sense of separateness with the work and the site.

I was helping move some small buckets of dirt over to the screening area when I heard Evelyn's granddaughter's trowel go *clink*! She was wearing earbuds, and she loudly proclaimed, "Hey, I think this is something!" A few of us gathered around as she carefully trowelled and brushed away the dark dirt, revealing a beautifully chipped bipoint. "Wow – how cool!" she exclaimed. "You're the first one to touch it in 2,000 years," we reminded her. While the artifact was labelled and bagged, the young woman jumped to her feet and did "the Artifact Dance," a joyous mashup of K-pop, Yup'ik, and hip-hop that made us all feel like we were levitating alongside her. It was an eternal moment. It felt as though the land – that site – knew we were there and somehow communicated with us.

There is awesome power inherent in what Westerners call "nature." As homo sapiens, we belong to the family of great apes. We are intelligent bipedal primates. Western urban life tends to dampen our sensibilities of the natural world, yet Indigenous Science teaches us how interconnected all life is. Humans who understand these complexities can adapt and survive in the ever-changing natural world. These survival skills and their unique world view are contained in and persist in songs and stories.

I have "bookmarked" in my mind those times with Evelyn Thomas, and I return to them quite often. I have thought deeply about the possibility that there are undiscovered connections in the natural world that indeed enable the land to remember. Perhaps this "memory" is currently beyond category and outside of our Western scientific ability to define it. Just as undiscovered aspects of physics such as dark matter are coming into focus scientifically, perhaps there exists something that forms and ties physical places to memory and existence. Or not.

Whatever the source, it was a hair-raising moment when time waved, wobbled, and then went still as the "zone" dissipated. Was it neurological? Charged particles in synch across membranes assumed to be impenetrable? Whatever it was, the Artifact Dance made it real.

Evelyn Thomas will always be, for me, a warm memory. She brought so much joy to those of us who worked and spent time with her. As time marches on, the past is "created" somehow. We know it may be something of an illusion. But Evelyn was real, and her memory – like the river's flow – is eternal.

Sunset at Caunaq Camp

Rachelle Persson

Yup'ik Transcription and Translation

The Central Alaskan Yup'ik language is spoken on the Bering Sea coast from Norton Sound to the Alaska Peninsula, as well as along the lower Yukon, Kuskokwim, and Nushagak Rivers. It is one of four Yupik languages, all of which are closely related to the Inuit/Iñupiaq languages of the arctic coast of Alaska, northern Canada, and Greenland, although they are not mutually intelligible. Together, Inuit/Iñupiaq and Yupik constitute the Eskimo branch of the Eskimo-Aleut family of languages. No apostrophe is used when speaking of Yupik languages generally, but an apostrophe is used for Central Alaskan Yup'ik and its dialects.

There are five dialects of Central Yup'ik: Norton Sound, Hooper Bay/Chevak (Cup'ik), Nunivak Island (Cup'ig), Egegik, and General Central Yup'ik. All are mutually intelligible with some phonological and vocabulary differences (Jacobson 2012:35-46; Woodbury 1984:49-63).

The Central Yup'ik language remained unwritten until the end of the nineteenth century, when Russian Orthodox, Moravian, and Jesuit Catholic missionaries, working independently of one another but in consultation with Native converts, developed a variety of orthographies. The orthography used consistently throughout this book is the standard one developed between 1967 and 1972 at the University of Alaska Fairbanks and detailed in works published by the Alaska Native Language Center and others (Reed, Miyaoka, Jacobson, Afcan, and Krauss 1977; Miyaoka and Mather 1979; Jacobson 1995).

The standard orthography for Central Yup'ik represents the language with letters and letter combinations, each corresponding to a distinct sound as follows:

Consonants

	labials	apicals	front velars	back velars
stops	p	t c	k	q
voiced fricatives	v	l s/y	g (ug)	r (ur)
voiceless fricatives	vv	ll ss	gg (w)	rr
voiced nasals	m	n	ng	
voiceless nasals	m	n	ng	

Symbols in parentheses represent the sounds made with the lips rounded.

Vowels

	front		back
high	i		u
mid		e	
low		a	

The apostrophe indicates consonant gemination, or doubling (and serves several other less important functions). There are also conventions for undoubling the letters for voiceless fricatives under certain circumstances (Jacobson 1995:6-7). This standard orthography accurately represents the Yup'ik language in that a given word can be written in only one way and a given spelling can be pronounced in only one way. Note that certain predictable features of pronunciation, specifically automatic gemination and rhythmic length, are not explicitly shown in the spelling.

Translation

Most of the translations in this book were done by either Alice Rearden or Marie Meade. As translators, Alice and Marie offer distinctive strategies for bridging differences between Yup'ik and English without erasing them. For both, the goal has been a natural-sounding, free translation, as opposed to either literal translation (at one extreme) or paraphrasing (at the other). Paraphrasing may communicate some of the sense of the original, but such interpretive translations modify the original to the point where the speaker's voice is alternately erased or transformed. Literal, word-for-word translation also falls short. At best, it is awkward, and at worst, it makes no sense. The narrator's choice of words is respected in this book, although translators may modify word order and sentence structure slightly to communicate original meaning. They do this in different ways. Marie Meade, for example, is freer with English word choice, paragraphing, and paraphrasing in contrast to Alice Rearden, who retains a more literal word choice and style.

Because their primary goal is communication, no translation in this book mechanically follows the structure of the original language. For example, Yup'ik word order is "English turned on its head," in which suffixes indicating tense, person, case, and other units of meaning are appended to verb and noun bases. Thus, the English phrase "my little boat" corresponds to the single Yup'ik word *angyacuarqa*, which consists of *angya-* "boat," plus *-cuar-* "little," plus *-qa* "my," so that the order of the parts within the Yup'ik word is "boat, little, my." In Yup'ik discourse, the object also typically precedes the verb. A literal translation of *qaltarpaliunga* might read "bucket/big one/to make/I." A more natural translation would employ typical English word order, that is, verb followed by object, and would read "I/make/a big bucket." Thus, translation involves a continuous process of reordering.

Other characteristics of Yup'ik oratory have been carefully retained. For example, redundancies and repetitions are important rhetorical devices in Yup'ik narrative. Narrators frequently restate important points, often phrased somewhat differently, at the beginning and end of an account, both to enhance memory and to add emphasis and depth. Use of repetition gives Yup'ik texts a denser texture than typical English phrasings, which careful attention in the translation can retain. Structured repetitions are characteristic of Yup'ik narrative art and vital to its structural integrity. To smooth them over or omit them would impoverish the translations.

Several grammatical features of the Yup'ik language pose potential problems for translators. First, relatively free word order characterizes the Yup'ik language.

For example, the meaning of the English sentence “The man lost the dog” can only be conveyed by placing the words “man,” “lost,” and “dog” in this order. A Yup’ik speaker, however, can arrange the three words *angutem* (“man”), *tamallrua* (“s/he lost it”), and *qimugta* (“dog”) in any of six possible word orders with no significant change in meaning. Nevertheless, word order is not totally irrelevant to interpreting Yup’ik sentences. Word order may be the only key to appropriate interpretation when the ending alone is insufficient. For example, the sentence *Arnam atra nallua* (lit., “woman//his/her name//s/he not knowing it”) can mean either “The woman does not know his name” or “He does not know the woman’s name.” The same three words in a different word order, however, are less ambiguous. *Arnam nallua atra* is commonly taken to mean “The woman does not know his name.” In contrast with other languages that have a free word order, the relative position of postbases inside a Yup’ik word is very rigid. Consequently, syntactic problems may occur in words that occur only in sentences in translation.

Translation is further complicated by the fact that the Yup’ik language does not specify gender in third-person endings. The listener is left to deduce gender from the context of the account. When a speaker describes women’s tasks, we have translated the pronominal ending as “she,” as that is the way an English speaker can best understand the speaker’s intent. Conversely, pronominal endings are translated as “he” when the speaker is describing a man’s activities. In general discussions, we have used either “it” or “he,” depending on the context. Readers should also know that Yup’ik orators sometimes mix singular and plural endings in a single oral “sentence,” and we have retained these grammatical variations to reflect the complexity of the Yup’ik original.

Yup’ik verb tenses also differ from English tenses. Although some postbases place an action clearly in the future and others place action definitely in the past, a verb without one of these time-specific postbases may refer to an action that is happening in either the past or the present (Jacobson 1984:22). Accounts of events or customs that are no longer practiced in southwest Alaska have been translated in the past tense. Readers should also note that tense may vary within a paragraph, especially in discussions of *qanruyutet* (oral instructions) marked by the enclitic “*-gguq*,” which can be translated “they said,” “they say,” or “it is said,” depending on the context. Traditional *qanruyutet* that speakers indicate still apply are translated using the present tense.

Our narrators also frequently used nonspecific pronouns and phrases that are difficult for English readers to follow. For example, a speaker may say “that one who told the story,” rather than naming a specific person. Narrators also often use phrases such as “he went down” or “he arrived” without specific places mentioned. Readers should note that the Yup'ik language has an elaborate set of demonstratives that situate listeners and that indicate relative placement of action and movement of people--often very specifically--without ever mentioning places directly. These include terms such as *pikavet* (toward the area up above), *piavet* (up the slope), *kanavet* (down the slope, toward the area down below), and *uavet* (toward the mouth of a river, toward the door), to name but a few (Jacobson 2012:963-967). Demonstratives also distinguish between things upslope, downslope, etc., that require more than a single glance to be seen, things that can be seen fully in a single glance, and things that are obscured from view. Where necessary we have tried to clarify these phrases using brackets to indicate the narrator's intent. We have used parentheses to designate passages where narrators themselves offer explanations important for the reader but not necessarily part of the account.

Many narrators attach the postbase "miut" (people of) to the name of a river or slough to designate the people living there, as in Kusquqvagmiut (the people of the Kusquqvaq [Kuskokwim River]). The names of many villages also derive from the name of the river or lake where they are located, for example, the old village of Luumarvigmiut on the Luumarvik River. However, narrators may also use the name Luumarvik for the village itself, and in fact often do so. Other village names may be rendered with or without the "miut" ending. The maps that accompany this text show the most commonly used place name. The text, however, reflects what narrators actually said, designating the place with or without the "miut" ending.

Yup'ik oral rendering values close attention to detail and consistent retellings, and whatever their stylistic preferences, Marie and Alice continue to work in that tradition. As Yup'ik scholar Elsie Mather (1995:32) notes, "The most respected conveyers of Yup'ik knowledge are those who express things that listeners already know in artful or different ways, offering new expressions of the same."

Transcription

As if translation from one language to another were not challenging enough, this book involves the movement from oral to written language. Our starting point is the verbal artistry of individual elders, but critical to understanding their words is the transfer of their voices onto the page. Through the 1970s, little attention was given to reflecting the dynamics and dramatic techniques of the performance, including the speakers' shifts in tone and rhythm. The oral origins of texts were all but hidden from view. Texts were routinely transcribed in paragraph form, as if the paragraph were the "natural" form of all speech.

Beginning in the 1980s, when so many basic tenets of anthropology were being scrutinized, the ubiquitous paragraph came under attack, especially in the work of Dell Hymes (1981) and fellow linguist Dennis Tedlock (1983). Together Tedlock and Hymes inspired a generation of linguists and anthropologists who have since adopted and adapted their insights in a variety of sociolinguistic transcription styles, igniting a veritable "renaissance" in the translation of Native American literature (Swann 1994:xxviii). Although neither Alice or Marie have chosen to employ the "short line" verse format favored by many translators, they use the prose format with a new sensitivity. In their work, paragraphs are no longer arbitrary groupings disconnected from the speaker's original oral performance but are distinguished by prominent line-initial particles like *tua-i-llu* ("so then"), by cohesion between contiguous lines, and by pauses between units. This is by no means a mechanical process, however, and different translators make different choices about what markers require a new paragraph.

As we think about both the limitations and the power of translation to communicate meaning across cultural and linguistic boundaries, it is useful to recall that translation is not the endpoint of understanding, but the beginning (Becker 2000:18). Similarly, the reader is invited to engage these translations and use them as starting points for understanding and respecting the profound differences between literary traditions that, in turn, make it possible for us to better understand ourselves.

Glossary

Note: In the Yup'ik language, nouns ending in "q" are singular, nouns ending in "t" are plural, and dual nouns end in "k". Middle Kuskokwim speakers often end Yup'ik nouns in "s" (as in English) to form the plural (for example, calling fish traps *taluyaqs* rather than *taluyat*). An "ing" ending is also sometimes added to verbs, as in *manaqing* (hooking for fish). This is standard on the middle Kuskokwim and clearly understood by those familiar with the region, and we respect their choices.

aanaq mother

aataq father

alangruq / alangrut ghost(s), apparition(s), thing(s) that appear unexpectedly

angak maternal uncle, mother's brother

angalkuq / angalkut shaman(s), healer(s)

ap'a grandfather

arnassagaq old woman

ataata paternal uncle

atkuk parka

aviukaq / aviukarrluku giving an offering of food and water

aviukaqsaraq the practice of giving an offering

ciuliaq ancestor

curukat guests invited to a dance festival (lit., "attackers")

ella maliggluku following *ella* (the universe), clockwise

eyagyaraq / eyagyarat abstinence practice(s) following birth, death, illness, and first menstruation

ilat / ilaqs relatives

ilungaq / ilungat female cross-cousin(s) of a female

iluraq / ilurat male cross-cousin(s) of a male

ircenrraq / ircenrraat little person/people, other-than-human person(s)

kalukaq feast

kass'aq / kass'at white person / people, Caucasian(s), non-Native(s)

Kassiyuq Dance Festival

maqivik bath house

munaq dexterous

nayuryarluni lying concealed, watching for animals and birds to come

nukalpiaq good hunter and provider

nuliacungaq / nuliacungat female cross-cousin(s) of a male

pall'itaak removable log frame entrance to the underground tunnel passageway into the *qasgiq*

pupicuk infected sore, impetigo

qanemciq / qanemcit story / stories (from *qaner-,* "to speak")

qaneryaraq / qaneryarar / qaneryaraat teaching(s), admonition(s), word(s) of advice (lit., "that which is spoken")

qanruyun / qanruyutet oral instruction(s); teaching(s)

Qaugkumiut people from the upper Kuskokwim, upriver people (from *qaugna*, "the one upriver")

qasgiq / qasgit communal men's house(s)

quliraq / quli'ir / qulirat traditional tale(s), legendary tale(s) or place(s)

tuunrat spirit helpers

tuyuq lay pastor, village chief

uicungaq woman's male cousin

ukurraq daughter-in-law

Unegkumiut downriver people (from *unegna*, "the one down(river) there")

Uurayuli lit., "One who whistles"

yuarukaraat dance songs requesting specific gifts

yuarulluk / yuarulluut song(s) of incantation

yugaq / yugat nonhuman being(s)

yuguaq pretend person

yuraq / yuraqing (English-ized) Yup'ik dance

Yurialnguut Upper Kuskokwim Athabascans

Fish

aciirtuurta / aciirturtet first king salmon under the ice (lit., "those underneath")

akakiik / akakiiget broad whitefish (from *akag-*, "to roll"); also ***qaurtuq***

amaqaayak / amaqaayiit pink salmon, humpies (from *amaq*, "something carried on the back")

anerrluat springtime Dolly Varden trout

can'giiq / can'giiret blackfish

cavirrutnaq / cavirrutnat round whitefish

ceturrnat tomcod

ciiq / ciiret sheefish

cikignaq lake trout

cimerliq / cimerlit rainbow smelt; also ***qusuuq / qusuuret***

cingikeggliq / cingikegglit humpback whitefish

culugpauget arctic grayling

iituliar(aq) / iituliyagaat whitefish fry, young whitefish

imarpinraq / imarpinraat Bering cisco (lit., "ones from the ocean")

inarneret dead fish, including spawned-out fish (from *inarte-,* "to lie down")

iqallugpik / iqallugpiit Dolly Varden trout; also ***yugyaq / yugyiit***

iqalluk / iqalluut chum or dog salmon; also ***kangitneret***

itret whitefish swimming upriver from the Kuskokwim and its tributaries in spring (from *iter-*, "to enter")

kapatiit bullheads

luqruuyak / luqruuyiit pike

manignaq / manignat lush fish, burbot

meluk / meluut fish eggs / roe

masseq / massret old salmon near spawning

nemeryaq / nemeryat eels, Arctic lampreys

neqet fish, food

neqyagaat small fish or whitefish (least cisco)

nutemllayagaat young salmon before going out to the ocean (lit., "little original ones")

patqayulit "kissing fish," round fish, but not eels

qakiiyaq / qakiiyat silver salmon, cohos

qaurtuq / qaurtut broad whitefish; also ***akakiik***

qusuuret rainbow smelt

sayak / sayiit red salmon, sockeyes; also ***qaktaalriit***

talaariq / talaarit rainbow trout

taryaqvak / taryaqviit king salmon

tulimararualget chum salmon entering rivers closer to Bethel (lit., "ones with *tulimararuat* (pretend ribs)")

uqurlit fatty king salmon from the Yukon

yugyaq / yugyiit Arctic char

Land animals and birds

aqsatuyaaq small beaver

cikultaal, cikultall stonefly (order *Plecoptera*), cold-hardy insect that spends its larval stage in water

cuignilnguq river otter

iggiayulit great horned owls

ilegvak muskrat

issaluuq porcupine

itrat surf scoters; also ***akacakayiit***

kauturyaraat tree swallows

maqaruaq rabbit

palugtaq beaver

peleqpalaat frogs

qakurtat hawk owls; also ***eskaviat***

tekciuk Savanah sparrow

Plants

angeryuk spruce sap, tree pitch

ayuq / ayut Labrador tea plant(s)

caiggluk wormwood

elagat alpine sweet vetch or "Eskimo potatoes" (lit., "things dug from underground")

enrilnguat soft willow shoots

kaviqsuyagaat little red-barked willows

qet'get, qetek waterberries, root nodules of horsetail plants

qikmiruat pussy willow catkins

teptukuyiit valerian (from *teptu-,* "to be odoriferous")

tumaqliq / tumaqlit low bush cranberries (red berries)

uruneq low bush cranberries (red berries) in spring (from *urunret*, "open ground surrounded by snow")

Land and water features

akuluraq stream between two bodies of water

currluk murky water

kuignayuk valley with a stream

pellat places where one gets lost

qecikluut clear creeks, creeks with warm spots that do not freeze

qamanret eddies, places without currents

tevenret portages, high places

umcik closed up (from *umcig-,* "to be airtight")

uyangteq look out on

yuilquq wilderness

Foods

akutaq festive mixture of berries, fat, boned fish and other ingredients (lit., "a mixture")

anauteq large intestine, colon

aqlitnguat split fish attached at the tail, with grooves to promote drying (lit., "imitation earrings")

assaliaq fry bread, pancakes

caayuq tea

cin'at whole king salmon fermented in an underground pit

cungak bile, gall

egamaarrluk / egamaarrluut half-dried fish or meat boiled before serving

erurciigalnguq moose's second stomach, also called the honeycomb or towel (lit., "one that cannot be washed")

igyamcuut dried fish esophagus and stomachs (from *igyaraq*, "throat")

kanartaq / kanartat dried burbot

kiagcetaq / kiagcetat (lit., "thing(s) of last summer") such as whitefish caught in the spring or dry fish from the previous summer

kumlaneq / kumlanret frozen fish eaten raw

kuucenak hind quarters, pelvic bone, rump

mak'aq fish roe *akutaq* made from mashed roe, oil, and salmonberries

neqerrluk dry fish

palugtem it'gai beaver feet

paraluruaq rice

passiaq *akutaq* made from crushed, aged fish eggs and berries, oil, and sugar

pateq marrow

patruciq moose or caribou intestines stuffed with meat and marrow

piitnaq famine, food shortage

pukuk bones with meat

qageq / qagret boiled and cooled fish allowed to set in their congealed broth

qamiqurrluut dried and smoked salmon heads (from *qamiquq*, "head")

qanruagtat whole fish strung through the mouth to dry (from *qaneq*, "mouth")

qassayaaq / qassayaat / qassayagaat aged frozen whitefish

qayussaak mixture of broth, greens, oil, and fish eggs; also ***yuurqaaq***

qecaruaq tripe, stomach lining tissue of caribou or moose

qercuqat hard frozen fish

qerpertaq *akutaq* made with fresh whitefish or pike roe and mashed cranberries

segglaruat / segg'aruat split and dried fish

sulunaq / sulunat salted fish

tamuanat spawning fish hung to dry (lit., "those that require chewing")

tatangquq cartilage

tenguggluk *akutaq* made from *tenguk* (liver) and berries

tepeq aged fish

tep'ngaayak / tep'ngaayagaat slightly aged frozen whitefish

tuntuvak qengaq moose nose

tunuq tallow, back fat

uquaq whitefish stomach oil

yualuq tendons, sinew, thread

yuurleqtaaq moose hoof Jell-O

Tools / boats / clothing

aamak beaded collar, worn by young girls until marriage; also ***uyamik***

aliimatek mittens

anguarun propeller blade

angyaq open skin boat

angyaqatak shallow-draft skin boat meant for one-time use (from *angyaq*, "open skin boat" plus *qatak*, "about to be")

atkuk parka

ayakutaq willow side pieces for a fish trap

ayaurutet boat poles

camataq dance headdress

canassuun carving knife

cauyaralget round-bottomed boats (lit., "ones / boats with *cauyarat*, curved ribs")

cavget toggling harpoon points

ceterat tassels; also ***alngat***

ciuqalek fancy skin boots, made with a piece of dark fur over the shin

cuukiit socks

elagyat caches, originally underground (from *elag-*, "to dig")

ellin / sellin whetstone used to sharpen knives

ellumerrun skin scraper

imarnin gut rain parka

inivik / iniviit fish drying rack(s)

ipuun / ipuutet spoon(s), ladle(s)

kaapaq beaded hairnet

kameksak ankle-high skin boots, mukluks

kaputaq poker

kepun adze

kic'arat sinkers

kuvyaq fishnet

levaat boat motors

malagg'aayaq fur hat with ear flaps

manaq fishing lure with hook

manaqing (English-ized) fishing with hook, line, and lure; hooking for fish

nemerqutaq / nemenglluk foot wrapping used in place of socks

neqlivik fish camp

nillarcuun, nillat skin stretching frame(s)

palayat large skin boats, some with sails

pelutsiaq saucer; also ***acliq***

piicikaq / piicikat birch-bark basket(s)

piineq grass insole, bootliner

pitegcaun arrow

pugtaqutat floats

qantat bowls

qaspeq / qasperet thin hooded pullover garment(s)

qilakutaq canopy

qer'aq fish rack

qulvarviit elevated fish caches

quutaaryaraq seine fishing (lit., "way of repeatedly closing in")

salayaq summer storehouse and smokehouse for fish

segvik "fish pond," dock for fish processing, including holding tank and cutting tables

taassiq dishpan, large bowl

taluyaq / taluyat conical wooden fish trap(s)

taluyarpak / taluyarpiit large conical wooden fish trap(s)

tangluq / tangluk / tanglut snowshoe(s)

uluaq / uluat semilunar woman's knife / knives

urluveq bow

uyamik necklace, pendant, neckpiece; also ***aamak***

Notes

1. My discussion of topic-specific gatherings draws from our book, *Ellavut/ Our Yup'ik World and Weather* (Fienup-Riordan and Rearden 2012). I have also drawn from an essay I published in Roger Sanjek's 2015 edited volume, *Mutuality: Anthropology's Changing Terms of Engagement* (Fienup-Riordan 2015).
2. Along with poverty, the loss of dignity, issues of individual and cultural identity, and the history of multi-generational suffering associated with population loss and concentration are undeniable aspects of this complex contemporary situation (see Doak and Nachmann 1987; Ducker 1996, 2000; Fienup-Riordan 2010; Napoleon 1996; Oswalt 1990; and Wolsko et al. 2007).
3. See Moncrieff and Klein 2003 for correlative indicators of salmon arrival and abundance on the Yukon River.
4. See Coffing (1991:11) for a census of fish camps and salmon production units in Kwethluk in 1986.
5. Willow grouse (also known as ruffed grouse) are *temtemtaaq* in Yup'ik and *Bonasa umbellus* in Latin.

References

Alaska Department of Labor. 2010. American Community Survey Site. *http://live.laborstats.alaska.gov/cen/acsarea.cfm*

Alaska Injury Prevention Center. 2007. "Suicide in Alaska." Juneau, AK: Alaska State Department of Health and Social Services.

Albrecht, D. E. 1990. *Co-management as Transaction: The Kuskokwim River Salmon Management Working Group*. Master's thesis, McGill University, Montreal, Canada.

Anderson, Eva G. 1940. *Dog-team Doctor*. Caldwell, Ida: Caxton.

Avakumoff, John. 1987. Taped interview. Joseph Bartolini, interviewer. Fish Camp near Napaimiut. 15 June. Tape 87LMVO6; BIA ANCSA Office, Anchorage.

Bartolini, Joseph. 1991. "Report of Investigation for Arnasagaq, Calista Corporation BLM AA-9852, BLM AA-9853." BIA ANCSA Office, Anchorage, Alaska.

Becker, A. L. 2000. *Beyond Translation: Essays toward a Modern Philology.* Ann Arbor: University of Michigan Press.

Berman, Matthew. 2014. "Suicide Among Young Alaska Native Men: Community Risk Factors and Alcohol Control." *American Journal of Public Health*. Published online April 2014 at *www.iser.uaa.alaska.edu.*

Boas, Franz. 1901-1907. *The Eskimo of Baffin Land and Hudson Bay*. Bulletin of the American Museum of Natural History, Vol. 15, Pts. 1-2. New York: Trustees of the American Museum of Natural History.

Bobby, Pete. 1987 Taped interview. Robert Waterworth and Marjorie Connolly, interviewers. Lime Village vicinity. 25 June. Tape 87LMV19, BIA ANCSA Office, Anchorage.

Brazil, C., D. Bue, H. Carroll, and T. Elison. 2011. *2010 Kuskokwim Area Management Report*. Alaska Department of Fish and Game, Fishery Management Report No. 11-67, Anchorage.

Brelsford, Taylor, and Mike Williams. 2018. "Salmon Governance Dynamics: The Emerging Institution of the Kuskokwim River Inter-Tribal Fisheries Commission." State of Alaska's Salmon and People presentation, Anchorage, AK.

Burch, Ernest S. and T. C. Correll. 1972. "Alliance and Conflict: Inter-regional Relations in North Alaska." In: Lee Guemple (ed.), *Alliance in Eskimo Society*. Proceedings of the American Ethnological Society, 1971. Supplement, pp. 17-39. Seattle: University of Washington Press.

Charnley, Susan. 1984. "Human Ecology of Two Central Kuskokwim Communities: Chuathbaluk and Sleetmute." Technical Paper No. 81, Alaska Department of Fish and Game, Division of Subsistence, Juneau.

Coffing, M. W. 1991. *Kwethluk Subsistence: Contemporary Land Use Patterns, Wild Resource Harvest and Use, and the Subsistence Economy of a Lower Kuskokwim River Area Community*. Alaska Department of Fish and Game, Division of Subsistence, Technical Paper No. 157, Juneau.

Cooper, Rachel and Alan Dick. 2016. *Tatiana: Cook Inlet Alaska Early 1800s*. Publication Consultants.

Cussack-McVeigh, Holly. 2002. Collection notes on pieces made by Bedusa Derendy. Manuscript. University of Alaska Museum of the North.

Doak, B. and B. Nachmann. 1987. *Violent Deaths Among Young Adults in Southwest Alaska Villages: A Subgroup of Longitudinal Cohort Study*. Alaska Native Medical Center, Anchorage, AK.

Ducker, James H. 1996. "Out of Harm's Way: Relocating Northwest Alaska Eskimos 1907-1917." *American Indian Culture and Research Journal* 20(1):43-71.

2000. "Curriculum for a New Culture: A Case Study of Schools and Alaska Natives, 1884-1947." *Pacific Northwest Quarterly* 91(2):71-83.

Egnaty, Jack. 1987. Taped interview. Joseph Bartolini and Terry Fiffield, interviewers. Sleetmute. 19 June. Tape 87LMV12, BIA ANCSA Office, Anchorage.

Fienup-Riordan, Ann, ed. 1988. *The Yup'ik Eskimos as Described in the Travel Journals and Ethnographic Accounts of John and Edith Kilbuck, 1885-1900*. Kingston, Ontario: Limestone Press.

Fienup-Riordan, Ann. 1990. *Eskimo Essays: Yup'ik Lives and How We See Them*. New Brunswick, NJ: Rutgers University Press.

1991. *The Real People and the Children of Thunder: The Yup'ik Eskimo Encounter with Moravian Missionaries John and Edith Kilbuck*. Norman, OK: University of Oklahoma Press.

1994. *Boundaries and Passages: Rule and Ritual in Yup'ik Eskimo Oral Tradition*. Norman, OK: University of Oklahoma Press.

2000. *Hunting Tradition in a Changing World: Yup'ik Lives in Alaska Today*. New Brunswick, NJ: Rutgers University Press.

2010. "Yup'ik Perspectives on Climate Change: 'The World is Following Its People.'" *Études/Inuit/Studies* 34(1).

2015. "If you want to go fast, go alone. If you want to go far, go together: Yup'ik elders working together with one mind." In: *Mutuality: Anthropology's Changing Terms of Engagement*. Roger Sanjak, ed. pp. 61-78. Philadelphia: University of Pennsylvania Press.

Fienup-Riordan, Ann, and Alice Rearden. 2012. *Ellavut/Our Yup'ik World and Weather: Continuity and Change on the Bering Sea Coast*. Seattle: University of Washington Press.

2016. *Anguyiim Nalliini/Time of Warring: The History of Bow-and-Arrow Warfare in Southwest Alaska*. Fairbanks: University of Alaska Press.

Fienup-Riordan, Ann, Alice Rearden, and Marie Meade. 2025. *Angalkut / Shamans in Yup'ik Oral Tradition*. Fairbanks: University of Alaska Press.

Fortuine, Robert. 1992. *Chills and Fever: Health and Disease in the Early History of Alaska*. Fairbanks: University of Alaska Press.

Gordon, George Byron. 1917. *In the Alaskan Wilderness*. Philadelphia: John C. Winston Company.

Hays, J., J. Reuther, C. Wooley, J. Rogers, M. Proue and R. Bowman. 2012. *Life on the River: Community Archaeology at SLT-094, Middle Kuskokwim River, Alaska*. Report submitted to Donlin Creek LLC, Anchorage by Northern Land Use Research, Inc., Fairbanks, and Chumis Cultural Resources Services, Anchorage, January 2012.

Henkelman, James, and Kurt Vitt. 1985. *Harmonious to Dwell: The History of the Alaska Moravian Church, 1885-1985*. Bethel, AK: Moravian Seminary and Archives.

Hrdlička, Aleš. 1943. *Alaska Diary, 1926-1941*. Lancaster, PA: Cattell Press.

Hutchinson, Lisa. 1991. "Report of Investigation for Arnasagaq. BLM AA-9852, BLM AA-9853." BIA ANCSA Office, Anchorage.

Hymes, Dell. 1981. *"In Vain I Tried to Tell You": Essays in Native American Ethnopoetics*. Studies in Native American Literature 1. Philadelphia: University of Pennsylvania Press.

Ikuta, H., A. R. Brenner, and A. Godduhn. 2013. *Socioeconomic Patterns in Subsistence Salmon Fisheries: Historical and Contemporary Trends in Five Kuskokwim River Communities and Overview of the 2012 Season*. Alaska Department of Fish and Game, Division of Subsistence Technical Paper No. 382, Fairbanks.

Jacobsen, Johan Adrian. 1977. *Alaska Voyage, 1881-1883: An Expedition to the Northwest Coast of America*. Erna Gunther, translator. Illinois: University of Chicago Press.

Jacobson, Steven A. 1984. *Yup'ik Eskimo Dictionary*. Fairbanks: Alaska Native Language Center, University of Alaska.

1995. *A Practical Grammar of the Central Alaskan Yup'ik Eskimo Language*. Fairbanks: Alaska Native Language Center, University of Alaska.

2012. *Yup'ik Eskimo Dictionary*. Second Edition. Fairbanks: Alaska Native Language Center, University of Alaska.

Jerabek, Cheryl. 2014. "Russian Impact on Cultural Identity and Heritage in the Middle Kuskokwim Region of Alaska." Ph.D Dissertation, University of Alaska Fairbanks, May 2014.

Kari, Priscilla. 1985. "Wild Resource Use and Economy of Stony River Village." Technical Report No. 108. Division of Subsistence, Alaska Department of Fish and Game, Juneau.

Krauss, Michael. 2007. "Native Languages in Alaska." In *The Vanishing Voices of the Pacific Rim*. Osahito Miyaoka, Osamu Sakiyama, and Michael E. Krauss, ed. Oxford: Oxford University Press.

Lantis, Margaret. 1950. "The Reindeer Industry in Alaska." *Arctic* 3(1):27-44.

Linn, Angela J. 2013. "An American Treasure in Fairbanks: The Rehabilitation of the Kolmakovsky Blockhouse." *Alaska Journal of Anthropology* 11(1&2):93-100.

Maddren, A. G. 1914. Photograph albums, 1906-1914. Manuscript Collection, University of Alaska Anchorage Archives and Special Collections.

Mather, Elsie P. 1995. "With a Vision Beyond Our Immediate Needs: Oral Traditions in an Age of Literacy." In: *When Our Words Return: Writing, Hearing, and Remembering Oral Traditions of Alaska and the Yukon*. Phyllis Morrow and William Schneider, eds. pp. 13-26. Logan: Utah State University Press.

McAtee, June. 2010. "Reindeer and potatoes on the Kuskokwim River: A family history in western Alaska." *Alaska Journal of Anthropology* 8(1):23-38.

Michael, H. N., ed. 1967. *Lieutenant Zagoskin's Travels in Russian America, 1842-1844*. Toronto: University of Toronto Press.

Miyaoka, Osahito, and Elsie Mather. 1979. *Yup'ik Eskimo Orthography*. Bethel, AK: Kuskokwim Community College.

Moncrieff, C., and J. Klein. 2003. "Traditional ecological knowledge of salmon along the Yukon River." Yukon River Drainage Fisheries Association, Anchorage.

Napoleon, Harold. 1996. *Yuuyaraq: The Way of the Human Being*. University of Alaska Fairbanks: Alaska Native Knowledge Network.

Nelson, Edward William. 1899. *The Eskimo about Bering Strait*. Bureau of American Ethnology Annual Report for 1896-1897, Vol. 18, Pt. I. Washington, D.C.: Smithsonian Institution Press (Reprinted 1983).

Oleksa, Michael J. 1992. *Orthodox Alaska: A Theology of Mission*. Crestwood, NY: St. Vladimir's Seminary Press.

Osgood, C. 1958. *Ingalik Social Culture*. New Haven: Yale University Press.

Oswalt, Wendell H. 1962. "Historical Population in Western Alaska and Migration Theory." *Anthropological Papers of the University of Alaska* 2(1):1-14.

1980a. *Historic Settlements Along the Kuskokwim River, Alaska*. Alaska State Library Historical Monograph No. 7. Juneau: Alaska Division of State Libraries and Museums.

1980b. "Kolmakovskiy Redoubt." *Monumenta Archaeologica,* No. 8. University of California, Los Angeles.

1990. *Bashful No Longer: An Alaskan Eskimo Ethnohistory, 1778-1988*. Norman: University of Oklahoma Press.

Pierce, Richard, ed. 1984. *The Journals of Iakov Netsvetov: The Yukon Years 1845-1863*. Lydia Black, translator. Kingston, ON: Limestone Press.

Rasmussen, Knud. 1921-1925. *Myter og Sagn fra Grønland, I-III*. Copenhagen: Gyldendal.

1938. "Knud Rasmussen's Posthumous Notes on the Life and Doings of the East Greenlanders in Olden Times" ed., H. Osterman. Meddr Grønland 109(1).

Rearden, Alice, and Ann Fienup-Riordan. 2016. *Ciulirnerunak Yuuyaqunak/Do Not Live Without an Elder: The Subsistence Way of Life in Southwest Alaska*. Fairbanks: University of Alaska Press.

Rearden, Alice, Marie Meade, Mark John, and Ann Fienup-Riordan. 2021 *Ircenrraat/Extraordinary Persons in Southwest Alaska*. Fairbanks: Alaska Native Language Center.

Redding-Gubitosa, Donna. 1992. "Excavations at Kwigiumpaingukmiut: A Multi-Ethnic Historic Site, Southwestern Alaska." Ph.D Dissertation, University of California, Los Angeles.

Reed, Irene, Osahito Miyaoka, Steven Jacobson, Pascal Afcan, and Michael Krauss. 1977. *Yup'ik Eskimo Grammar.* Fairbanks: Alaska Native Language Center, University of Alaska.

Runfola, David. 2013. "2012 Update." In: *Socioeconomic Patterns in Subsistence Salmon Fisheries: Historical and Contemporary Trends in Five Kuskokwim River Communities and Overview of the 2012 Season*. Ikuta, H., A. R.

Brenner, and A. Godduhn, pp. 121-26. Alaska Department of Fish and Game, Division of Subsistence Technical Paper No. 382, Fairbanks.

Smith, Barbara S. 1980. *Russian Orthodoxy in Alaska: A History, Inventory, and Analysis of the Church Archives in Alaska with an Annotated Bibliography.* Anchorage, AK: Alaska Historical Commission.

Søby, R. 1969. "The Eskimo Animal Cult." *Folk* 11-12:43-78.

Street, Steve. 1998. Archaeological Inventory and NHPA Section 106 Review: Woodrow Wilson Vanderpool Native Allotment FF-016757, Parcel C, Napaimute, Alaska. August 1998. AVCP, Bethel.

Swann, Brian. 1994. *Coming to Light: Contemporary Translations of the Native Literatures of North America.* New York: Random House.

Tedlock, Dennis. 1983. *The Spoken Word and the Work of Interpretation.* Philadelphia: University of Pennsylvania Press.

Tundra Drums. September 13, 1984, and October 3, 1984.

VanStone, James. 1974. *Athapaskan Adaptations: Hunters and Fishermen of the Subarctic Forests.* Chicago: Aldine Publishing Company.

Webber, E.J. 1943. Book II, #717. US Geological Survey Records, National Archives, Washington D.C.

Williams, Sinka and Stanley Nook. 1988. Tape recorded interview and transcript. Philippa Coiley, interviewer. Lower Kalskag, AK. July 20. 88CAL081. Transcribed and translated by Monica Shelden. BIA ANCSA Office, Anchorage.

Wolfe, Robert. 1982. "Alaska's Great Sickness, 1900: An Epidemic of Measles and Influenza in a Virgin Soil Population." *Proceedings of the American Philosophical Society* 126(2):91-121.

Wolsko, C., C. Lardon, G. V. Mohatt, and E. Orr. 2007. "Stress, Coping, and Well-being among the Yupik of the Yukon-Kuskokwim Delta: The Role of Enculturation and Acculturation." *International Journal of Circumpolar Health* 66:51-61.

Woodbury, Anthony C. 1984. "Eskimo and Aleut Languages." In *Arctic*, Vol. 5, *Handbook of North American Indians.* David Damas, ed. pp.49-63. Washington, D.C.: Smithsonian Institution Press.

Wooley, Chris, Chumis Cultural Resource Services, Joshua D. Reuther, Justin M. Hays, Molly M. Proue, and Molly Odell. 2008. *2007 Cultural Resources Survey for the Donlin Creek Project, Alaska.* Chumis Cultural Resources Services, Anchorage, AK.

Wooley, Chris and Evelyn Thomas. 2011. "Return with a Sharing: Coming Home to the Kuskokwim." *Alaska Journal of Anthropology* 9(2):73-79.

Index

Page numbers in italics indicate illustrations.